Social Conflict

ESCALATION, STALEMATE, AND SETTLEMENT

McGraw-Hill Series in Social Psychology

CONSULTING EDITOR, Philip G. Zimbardo

Leonard Berkowitz:	Aggression: Its Causes, Consequences, and Control
Sharon S. Brehm:	Intimate Relationships
Susan T. Fiske and Shelley E. Taylor:	Social Cognition
Stanley Milgram:	The Individual in a Social World
David G. Myers:	Exploring Social Psychology
Ayala Pines and Christina Maslach:	Experiencing Social Psychology: Readings and Projects
Scott Plous:	The Psychology of Judgment and Decision Making
Lee Ross and Richard E. Nisbett:	The Person and the Situation: Perspectives of Social Psychology
Jeffrey Z. Rubin, Dean G. Pruitt, and Sung Hee Kim:	Social Conflict: Escalation, Stalemate, and Settlement
Harry C. Triandis:	Culture and Social Behavior
Philip G. Zimbardo and Michael R. Leippe:	The Psychology of Attitude Change and Social Influence

Social Conflict

ESCALATION, STALEMATE, AND SETTLEMENT

SECOND EDITION

Jeffrey Z. Rubin
Tufts University

Dean G. Pruitt
State University of New York at Buffalo

Sung Hee Kim
University of Kentucky—Lexington

McGraw-Hill, Inc.

New York St. Louis San Francisco Auckland Bogotá Caracas Lisbon London Madrid Mexico City Milan Montreal New Delhi San Juan Singapore Sydney Tokyo Toronto

SOCIAL CONFLICT

Escalation, Stalemate, and Settlement

This book is printed on acid-free paper.

6 7 8 9 0 DOC DOC 9 0 9

ISBN 0-07-054211-2

This book was set in Palatino by The Clarinda Company.
The editors were Christopher Rogers, Laura Lynch, and Fred H. Burns;
the production supervisor was Denise L. Puryear.
The cover was designed by Carla Bauer.
R. R. Donnelley & Sons Company was printer and binder.

Library of Congress Cataloging-in-Publication Data

Rubin, Jeffrey Z.
Social conflict: escalation, stalemate, and settlement / Jeffrey Z. Rubin, Dean G. Pruitt, Sung Hee Kim.—2nd ed.
p. cm.
Dean G. Pruitt's name appears first in the 1986 ed.
Includes bibliographical references and index.
ISBN 0-07-054211-2
1. Social conflict. 2. Social conflict—Psychological aspects.
3. Interpersonal conflict. 4. Problem solving. I. Pruitt, Dean G.
II. Kim, Sung Hee, (date). III. Title.
HM291.P725 1994 93-24557
303.6—dc20

About the Authors

Jeffrey Z. Rubin is professor of psychology at Tufts University, adjunct professor of diplomacy, Fletcher School of Law and Diplomacy, Tufts University, and senior fellow, Program on Negotiation at Harvard Law School. Rubin received his Ph.D. degree in social psychology from Columbia University. A Fulbright and Guggenheim fellow, Rubin is a fellow of the American Psychological Association and the American Psychological Society. Editor of *Negotiation Journal* since its inception, Rubin is the author or co-author of more than a dozen books, many dealing with conflict and negotiation. Among his publications are *When Families Fight, Leadership and Negotiation in the Middle East, Negotiation Theory and Practice, Mediation in International Relations, Dynamics of Third Party Intervention, Culture and Negotiation,* and *The Social Psychology of Entrapment.*

Dean G. Pruitt is distinguished professor at the State University of New York at Buffalo. He received his Ph.D. degree in psychology from Yale University. He is author or co-author of *Theory and Research on the Causes of War, Negotiation Behavior, Mediation Research, Negotiation in Social Conflict,* and numerous articles and chapters. He is a fellow of the American Psychological Association and the American Psychological Society. He is a recipient of the Harold D. Lasswell Award for Distinguished Scientific Contribution to Political Psychology and has been president of the International Association for Conflict Management and former vice president of the International Society of Political Psychology.

Sung Hee Kim teaches at University of Kentucky. She received her Ph.D. from Tufts University in 1991 and is a recent recipient of a Peace Scholar Fellowship from the United States Institute of Peace. She has published articles on conflict, attribution processes, and social comparison-based emotions. Her most recent research involves the role of vengeful emotions in conflict escalation.

For Our Children

Contents

Foreword

Conflict has been a driving force in the development of social psychology. It could reasonably be argued that modern social psychology in the United States began from a broad thematic interest in the nature of human conflict in the era around World War II. Psychologists of that time were living in a cauldron of social conflict. It was a time of national fascism with its charismatic leaders and mass followers, power and dominance, war and violence, prejudice and discrimination; of tensions from changing work demands and new employment strategies; and of assimilation of immigrants from diverse backgrounds, as well as urban relocation of rural migrants. Some of those investigators analyzed the forces of change and resistance, as well as the conflict between the needs of a democratic society that requires consensus and conformity and the values of individual independence and autonomy. Other researchers recognized the role of persuasive rhetoric as central to democratic decision making, while allowing for a diverse audience to oppose some aspects of every message.

This generic involvement of social psychological researchers in conflict became ever more focused into the personal tension states it created within individuals. Kurt Lewin emphasized the motivational force of perceived discrepancies between the person's needs and goals and the norms of the group. His premier student, Leon Festinger, helped move social psychology toward a more cognitive orientation by recasting the tension-inducing nature of such discrepancy as taking place within a single person's cognitive system when private beliefs become dissonant with one's public actions. Contemporary social psychology is now heavily influenced by the cognitive dimension of human functioning. During the many decades that general psychology was held captive by the mindless, valueless doctrines of behaviorism, it was social psychology that remained rebellious, fighting the guerrilla wars of situationism, constructivism, Person X Stimulus interactionism, and cognitive involvement in human action. Social psychologists were also the ones who raised the banners of practical applications and socially responsible research. Social psychological researchers learned from their experimentalist brethren the tenets of rigorous, carefully controlled laboratory research, but added a new flair and ingenuity that infused the artificial setting with "mundane realism." But many social psychologists went beyond the confines of the laboratory testing of causal hypotheses; they got their notebooks dirty in the muck and mire of everyday life in the varied fields of humanity-at-work. They have brought their abiding curiosity for understanding the whys, whens, and hows of human experience and behavior into a seemingly endless array of vital venues—of education, health, law, politics, business, environment, and culture, to name but a few.

This innovative *McGraw-Hill Series in Social Psychology* has been designed as a celebration of the fundamental contributions being made by researchers, theorists, and practitioners of social psychology in improving our understanding of human nature and enriching the quality of our lives. It has become a showcase for presenting new theories, original syntheses, analyses, and current methodologies by distinguished scholars and promising young writer-researchers. Common to all of our authors is the commitment to sharing their vision with an audience that starts with their colleagues but extends out to graduate students, undergraduates, and all those with an interest in social psychology. Some of our titles convey ideas that are of sufficient general interest that their message needs to be carried out into the world of practical application to those who may translate some of them into public action and public policy. Although each text in our series is created to stand alone as the best representative of its area of scholarship, taken as a whole, they represent the core of social psychology. Teachers may elect to use any of them as "in-depth" supplements to a general textbook, while others may choose to organize their course entirely around a set of these monographs. Each of our authors has been guided by the objective of conveying the essential lessons and principles of his or her area of expertise in an interesting style that informs without resort to technical jargon, that inspires others to share their excitement by utilizing these ideas or creating new and better ones through research.

Let's return to our opening theme of social conflict in introducing this special work by Jeffrey Rubin, Dean Pruitt, and Sung Hee Kim. All social conflict begins with one party wanting something that another party resists doing or giving. Those conflicts stretch from the mundane interactions of parents wanting reluctant children to clean their rooms or do homework, to challenges between legal adversaries in courts of law, to salespeople negotiating deals with customers, to political opponents compromising on line items in national or local budgets, to international peace conferences that can prevent war. Are there similar basic principles operating across such diverse settings? Does our understanding of how such conflicts between individuals (acting alone or as representatives of agencies) escalate, reach plateaus of stalemates, and become settled help us to reduce the destructive aspects of such conflict by avoiding them or providing appropriate counsel to the conflicting parties? The authors of *Social Conflict* answer these questions in the affirmative, going on to illustrate exactly how each stage in a host of different conflict scenarios is best parsed, or perceptively analyzed, into underlying processes and paths that lead to desirable or undesired outcomes. Their wisdom guides the reader to see how effective problem solving strategies result in the most equitable resolution of human conflicts when they replace contentious strategies of domination or the unsatisfying strategies of yielding.

The success of the first edition of *Social Conflict* created a challenge for the authors and editor to enhance its strengths while overcoming some of its limitations, yet not to overfix such a good product. They have succeeded admirably in meeting these goals. The dedicated scholarship, breadth of coverage, and currency of information shown in the second edition goes beyond what was admirable previously. The theoretical orientation has become more coherent and tightened, and more systematically applied throughout the presentation. More emphasis has been focused on the settlement phase of social conflicts, perhaps in the hope of providing more sensible guidance to "real-world" practitioners of conflict resolution. Readers who enjoyed and learned from the first edition will be delighted by the range of updated examples of domestic and racial conflict, as well as source material on current national and international conflict. Among the most valuable additions to this popular text is the extended coverage of cross-cultural and multicultural conflicts. Perhaps the addition of new co-author, Sung Hee Kim, may have influenced the decision to expand the perspective on how cultural differences, values, and normative rules impact on creating conflicts and resolving them. Finally, all readers will enjoy the smoother flow of the narrative style and the improved graphic illustrations, which combine to make learning the lessons of social conflict readily accessible and memorable. I suspect that in the final analysis the enduring value of *Social Conflict* will lie in helping each of us become more savvy about dealing intelligently and sensitively with conflicts in our own daily lives.

Philip G. Zimbardo
Consulting Editor

Preface

❖

When the first edition of *Social Conflict* was published in 1986, two of us (JZR and DGP) laid our pencils to rest, contented ourselves with a job well done, and expected never to work on this project again. To our pleasant surprise, however, the first edition was well received, and we began to think about the possibility of revision. Busy as we each were with other pursuits, and intimidated as we were at the thought of revisiting a conflict literature that had grown with lightning speed, we were reluctant to go forward with a second edition.

Enter author number three (SHK), a young social psychologist with an abundance of energy, rich cultural experience, lively interest in conflict studies, and the questionable judgment to join the two of us. Join us she did, and we believe that the book is stronger as a result.

Readers of the first edition of *Social Conflict* will find that this book looks familiar in some ways, and different in others. We have retained the book's broad focus on conflict escalation, stalemate, and settlement, the use of illustrations drawn from the many contexts in which conflict arises, and a simple conceptual foundation on which subsequent chapters build in a reasonably orderly way. We have updated our report on the most recent developments in the proliferating research and theoretical literature, and this is reflected in a more extensive bibliography. Finally, we have gone out of our way to keep the book brief and (we hope) readable.

There are also some important differences between the two editions. First, we have reorganized the center section on escalation to clarify further the processes by which conflicts and relationships deteriorate, and the conditions that encourage these processes. This section, while not much longer than it was originally, is now four chapters instead of three.

Second, we have devoted proportionally more of the book to stalemate and settlement; this reflects the dramatic growth of research and theory in these areas.

Third, we have simplified the conceptual foundation; where we once discussed five strategies for the settlement of conflict, we now focus on only *three* key coping strategies: contending, yielding, and—most importantly—problem solving.

Fourth, we have included new literature, both experimental and applied, on the increasingly important topic of culture. Aware that the first edition largely ignored the body of work developed outside the United States, while blithely assuming the generalizability of our observations from one culture to the next, we have now tried to examine this assumption more carefully.

Fifth, in order to keep the book's narrative flowing as smoothly as possible, while giving us an opportunity to add various asides, we have introduced footnotes for the curious reader who wants more than the text provides. We have also simplified our use of gender pronouns (always a problem in descriptions of interaction between two individuals) by using the terms Party and Other whenever appropriate.

Finally, in order to keep pace with recent changes in world affairs, we have shifted our emphasis a bit in the choice of illustrations used throughout the book. The Cold War may be over but conflict rages on, in states across the sea and in the tinderbox of our nation's families and inner cities. We have therefore made every effort to be as current in our coverage as possible.

As is always the case with a complex project, we are grateful to many people for their assistance and support along the way. We especially thank Laura Lynch, Chris Rogers, and Fred Burns of McGraw-Hill for their editorial guidance; they coaxed us, gently but firmly, from start to finish. Thanks too to the students of the Fletcher School of Law and Diplomacy, Tufts University, who shared their candid observations in a seminar on international negotiation processes, and to the psychology students (both graduate and undergraduate) at the State University of New York at Buffalo, who performed a similar function. A special thank you to the three reviewers that McGraw-Hill asked to comment on the first edition—George Levinger, University of Massachusetts, Amherst; James Sebenius, Harvard Business School; and William P. Smith, Vanderbilt University. Their comments were a judicious mix of constructive criticism and detailed advice, and they made the task of revision far easier than we had anticipated.

Finally, the work leading up to the second edition would never have been completed without the support and encouragement of our spouses, Carol, France, and Richard. To them we owe our boundless thanks and love; with their knowledge and support, we again dedicate this book to our children.

Jeffrey Z. Rubin
Dean G. Pruitt
Sung Hee Kim

1

Overview

Toward a Theory of Conflict • What Is Conflict? • Some Good News and Some Bad News about Conflict • *The Good News* • *And the Bad News* • Plan of the Book

- Ben, age 18, has borrowed the family car, then forgotten to fill it up with gasoline. The next morning, Dad is late for work because he has to wait for gas in the middle of rush hour traffic. That night Dad lets his son know what inconvenience his forgetfulness has caused. Ben's apology is half-hearted, so Dad heats things up a bit. He complains about Ben's generally inconsiderate and irresponsible behavior on a number of fronts. Eventually Ben is provoked into yelling at his father, who, outraged by this uncalled-for behavior, demands the car keys back and announces that until further notice, Ben will no longer be allowed to use the family car. Around this time, Mom (with Sis looking on) intervenes in Ben's behalf, trying to persuade Dad that maybe he's being too hard on their son. When Dad tells Mom to mind her own business, Mom (as well as Ben and Sis) walk out the door, leaving Dad to wonder what went wrong.[1]
- Sales and Production are in the throes of an intense exchange regarding the delivery date for their company's new product. Sales argues that unless a delivery date can be scheduled no more than *three* months from now, potential new customers will be lost to the competition, visiting a minor disaster upon Sales and the company as a whole. Production argues in return that it has a carefully organized and sequenced production schedule that

[1] This story is adapted from *When Families Fight* by Jeffrey Rubin and Carol Rubin (1989).

must be maintained. Breaking that schedule, by making the new product available for distribution earlier than Production intends, would incur costs in time and money that would be detrimental to Production and the company. No, insists Production, the new product is scheduled for introduction *nine* months hence, and that's when it will appear! After days of acrimony, an agreement is reached in which each department settles for less than it originally wanted: a production schedule of *six* months.

- When U.S. President Jimmy Carter brought Egypt's President Anwar Sadat and Israel's Prime Minister Menachem Begin together at Camp David in October, 1978, it seemed that Carter, the would-be mediator, had taken on an impossible task. The conflict over the Sinai Peninsula appeared entirely intractable, since Egypt demanded the immediate return of the entire Sinai; Israel, in turn, having occupied the Sinai since the 1967 Middle East war, refused to return a centimeter of this land. Carter's initial efforts to mediate a settlement, proposing a compromise in which each nation would retain half of the Sinai, proved completely unacceptable to both sides. President Carter and his staff persisted, eventually discovering that the seemingly irreconcilable positions of Israel and Egypt reflected underlying interests that were not incompatible at all. Israel's underlying interest was *security;* Israel wanted to be certain that its borders would be safe against land or air attack from Egypt. Egypt, in turn, was primarily interested in *sovereignty*—regaining rule over a piece of land that had been part of Egypt as far back as biblical times. After thirteen days of hard work, and twenty-three draft agreements developed by Assistant Secretary of State Harold Saunders, Carter's persistence as a mediator paid off. Israel agreed to return the Sinai in exchange for assurances of a demilitarized zone and new Israeli air bases. This agreement was put into effect in April, 1982, and continues to the present day.[2]
- When Rodney King, an African American, was stopped after a high-speed police chase on March 3, 1991, then was subdued by the police after apparently resisting arrest, the incident seemed not particularly newsworthy. Thanks to a Los Angeles resident, however, who used his new video camera to record the arrest of King, the ordinary became extraordinary. The videotape clearly showed Rodney King being kicked and pummeled, hit with nightsticks forty times by some of the police officers, while others stood nearby, observing impassively. More than a year later, in late spring of 1992, a

[2] This analysis of mediation in the Camp David negotiations—particularly, the emphasis on the value of identifying underlying interests as a way of moving toward agreement—is adapted from Fisher, Ury, & Patton's *Getting to YES* (1991).

jury in Ventura, California, found the four patrolmen accused of the beating to be innocent of the charge of using undue force. Within hours, the city of Los Angeles erupted in riots. Buildings were burned to the ground as citizens, mostly African American residents, vented their rage at the police and at the government more generally. It took an appearance by President Bush and the intervention of 2,000 National Guard troops to quell the three-day uprising.

TOWARD A THEORY OF CONFLICT

Though strikingly different in scale and significance, the four incidents just cited have a great deal in common. They all describe a conflict between two or more sides, a situation in which each party aspires to an outcome that the other is apparently unwilling to provide. The outcome may involve access to the family car, time, ease of scheduling, land, security, justice, tolerable living conditions—or any of myriad other possibilities. Note, moreover, that each example of conflict involves a distinctive set of moves, ways of pursuing the conflict in an effort to settle it. Are these moves similar? Not superficially. But they can be sorted into three main classes or strategies that reveal continuity from case to case. Indeed, one of the major objectives of this book is to describe in detail the different sorts of strategies used by parties experiencing conflict and to examine the causes and consequences of the use of these strategies.

One basic strategy is *contending*—trying to impose one's preferred solution on the other party. Dad presumably wanted an apology from his son, Ben, and tried to impose this by venting his anger and frustration. Sales and Production tried at first to argue each other into submission, as did Israel and Egypt in the early stages of the Camp David negotiations. In the dispute between Rodney King and the Los Angeles police, contending assumed a distinctly physical form, as did the response by angry Los Angeles residents to the jury verdict in the subsequent trial of the police officers.

A second strategy is *yielding*—lowering one's own aspirations and settling for less than one would have liked. This is the way Sales and Production resolved their dispute over timing. Each side settled for less than it aspired to and, in so doing, the parties managed to carve out a compromise agreement. Is the agreement a good one? That is, is it likely to be mutually satisfactory? We cannot be sure, but there is reason to wonder whether a "worst of both worlds" solution may have evolved. A delay of three months may have been sufficient to erode the profits that Sales hoped for, and moving up the production schedule by three months may have seriously disrupted the efficiency of Production's plan. Yielding created a solution, but not necessarily a solution of high quality.

A third fundamental strategy is *problem solving*—pursuing an alternative that satisfies the aspirations of both sides. With the mediation assistance of President Carter and his aides, Egypt and Israel engaged in just such a process when they moved toward an agreement to disengage in the Sinai Peninsula. In theory, Egypt and Israel could have engaged in problem solving without U.S. assistance as a mediator; they could have identified their respective underlying interests and, on that basis, moved to satisfy them by developing a mutually acceptable solution. Because the two sides had a long history of intense conflict with each other, President Carter's intervention as a mediator offered a perspective that perhaps made more likely both sides' satisfaction of their aspirations.

It is well to note several things about these three strategies for dealing with conflict. First, most conflict situations—be they armed exchanges, labor strikes, international negotiations, family squabbles, or the tacit exchanges that occur when two drivers vie for position at an unmarked intersection—call forth a *combination,* and often a *sequence,* of the preceding strategies. Rarely is one strategy used to the exclusion of the others.

Second, each strategy may be implemented through a wide variety of tactics. The terms *strategy* and *tactics* differ in scope. A strategy constitutes a set of (macroscopic) objectives or ends, and tactics are the (relatively microscopic) means to these ends. As will become apparent, achieving a strategic objective requires individual tactical maneuvers. In this book we look primarily at strategic considerations, but we also keep a careful eye on the tactics that help transform strategic objectives into reality.

Third, contending, yielding, and problem solving are each *coping* strategies, in the sense that each involves a relatively consistent, coherent effort to settle conflict: by taking something away, giving something up, or working jointly to solve the problem at hand.[3] Contending and yielding are coping strategies that are mirror images of each other. Together they cause conflicts to escalate, and the details of their operation are the focus of the first part of the book. Problem solving is a coping strategy whose objective is to produce a mutually acceptable settlement—either through negotiation or with the assistance of an outside intervenor, perhaps a mediator like President Carter at Camp David. The conditions that give rise to problem solving, as well as methods for engaging in this strat-

[3] In contrast, we can point to two very different strategies—withdrawing and inaction—that deal with conflict by *avoiding* it. Although we do not address either of these strategies in this book, a few words about each are in order. *Withdrawing* involves choosing to leave the scene of the conflict, either physically or psychologically, as when a small child walks away from a fight with an older sib. Although withdrawal can lead to victory (witness the strategic retreat of the Soviet army during World War II in the face of a blitzkrieg Nazi advance), it typically involves abandonment of conflict. *Inaction* involves doing nothing, simply waiting for the other side to move.

egy through negotiation or third party intervention, are the focus of the second part of this book. In between the stages of escalation and settlement lies a transitional period: the stage of stalemate.

As the four opening examples illustrate, conflicts differ in their complexity and importance, in the strategies to which they give rise, and in the solutions to which they lead. Despite these differences, we believe that—regardless of the segment of society in which they occur—conflicts have much in common.[4] Conflicts at the interpersonal, intergroup, interorganizational, and international level are clearly not the same. Nevertheless, we believe it is possible to develop generalizations that cut across, and shed light on, most or all conflicts. Our aim in this book is to organize and report existing contributions to an emerging theory of social conflict and to add ideas of our own. Although we wish to improve the practice of dispute settlement, and therefore occasionally introduce prescriptive advice for doing so (particularly in Chapters 10 and 11), our aim is primarily *descriptive:* to account, as best we can, for the many interesting ways in which people go about addressing social conflict.

WHAT IS CONFLICT?

According to Webster (1983), the term *conflict* originally meant a "fight, battle, or struggle"—that is, a physical confrontation between parties. But its meaning has grown to include a "sharp disagreement or opposition, as of interests, ideas, etc." The term now embraces the psychological underpinnings of physical confrontation as well as physical confrontation itself. In short, the term *conflict* has come to be so broadly applied that it is in danger of losing its status as a singular concept.

Our solution to this problem has been to adopt a restrictive meaning that builds on Webster's second definition. For us, *conflict means perceived divergence of interest, or a belief that the parties' current aspirations cannot be achieved simultaneously.* We have chosen this meaning because it seems to be the best place to begin building theory. We are able to construct a simple yet powerful theory (presented in Chapters 2 and 3) by trying to explain the origins of perceived divergence of interest and the impact of this perception on strategic choice and outcome. Undoubtedly our decision in this matter was influenced by the fact that all three of us are social psychologists and hence are accustomed to thinking in terms of the impact of mental status on social behavior. Nevertheless, we believe that this ap-

[4] Harvard Law School Professor Roger Fisher gave a talk some years ago, entitled "Negotiating with the Russians and Negotiating with One's Spouse: Is There a Difference?" His answer, and ours as well: "Not as much as you might think."

proach will be of value to scholars and practitioners from many other disciplines.[5]

Implicit in our definition of conflict is the deliberate exclusion of certain topics from further analysis. We will have little to say about differences of opinion concerning facts, or arguments of interpretation over objective reality. Nor will we have much to say about overt conflict in the form of physical violence, armed insurrection, or war.

Each of the foregoing topics is important and worthy of attention in its own right, but we cannot cover everything. Instead, we wish to examine the psychological realm of perceived divergence of interest and to emphasize conflict as it occurs in the present—with its attendant implications for the future. What will be the disposition of the Sinai? How long will Production take to fill the order? Why did the Rodney King incident turn into a major urban crisis? How can Ben and Dad settle their conflict over the family car? These are the sorts of questions we wish to address, although we cannot ignore the past altogether (past frustrations can make people concerned about precedents for the future and breed hostility that encourages the future use of heavy contentious tactics).

Our analysis of conflict has been informed, whenever possible, by the awareness that conflict is waged in diverse settings, often involving multiple parties, and much of our analysis attempts to take such complexity into account. Still, we have focused primarily on dyadic conflict—that is, conflict between two parties—for several reasons. First, although we have tried to make use of the limited field research available on social conflict, most of the relevant conflict research has in fact been conducted in laboratory settings, and it has typically involved the dyad. Second, as social psychologists we find ourselves best able to construct a plausible theory based on the unit of analysis we know best: the interface between two individuals, two groups, or two organizations. Similarly, we believe that the dyad is a good starting place from which to analyze more complex conflictual relations; often, analysis of even the most complex of conflicts can be facilitated by understanding the polarities that produce those who are in favor of some course of action versus those who are equally opposed. Although the fight between Ben and Dad escalates to include Mom and Sis, what remains in the last analysis is the "we versus they," two-sided quality of the conflict.

Because much of our analysis pivots around the dyad, we use a bit of jargon throughout the book. When our analysis is presented from one

[5] By defining conflict as *perceived* rather than *true* divergence of interest, we depart from custom in the social sciences. We believe that this departure has merit because perceived divergence of interest is more useful in predicting what people actually will do. This is because *perceptions ordinarily have an immediate impact on behavior* (that is, in the case of conflict, on the choice among strategies), *whereas reality works more slowly and with less certainty.* We acknowledge that defining conflict in perceptual terms leaves open the possibility that one party will believe that there is a conflict of interest while the other does not. In such a case, one party must clearly be wrong, although each will probably act on its perceptions anyway.

side in a relationship, we refer to that person or group as *Party* and to the other person or group—the one to whom things are done to or with—as *Other*.

SOME GOOD NEWS AND SOME BAD NEWS ABOUT CONFLICT

Although conflict is found in almost every realm of human interaction, and although episodes of conflict are among the most significant and newsworthy events of human life, it would be a mistake to assume that interaction necessarily involves conflict. People manage to get along remarkably well with other individuals, groups, and organizations; they do so with consideration, helpfulness, and skill, and with little evidence of conflict along the way. When conflict *does* arise, more often than not it is settled, even resolved, with little acrimony and to the mutual satisfaction of the parties involved.

People have been interested in the study of conflict at least since biblical times. The nineteenth century provided a dramatic, energetic thrust whose impact is still felt today. Charles Darwin was interested in the struggle within species for "survival of the fittest." Sigmund Freud studied the internal combat of various psychodynamic forces for control over the ego. And Karl Marx, reflecting the dialectical philosophy that preceded him, developed a political and economic analysis based on the assumption that conflict is an inevitable part of society.

If we conclude, on the basis of the ideas of these three profound nineteenth-century thinkers, that conflict is necessarily destructive, we miss the point of their work. For Darwin, the productive outcome of the struggle for survival was the emergence of an individual who happens to have a genetic anomaly that fosters survival; new species arise because of the genetic adjustments occasioned by the struggle to survive. Freud similarly envisioned individual growth and insight to result from the struggle to understand and address the conflicts within. And Marx, in his dialectical materialism, determined that conflict promotes further conflict; that change is inevitable; and that, at least in his judgment, this change moves inexorably in the direction of an improved human condition. All three men were keenly aware of the virtues and necessity of conflict; they all saw the beneficial as well as the costly consequences of conflict.

The Good News

First, conflict is the seedbed that nourishes social change. People who regard their situation as unjust or see current policies as foolish must usually do battle with the old order before they can be successful. Almost every new piece of legislation in the Congress of the United States is enacted after a period of debate and cross pressures from opposing interest groups. Where would we be if, in the interest of avoiding conflict, we routinely stifled reformers or they stifled themselves?

A second positive function of social conflict is to facilitate the reconciliation of people's legitimate interests. Most conflicts do not end with Party winning and Other losing. Rather, some synthesis of the two positions—some integrative agreement—often emerges that fosters the mutual benefit of Party and Other, as well as the larger collectives of which they are members. If union and management, Egypt and Israel, Sales and Production, or two people arguing over an automobile can manage to reconcile their interests, they will contribute to their own individual outcomes and, indirectly, to the well-being of the larger organization, world community, or neighborhood of which they are members. If, in an effort to avoid conflict, they are not allowed to make claims against one another, such deep-seated reconciliation will seldom be possible. In this sense, conflict can be considered a creative force.

The third positive effect is that by virtue of its first two functions, conflict fosters group unity. Without the capacity for social change or the reconciliation of individual interests, group solidarity is likely to decline—and with it group effectiveness and enjoyment of the group experience (Coser, 1956). The eventual result is often group disintegration. Without conflict, groups are like the married couple in Ingmar Bergman's film *Couples,* who fail to recognize and confront the issues in their marriage and eventually split up because neither is getting anything out of their relationship.

And the Bad News

We have seen that much social exchange does not give rise to conflict. Moreover, when conflict does arise, it is often settled without pain and rancor while serving a number of positive functions. However, the fact remains that conflict is fully capable of wreaking havoc on society. Marriages succumb to conflict at an alarming rate. Our daily newspapers are replete with accounts of controversies that—if not especially common—are certainly compelling in their terrible intensity and consequences. And although the Damoclean sword of nuclear annihilation no longer looms over our collective heads, it would be hard to deny that conflict remains the major problem of our times.

It may seem paradoxical that conflict can have both harmful and beneficial consequences, but this paradox is more apparent than real. What often happens is that the positive functions of conflict are swamped by the harmful consequences that derive from the use of heavy contentious tactics. In the throes of insult, threat, and even physical assault, it is difficult to savor the positive functions of conflict.

When people deal with conflict by contending, each trying to do well at the other's expense, they tend to engage in a set of moves and countermoves that intensifies conflict. We refer to this increase in intensity as *escalation.* The escalation of conflict is accompanied by a number of transformations, each of which is difficult—though not impossible—to reverse. These are explored in greater detail in Chapter 5.

Although conflict need not be destructive in its consequences, when it is bad, it may well be horrid. And because destructive conflict—although far less prevalent than its more constructive cousin—is capable of doing so much damage to the people who are caught in its machinery, we want to take a particularly close look in this book at the circumstances that lead conflict along a destructive, escalatory pathway.[6]

PLAN OF THE BOOK

The book's organization reflects the set of guiding assumptions and interests that have characterized our introductory remarks. Chapter 2 elaborates on our definition of conflict, introduces simple graphic analysis to clarify the definition, and summarizes the causes of conflict as well as the conditions that make conflict less likely to erupt. Chapter 3 deals with the topic of strategic choice. We first describe in more detail the three strategies for coping with conflict. We then turn to the set of considerations that lead Party to choose one strategy over another. Together, Chapters 2 and 3 comprise the theoretical heart of the book, inasmuch as they present concepts that are used in most of the later chapters.

The next five chapters focus, in one way or another, on the important topic of escalation. Chapter 4 explores the set of contentious tactics that Party typically uses in an effort to prevail at Other's expense. Conflict escalation is most likely to occur when such contentious tactics are used. Chapter 5 details the transformations that occur during escalation. It also examines two conflict models that have been used to explain the escalation of conflict, the aggressor-defender and conflict spiral models. Chapter 6 examines the structural changes that often occur during conflict escalation, which explain why escalation tends to persist and recur. Chapter 6 also introduces a third conflict model, the structural change model.

[6] Or to put this point another way, escalation and de-escalation are not weighted equally. It is a lot easier to move up the escalation ladder than to come back down. This is because (1) people are usually more frustrated by being deprived than they benefit from being rewarded, (2) experiencing inequity against us is more disturbing than experiencing inequity in our favor, and (3) fear is a more powerful motivator than a sense of safety. As a result, people are more prone to retaliate and engage in defensive actions when challenged than to reciprocate when they are treated well.

Chapter 7 looks at the mechanisms that cause structural changes to endure; it is these mechanisms that underlie the tendency of escalation to persist and recur, and that help us understand the deterioration of human relationships. Finally, Chapter 8 completes our look at conflict escalation by examining the conditions that increase or reduce stability—that is, the likelihood and extent of escalation during conflict.

The focus of Chapter 9 is stalemate, the point at which Party and/or Other comes to believe that it is no longer capable or willing to continue expending the effort necessary to sustain an escalating exchange. Stalemate represents the point of transition in a conflict-intensified exchange between the trajectory of escalation and the pathway of de-escalation and eventual problem solving.

Chapter 10 addresses the extremely important, constructive, and often creative strategy of problem solving. Problem solving, a commonly used and often highly effective solution to conflict, need not occur only in the wake of conflict escalation and stalemate. This chapter describes the several methods of moving toward an integrative solution that satisfies the aspirations of all concerned.

The final chapter, Chapter 11, addresses the roles and functions of third parties, particularly mediators. Although third parties can involve themselves in disputes at any point along the way, we are particularly interested in exploring the several things that third parties can do to ease disputants away from contentious behavior and in the direction of problem solving.

2

Nature and Sources of Conflict

Defining Components of Conflict • *The Role of Relative Deprivation* • *Sources of Intergroup Conflict* • Conditions that Encourage Conflict • Conditions that Discourage Conflict • *Problems with Too Much Suppression of Conflict* • Conclusions

In Chapter 1 we defined *conflict* as perceived divergence of interest. In Chapter 2 we elaborate on this definition by examining the several components that define conflict—whether such conflict takes place between individuals, groups, or nations. In other words, how can we know when conflict exists? Next, we look at the conditions that encourage conflict. Finally, we review the conditions that make conflict less likely to occur.

DEFINING COMPONENTS OF CONFLICT

By the term *interests* in our definition of conflict, we mean most generally people's feelings about what is basically desirable. We use the term where others (Burton, 1979) use *values* or *needs*. Interests tend to be central to people's thinking and action, forming the core of many of their attitudes, goals, and intentions.

There are several dimensions that can be used to describe interests. Some interests are virtually universal (such as the needs for security, identity, social approval, happiness, clarity about the nature of one's world, and some level of physical well-being). Other interests are specific to certain actors (such as the Palestinians' desire for a homeland or Ben's wish to have access to the family car). Some interests are more important (higher in priority) than others, and such priorities differ from person to person. Some interests underlie other interests; for example, America's interest in security underlies its interest in maintaining a strong Western alliance.[1]

Before Party's interests can clash with those of Other, these interests must be translated into *aspirations*, a behavioral representation of the things that Party strives for or believes it must exceed.[2] Aspirations, in turn, have several sources, including Party's past achievement, the achievement of Other (or various Others), the perceived power relations between Party and Other, and social norms (including principles of fairness).

Conflict exists when Party sees its own and Other's aspirations as incompatible. Such perceived incompatibility depends on the extent to which the available alternatives (options) seem capable of satisfying the aspirations of Party and Other. When available alternatives are compatible with these aspirations, no conflict is experienced. The poorer the perceived fit between the pool of available alternatives and the aspirations of Party and Other, the more severe the conflict.

A few graphs may help to clarify what is meant by perceived incompatibility of aspirations. Figure 2.1 represents Party's conception of the joint outcome space for itself and Other.[3] The horizontal axis represents some dimension or combination of dimensions of value to Party, and the vertical axis represents a similar value dimension for Other. The dashed lines represent perceived aspirations. The line marked P represents Party's own aspirations; that marked O, Party's view of Other's aspirations. The points in the space represent various known alternatives. These alternatives can be a matter of Party's behavior, Other's behavior, or joint action by Party and Other. A and B can be thought of as partisan alternatives, providing value only to Party (A) *or* Other (B); C is moderately favorable to both, a form of compromise; and D is highly favorable to both, an integrative alternative.

Alternatives such as D in Figure 2.1 are called *integrative* because they integrate—that is, reconcile—the two parties' interests. Anything that

[1] Note that our definition of *interests* is deliberately broader than, and is meant to subsume, the term as used in popular treatments of negotiation, such as Fisher, Ury, and Patton's (1991) *Getting to YES.* In their illustration of two sisters arguing over the division of an orange, "positions" describes how much of the orange each would like. "Interests" denotes their respective underlying concerns, where one sister wishes to bake a cake (and wants only the peel of the orange) while the second is thirsty (and cares only about the fruit of the orange).

[2] Aspirations may take the form of *goals* that Party is striving for, such as a $2,000 raise or a moderate level of respect within Party's profession. Or aspirations may be represented by certain minimal *standards* that Party aspires to meet or exceed, such as a rock-bottom salary requirement of $32,000 or a 98% certainty of being able to repel an enemy attack.

[3] This and subsequent diagrams have elements in common with those used by Thomas (1976).

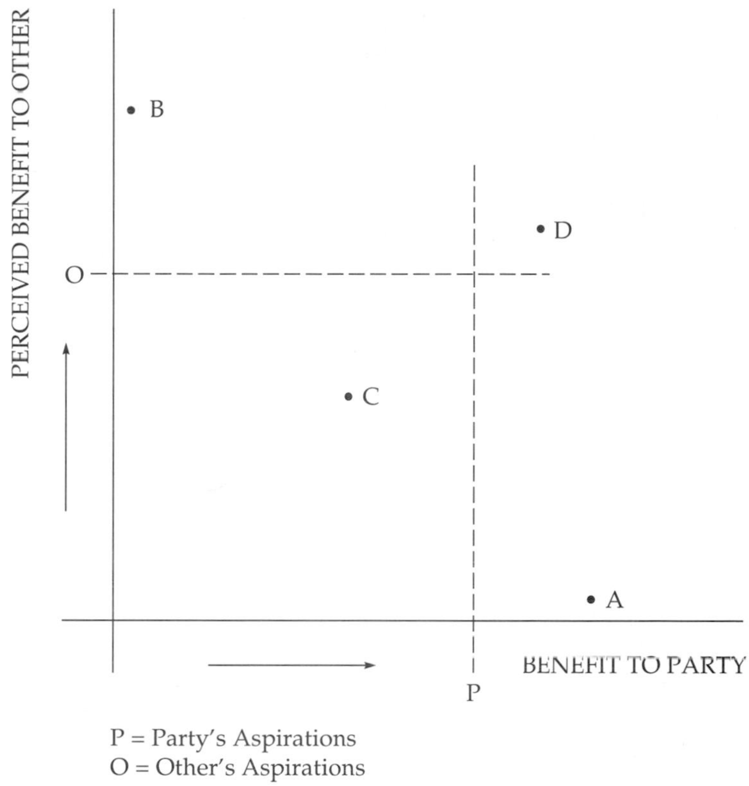

FIGURE 2.1
Party's conception of a joint outcome space with Other.

provides a glimmer of hope of finding an integrative alternative diminishes perceived conflict. For example, when Sadat made his famous trip to Jerusalem in 1977, it began to seem possible that a solution could be found to the major differences between Egypt and Israel. As a result, the tension between Egypt and Israel diminished in the eyes of most people on both sides.

Figure 2.2 shows four possible patterns of perceived alternatives and aspirations. In Figure 2.2*a*, there is no perceived divergence of interest because a known alternative satisfies both parties' aspirations. (It is represented by the point that lies above and to the right of the intersections of the two dashed lines.) Figures 2.2*b* through 2.2*d*, which can be contrasted with Figure 2.2*a*, depict various ways in which perceived divergence of interest can develop. In Figure 2.2*b*, Party's own aspirations have risen to a level where there is no viable alternative. In Figure 2.2*c*, Other's aspirations are perceived to have risen to such a level. In Figure 2.2*d*, the mutually acceptable (integrative) alternative that appeared in Figure 2.2*a* is no

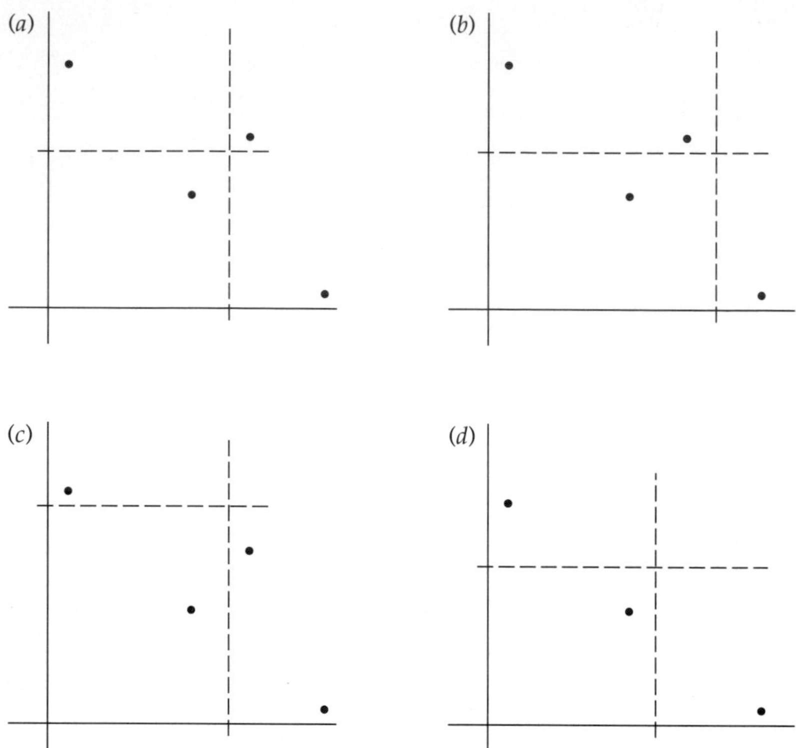

FIGURE 2.2
Four possible patterns of perceived alternatives and aspirations.

longer available, and the remaining alternatives have the character of a zero-sum game, where Party's advantage implies Other's disadvantage.[4]

Figure 2.2 shows that conflict looks larger as Party's and Other's aspirations rise in relation to the available alternatives. In addition, people judge conflict on the basis of the apparent *rigidity* of these aspirations. When aspirations seem incompatible, conflict is judged to be more profound when the apparent aspirations on both sides are rigid. The reason for this is that rigid aspirations resist lowering; hence, conflict seems more difficult to resolve.

[4] Though they do provide an intuitive understanding of our ideas about conflict, graphs of the kind shown in Figures 2.1 and 2.2 have serious limitations in that they treat utility (an individual's level of benefit) as a single dimension. In reality, human needs in most situations are multidimensional. For example, people need both food and adequate housing, and they cannot readily trade more of one for less of the other, as implied by a simple utility concept. Rather than having a single level of aspiration, as implied by Figures 2.1 and 2.2, people are likely to have multiple aspirations, one for each realm of need involved in the controversy. A more sophisticated analysis would employ multidimensional graphs.

Aspirations tend to be rigid when one or both of two conditions obtains: first, when very important values underlie the aspirations (security, identity, and recognition, for most people and probably for all nations); and second, when the values underlying the aspirations are of the either-or variety (Party either achieves them or it does not). Such values produce rigid aspirations because making any concession requires giving up the value altogether.

Conflict is likely to seem particularly profound when Party regards its aspirations as legitimate or rightful, that is, as outcomes to which Party is entitled. This is partly because rightful aspirations tend to be rigid and partly because failure to achieve rightful aspirations is a source of special distress. For example, prior to the 1971 prison revolt at the Attica correctional facility in upstate New York, prisoners were led to believe (based on promises made by State Corrections Commissioner Russell Oswald) that they were entitled to numerous improvements in prison conditions. When, for a variety of reasons, these improvements were not forthcoming, the prisoners felt deeply disappointed. An extremely costly prison revolt was the result, in which nearly forty prisoners and corrections officials lost their lives (*Attica: The Official Report of the New York State Special Commission on Attica*, 1972).

We see that conflict, defined as perceived divergence of interest, occurs when no alternative seems to exist that will satisfy the aspirations of both Party and Other. This can occur because Party or Other has high aspirations or because integrative alternatives seem to be in short supply. When such conflict exists, it seems especially severe if Party and Other have rigid aspirations that they regard as legitimate.

The Role of Relative Deprivation

Divergence of interest is often discovered as a result of harsh experience in which Party fails to achieve its aspirations. Such an experience is called *relative deprivation*. One example in this regard is the 1971 Attica uprising. Or consider the experience of the African American residents of Los Angeles in the aftermath of the Rodney King beating. Many people expected that the police officers responsible for this savage beating would be brought to trial, convicted, and punished. When the officers were found innocent, this outcome inflamed the passions of a great many people.

Relative deprivation has two effects: First, it alerts Party to the existence of incompatible interests. Second, the frustration and indignation associated with relative deprivation are a source of energy which increases the likelihood and vigor of coping activity. If Other is held responsible (i.e., blamed) for Party's relative deprivation, this energy takes the form of anger, which is particularly likely to produce contentious action.

If relative deprivation continues, a sense of hopelessness may develop. This usually diminishes conflict behavior, and hence, overt conflict. The most common reason for this is that Party adjusts its aspirations to fit reality, reducing the perceived divergence of interest.

The role of relative deprivation is so common in the development of conflict that some theorists view it as a sine qua non for the emergence of conflict (Davies, 1962; Gurr, 1970; Kriesberg, 1982). We differ with this point of view, since we believe that Party can draw conclusions about divergence of interest from other evidence than that provided by relative deprivation, including Other's statements about its motives and a lack of trust in Other.

The term *trust* has many meanings, but in this context it implies a belief that Other is positively concerned about Party's interests. The concern need not be genuine, in the sense of being based on positive feelings toward Party. It is quite possible for Party to trust Other because it believes that Other is dependent on Party and for this reason unlikely to risk Party's anger.

Distrust is the opposite of trust. It is a belief that Other is hostile or indifferent to Party's interests, in other words, a perception that there is a divergence of interest with Other. Distrust encourages a perception that Other's aspirations are incompatible with Party's. For example, as the Muslims of northern Sudan seek closer relations with Egypt (their Muslim neighbor to the north) the northern Sudanese are likely to view their adversary, the animist peoples of southern Sudan, as opposed to the establishment of such relations. This perception, in turn, leads the northerners to distrust the southerners, thereby encouraging conflict. Trust, on the other hand, discourages conflict by fostering the belief that Other will try to accommodate Party's interests in areas of special importance to Party. We have more to say about trust and distrust in Chapter 6.

Sources of Intergroup Conflict

When groups rather than individuals are in the throes of conflict, several additional mechanisms come into play. Group support can make people more confident of the legitimacy of their aspirations, enhancing the likelihood of conflict. When several people with similar latent (unrecognized) interests begin to talk with one another, they may begin to develop and pursue new aspirations, which can lead to conflict with others whose interests are opposed to these aspirations. Such a result is particularly likely if they begin to identify themselves as a group apart from other groups.[5]

For intergroup conflict to develop, a sense of group bonding is

[5] Consider the formation of, and struggle between, various ethnic groups in the former Yugoslavia.

needed. One of the most important sources of bonding is common group membership—the perception that Other is a member of a group to which Party also belongs. A good deal of experimental research has been conducted on the relationship between this phenomenon and *ethnocentrism,* the tendency to favor the ingroup over the outgroup and to derogate the outgroup (Brewer, 1979, 1986; Fisher, 1990; Stroebe et al., 1988; Tajfel, 1970). Even the most minimal common group membership—being classified by outsiders with some people and not with others—tends to produce ethnocentrism. People like better, think more highly of, and discriminate in favor of other people with whom they are classed, regardless of the basis for the classification (Brewer, 1979; Messick & Mackie, 1989; Tajfel et al., 1971). This is the social categorization or "minimal group" effect. It helps to explain why ethnocentrism is so universal a human characteristic (Sumner, 1906).[6]

Conflict may be more common in relations between groups than in relations between individuals, and more common in relations between individuals who do not see themselves as sharing a common group membership than in relations between those who do. Evidence favoring the first of these two generalizations (more escalation between groups than between individuals) has been found in two studies (Komorita & Lapworth, 1982; McCallum et al., 1985).

What mechanism can account for the social categorization effect? There are two popular explanations. Allen and Wilder (1975) propose that common group identity produces perceived similarity with other members of one's group, which leads to positive sentiments toward these people. Turner (1981) postulates that social categorization produces competition for status between the ingroup and the outgroup, motivated by the fact that people's self-concepts are very much wrapped up in their social identities.

The latter, "social identity" explanation is supported by three findings. One is that personal failure leads Party to voice more positive images of its own group and more negative images of Other's group (Cialdini & Richardson, 1980). This finding can be deduced from the social identity explanation because personal failure threatens Party's self-concept. The second is that there is more bias against groups that are more similar in status to Party's own (Turner, 1981). This finding can also be deduced from the social identity explanation because groups that are roughly equal in status are more likely to compete for status. The third finding is that there is more bias against an outgroup of a different status from Party's

[6] One of the authors (JZR) has had the experience, at the YMCA pool at which he swims each morning at 6 A.M., of discovering how quickly bonds form among the mixed-sex swimmers who happen to frequent the pool's "moderate circle" at that ungodly hour. Indeed, the sense of "groupness" is sufficiently compelling that newcomers to the pool are typically treated with hostility and contempt simply because they are *new*. They have to earn their way into the group's good graces.

own to the extent that there is uncertainty about Party's own or the Other group's status (Turner, 1981). This can be deduced by the same reasoning.

Thus, intergroup conflict is more likely to develop when group identity exists. Such group identity, in turn, is stronger when groups are homogeneous (Wilder, 1984) and when group boundaries seem immutable with no chance of transition to another group (Kriesberg, 1982).

Group identity leads to aspirations for Party's group. This sets the stage for fraternalistic deprivation, the sense that one's group has been deprived, which has been identified empirically as a major source of intergroup conflict (Abeles, 1976; Guimond & Dubé-Simard, 1983; Runciman, 1966; Vanneman & Pettigrew, 1972; Walker & Mann, 1987). The result is often the development of a *struggle group* consisting of people who espouse a common cause. One example of a struggle group in formation can be seen in the sequence of steps during the 1960s by which individual students' distress about the Vietnam War was transformed into a massive student movement that came into conflict with various adult institutions, including many university administrations.[7]

CONDITIONS THAT ENCOURAGE CONFLICT

A number of conditions serve to encourage conflict, that is, perceived divergence of interest. These include the following:

1. *Periods of rapidly expanding achievement.* People become more hopeful as things get better, causing their aspirations to rise. In periods of rapidly expanding achievement, such rising aspirations can sometimes outstrip reality. A case in point is the period of growing African American awareness, self-confidence, and agitation during the 1960s, after two centuries of subjugation. Enforcement of civil rights had improved markedly in the prior decade, especially with the landmark Supreme Court decision outlawing school segregation; and the pace of this advance was accelerated in the 1960s, which saw the passage of much new legislation and widespread changes in the attitudes of whites. Paradoxically, this period also saw more discontent and agitation among African Americans than any other time before or after. What may well have happened is that the progress made in civil rights encouraged expectations of rapid further change, producing unrealistic aspirations. We do not contend that these aspirations were illegitimate, only that they were inconsistent with the aspirations of others and therefore produced conflict.

Conflict is especially likely to occur after a period of expanding

[7] Dahrendorf (1959) has specified three conditions that foster development of a struggle group and thereby encourage conflict: (1) continuous communication among the people in question; (2) availability of leadership to help articulate an ideology, organize a group, and formulate a program for group action; and (3) group legitimacy in the eyes of the broader community—or at least the absence of effective community suppression of the group.

achievement if there is a slowdown or reversal in this achievement. Thus Davies (1962) presents evidence that revolutions occur when a period of expanding "economic and social development is followed by a short period of sharp reversal" (p. 5).

2. *Ambiguity about relative power.* Conflict is especially likely when ambiguity exists about the nature of power such that each party can conclude—through a process of wishful thinking—that it is stronger than the other. This state of affairs tends to produce incompatible aspirations, leading to conflict. The Vietnam War offers a good example. Because of differing military technologies, both the United States and North Vietnam inferred that they were the probable victor. Many years of war were required to demonstrate which of these parties had drawn the right conclusions (it was North Vietnam).

3. *Invidious comparison.* Conflict is also encouraged when Party develops the awareness that Other is of no greater merit than Party, yet Other is afforded greater privilege. This leads to an *invidious comparison,* in which aspirations rise for both realistic reasons (because it seems reasonable that Party can do as well as Other) and idealistic reasons (because Party thinks that its outcomes should be as good as Other's).

The importance of a comparison figure in the development of conflict is illustrated by the events in Henrik Ibsen's classic play *A Doll's House.* The heroine, Nora, is a traditional housewife who is dominated by her husband. She becomes acquainted with Christine, a more liberated woman, and the contrast between their two conditions causes Nora to aspire to greater freedom and privilege. This brings her into conflict with her husband, whom she eventually leaves.[8]

4. *Status inconsistency.* Invidious comparisons are particularly likely when there is status inconsistency (Kriesberg, 1982). Status inconsistency (also called *rank disequilibrium*) exists when there are multiple criteria for assessing people's merit or contributions, and some people are higher on one criterion and lower on another criterion than others. In our society, for example, both experience and education are sources of on-the-job status. People with experience tend to believe that experience makes the most relevant contribution, whereas people with education tend to believe the opposite. When these two kinds of people have to work together, each is likely to feel more deserving of rewards than the other, and conflict is especially likely to develop.

5. *Weakening normative consensus.* Societies and the groups within them are constantly developing rules to govern the behavior of their members. Broader and longer-lasting rules are called *norms.* A major function of such rules is to dovetail the aspirations of potential opponents

[8] Equity theorists (Adams, 1965; Walster et al., 1978) argue that invidious comparisons are especially likely to be made when people whose outcomes are better than our own seem similar to us in basic merit (the technical term for merit is *contributions*) or when people whose outcomes are equal to our own appear to have lower merit than we do.

and hence reduce the likelihood of conflict (Thibaut & Kelley, 1959). An example is the norm against stealing. If this norm did not exist, conflict would be so pervasive and severe that society would be virtually unworkable. A less earthshaking example is the minimum wage law. By specifying a single wage level for routine jobs, this law limits the aspirations of both workers and employers and thus reduces the likelihood of conflict between them. A similar function is played by the rule, subscribed to in many families, that one spouse cooks and the other does the dishes.

Norms are relevant to conflict because they specify the outcomes to which Party is entitled and hence the aspirations to which Party has a right. When Party's rightful aspirations seem incompatible with Other's apparent goals, the result is often quite explosive.

The points just made imply that conflict is particularly common at times when social norms are weak and changing. In such periods, Party is especially likely to develop idiosyncratic views of its rights, views that do not dovetail with those developed by Other. The present troubled period in relations between husbands and wives is a case in point.

6. *Zero-sum thinking.* The view that Other's gain is Party's loss, and vice versa, is zero-sum thinking (also known as the "fixed-pie" assumption). This is another important condition that encourages conflict. Often issues really are zero-sum in nature, as when Party and Other are to divide a resource of limited magnitude between them: the more one gets, the less there is for the other. At least as often, however, conflict is encouraged not because issues are truly zero-sum in nature[9] but because they are treated this way by Party and Other. One of the characteristics of many escalating conflicts is that Party's aspirations shift (see Chapter 5) from doing well, to avoiding doing poorly, to harming Other as much as possible. In the throes of such shifts in motivation, zero-sum thinking is quite commonplace.

7. *Communication among group members.* Each of the sources of intergroup conflict described earlier in this chapter (e.g., common group identity, fraternalistic deprivation) is encouraged by communication among group members (Dahrendorf, 1959; Kriesberg, 1982). This means that conflict is especially likely to be produced when group members are in close proximity to one another, are involved in common activities, and/or have access to the technology of communication.

8. *The availability of leadership.* Intergroup conflict is especially likely when leaders feel a sense of fraternalistic deprivation and are ready to organize a struggle group (Coleman, 1957; Dahrendorf, 1959; Kriesberg, 1982). In William Golding's novel *Lord of the Flies,* two leaders rapidly emerge: Ralph and Jack. In Golding's fantasy about survival of a band of shipwrecked children on an isolated island, Ralph is inclined to lead by orienting the small children to the circumstances that will facilitate their

[9] Indeed, even when they are, it is often possible to find ways to transform a zero-sum into a non-zero-sum arrangement. Some of these ways are described in Chapters 9 through 11.

escape and rescue. Jack, in contrast, seems motivated to turn the band of fearful children on the island into a struggle group prepared to combat all forms of authority except Jack's own. Jack prevails, at least for a while.

CONDITIONS THAT DISCOURAGE CONFLICT

It is possible to develop a listing of conditions that discourage conflict simply by turning to the previous section and standing each point on its head. We will discuss some of these conditions, along with several others that are best presented solely in this context.

1. *Consensus about norms.* Low-conflict communities typically have a broad normative consensus regarding certain goals, rules of conduct, role definitions, procedures for decision making, and authority and status systems. In a smoothly functioning automobile assembly plant, for example, established authority relations and work rules ensure the compatibility of most people's aspirations. And in small New England towns in the nineteenth century, the common cultural heritage and the Protestant church served as social cement. In contrast, conflicts are often found in communities whose norms are breaking down, because some community members begin to aspire to outcomes that others are not willing to let them have. For example, many difficulties that arise in the two-person "community" of marriage today can be traced to uncertainties in our society about what spouses can reasonably expect from each other (Rubin & Rubin, 1989).

When a set of norms has broad support among the more powerful segments of a community, disadvantaged groups—even if they are sizable—are relatively unlikely to develop aspirations that threaten these norms. Most people learn to fit in and make the most of what may be a constricted set of options. Their aspirations fit social reality.

This does not mean that everybody is happy in a community with a broad normative consensus. The least advantaged—be they African Americans, women, students, or slaves—may be quite unhappy. But most of them are sufficiently discouraged (by the fact that everyone else seems to support the norms) or frightened (by the techniques used to enforce the norms) to aspire to no better than they have. Of course, there are always people in such settings who are restless about their rights and benefits. Community stability, in the sense of an absence of conflict, is enhanced if these people can readily escape, as many did by moving to the western frontier from nineteenth-century New England.[10]

[10] Cross-cultural research indicates that many individualistic cultures, like the United States, Great Britain, Germany, and France, highly value autonomy, independence, and individual achievement. In contrast, collectivistic cultures found in South America and Asia highly value interpersonal harmony, conformity, and ingroup achievement (Hofstede, 1980; Triandis, 1989; Triandis et al., 1988). On the basis of these findings, it could be argued that there will be stronger consensus about norms in collectivistic cultures than in individualistic ones; furthermore, there will be stronger social sanctions against nonconformity in the former than in the latter.

Stable communities have particularly clear norms governing those interpersonal relationships that are most prone to conflict, such as authority and status relationships. For example, employers and workers have plenty of opportunity for conflict because their activities and wishes are so intimately linked. But most people go into the job situation with a fairly clear idea of their appropriate roles. Workers expect to do more or less as they are told and to try to make a good impression; employers expect to provide clear direction and both positive and negative reinforcement. Considering the potential for conflict, things work amazingly well.

2. *Lack of information about Other's attainments.* One method of preventing invidious comparisons on the job is to conceal information about employee rewards. Salary information is particularly easy to conceal, and many organizations do so in an (often fruitless) effort to avert conflict. Another approach is to develop a firm set of norms that link rewards to a single, easily measured criterion, such as seniority or educational attainment. This is the method used to minimize invidious comparisons in the United States civil service system.

3. *Physical and psychological segregation.* This is the approach of "divide and rule." Two forms of segregation can be distinguished: psychological segregation, in which social groups do not identify with one another, and physical segregation, in which they do not come in contact with one another. Psychological segregation is self-imposed, whereas physical segregation can be either self-imposed or imposed by the community. An example of psychological segregation is the tendency of men to compare themselves with other men, and women with other women, in deciding how much money to ask from an employer (Major & Forcey, 1985). This tendency may well contribute to the perpetuation of lower pay for women. An example of self-imposed physical segregation is the tendency of African Americans and whites to sort themselves out according to race in dining halls (Schelling, 1978). Psychological and physical segregation tend to diminish invidious comparisons between social groups, making conflict less likely to occur.

4. *Existence of a strict status system.* Such a system eliminates status inconsistency and reduces comparisons between groups of different status. These systems are most effective when backed up by myths that picture the more advantaged segments of society as more deserving. For his ideal state, the republic, Plato recommended the establishment of such a myth: the rulers should be viewed as containing gold in their makeup, the auxiliaries silver, and the farmers and other workers iron and bronze. Myths about racial and sexual inferiority serve a similar purpose. In our society, African Americans and women have traditionally been viewed as intellectually and emotionally deficient and hence less deserving of reward. Quite often they have subscribed to these myths themselves. Such myths encourage the belief that the more advantaged segments of a community are the more deserving, thereby discouraging the "upward comparison"

that often produces feelings of relative deprivation (Wood, 1989). Hence, they promote social stability (though often at the expense of social justice).

5. *Social mobility.* Both social mobility and the myth of social mobility help to discourage conflict when strict status systems do not exist. The myth of social mobility (Apfelbaum, 1979) holds that anyone with ability can advance. This myth implies that if Party's outcomes are lower than Other's, it is because of Party's inferior ability. Accordingly, Party has no legitimate claim to greater reward, and no legitimate basis for making invidious comparisons. Because there is some truth to the myth of mobility in America—almost everybody knows someone who has risen from disadvantaged beginnings—it is a particularly important source of stability in our society.

6. *Physical and social barriers to communication.* When such barriers to communication exist, particularly among like-minded people, conflict is likely to be discouraged. This is one method used by elites to prevent the development or continuation of conflict that may challenge the elite's privileged social position.

Psychological and physical separation of potential dissidents makes it difficult for them to join together. In the psychological realm, if they do not trust, respect, or identify with one another, they are unlikely to find common cause. For example, low-status people often do not respect one another because of the myth of their own inferiority. Hence, they have difficulty working together on common problems. Rulers sometimes follow a policy of divide and rule, contriving controversies between potential opponents who might otherwise unite against them.

Keeping people apart physically can have a similar impact. Separating prison chums is a time-honored method for averting prison revolts. The rules against forming organizations without the approval of the Communist party, which were found in all communist countries, have similar objectives. So do rules that deny legitimacy to collective dissent. An example of what can happen when dissenters are given legitimacy occurred in the academic department of one of the authors (DGP). Associate professors who were unhappy with the organization of the department were allowed to form a committee to recommend changes. With their common interests legitimized in this way, they felt free to push for a sweeping reform of the department's structure, which reduced the power of the chairperson who had allowed them to organize.

The reader may have noticed a seeming contradiction between this policy of separating potential deviants and the policy of segregation that was mentioned earlier as a condition discouraging conflict. The contradiction is due to the fact that segregating low-status people from the rest of society has two rather different effects. It reduces social comparison with high-status people and hence makes the low-status group more content with their inferior rewards. Yet the enforced association of segregated people also makes it easier for them to find common cause and to organize for struggle, making conflict more likely under certain circumstances.

It is not yet clear under which conditions each of these opposing effects will prevail, but we can gain some insight into this issue by watching the behavior of successful ruling elites. Ruling groups usually segregate low-status people, distancing themselves from these people but allowing them free association with one another. However, when there is reason to believe that a struggle group is developing, a policy of divide and rule is often substituted. Known dissidents are jailed or exiled, and others of the disadvantaged are "co-opted," or brought into closer association with the ruling group. This often nips conflict in the bud.

This combination of tactics was employed by administrators at the University of Chicago, which survived an undergraduate crisis in the late 1960s without the sort of serious conflict that engulfed many other schools. At the start of the crisis, the undergraduates were segregated from the faculty and administration in the usual dormitory and classroom configurations. The crisis was initiated by a student sit-in designed to reverse a decision to deny tenure to a leftist professor. The administration immediately organized a series of meetings between the faculty and all students who would participate, with the aim of revising the curriculum to make it conform more closely to the students' wishes. This dramatic activity produced bonds between the faculty and the bulk of the student body, psychologically separating the latter from the students who were sitting in. At the same time, a student court began systematically expelling hard-core members of the sit-in. As a result, the sit-in diminished in numbers and finally ended with its leaders admitting defeat.[11]

7. *Removal of actual or potential leadership.* Group formation usually requires leadership. Some individual or small group must articulate and codify the interests of the larger group, formulate a program, and organize people behind it (Dahrendorf, 1959). Whether a dissident movement can get off the ground is largely a function of whether leadership is available and able to operate. It follows that one method of containing the development of a struggle group is to remove potential leaders. Another method, which is effective in somewhat aroused situations, is for moderate and respected community members to speak against, and thus discredit, emerging radical leadership (Coleman, 1957). A third method is to win the leadership over. A tactic that the Korean government formerly used was to give a dissident leader an important position in the government. For example, a university president attracted much support from radical students mainly because of his criticism of the government's plans for educational reform. The government appointed him the secretary of

[11] The all-white government in South Africa followed such a policy over the years preceding the release of Nelson Mandela, the leader of the largest black opposition party, the African National Congress. More militant opponents like Mandela were put in jail, while less militant opponents like Mongosuthu Buthelezi, the leader of the smaller Inkatha Freedom party, were given limited status and rights.

education. Once he assumed that position, he not only withdrew his initial position but also began to support the government's stand.

8. *Blocking outside support.* The success of struggle groups often depends on support from outside their community. During the Cold War (see Chapter 5), much was made of tangible (e.g., military) support for guerrilla groups in countries like South Vietnam and El Salvador. But the issue is more complicated, as there are many forms of intangible support. Community dissent often grows out of a broad social movement at the national or even worldwide level. A case in point is the radical student movement of the late 1960s, which permeated the United States and had its counterparts in France, West Germany, Mexico, and many other countries. Some people thought that national or international leaders were pulling the strings in local communities, but this was seldom the case. The leadership was usually local in origin, and the main contributions of the national and international movements were moral support and examples that could be imitated. Student demonstrations, which spread rapidly in 1968 and 1969, often seemed to contain an element of "keeping up with the Joneses." The news that students had started to demonstrate in one location encouraged the belief that it was possible elsewhere. Pride in one's own local movement depended in part on having a demonstration comparable to those that had occurred on other campuses.

It follows that communities are less stable when there exists a national or international movement consisting of struggle groups in other communities (Coleman, 1957). Once such a movement gets started, it is hard to put the genie back in the bottle. Each struggle action serves as an example to other communities, which then serve as examples to still others in a chain reaction. An example is the overthrow of one communist regime after another in Eastern Europe in 1990.[12]

Problems with Too Much Suppression of Conflict

As mentioned in Chapter 1, conflict has a number of positive functions. Hence, conditions that discourage conflict are a mixed blessing. One problem with discouraging conflict is that archaic policies that advance few people's interests may be preserved. Communities that are averse to conflict typically fail to make needed changes, because there are almost always some proponents of the status quo, however unfavorable it may be for the majority of citizens. In Coser's (1956) words, "Conflict prevents the ossification of the social system by exerting pressure for innovation and creativity" (p. 197). A second danger of putting a cap on conflict is

[12] A conceptual cousin of blocking outside support is introducing a common enemy, the effect of which is to increase group cohesiveness and promote intragroup cooperation. This is why many a leader has created a common enemy or exaggerated the threat of a common enemy. A recent example is the behavior of Iraq's Saddam Hussein in the post–Gulf War period.

that doing so may encourage premature decision making. A group that fears internal conflict may adopt the first plausible suggestion in order to close off debate among its members.[13] Premature decisions are often poor decisions. A third danger is that benign misunderstandings that serve nobody's interests may arise. Research (Fry et al., 1983) suggests that such misunderstandings are sometimes found in courtship. Party is so afraid of antagonizing Other that it fails to push its viewpoint sufficiently for Other to understand it.

Conflict is also often necessary to achieve justice. Many of the techniques for discouraging conflict are used by tyrants and other unfeeling elite groups to prevent agitation for the redress of legitimate grievances. A seemingly tranquil situation may serve to mask gross inequities and interpersonal exploitation.

Nevertheless, there is a limit to the amount of conflict that society can tolerate, even conflict of the most productive sort. Conflict takes time and energy away from other pursuits. A group, organization, or country can become so embroiled in controversy that it is unable to cope with basic environmental demands.[14]

Individuals, groups, and societies must tread a fine line between too little and too much stability. Some element of stability is essential because it is necessary to keep the total amount of conflict between group members within bounds. If most issues were under debate most of the time, there would be no time or energy for coping activities. But too much stability can be maladaptive because efforts to avert conflict run the risk of producing premature decisions and perpetuating outdated policies.

CONCLUSIONS

In this chapter, we have examined the causes of conflict and the conditions that reduce the likelihood of conflict. Stability, in the sense of the absence of conflict, seems superficially attractive, but efforts to achieve this goal can easily be counterproductive. They may consign society to a state of affairs that is static, sometimes unjust, and often unworkable in the long run.

We turn now to strategic choice. Chapter 3 deals with the conditions that determine how Party chooses among the three strategies for coping with conflict: contending, yielding, and problem solving.

[13] It has been widely speculated that one reason the Wang Computer Company failed in the period after its founder's death has to do with an organizational culture that emphasized harmony and the avoidance of conflict. Because of anxiety about conflict, managers were reluctant to make difficult decisions on their own. Rather than confront those with whom they disagreed, the managers waited for An Wang to intervene. As a result, the company had difficulty adjusting to Wang's death and a rapidly changing market.

[14] Something like this appears to have happened in Poland during 1981 and 1982, when the struggle between the government and the popular union Solidarity greatly diminished industrial productivity.

3

Strategic Choice

Peter Colger has to make a decision. For months he has been looking forward to taking his two weeks of vacation at a quiet mountain lodge where he can hunt, fish, and hike to lofty scenic overlooks. Now his wife Mary has rudely challenged this dream. She has told him that she finds the mountains boring and wants to go to Ocean City, Maryland, a busy seaside resort that Peter dislikes intensely. Peter must decide what strategy to employ in this controversy.

As we saw in Chapter 1, three basic strategies are available to Peter. He can engage in *contentious behavior* and try to prevail—for example, by arguing for the merits of a mountain vacation, indicating that he had already made up his mind, threatening to take a separate vacation if Mary does not agree, or even making a large deposit on a room in a mountain hotel. He can take a *problem-solving approach* and try to find a way to go to both places or to a vacation spot that satisfies both sets of interests. He can *yield* to Mary's demands and agree to go to the seashore. And there is another, less interesting approach: he can *avoid* the conflict altogether by being inactive (doing nothing) in the hope that the issue will simply go away or by withdrawing from the controversy—for example, by deciding not to take a vacation.

This chapter examines the conditions that determine how Peter (and, more generally, anyone facing a conflict) decides among these basic strategies.

NATURE OF THE STRATEGIES

Contending refers to any effort to resolve a conflict on Party's terms without regard to Other's interests. When Party employs this strategy, it maintains its own aspirations and tries to persuade or force Other to yield. Various tactics are available to Party when it chooses this strategy. They include making threats, imposing penalties with the understanding that they will be withdrawn if Other concedes, and taking preemptive actions designed to resolve the conflict without Other's consent (in our example, perhaps by making a deposit at a mountain hotel). If Party is trying to reach a negotiated settlement of the controversy, contending may also involve presenting persuasive arguments, making demands that far exceed what is actually acceptable, committing itself to an "unalterable" position, or imposing a deadline.

In contrast, *problem solving* entails an effort to identify the issues dividing the parties and to develop and move toward a solution that appeals to both sides. When Party employs this strategy, it maintains its own aspirations and tries to find a way of reconciling them with Other's aspirations.

Various tactics are available to implement the strategy of problem solving. These include risky moves, such as conceding with the expectation of receiving a return concession, mentioning possible compromises as talking points, and revealing Party's underlying interests. They also include cautious moves, such as hinting at possible compromises, sending disavowable intermediaries to discuss the issues, communicating through back channels, and communicating through a mediator.

Yielding, which involves lowering Party's aspirations, need not imply total capitulation. It may also imply a partial concession. For example, Peter Colger might decide to give up his secondary goal of hiking to mountain overlooks in order to make it easier to find a mutually acceptable agreement. He could then engage in problem solving, seeking a quiet resort that permits fishing and hiking where his wife can also accomplish her major goals of spending time at a busy seaside resort.

CHOOSING A STRATEGY

There are trade-offs among the three basic strategies, in the sense that choosing one of them makes choosing the others less likely. Though sometimes found in combination with each other, these strategies are somewhat incompatible, for three reasons. First, the strategies are alternative means of moving toward the same end, agreement with Other. If it is not possible to use one of them, Party is more likely to employ the others. Second, the strategies require different psychological orientations; for example, it does not seem quite right to try to push Other around while yielding to or working with Other. Third, the strategies tend to send out contradictory signals to Other. Yielding often implies weakness, which is incompatible with putting effective pressure on Other. Contending may undermine Other's trust, reducing the likelihood of effective problem solving.

Because of these trade-offs, there are indirect as well as direct antecedents or conditions that favor all three strategies. Indirect antecedents affect the likelihood of adopting a strategy by encouraging or discouraging one of the other strategies.

Most of the rest of this chapter is devoted to two theoretical notions about the conditions that affect choice among the basic strategies. The first, which is summarized in a *dual concern model*, traces strategic choice to the relative strength of concern about Party's and Other's outcomes. The second, which we call the *perceived feasibility perspective*, attributes this choice to the perceived likelihood of success and the cost of enacting the various strategies. These two theoretical notions are complementary in the sense that each deals with issues ignored by the other.[1]

The chapter ends with a discussion of the forces that determine the vigor with which the three strategies are enacted.

THE DUAL CONCERN MODEL

The dual concern model appears in Figure 3.1. It postulates two types of concerns: *concern about Party's own outcomes*, which is shown on the hori-

[1] A good deal of evidence will be cited in support of these theoretical notions, most of it derived from laboratory experiments on simulated negotiation. *Negotiation*, a form of conflict behavior, occurs when two or more parties try to resolve a divergence of interest by means of conversation. Much of the material presented in Chapter 10 (Problem Solving) is in fact descriptive of aspects of negotiation. Laboratory studies of negotiation typically place subjects (often college students) in a simulated negotiation setting and manipulate theoretically relevant variables. Careful measurements of reactions to these variables are taken. Detailed discussion of this kind of research can be found in Pruitt (1981), Pruitt & Carnevale (1993), and Rubin & Brown (1975).

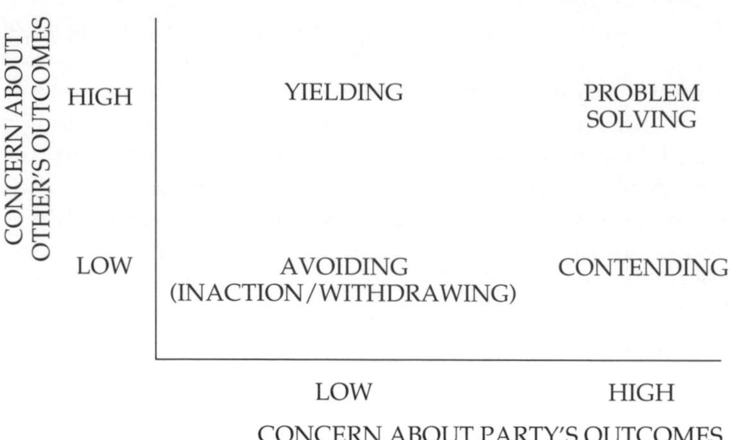

FIGURE 3.1
The dual concern model.

zontal axis, and *concern about Other's outcomes*, which is shown on the vertical axis. These concerns are portrayed as ranging from indifference (at the zero point of the coordinates) to high concern.[2]

The two concerns in this model are defined as follows: Concern about Party's outcomes means placing importance on its interests in the realm under dispute. When Party has a strong concern about its own outcomes, it is highly resistant to yielding; in other words, its aspirations tend to be rigid and high.[3] Concern about Other's outcomes implies placing importance on Other's interests—feeling responsible for the quality of Other's outcomes. This concern is sometimes *genuine*, involving an intrinsic interest in Other's welfare. It is more often *instrumental* (strategic), being aimed at helping Other in order to advance Party's interests. For example, dependence on Other often encourages Party to build a working relationship by trying to satisfy Other's needs.

The dual concern model makes the following predictions about the antecedents of strategic choice: Problem solving is encouraged when Party has a strong concern about both its own and Other's outcomes. Yielding is encouraged when Party has a strong concern about only

[2] Although not shown in Figure 3.1, it is theoretically possible for Party to have negative concerns about Other's outcomes and even about Party's own outcomes. In other words, we might have extended the coordinates in the figure downward and to the left. A few points about negative concerns will be made in this chapter, but not enough to warrant introducing further complexity into the formal statement of the model. See McClintock (1988) for a discussion of negative concerns about Party's and Other's outcomes.
[3] See Kelley et al. (1967) for a sophisticated discussion of the concept of resistance to yielding.

Other's outcomes. Contending is encouraged when Party has a strong concern only about its own outcomes. Avoiding—and inaction, in particular—is encouraged when Party has a weak concern about both its own and Other's outcomes.[4]

Thomas (1976) notes that the two concerns in the dual concern model are often erroneously reduced to a single dimension, with selfishness (concern about Party's own outcomes) on one end and cooperativeness (concern about Other's outcomes) on the other. This is an incorrect simplification, because it is clear that both concerns can be strong at the same time. Party can be both selfish and cooperative (leading it to engage in problem solving in an effort to reconcile the interests of both Party and Other). By postulating dual concerns, we are forced to distinguish between two ways of cooperating with Other, yielding and problem solving. These were not sufficiently separated in a prior theory of strategic choice (Deutsch, 1973), which proposed only a single motivational dimension ranging from competition to cooperation. Postulating dual concerns also forces us to distinguish between two ways of advancing Party's interests, contending and problem solving.

The Dual Concern Model as a Theory of Conflict Style

The dual concern model was originally developed as a theory of individual differences in conflict style (Blake & Mouton, 1964; Filley, 1975; Rahim, 1983; Rahim & Bonoma, 1979; Thomas, 1976). Conflict style is the way a person most commonly deals with conflict (Pruitt & Carnevale, 1993). The dual concern model implies that conflict style is determined by the strength of two independent individual difference variables—concern about Party's own outcomes and concern about Other's outcomes.

This view of the dual concern model has generated two lines of research. The studies in the first tradition typically perform a multidimensional scaling analysis on Party's self-report about the methods it uses in dealing with conflict (van de Vliert, 1990; van de Vliert & Prein, 1989). The findings of these studies are largely consistent with the predictions of the dual concern model: a two-dimensional solution is found, with the largest distances between contending and yielding, and between problem solving and avoiding. The only discrepancy from the dual concern

[4] The dual concern model has its origins in Blake and Mouton's (1964) managerial grid and has been adapted to the analysis of conflict by various authors (Blake & Mouton, 1979; Filley, 1975; Gladwin & Walter, 1980; Rahim, 1983, 1986; Ruble & Thomas, 1976; Thomas, 1976; van de Vliert & Prein, 1989). Other labels are sometimes given to the dimensions in this model. For example, concern about Party's own outcomes is sometimes called *assertiveness*, and concern about Other's outcomes is sometimes called *cooperativeness*.

model is that yielding and avoiding are closer to each other than the model predicts.[5]

The second tradition, largely emerging from organizational settings, focuses on the development of instruments designed to measure Party's preferences for the various conflict styles: problem solving, contending, yielding, avoiding, and compromising (Hall, 1969; Kilmann & Thomas, 1977; Lawrence & Lorsch, 1967; Rahim, 1983). These instruments have been used to examine issues such as the relationship between personality characteristics and conflict style (Kabanoff, 1987) or the impact of status difference on conflict style (Musser, 1982; Putnam & Poole, 1987; Rahim, 1986). For example, Rahim (1986) found that managers use different styles in handling interpersonal conflict with superiors, subordinates, and peers. With superiors they resort to yielding, with subordinates they engage in problem solving, and with peers they use compromising.

Although factors such as status differences may affect conflict style, people often show consistency in their conflict style across various conflict situations. Work by Sternberg and his associates (1984, 1987), although not a direct test of the dual concern model, indicates that Party can indeed be highly consistent in its style across various conflict situations. For example, in one study (Sternberg & Dobson, 1987), college students described recent interpersonal conflict episodes with a same-sex peer, an opposite-sex peer, and a parent. After finishing these descriptions, the participants rated the extent to which each of several styles of conflict resolution was characteristic of their own style. Not only did subjects show strong preference for certain styles of conflict resolution over other styles, but they also exhibited strong consistency in their styles across different interpersonal conflicts.

The Dual Concern Model as a Theory of the Impact of Conditions on Strategic Choice

The dual concern model also serves as a theory about the impact of various conditions on strategic choice. Some of these conditions affect Party's concern about its own outcomes; others affect Party's concern about Other's outcomes.

[5] Note that these studies, unlike the dual concern model shown in Figure 3.1, often include a "compromising" style, which involves working toward an agreement by making concessions. In earlier versions of this model (Blake & Mouton, 1964; Rahim, 1983; Thomas, 1976), this style is centrally located and thus equidistant from the other four styles. However, the results of recent studies indicate that the compromising style may be better placed between problem solving and yielding, but far from avoiding and contending (van de Vliert & Prein, 1989). It seems that a compromising style results from high concern about Other's outcomes combined with moderate concern about Party's outcomes (Pruitt & Carnevale, 1993).

Determinants of Party's Concern about Its Own Outcomes

The strength of Party's concern about its own outcomes differs from situation to situation and from person to person. For example, Party A may be relatively indifferent about the location and quality of his or her vacation, whereas this may be a matter of great concern for Party B. A, on the other hand, may have a much deeper concern about the quality of work on the job.

Concern about Party's outcomes can be traced to a number of determinants. One is the importance of the interests affected by these outcomes. As noted in Chapter 2, important interests produce high, rigid aspirations, which is the same thing as having a strong concern for Party's outcomes. For example, suppose that Party A does not have strong preferences about vacation plans, while B has an extremely taxing job and has a great need for rest and relaxation during vacation. If these vacation preferences are challenged by another person (C), Party A is likely to yield or avoid, whereas Party B will make an effort to salvage its preferences via contentious or problem-solving activities.

Another determinant of Party's concern about its own outcomes in any one realm is the importance of outcomes in other realms. Party does not have an infinite amount of time or energy, so it cannot pursue all of its interests with equal intensity. A strong concern about one issue often leads to a weak concern about others. For example, Party A may be relatively indifferent to the issue of quality of vacation because of being wrapped up in job-related issues, a political campaign, or some other absorbing activity.

Party's concern about its own outcomes is also affected by the way these outcomes are framed. When Party focuses on its potential losses in a conflict, it employs a negative frame. But when Party focuses on its potential gains, it employs a positive frame.[6] Interestingly, research on framing effects in negotiation (Neale & Bazerman, 1985; Thompson, 1990a) shows that negotiators with a positive frame make more concessions than those with a negative frame. Seeing outcomes as various degrees of loss highlights the potential costs of concessions, making it hard for Party to give up its position. This suggests that negative framing produces more concern about Party's outcomes than positive framing.

Fear of conflict is another determinant that leads concern about Party's outcomes to be low. This is because resistance to yielding, which is produced by a high concern about own outcomes, tends to engender conflict. Fear of conflict is a personality predisposition for some

[6] For example, consider a wage dispute between labor and management. Suppose the workers demand $16 per hour, while management insists on $12 per hour. One option would be "splitting the difference," that is, agreement on $14. If the workers see this as a $2 loss (since $14 is $2 less than their original demand), they are employing a negative frame. In contrast, if they see the option of $14 as a $2 gain (since $14 is $2 more than management's initial offer), they are employing a positive frame.

people. It is also produced by certain situations, such as when Party is attracted to (or dependent upon) Other but is uncertain about Other's opinion of Party (Hancock & Sorrentino, 1980). Situations such as this, which are said to involve "false cohesiveness" (Longley & Pruitt, 1980), are especially common at the beginning of a relationship when people are getting to know each other. Research on newly formed romantic couples suggests that such sentiments can block all forms of assertiveness, including both contentious and problem-solving behavior (Fry et al., 1983).

The conditions mentioned so far affect individuals acting on their own behalf. But the parties to conflict are often groups. Hence, we must inquire into the antecedents of the concern that group members feel about the outcomes achieved by their group.

Especially strong concerns about the fate of the group tend to develop in cohesive groups whose members share a similar life situation and discuss their common fate with one another. This is particularly likely when the members of such groups regard themselves as part of a broader social movement, making common cause with similar groups in other locations (Kriesberg, 1982).

When the parties are groups or organizations, actual conflict behavior is usually carried out by representatives (e.g., a labor-management dispute). Research on negotiation (Benton & Druckman, 1973; Neale, 1984; Smith, 1987; Tjosvold, 1977) suggests that representatives are usually more reluctant to yield than are individuals bargaining on their own behalf. This is because they are trying to please their constituents and typically view their constituents as nonconciliatory. The effect disappears in those infrequent cases where the constituent is revealed to have a conciliatory bias (Benton & Druckman, 1974; Tjosvold, 1977).

Other studies suggest that representatives are especially reluctant to yield under conditions that make them anxious to please their constituents, such as when they have low status in their groups (Kogan et al., 1972), are distrusted by their constituents (Wall, 1975), wish to continue associating with their constituents (Klimoski, 1972), think that their constituents depend on them (Enzle et al., 1992), or have female as opposed to male constituents (Pruitt et al., 1986). All of these conditions can be viewed as enhancing Party's concern about the outcomes of its group.

Accountability to constituents has much the same effect. A representative is accountable to the extent that it must report negotiation outcomes to powerful constituents. Accountable representatives are especially reluctant to concede in negotiation (Bartunek et al., 1975), suggesting that they are particularly concerned about own-group outcomes. As a result, they are more likely to adopt a contentious or problem-solving approach than to yield (Ben-Yoav & Pruitt, 1984b; Neale, 1984).

Quite often, constituents instruct their representatives to achieve high outcomes and are dissatisfied when they come home with less. This also serves to bolster the concern felt by representatives for their side's outcomes.

Determinants of Concern about Other's Outcomes

As mentioned earlier, concern about Other's outcomes takes two basic forms: genuine concern, based on an intrinsic interest in Other's welfare, and instrumental concern, aimed at advancing Party's own interests. There is an important difference between the two. Because instrumental concern is aimed at impressing Other, it is stronger when Other is more concerned about its own outcomes. By contrast, genuine concern aims at serving Other, regardless of Other's degree of self-interest.

Genuine concern about Other's outcomes is fostered by various kinds of *interpersonal bonds,* including friendship or love (Clark & Mills, 1979; Clark & Reis, 1988), perceived similarity (Hornstein, 1976), and kinship or common group identity (Brewer & Kramer, 1986; Fisher, 1990). Genuine concern is also fostered by a positive mood, which may result from succeeding in an important task, getting a small gift, eating good food, imagining a vacation, hearing humorous remarks, and so on. A positive mood enhances cooperation in negotiation (Baron, 1990; Carnevale & Isen, 1986; O'Quin & Aronoff, 1981; Pruitt et al., 1983) and fosters helping behavior (Cunningham et al., 1990; Isen & Levin, 1972; Salovey et al., 1991).[7]

Instrumental concern about Other's outcomes is common whenever Party sees itself as dependent on Other—when Other is seen as able to provide rewards and penalties. An example is the expectation of further negotiation in the future, which has been shown to encourage concession making (Gruder, 1971) and problem solving (Ben-Yoav & Pruitt, 1984a, b). Dependence leads to the conclusion that it is desirable to build a relationship with Other now. Hence, Party tries to impress Other with its concern about Other's welfare.[8]

Dependence is by no means a one-way street. Mutual dependence is quite common and can encourage either mutual yielding or mutual problem solving. The impact on mutual problem solving is illustrated by a case study of mediation between two managers in the same company (Walton, 1969). It was not until both men discovered that they could be hurt by each other that they began trying to solve their problems.

For Party to be aware of its dependence on Other, it is often necessary for Party to project itself into the future. This point is important for un-

[7] Paradoxically, some kinds of negative moods have also been shown to enhance helping behavior (Carlson & Miller, 1987; Cialdini & Kenrick, 1976). One explanation for this is that helping someone gets rid of Party's bad mood (Carlson & Miller, 1987). It appears that helping behavior following a negative mood may sometimes be motivated by concern about the way Party is feeling rather than by genuine concern for Other.

[8] Rusbult and her associates (Drigotas & Rusbult, 1992; Rusbult et al., 1991) call the desire to build a relationship *commitment* and have shown that it is central to accommodation in marital conflict.

derstanding conflict because people embroiled in escalating conflicts often lose awareness of the future. They concentrate so hard on winning in the present that they lose track of the importance of maintaining good relations. In such situations, future perspective can be regained in a number of ways. One is to take time out from the controversy—to become disengaged for a while.

Although bonds and dependencies usually foster concern about Other's outcomes, under certain conditions they can produce exactly the opposite reaction—antagonism toward Other and adoption of contentious tactics. Indeed, conflict between people in close relationships tends to breed more intense emotions—such as anger, hatred, and contempt—than that among strangers (Bersheid, 1983; Peterson, 1983). This reaction occurs when people to whom we are bonded—friends, relatives, people we admire—fail to fulfill their minimum obligations or severely frustrate us. Our bonds to these people can actually encourage more anger and aggression than we would otherwise feel, because we believe they owe us preferential treatment. A similar reaction occurs when people on whom we are dependent are unresponsive to our needs (Gruder, 1971; Tjosvold, 1977). The ordinary reaction to dependence is concern about Other's outcomes. But if Other is perceived as taking advantage of this concern, it often seems necessary to reverse gears and retaliate in order to motivate Other to be more responsive.[9]

Experimental Support for the Dual Concern Model

Four experimental studies of negotiation behavior (Ben-Yoav & Pruitt, 1984a, b; Carnevale & Keenan, 1990; Pruitt et al., 1983) provide evidence in support of the dual concern model. In all four studies, the two concerns specified in the model were independently varied. High concern about Party's own outcomes was created either by asking negotiators to achieve an explicit profit level (Ben-Yoav & Pruitt, 1984a; Pruitt et al., 1983), by giving them a negative rather than a positive frame (Carnevale & Keenan, 1990), or by making them accountable to constituents (Ben-Yoav & Pruitt, 1984b). High concern about Other's outcomes was induced either by giving negotiators a small gift so as to induce a positive mood (Pruitt et al., 1983), by making them expect cooperative future interaction (Ben-Yoav & Pruitt, 1984a, b), or by instructing them to care about Other's outcomes (Carnevale & Keenan, 1990).

The predictions of the model were largely confirmed: high concern about Party's outcomes coupled with high concern about Other's out-

[9] These reactions are outside the scope of the dual concern model, which deals only with positive concern about Other's outcomes. A fuller discussion of bonds and their effect on conflict can be found in Chapter 8.

comes produced higher joint outcomes, suggesting that some form of problem-solving strategy was used. High concern about own outcomes coupled with low concern about Other's outcomes led to the use of contentious tactics such as threats and persuasive arguments. Low concern about own outcomes coupled with high concern about Other's outcomes produced the lowest joint benefit in most of the studies, suggesting yielding (aspiration collapse) as predicted by the dual concern model.

The dual concern model postulates that strategic choice is determined by the strength of two concerns: concern about Party's own outcomes and concern about Other's outcomes. When both concerns are strong, people prefer problem solving; when the former concern is strong, they prefer contending; when the latter concern is strong, they prefer yielding; and when both concerns are weak, avoiding is likely. Party's concern about its own outcomes, which produces high rigid aspirations, tends to be strong when the interests at stake are important, when outcomes in other realms are unimportant, when a negative frame is employed, when there is low fear of conflict, when there is high accountability to constituents, and when constituents insist that their representative achieve a high level of benefit. Concern about Other's outcomes can be either genuine or instrumental. Genuine concern is fostered by interpersonal bonds of all types and by good mood. Instrumental concern is fostered by a desire to develop a working relationship with a person on whom one is dependent.

THE PERCEIVED FEASIBILITY PERSPECTIVE

Choice among the three basic strategies is also a matter of perceived feasibility—the extent to which the strategy seems capable of achieving the goals that give rise to it and the cost that is anticipated from enacting each strategy. Considerations of feasibility supplement those specified by the dual concern model. The dual concern model indicates the strategies preferred under various combinations of concern about Party's and Other's outcomes. But for a strategy actually to be adopted, it must also be seen as minimally feasible. If not, another strategy will be chosen, even if it is less consistent with the current combination of concerns.

For example, consider the situation when Party is concerned about both its own and Other's outcomes. Problem solving is its preferred strategy. But if this strategy seems infeasible or too risky, Party is likely to shift to yielding or contending, its next best alternatives. Which of these is chosen is determined both by the relative strength of the two concerns and by other considerations of feasibility and cost. If Party is more concerned about Other's outcomes than its own, it will adopt a yielding approach, provided that this seems reasonably feasible. If Party is more concerned about its own outcomes than Other's, it will shift to contentious behavior, also provided that this seems reasonably feasible.

As another example, take the Party who is concerned mainly about its own outcomes. Contending is Party's preferred strategy because it holds the promise of getting something for nothing. But problem solving is a close second if the contentious approach appears infeasible or costly. Indeed, problem solving often seems the most feasible way of allowing Party to pursue its interests.

The next three sections deal with the perceived feasibility of problem solving, contending, and yielding.

Perceived Feasibility of Problem Solving

Perceived Common Ground

Problem solving seems more feasible the greater the *perceived common ground (PCG)*. PCG is Party's assessment of the likelihood of finding an alternative that satisfies the aspirations of Party and Other. The more likely it seems that such an alternative can be found, the more feasible problem solving appears to be. PCG is greater (1) the lower Party's own aspirations, (2) the lower Other's aspirations as perceived by Party, and (3) the greater the perceived richness of the set of integrative alternatives—that is, Party's belief that integrative solutions (alternatives favorable to both parties) exist or can be devised.[10]

This definition implies that PCG is the mirror image of perceived conflict. As PCG goes up, conflict, in the sense of perceived divergence of interest, goes down.[11]

The graphs in Figure 3.2 further explain PCG. The abscissa in these graphs maps Party's own benefits; the ordinate, Party's perception of Other's benefits. The large dots in these graphs refer to known alternatives, the medium-sized dots to alternatives that seem potentially discoverable, and the smallest dots to long shots. As before, the location of a point in the space shows the perceived value of that alternative to the two parties. The vertical lines in these graphs refer to Party's own aspirations and the horizontal lines to the aspirations Party perceives Other to hold.

PCG is greater the more points there are to the northeast (above and to the right) of the intersection of the aspiration lines and the darker these

[10] Party's belief in the existence of integrative solutions will be affected by many considerations, but one in particular has received considerable attention in recent years. This is the "fixed-pie" assumption, whereby Party (independent of objective reality) proceeds from the view that the conflict is zero-sum.

[11] The reader may be surprised to learn that lower aspirations make problem solving seem more feasible. Superficially, this seems inconsistent with the point made earlier that lack of concern about own interests (which produces low aspirations) reduces the likelihood of problem solving. However, these two points are not contradictory. We are talking about two countervailing forces that are simultaneously activated when concern about own interests is low. The one makes problem solving seem more feasible, and the other (by permitting the strategy of yielding) makes problem solving seem less necessary.

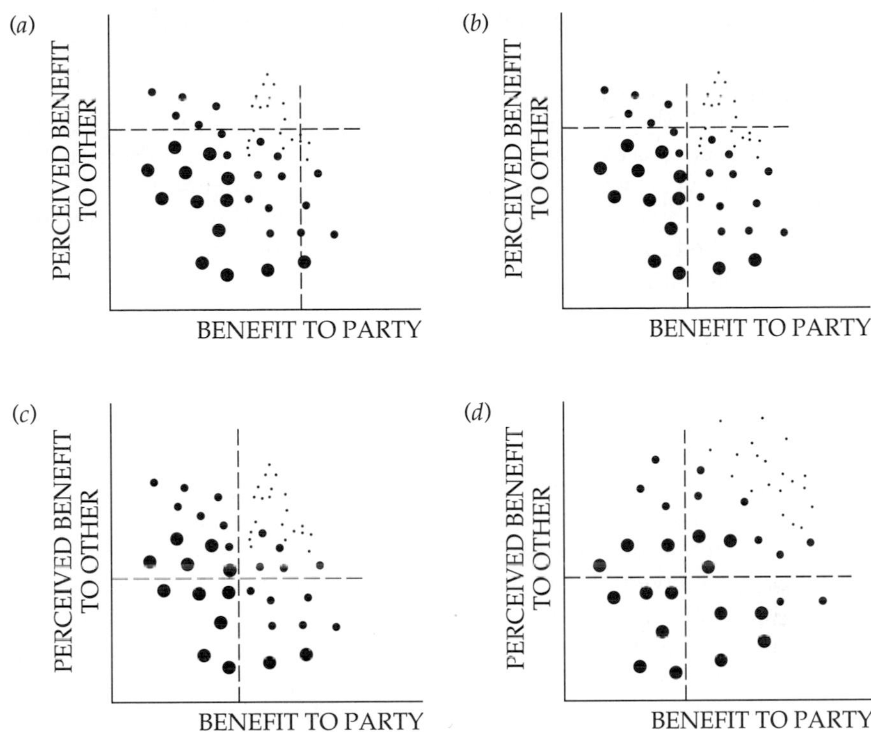

FIGURE 3.2
Four levels of perceived common ground (PCG), ranging from none in *a* to high in *d*.

points are. In Figure 3.2, PCG is greater in *b* than in *a* because Party's own aspirations are lower. It is greater in *c* than in *b* because Other's perceived aspirations are also lower. It is greater in *d* than in *c* because there appears to be a richer set of available alternatives—that is, there is greater perceived feasibility of developing integrative solutions (as shown by the fact that the darker points are farther from the origin in the northeast direction).

A number of conditions contribute to Party's choice of problem solving by enhancing PCG, the perceived likelihood that integrative solutions can be developed. These include the following:

1. *Faith in own problem-solving ability.* Party may be a good communicator and/or may understand how to devise mutually beneficial alternatives. Hence, Party's experience may lead it to see considerable integrative potential in almost any situation. Or Party may be less capable, likely to view conflict as more intractable and to

adopt strategies of yielding or contending rather than problem solving.

2. *Momentum.* Momentum refers to prior success at reaching agreement in the current controversy. The more frequent and recent such successes have been, the greater will be Party's faith that these successes can be reproduced in the future and that problem solving is worthwhile. Momentum can sometimes be encouraged by scheduling easier issues earlier in a negotiation agenda, so that a solid foundation of success has been built by the time more difficult issues are encountered.
3. *Availability of a mediator.* Mediators often serve as communication links between the parties, coordinating movement toward compromise or helping to develop integrative solutions. Their availability should make problem solving more likely to be successful.[12]
4. *Other's perceived readiness for problem solving.* Problem solving seems more feasible to the extent that Other seems ready to participate in this process. There are two reasons for this. One is that the perceived likelihood of developing integrative solutions is enhanced because joint problem solving is usually more efficient than unilateral problem solving. The other is that problem solving seems less risky when Other is not taking a contentious approach because under those conditions there is less danger in allowing oneself to look weak.

Trust

The perception that Other is ready for problem solving, and hence that there is a likelihood of developing solutions, is sometimes a function of trust—that is, of Party's perception that Other is concerned about Party's interests. Trust encourages problem solving when Party is otherwise reluctant to adopt this strategy, presumably by making problem solving seem more feasible (Kimmel et al., 1980).

Although trust allows Party to adopt a problem-solving strategy, it is no guarantee that this strategy will be adopted. Indeed, trust can sometimes have quite the opposite effect, encouraging high, rigid aspirations defended by contentious behavior.

[12] An example of the latter mechanism can be seen in the British reaction to the Argentine occupation of the Falkland/Malvinas Islands in 1982. Yielding was ruled out on the grounds of cost to the British image. Avoiding seemed inadvisable because every day of the occupation enhanced the legitimacy of the Argentine action. In short, the choice was between contending and problem solving. At first it appeared that there might be integrative potential; American Secretary of State Alexander Haig was trying to mediate the crisis. Hence the British adopted a problem-solving strategy, working with Haig while defending their basic interests by moving their fleet slowly toward South America. However, the perceived likelihood of developing integrative solutions disappeared with the failure of Haig's mission, making problem solving seem quite infeasible. As a result, the British adopted an exclusively contentious approach, an all-out invasion of the islands.

Whether trust encourages problem solving or contending depends at least in part on Party's perception of Other's resistance to yielding—that is, the apparent firmness of Other's aspirations. A trusted Other whose aspirations do not seem firm will be expected to give in to Party's demands. Hence, contentious behavior seems especially feasible and will be often adopted. But if Other's aspirations seem firm, trust implies instead that Other will cooperate only if Party cooperates. This encourages Party to adopt a problem-solving strategy.

Evidence that problem solving is encouraged by a combination of trust and perceived firmness comes from several negotiation studies. All examined Party's response to helpful actions (which presumably generated trust) by Other. When Other had been helpful, Party was more willing to cooperate if Other also (1) had high threat capacity (Michener et al., 1975; Tjosvold & Okun, 1976), (2) had a tough constituent (Wall, 1977), (3) had been unyielding or competitive in the past (Deutsch, 1973; Harford & Solomon, 1967; Hilty & Carnevale, 1992), or (4) had been unwilling to make unilateral concessions in the past (Komorita & Esser, 1975; McGillicuddy et al., 1984). These findings suggest that trust encourages problem solving when Party believes that Other has firm aspirations.

Trust develops in a number of ways. It is encouraged by a perception that Other has a positive attitude toward Party, is similar to Party, or is dependent on Party. As an example of the latter point, Solomon (1960) has shown that trust is greater when Party sees itself as having a capacity to punish Other for failing to cooperate. Trust is also likely to develop when Other is a member of Party's own group (Kramer & Brewer, 1984; Yamagishi & Sato, 1986) or when Party expects that third parties will punish Other for being uncooperative (Yamagishi, 1986). Furthermore, trust tends to develop when Party has been helpful toward Other (Loomis, 1959), since Party assumes that Other will reciprocate Party's helpful behavior.

Party tends to trust Other when Other has been helpful or cooperative, especially if its help is directed toward Party (Cooper & Fazio, 1979) and has occurred recently (Kelley & Stahelski, 1970). Trust is an especially common response when Other's helpful behavior is seen as voluntary and not as a product of environmental forces. Hence, Party tends to trust Other when Other's helpful behavior is not required by its role (Jones & Davis, 1965) or seems to be costly to Other (Komorita, 1973).

Perceived Cost

Despite the existence of PCG, parties may not necessarily adopt a problem-solving strategy. This is because the adoption of problem solving is subject to at least three risks: image loss, position loss, and information loss (Pruitt, 1981). Image loss is a perception by Other that Party is weak and thus willing to make extensive concessions. This perception, an unintended potential result of using problem solving, encourages Other to use a contending strategy in an effort to pressure Party to make those concessions. Position loss is a perception by Other that Party has conceded from a previous position. Problem-solving efforts by Party sometimes involve tentative suggestions of other possible options, which may unintentionally produce such a perception. The third risk, information loss, occurs when Party reveals its underlying interests or lower limit. Other can use this information to gain an advantage.

Perceived Feasibility of Contending

Contending seems more feasible the lower Other's apparent resistance to yielding. There is not much point in putting pressure on an opponent who has extremely strong feelings, has powerful and resolute constituents, or has already yielded as much as possible. Moreover, there is not much point in applying pressure on an opponent who, in negotiation, has more attractive alternatives away from the table.[13] Other tactics, such as yielding and problem solving, are more likely to be adopted. But if Other's aspirations (however high they may be) seem relatively easy to dislodge, contentious behavior gets a boost.

The points just made imply that contentious behavior is often self-liquidating, a victim of both failure and success. If it fails, this indicates that Other's resistance is greater than originally thought, so Party will abandon the tactic. If it succeeds and Other yields, Other's resistance to further yielding is likely to grow because Other will come closer and closer to its limit. Again, Party must eventually abandon the tactic.

The feasibility of contending is also a function of Party's apparent capacity to employ contentious tactics and of Other's apparent capacity to counter them. Does Party have good arguments? Does Other have counterarguments? Is Party adept at arguing its case? How effective is Other as a debater? Can Party punish Other? How good are Other's defenses against such tactics? Does Party have ways to commit itself credibly? Is Other capable of undoing these commitments?

Capacities such as these are sometimes lumped together under the familiar concepts of *power* and *counterpower*. These concepts have some merit in that they allow us to make a few broad generalizations. For example, we can generalize that more powerful people have higher aspirations and make greater use of heavy contentious tactics, regardless of the source of their power. But there is a tendency to overuse these concepts in social science theory, making facile generalizations with little real meaning (see, for example, Blalock, 1989; Morgenthau, 1967). The problem is

[13] This is the concept of BATNA (best alternative to negotiated agreement), as described by Fisher et al., (1991). If Other has a strong BATNA, contending may drive Other to take that best alternative.

that there are many kinds of power, each with a different set of properties (French & Raven, 1959; Raven & Rubin, 1983).

Perceived Cost

Contentious behavior, particularly in its more severe forms, runs the risk of alienating Other and starting a conflict spiral. There is also some danger of third party censure. Such considerations may deter contentious behavior, particularly when Party is dependent on Other or on watchful third parties.

Costs are also associated with constituent *surveillance,* which has a complicated relationship to the use of contentious tactics. Surveillance must be distinguished from accountability to constituents. Representatives are accountable to the extent that they can be rewarded or punished on the basis of the outcomes they generate for their constituents. They are under surveillance when their actual conflict behavior (for example, how they negotiate) is being observed. Representatives who are being observed by their constituents usually worry about getting out of line with these constituents' expectations. If they believe the constituents favor toughness, they will tend to adopt contentious behavior; if they see the constituents as conciliatory, they will avoid contending. These points are supported by a study of the joint effect of surveillance and sex of constituent (Pruitt et al., 1986) on strategic choice. Surveillance by male constituents was found to enhance negotiator contentiousness, whereas surveillance by female constituents was found to diminish contentiousness. This makes sense if we assume that the subjects subscribed to the usual stereotype that men favor a tough approach and women a conciliatory approach to interpersonal relations.[14]

Perceived Feasibility of Yielding

The success of problem solving and of contending are sometimes in doubt because they depend on Other's responses, which are not under Party's control. In contrast, it is much easier for Party to yield, because this strategy relies primarily on Party's own behavior—subject to Other's acknowledgment. This does not mean that yielding is always a feasible or effective strategy.

Several conditions encourage yielding. One is time pressure. In the

[14] Research on how men and women actually negotiate paints a more complex picture than this stereotype. Findings are inconclusive. Some studies indicate that women are more socially attuned than men and therefore more likely to vary their negotiating behavior in response to social cues, such as Other's attractiveness or Other's response to Party's cooperative initiatives (Rubin & Brown, 1975; Swap & Rubin, 1983). Women are also more likely than men to handle isolated negotiations in light of long-term relationships (Greenhalgh & Gilkey, 1984). Men are more likely than women to use a forceful style (Kimmel et al., 1980; Lim & Carnevale, 1990). Men also tend to obtain better outcomes than women through negotiation (Gerhart & Rynes, 1991; Rifkin, 1984). Still other studies show no gender differences (Nadler & Nadler, 1984). See Kolb and Coolidge (1991) for a more detailed discussion of gender and negotiation.

face of time pressure, all three strategies are possible, but research (Hamner, 1974; Pruitt & Drews, 1969; Smith et al., 1982) suggests that the favorite strategy is yielding. This is presumably because yielding is the fastest way to move toward agreement. Contending and problem solving are adopted in the face of time pressure only when there is heavy resistance to yielding.

There are two sources of time pressure: cost per unit time of engaging in the controversy and closeness to a deadline. In negotiation, time pressure may be due to any cost of continued negotiation, including time lost from other pursuits, the expense of maintaining negotiators in the field, or rapid deterioration of the object under dispute (such as fruits and vegetables). Deadlines are points in the future at which significant costs are likely to be experienced if the controversy has not been resolved. At a strike deadline, the union pulls workers out of the factory; at a hiring deadline, the job offer is withdrawn. The closer Party is to a deadline and the larger the penalty for passing that deadline without agreement, the greater the time pressure and hence the more likely Party is to yield.

Perceived Cost

Because it can be seen as a sign of weakness, yielding may result in image loss. This may be costly as it encourages Other to use a contentious strategy. Other may jack up the pressure to lower Party's aspirations. Furthermore, the image of being weak also invites future exploitation from third parties. In interactions with someone who is known as a "pushover," contentious strategies may be the first and immediate course of action. Other parties are emboldened by Party's reputation and may make quick, contentious moves. Fear of image loss discourages yielding.[15]

We have argued that perceived feasibility—assessment of effectiveness and cost—affects strategic choice. This consideration supplements the forces specified in the dual concern model. For example, problem solving is adopted when Party is concerned about both its own and Other's outcomes, provided that there is some perceived possibility of success at a reasonable cost. The perceived feasibility of problem solving is a function of perceived common ground (PCG), the perception that an alternative can be found that satisfies the aspirations of both Party and Other. PCG, in turn, depends on Party's own and Other's perceived aspirations and the perceived likelihood of developing integrative solutions. Perceived feasibility of contending is a positive function of perceived power and an inverse function of Other's apparent resistance to yielding.

[15] Note that yielding can also be costly to Other, however, in the sense that its use can result in low mutual benefits (Ben-Yoav & Pruitt, 1984a; Pruitt et al., 1983). This is because contentious behavior, encouraged by Party's yielding, prevents the exploration of integrative solutions that are actually more beneficial (for both parties) than those resulting from contentious strategies (Pruitt & Carnevale, 1993).

Perceived feasibility of yielding is affected by time pressure and the cost that is anticipated from enacting it.

THE VIGOR OF STRATEGIC BEHAVIOR

Implementation of the three basic strategies can be more or less vigorous. In the case of contentious behavior, vigor refers to the heaviness of the actions taken. Shouts are more vigorous than persuasive communications, blows more vigorous than shouts, shots more vigorous than blows. In the case of problem solving, vigor refers to the creativity of the problem-solving effort. At the low end of vigor is a simple, dull effort to coordinate the making of concessions toward an obvious compromise. At the high end is an active effort to understand Other's interests and a thoughtful search for a way to reconcile these interests with Party's own. In the case of yielding, vigor refers simply to how far Party drops its aspirations.

There are various determinants of how vigorous a strategy will be. One set of determinants is embodied in the dual concern model (Figure 3.1). The stronger the concerns specified by this model, the more vigorous will be the predicted strategy. Thus, if Party's concern about its outcomes is weak, greater concern about Other's outcomes will produce deeper yielding. If concern about Other's outcomes is weak, greater concern about Party's outcomes will encourage more extreme contentious behavior. If neither concern is weak, problem solving will be more vigorous and creative when the dual concerns are stronger.

It is common for Party who has adopted a coping strategy to begin less vigorously and move toward greater vigor if earlier efforts do not achieve agreement. Such gradualism ensures that no greater costs will be incurred than are necessary to achieve Party's goals. This point is most obvious in the realm of contentious behavior. Like the United States in the Vietnam War, Party usually begins cautiously and escalates only if its efforts become unsuccessful.[16]

Two of the coping strategies—contending and problem solving—appear to have a paradoxical feature: If adopted, the vigor with which they are enacted is a function of some of the same conditions that *discourage* their being adopted in the first place.

As mentioned earlier, the expectation of resistance from Other discourages contentious behavior. But suppose that other conditions (such as being a highly accountable representative with no dependence on Other) predispose Party to contend. What is the effect of expected resistance then? Our hypothesis is that it promotes the use of heavier contentious

[16] Sometimes a different sequence is found: one side makes a large, early commitment in the hope of successfully contending through a preemptive strike (e.g., Iraq's 1990 invasion of Kuwait).

tactics. If Other looks like a pushover, it should be easy to get a concession by simple stonewalling or persuasive argumentation. But if Other's position seems engraved in stone, heavier tactics will be needed, in the form of threats or other coercive actions.

Problem solving also exhibits this paradoxical feature: low PCG discourages problem solving, but it also encourages a creative form of problem solving when this strategy is adopted for other reasons. Suppose, for example, that there is a mutually perceived stalemate—Party and Other are unwilling to yield and contentious tactics seem useless. If avoiding is infeasible, problem solving is the only possible approach. To the extent that PCG is low (whether because of high aspirations, a perception that Other has high aspirations, or minimal perceived likelihood of developing integrative solutions), it will seem necessary to employ a more creative effort in order to reach agreement.

The latter point can be illustrated by reference to Figure 3.2. PCG is lower in Figure 3.2*a* than in any of the other three cases. Hence, problem solving seems infeasible and is unlikely to be elected. But suppose that problem solving *must* be employed despite its infeasibility. Then a greater creative effort will be needed to resolve the conflict in Figure 3.2*a*, because the viable options seem more remote.

CONCLUSIONS

Chapter 3 has presented a preliminary theory about the conditions that affect the choice Party makes among the three coping strategies available to it in conflict: contending, problem solving, and yielding. This theory consists mainly of a dual concern model, supplemented by some ideas about the effect of feasibility considerations. The theory also implies some paradoxical hypotheses about determinants of the vigor with which certain of the strategies are employed; for example, the same conditions that make contending and problem solving seem less feasible probably cause these strategies to be employed with greater vigor if they happen to be adopted. We turn in the next chapter to a detailed consideration of one of the three strategies, contending.

4

Contentious Tactics

Most exchanges and encounters do not result in conflict, let alone the use of contentious tactics (moves designed to get one's way at another's expense). As we saw in Chapter 1, Party is generally able to deal with Other without getting into conflict. Moreover, many of the conflicts that arise can be addressed through the collaborative problem-solving efforts of the parties involved. On the other hand, when conflicts *do* arise, and when Party employs contentious tactics, powerful and destructive forces are often unleashed. This alone makes it important to understand these events better.

All three of the primary strategies for dealing with conflict—contending, yielding, and problem solving—depend for their effectiveness on social influence processes. I can do well at your expense (contending), and I can let you do well at my expense (yielding), only if you allow me to. Moreover, I can successfully engage in problem solving only if you work with me to find a jointly satisfactory solution. These three strategies—more specifically, contending and problem solving (since we regard yielding as the mirror image of contending)—are of particular interest. This chapter focuses on the nature and variety of contentious tactics that Party uses in an effort to get Other to yield—how, in effect, Party gets

Other to accept that "what's mine is mine, and what's yours is mine."

As we saw in Chapter 3, contending is likely to be chosen in preference to the other conflict strategies when the following conditions obtain: Party is concerned about its own outcomes but not Other's outcomes; Party is antagonistic toward Other; Party's aspirations are high and are resistant to lowering; Party views Other's aspirations as also high, though not so resistant; little perceived common ground (PCG) is believed to exist, and alternatives therefore cannot be developed that satisfy both parties' aspirations; Party has the capacity for contending; and Other's resistance to lowering aspirations is deemed to be low. Under these circumstances, Party is likely to make use of contentious behavior in an effort to lower Other's aspirations, while keeping its own aspirations at their currently high level.

The basic strategy of contending is quite straightforward: Party seeks to find a solution at Other's expense. Of greater interest are the contentious *tactics* themselves—the detailed moves and countermoves, the gestures, positions, and ploys, the things that Party actually *does* to Other.

The tactics to be explored here are an assortment of odd bedfellows ranging from ingratiation, gamesmanship, and guilt trips to persuasive argumentation, threats, and irrevocable commitments. Our analysis of these tactics is guided by the following premises:

First, there is nothing inherently destructive or baleful about contentious tactics. Rather, it is the end to which these tactics are used that renders them harmful. For example, although threats (involving Party's effort to impose its will through the contingent statement of intention to use force) are most easily conceived of as instruments of destruction or malevolence, they may also be used to signal Party's unwillingness or inability to bend beyond some critical point in a generally collaborative arrangement. Similarly, irrevocable commitments can be used not only in the service of imposing Party's will on Other but to signal Party's determination to keep the relationship together, under even the most difficult circumstances. In short, contentious tactics can often be used to advance the interest of collaboration as well.

Second, we assume that contentious tactics differ along a dimension of lightness-heaviness. We define *light tactics* as those whose consequences for Other are favorable or neutral. By contrast, *heavy tactics* impose, or threaten to impose, unfavorable or costly consequences on Other. Guilt trips are lighter than threats, and threats are lighter than irrevocable commitments to coercion.

Third, we assume that contentious tactics are more often than not deployed in an escalative sequence, moving from light to progressively heavier. One reason for this sequence is that light tactics are typically less costly for Party than heavier ones. Such a sequence serves notice on Other, and on any bystanders who may happen to be observing, that Party is a "reasonable" person, someone who is moved to heavy tactics only as a last resort. The transition from light to heavy implies that Party has tried to prevail by utilizing carrots and has been dragged only reluctantly into the use of sticks as a result of Other's intransigence. The light-to-heavy shift thus permits Party to blame its own contentious behavior on Other.

One can better appreciate the general psychological sense of this light-to-heavy shift by considering the consequences of efforts to implement the reverse sequence. If Party first makes use of heavy tactics (such as irreversible commitments to particular positions) and then subsequently uses light tactics (such as ingratiation), it is in danger of conveying to Other and to any onlookers the impression of being a bully who tries to force its will on others. Moreover, the eventual shift to lighter tactics may create an impression of weakness—the view that Party has been unable to prevail with heavy tactics and has been forced to adopt a more conciliatory stance. Under these circumstances, light tactics may even be seen as an attempted bribe, as when failed attempts to influence Other leads Party to try buying its way out.

Of course, there *are* occasions when the light-to-heavy shift in tactics seems inappropriate. And it is not uncommon for Party to employ heavy tactics such as threats to "soften up" Other before resorting to light tactics such as ingratiation. The light tactics seem so appealing in contrast to their heavier counterparts that they are likely to be quite effective. Such an effect is particularly compelling when different members of Party's team utilize the heavy and light contentious tactics, creating a "bad cop" and "good cop," respectively.[1] However, we contend that the sequence from light to heavy tactics is more common.

In keeping with the preceding analysis, the order of presentation of contentious tactics in this chapter conforms roughly to the light-to-heavy sequence. We will look first at the tactics of ingratiation and "feather ruffling," both of which constitute relatively lightweight maneuvers designed to make subsequent moves more effective. Next we will look briefly at guilt trips and persuasive argumentation before turning to such heavier contentious tactics as threats. We close with an examination of coercive commitments that appear irrevocable.[2]

INGRATIATION: THE ART OF RELATIONSHIP BUILDING

Some of the most effective contentious tactics involve little understanding by Other that it is the target of an influence attempt. Indeed, the effectiveness of a tactic such as ingratiation stems from Other's very ignorance of

[1]This is also called the black hat/white hat or bad guy/good guy routine.

[2]While we believe that the contentious tactics explored here are among the more interesting and important, there are many other such tactics. These include harming Other or something that Other values (Averill, 1982); fait accompli (Falbo, 1977; Falbo & Peplau, 1980); harassment (Pruitt & Carnevale, 1993); and more indirect approaches, such as hinting (Falbo & Peplau, 1980).

Party's ultimate designs. To the extent that Other is able to "see through" Party or discern Party's true intentions, these tactics are likely to prove ineffectual and may even backfire.

As defined by Jones and Wortman (1973),[3] ingratiation is "a class of strategic behaviors illicitly designed to influence a particular other person concerning the attractiveness of one's personal qualities" (p. 2). Successful ingratiators enhance their own perceived attractiveness in an effort to prepare the target for subsequent exploitation.

Ingratiation is characterized by an interesting and important dilemma: it is easiest to achieve when it is needed least. It is precisely when Other's positive feelings are most in demand that these feelings are hardest to cultivate. Why? Because to the extent that Other is aware that Party has something to gain by creating a favorable impression, Other will be suspicious of attempts in this direction. The more help Party needs from Other, the more likely it is that Other will interpret Party's ingratiating behavior as a sign of manipulative intent rather than a genuine expression of liking and regard. Ingratiation can have some effect even when Other is suspicious or aware of Party's true intentions (Byrne et al., 1974; Drachman et al., 1978), but this effect is likely to be greatly attenuated.

How should ingratiators go about their business? Jones and Wortman (1973) make a number of tactical suggestions. First, they argue for the importance of flattery or "complimentary other-enhancement," a class of tactics that exaggerates Other's admirable qualities while soft-pedaling Other's weaknesses. This technique relies for its effectiveness on the assumption that people find it hard to dislike those who say kind things about them, as when a woman is told by her date that she is a "beautiful and sensitive person" or a subordinate heaps praise on a boss.[4]

Flattery is a useful tactic in settings that range from international diplomacy and business transactions to the most mundane everyday situations. Merely witness the litany of successful flatterers in history and literature, such as Machiavelli and Iago. If flattery is to be effective, Party must not sacrifice credibility. Are the date's compliments believable, or do they seem driven by some ulterior motive? It is possible for flattery to be so excessive that the tactic simply fails to work. This point has been documented experimentally in studies by Dickoff (1961); Fleinke et al. (1972); and Lowe and Goldstein (1970). Jones and Wortman (1973) suggest a number of ways an ingratiator can enhance the credibility of flattering overtures. These include avoiding excessive compliments, picking attributes to admire that Other may be a bit insecure about (and that therefore make Other vulnerable to flattery), making sure that all compliments are plausible, and carefully mixing negative with positive comments

[3]And described more recently in analyses and reviews of the experimental literature by Liden & Mitchell (1988), Schlenker (1980), and Tedeschi & Melburg (1984), among others.
[4]For writings on the use of ingratiation by employees in organizational settings, see Dipboye & Wiley (1977, 1978), Ralston (1985), and Wortman & Linsenmeier (1977).

(what Jones and Wortman describe as "a judicious blend of the bitter and the sweet," p. 9). Yet another possibility is to describe Other in flattering terms to a third person in the hope that this individual will then relay these flattering remarks to Other (Wortman & Linsenmeier, 1977).

The second major class of ingratiation tactics involves what Jones and Wortman describe as "opinion conformity." By expressing agreement with Other's opinions, Party attempts to create the impression of having attitudes that are similar to Other's—a state that social psychologists have found generally induces interpersonal attraction (Byrne, 1971; Clore & Byrne, 1974). There are at least two pitfalls, however, that Party must avoid in these efforts at opinion conformity. First, Party should try to avoid the impression that agreement is driven by some ulterior motive. On the basis of supportive research evidence (see Jones et al., 1963), Jones and Wortman advise ingratiators to try to anticipate Other's views rather than merely react to them. They provide the following example:

> If the target person says he thinks there should be more "law and order" and you indicate your agreement with his position, he may infer that you are agreeing in order to impress him. But if you cleverly intuit from his short hair, his manner of dress, and his other attitudes that he feels this way, and then spontaneously mention how concerned you are about the problem of law and order, such an attribution on his part is probably less likely. (p. 17)

Second, Party must avoid seeming to be the kind of person who goes around blindly agreeing with everybody's point of view (Gerard & Greenbaum, 1962; Jones & Wein, 1972). Party can accomplish this by systematically agreeing with some, but not all, of Other's positions—or, even better, by indicating disagreement with the views of people that Other can reasonably be assumed to disagree with.

A third set of ingratiation tactics involves the giving of favors, on the grounds that people tend to like those who do nice things for them (Greenberg & Frisch, 1972; Nemeth, 1970; Regan, 1971). Of course, if Other suspects Party of doing favors to get something in return, the tactic will backfire; Other must have no sense that strings are attached. Jones and Wortman suggest two ways in which Party can successfully avoid Other's suspicion in this regard: doing small rather than large favors, on the grounds that the latter will arouse the suspicion that something is desired in return; and performing favors that do not lead Other to feel constrained to respond in a particular way (Brehm & Cole, 1966)—for example, doing a favor in Other's absence that the latter will eventually learn about.

Finally, Jones and Wortman (and, more recently, Godfrey et al., 1986) describe several tactics of "self-presentation" that may be adopted by the successful ingratiator. The idea is for Party to present its own virtues in such a way that Other finds them attractive. Self-presentation is tricky business. Too forthright a description of one's virtues may lead Other to conclude that Party is conceited or has manipulative intentions; too subtle a description of Party's virtues may dilute the intended effect to the vanishing point (Jones & Gordon, 1972). Jones and Wortman advise ingratiators to address this dilemma by using indirect but clear-cut methods of "tooting their own horn," such as doing rather than merely saying self-aggrandizing things. "Rather than telling the target person that he is a good cook," they write, "an ingratiator can invite the target person to a gourmet dinner" (p. 23).

When used in a contentious exchange, ingratiation tactics soften Other up for later concessions not through coercion, assertion, or aggression but through charm and guile. How much easier and less costly it is to charm Other into surrendering something of value rather than extracting it through the imposition of will.

It is important for successful ingratiation that Other not attribute Party's behavior to ulterior motives. Paradoxically, the greater Party's power relative to that of Other, the more effective Party's ingratiation tactics are apt to be (because Other is less likely to attribute Party's behavior to ulterior motives)—but the less necessary such tactics are in the first place. Conversely, it is when Party is in a position of relatively low power vis-à-vis Other that Party is most dependent on ingratiation tactics—and these tactics are least likely to be effective. The more Party needs Other, the more suspicious Other is likely to be of Party's attempts to make a good impression.[5]

GAMESMANSHIP: THE ART OF FEATHER RUFFLING

Another class of tactics entails inducing a state of upset or unrest that has the effect of lowering Other's resistance to yielding. This is the art of "feather ruffling." If ingratiation is like the gift of a Trojan horse, lowering Other's suspicions and resistance and allowing Party to penetrate the walled city, feather ruffling resembles a diversionary blaze outside the walls that becomes the focus of so much attention that the enemy can scale another part of the city walls and have its way.

Perhaps nowhere have the tactics of feather ruffling been articulated more elegantly and creatively than in the writings of the British author Stephen Potter. In his book *The Theory and Practice of Gamesmanship: The Art of Winning Games Without Actually Cheating* (1948), Potter describes several key tactics and maneuvers that can be used to get, and keep, an adversary off guard. Although his book is written largely tongue in cheek

[5]Although ingratiation tactics may be unlikely to work when needed most, research has demonstrated that if they *do* work, the result is not only that Other does Party's bidding, but Party's self-esteem may increase as well (Jones et al., 1981; Rhodewalt & Agustsdottir, 1986).

and all his examples are drawn from the British sporting world of rugby, tennis, and golf, his analysis reveals some important varieties of contentious behavior.

The key to effective gamesmanship, writes Potter, is finding a way of creating a state of "muddled fluster." One important technique for accomplishing this objective entails behaving in a manner that is antithetical to the actions of Other. Thus, by deliberately playing against the opponent's tempo—by speeding up when Other wishes to slow down, or taking one's sweet time when Other seems in a rush—Party can break Other's rhythm and induce distraction. Among Potter's many amusing examples of this maneuver:

> . . . tying up a shoe-lace in a prolonged manner, after the opponent at squash or lawn tennis had served two or three aces running; the extended noseblow, with subsequent mopping up not only of the nose and surrounding surfaces, but of imaginary sweat from the forehead and neck as well. (p. 59)

Analogously, in *any* form of contentious encounter, it may make sense for Party to break Other's rhythm by insisting, for example, on more time to review the facts or on a faster pace of decision making.

Although Potter advises the artful gamesman against spending too much time looking for his or her own "lost ball," it makes good sense to make "a great and irritatingly prolonged parade of spending extra time looking for his *opponent's* ball" (p. 35). More generally, gamesmanship requires deflecting Other's suspicions by behaving in ways that appear to be in the interest of helping Other. For example, a negotiator who wishes to use contentious tactics effectively, in the service of disrupting Other's momentum, might suggest, "Let's slow down a bit, so that I can understand better exactly what it is that you want and how I can provide you with what you need."

Potter's second general bit of advice to the artful gamesman is to behave in ways that are likely to lead Other to feel either irresponsible or incompetent. As before, the key is to induce these feelings without arousing Other's suspicion or encouraging Other to blame Party in any way. Two of Potter's examples may suffice to make this point. First, there is the art of "limpmanship": "the exact use of minor injury, not only for the purpose of getting out of, but for actually winning difficult contests" (p. 36). For example, Potter recommends intense and ferocious play by an inadequate tennis player. At some point the gamesman pauses momentarily, as if lost in thought. When the adversary makes inquiries, the gamesman confesses to having an "ancient ticker" that is "not supposed to be used full out at the moment . . . only a temporary thing." Rather than creating the sense that Party is searching for an inappropriate excuse, this ploy has the effect of laying responsibility for Party's unhappy fate squarely on the shoulders of Other.

Potter's second example describes the Party who, when Other arrives to pick the former up by car, deliberately stalls by delaying answering the bell, not having things ready, and forgetting some necessary item of equipment. All of these moves are likely to increase Other's impatience, even agitation, and lead Other to feel incompetent—while lacking insight into the precise source of these feelings.

In the more general realm of contentious tactics, quite apart from the rarified atmosphere of Potter's sporting examples, one can see ploys like this being adopted by negotiators who subtly point out that their adversary seems to be having a bit of difficulty understanding the charts and statistical summaries of the issues in dispute.

The key to successful gamesmanship, then, like the key to ingratiation, is keeping Other blind to Party's true intentions. To this end, Potter advises successful gamesmen to "shield" themselves behind a set of situational circumstances. It is a favorable wind or an unusually effective piece of equipment in a tennis game, or fortuitous timing and a lucky break in a hard-fought negotiation, that explains Party's success—not Party's talent, skill, or artifice. As Potter writes, "Let the gamesman's advantage over an opponent appear to be the result of luck, never of play" (p. 45). By so doing, Party can deflect the anger or determination that might otherwise lead Other to respond effectively.

GUILT TRIPS

Some years ago, one of the authors and his spouse departed from East Tennessee (and a visit with the author's mother-in-law) to visit friends in Alabama. Although the couple had planned to return in time for dinner the following evening, they found themselves having so much fun with their friends that they called home in the late afternoon to inform Jeff's mother-in-law that they would not be home until late at night and would therefore make other dinner arrangements. When the couple arrived home, at perhaps 1 A.M., they found the dining room table still covered with a beautiful linen tablecloth, along with two perfect place settings—a subtle reminder of the missed dinner opportunity. When, the next morning, Jeff's mother-in-law was asked whether she was at all upset because her daughter and son-in-law had not made it home for dinner the night before, she said no. And when asked about the two place settings, she added, "Oh, I just didn't get around to putting those old dishes away." The couple felt bad, as if they'd wronged Jeff's mother-in-law in some way. They also felt they owed her something to atone for this (unintentional) offense. The mother-in-law, meanwhile, had complete and utter deniability.

This, then, is a guilt trip, often wrapped in the guise of innocuous observations about reality—that may have disruptive and distressing effects. We have seen that the key to ingratiation's effectiveness is Other's ignorance of Party's deliberate attempts to exert influence; Other is made to feel kindly toward Party and is thereby softened up. Similarly, feather-ruffling tactics work because Other is thrown off stride without knowing that Party has deliberately behaved in ways designed to produce exactly this effect. Guilt trips are a third member of this general family of contentious tactics. Other knows that something has been said or done by Party to make Other feel bad (or guilty), but Party can deny any intent to induce this consequence. Thus, Party can make Other feel bad about having behaved in ways that were hurtful to Party, while Party can insist that this consequence was entirely unintentional. If Other feels bad about having harmed Party, and is therefore inclined to do Party's unspoken bidding, Party can deny having intended to make Other feel bad—let alone behave in some compensatory fashion. Much of Stephen Potter's gamesmanship advice (recall the example of the tennis player with the "ancient ticker") follows this very pattern.

In another illustration from the realm of family relations, Monica is about to go out for the evening with several of her friends. The closer she gets to leaving the house, the more lonely and pathetic her husband Don's demeanor becomes. Finally, just as she is about to leave, Don—who by now is slouching around the house in a ratty old bathrobe, head down, slippers scuffing along the floor—says, "I hope you have a really good time, honey. I don't feel so well, but no need to worry. Have fun."

If Monica, feeling sorry for poor Don, decides to cancel her plans to go out for the evening, Don gets what he wants. If she instead goes out as planned, Don has perhaps succeeded in scoring a few guilt points that may be redeemed by him at a later time. And if Monica confronts Don with his guilt-inducing behavior, he can deny ever having had such an intention: "Honey, I really don't know what you're talking about. I'm standing here wishing you well, hoping you have a great time. What's the matter with that? Have you got some kind of problem? Are you feeling guilty?"

Guilt seems to be a powerful concern in many cultures. Among Americans, only depression makes people more uncomfortable than guilt (Izard, 1977), while for the Greeks and the Chinese, no emotion is more discomforting than guilt (Sommers, 1984). Moreover, as research over the last several decades has indicated, guilt trips often work. Freedman and his colleagues (1967) induced experimental participants to tell a lie (saying they have not heard about a test that has just been described to them by someone else), then found that participants were more likely to comply with a third person's request for help with a different experiment. Other ways of experimentally making someone feel guilty include inducing this person to upset a carefully arranged stack of index cards (Freedman et al., 1967), to break an expensive machine (Brock & Becker, 1966; Wallace & Sadalla, 1966) or camera (Regan et al., 1972), or to subject another person to a series of electric shocks or loud noises

(Carlsmith & Gross, 1969). Pratkanis and Aronson (1992) summarize three basic ways of inducing guilt: first, by reminding Other of past sins that have long since been atoned for; second, by making Other's small transgressions loom large; and third, by making it appear that Other is responsible for a wrong that it did not commit. Regardless of the way in which guilt is induced in Other by Party, Other is subsequently more likely to comply with a request made by Party or by someone else altogether.[6]

Guilt trips tend to be used as a contentious tactic for four general reasons. First, they are familiar. We all know the Jewish mother jokes, we have watched Woody Allen films ad nauseam, and most of us have been the recipient of guilt trips at the hands of others. Second, like ingratiation and feather ruffling, guilt trips have deniability. Since the relationship has not been threatened directly, there is little risk that the perpetrator will be accused of anger, intolerance, stubbornness, or provocation. Third, guilt trips work because, by definition, they are designed to make us feel personally to blame for the problem. This is not a pleasant feeling. It may often seem that the easiest way for Other to rid itself of the unpleasant feeling is to yield to Party's requests, so as to make amends for its "blameworthy" actions. And fourth, guilt trips seem safe. For Party to come right out and say what it feels or means or wants risks the possibility that Other will tell it to go to hell; to announce that Party depends on Other to do something invites rejection. When Don drags around the house wearing his hangdog look just as Monica is getting ready to go out, maybe what he's really feeling is that if he comes right out and says that he wants Monica to stay home with him, she'll laugh in his face, exposing him to feelings of powerlessness, abandonment, and humiliation. It's much safer simply to groan, mumble, and shuffle.

If these are the reasons why it is tempting to resort to guilt trips, then there are also several offsetting problems. First, guilt trips may not be effective simply because Other may not notice the things that Party does to induce guilt. Second, a guilt trip makes Other feel bad, without ever explaining why. And third, because the underlying issues tend not to be discussed, guilt trips have a way of allowing Party's underlying problem to continue—thereby paving the way for Party to become more upset than before.

PERSUASIVE ARGUMENTATION

Ingratiation, gamesmanship, and guilt trips are preparatory tactics in the sense that they erode Other's resistance to lowering aspirations rather

[6]The reader interested in learning more about research on guilt trips may wish to read a recent review of the experimental literature by Vangelisti et al. (1991). This paper also includes a typology of techniques that can be used to make others feel guilty in conversation.

than acting on these aspirations directly. In contrast, a number of contentious tactics are applied in a direct effort to induce Other to reduce aspirations. The lightest of these tactics is *persuasive argumentation,* a technique whereby Party induces Other to lower its aspirations through a series of logical appeals.

The skill required for successful persuasive argumentation should not be underestimated. Party must convince Other to surrender something that it holds dear and that Party covets—not through coercion or the lure of reward, but through persuasion. This is a tall order in a contentious encounter. Social psychological theory and research in the area of persuasion has received much attention over the years.[7] Rather than dwell on this broad issue, we shall simply describe two general types of appeals that can be useful when there is conflict of interest.

First, Party may try to persuade Other that Party has a legitimate right to a favorable outcome in the controversy. If I can persuade you that it is "your money or *my* life"—that is, I am in considerable jeopardy unless you grant my wish—I may be able to persuade you to lower your aspirations. Such is the case when negotiators argue that they are in danger of being fired, demoted, or replaced unless they can return a particularly favorable division of resources to their constituents. Prime Minister Begin of Israel and a number of his senior advisors managed to employ exactly such arguments with considerable success in the Middle East negotiations of the late 1970s and early 1980s.

A second major form of persuasive argumentation requires Party to convince Other that lower aspirations are in the latter's interest. This is really quite an extraordinary maneuver: I am persuading you that it is in your interest to permit me to prevail. Consider a failing business whose management persuades labor negotiators that unless workers accept pay cuts and layoffs, the business will go down with all hands aboard. Sound farfetched? If so, recall the successful effort by Chrysler management to persuade autoworkers to accept deep pay cuts in order to increase the chances of corporate survival. Similar efforts by commercial airlines and the Greyhound Bus Company succeeded in the early 1980s. In each of these examples, Party convinced Other to embrace lower aspirations by pointing to a credible alternative that appeared to be even less attractive.

THREATS

Threats are messages of intention by Party to behave in ways that are detrimental to the interests of Other, depending on what the latter does or

[7]See, for example, the volume by Zimbardo & Leippe (1991).

does not do.[8] We begin our analysis of threats with a review of their general characteristics, then consider both their potential advantages and drawbacks. Finally, we comment on the reasons why threats seem to emerge as a dominant form of social influence in contentious exchanges.

General Characteristics of Threats

Imagine, for the purposes of the following general analysis, a world in which there are two people—Party and Other—and three possible behaviors that Other can perform: X, Y, and Z. Imagine further that Party wishes to induce Other to do X, whereas Other prefers Y and to a lesser extent Z. Obviously we are describing here an ideal case; there are often more than two participants and more than three forms of available behavior. Still, such situations do exist in reality, as when Other is a child (Johnny) who has a plate with three foods remaining—spinach (X), mashed potatoes (Y), and steak (Z)—and Party is Johnny's father.

Assuming that Party is able and willing to mete out rewards and punishments to get its way, how might Party proceed to influence Other to do X rather than Y or Z? One approach would be for Party to say, in effect, "If you do X (the thing I want), I will reward you." Translated into English, his father says to Johnny, "If you eat your spinach now, I'll give you your favorite flavor of ice cream for dessert." Such a statement is a prototypical promise, providing a consequence (ice cream) that Other is believed to find desirable in exchange for compliance (eating the spinach now).

In contrast, Party might attempt to induce the performance of X by saying, "Unless you do X, I will punish you" ("Unless you eat your spinach now, I will send you to your room"). In this, a prototypical threat, Party is proffering a consequence that is presumed to be undesirable to Other (being sent to his room), contingent on Other's failure to comply with Party's wishes.

Where a promise offers the lure of a carrot, a threat influences through the menace of a stick. This difference—the positive or negative consequence implied—is the most important and obvious feature that distinguishes promises from threats. Less obvious is the fact that *threats ordinarily provide more information about how Party intends to behave than do promises.* To understand why this is so, take a look at Figure 4.1.

The typical promise designed to compel or induce the performance of some behavior (X) indicates what will happen if Other does the thing desired, but it leaves uncertain the consequence of noncompliance (doing Y

[8]Promises, in contrast, are contingent messages of intention by Party to behave in ways that are beneficial to the interests of Other. Because promises serve primarily to cement contractual relations (see Schelling, 1960) rather than to prevail in a contentious exchange, they are not central to a discussion of contentious tactics. However, because some of our observations about threats derive from a comparison with promises, we also have a few comments about the general nature of promises in this section.

	X (Spinach)	Y (Potatoes)	Z (Steak)
PROMISE	+	?	?

"If you do X, I will reward you."
("If you eat your spinach now, I'll give you your favorite flavor of ice cream for dessert.")

	X	Y	Z
THREAT	?	–	–

"Unless you do X, I will punish you."
("Unless you eat your spinach now, I will send you to your room.")

+ = Reward
– = Punishment
? = Uncertain outcome
(reward, punishment, neither, or both)

FIGURE 4.1
Information conveyed by a typical promise and a typical threat.

or Z). In contrast, the corresponding threat makes clear the negative consequences of not doing X and leaves uncertain the consequence of compliance. In the example of Johnny and the three remaining foods on his plate, his father's threat actually conveys twice as much unequivocal information about consequences (a minus sign for Y and for Z) than the corresponding promise (a plus sign for X). Extended to a more extreme case, we might imagine 1,000 things that poor Johnny can do, only one of which is the thing desired by his autocratic father. Whereas the promise informs Johnny about the consequences of doing only the one thing his father prefers, the threat clearly implies that Johnny is to be punished for doing any of 999 things![9]

[9]Note that our informational analysis has been based on compellent promises and threats (those designed to induce some desired behavior), primarily because these are the promises and threats that are typically used in most conflictual encounters. The same analysis can reasonably be applied to their deterrent counterparts (designed to deter the performance of some undesirable behavior), so long as the aim of these threats is to deter everything other than X. However, in the case of a deterrent promise or threat that aims to prevent the performance of X while tolerating Y and Z, the preceding informational analysis changes. The deterrent promise "If you do anything other than X, I will reward you" clearly contains more informational clarity than the corresponding threat "If you do X, I will punish you." Note that this deterrent promise may fail to work because it resembles a bribe. It is a bit like the Lord's promise in the Garden of Eden: "Eat the fruit of any tree but the Tree of Knowledge and all will go well with you." Such a promise invites the temptation to explore the one alternative for which reward is not forthcoming.

Research by Lewicki and Rubin (1973), Rubin and Lewicki (1973), and Rubin et al. (1973) has consistently pointed to the potential importance of differences in the informational clarity of promises and threats. This work indicates that the greater the amount of apparent information conveyed by a promise or threat, the more likely Party is to be rated by Other as powerful and in control of the interaction. As a result, compliance is rated as more likely in response to threats than to promises. This sort of analysis also reveals why Party, given a choice, might prefer to make use of threats. They help to foster the impression that Party is fully in control of the interaction—more so than would be implied by use of the corresponding promise.

Some Good News about Threats

Threats may not be so nice as promises, but they are more tempting to use as a means of eliciting compliance. This is so for several reasons:

First, the threat that works costs Party nothing; there is no reward to be doled out *and* no punishment to be imposed. It is the leverage provided by the desire to avoid a cost—rather than the cost itself—that makes the threat work. As Schelling (1966) observes, where brute force often fails because it increases Other's resistance and pluck, the *threat* of such force may succeed.

Consider, for example, the tragedy that swept through the Branch Davidian compound in Waco, Texas in the winter of 1993. Perhaps if the Bureau of Alcohol, Tobacco, and Firearms (ATF) had first *threatened* cult leader David Koresh with the use of all necessary force unless they surrendered their firearms at the outset (instead of launching a surprise attack that surprised no one), the ATF might have achieved their objective with less tragic results. And perhaps, at the close of the fifty-day siege, the outcome might have been different had the FBI and ATF leadership first *threatened* to use tear gas if Koresh and his followers did not surrender—instead of simply moving directly to coercive tactics. Often it is the threatened use of force, rather than force itself, that produces the results Party wants.

Second, threats are often highly effective; their value has been demonstrated repeatedly and consistently (for example, Black & Higbee, 1973; Bonoma et al., 1970; Bonoma & Tedeschi, 1973; Gahagan et al., 1970; Lindskold et al., 1969; Mogy & Pruitt, 1974). Indeed, it can be argued that threats are more effective at motivating Other to comply than are promises. This is in part because threateners usually seem more powerful and controlling than promisors, due to the fact that their messages provide more information about what is likely to happen (Levinger, 1987). It is also because threats have been found experimentally to be very credible forms of influence, often more so than promises (see Pruitt & Carnevale,

1993, and Rubin & Brown, 1975, for a review of this literature). And it is also because people are ordinarily more highly motivated to avoid a possible loss than to obtain a possible reward (Taylor, 1991). Hence, they are more likely to yield when confronted with a threat.

A third potential "virtue" of threats is that threateners can benefit even when they renege on a threat. If Party elects *not* to enforce the terms of a threat when Other fails to comply, this choice may be regarded by Other not as particularly weak or foolish but as humane. Whereas a reneging promisor is almost certain to be seen by Other as a person who cannot be trusted to do what he or she says, a reneging threatener may be regarded as powerful but compassionate—the sort of person (like a kindly parent) who understands the wisdom of forbearance. To be sure, one who reneges on either a threat or a promise runs the risk of reduced credibility in the eyes of Other. But the potential cost for Party associated with reneging on a threat may be offset, at least in part, by the possibility of a charitable interpretation of Party's actions.

A fourth virtue of threats, causing them to be used with considerable frequency by people in conflict, is that they are consistent with the sense of justice and rectitude that often accompanies such interactions. People in contentious encounters often believe, or act as though they believe, that they have God and Right on their side. Under these circumstances, what better way of exerting influence than by means of a threat? If Other does what Party demands, this is only right and proper and deserves no special reward. But if Other fails to do what Party requests, then punishment is the appropriate response to this wrong. ("If Johnny doesn't have the good sense and respect to do what I asked him to do, then he deserves his punishment. He knew what was coming to him.")

A Major Difficulty with Threats

The most serious problem associated with the use of threats is that they tend to elicit similar behavior from Other. Threats lead to counterthreats, so the effect of using them is often to escalate the controversy at a precipitous rate. Deutsch and Krauss (1960) and others have demonstrated that threats lead to increased suspicion and dislike by Other for Party, which in turn makes it more likely that Other will respond with threats of its own (Smith & Anderson, 1975; Youngs, 1986). In this way, a negative spiral of intensifying hostility is set in motion (McClintock et al. 1987), creating a pattern that is described in more detail in Chapters 5 and 6.[10]

Despite this disadvantage, threats are used because they are cheap, they often seem justified, and they may appear to be the only tactic that will

[10]For empirical evidence about the negative effects of threats in organizational settings, see Freedman (1981).

work. However, the resentment and hostility engendered by threats often motivate a response in kind from Other, creating an escalative spiral.

IRREVOCABLE COMMITMENTS

Threats are "if-then" messages, assertions by Party in the following form: "If you do (don't do) X, then I will punish you." By contrast, the coercive tactics that we are about to examine do not appear to contain this element of contingency. Instead, these threat tactics typically assume the following form: "I have started doing something that requires adjustment from you and will continue doing it despite your best efforts to stop me." Party guarantees to continue behaving in a certain way, and the coercive commitment that has been made is—or appears to be—an irrevocable one. In order to better understand the nature of these irrevocable commitments,[11] let us consider briefly two rather different examples, the first drawn from the fabled game of chicken, the second from the world of nonviolent resistance.

As it was played in old James Dean, Sal Mineo, and Marlon Brando movies, chicken involves two participants who are driving their cars at breakneck speed on a direct collision course. The loser in this game (the chicken) is the first person to turn aside in order to avert a head-on collision and almost certain death for both players. Researchers (such as Deutsch & Lewicki, 1970) and theorists (such as Schelling, 1960) have studied the game of chicken with interest because of its structural similarity to the contests of will that are occasionally played out in such international settings as the conflict between Great Britain and Argentina in the Falklands/Malvinas, the Cuban missile crisis, or the escalating conflict between the United States and Iraq in the Persian Gulf in 1990 and 1991. More generally, the game of chicken can be observed whenever two or more parties lock into a contest of wills in which neither side is willing to concede first and both stand to lose a great deal through joint intransigence. A divorcing couple in the throes of a nasty child custody dispute and the affected sides in a costly labor strike are also good candidates for a chicken analysis.

Because the game of chicken is a quintessential example of a test of grit and determination, the usual threats are not likely to work very well. Why should Other give in on a vitally important issue simply because Party has tendered some statement of contingency that may or may not be honored? No, more powerful influence medicine is required here, in the form of a (seemingly) irrevocable commitment. For instance, in the driving example already mentioned, Party could fling its steering wheel out the window in full view of Other (Schelling, 1960). The message conveyed through this

[11]Also called positional commitments (see Pruitt & Carnevale, 1993).

commitment is that now only Other has control over what will happen. Party has irrevocably committed itself to a potentially disastrous course of action. As a result, the locus of control over the outcome of the exchange has been shifted from the shoulders of Party to those of Other, who is now the only one capable of preventing mutual catastrophe.

As a dramatically different illustration of irrevocable commitment, let us consider some of the basic tactics of nonviolent resistance. By nonviolent resistance we mean such events as Mohandas K. Gandhi's fasts in order to secure concessions from the British forces that occupied India, the boycotts and sit-down strikes by courageous African Americans in the south of the 1950s and early 1960s, and refusal to register for the draft or to move out of the way of approaching tanks as a means of protesting a national war effort. Although many of us admire the courage, determination, and moral conviction that characterize such examples of nonviolent resistance, we must not lose sight of the essentially contentious tactics at work, which are designed to prevail in an intensely conflictual exchange.[12]

Nonviolent resistance is probably best thought of as a class of tactics rather than a monolithic entity; indeed, Sharp (1971) has distinguished nine different types of nonviolence. Nevertheless, certain central features are found in virtually every use of this approach. The most important of these is Party's apparently irrevocable commitment to a set of demands and a nonviolent course of action. If effectively conveyed to Other, such commitment shifts the locus of responsibility for what happens squarely onto Other's shoulders. In announcing his intention to begin fasting in protest of British policies in India, Gandhi served notice on the British that they now had exclusive responsibility for determining the outcome of the crisis. Nothing would budge Gandhi from this stance other than British surrender to his wishes, and it fell entirely to the British to decide whether to accede to the Mahatma's demands or let him die. As is well known, on virtually every occasion in which nonviolence was tried in India—both by Gandhi alone and as a form of mass, collective action—the tactic worked as intended.

Some Advantages of Irrevocable Commitments

We have looked at two very different styles of irrevocable commitment. The first, deliberately stripping oneself of control in the game of chicken, serves notice on Other of Party's commitment to a belligerent course of action. The

[12]We acknowledge that it may appear bizarre to liken hell-bent teenagers or world leaders in a highly competitive game of chicken to the moral appeal advanced through the nonviolent acts of Gandhi or Dr. Martin Luther King, Jr. At heart, the psychological features that lead each "game" to be effective are strikingly similar, even though their underlying motivation and moral or political consequences may be profoundly different.

second example, nonviolent resistance, is a demonstration of similar unswerving commitment—although typically to a moral stance rather than to outright belligerency. What the two examples have in common is that they place the onus for escaping mutual disaster entirely on Other. Let us now consider some of the several "virtues" of this tactic.

If used successfully, irrevocable commitments force Other to do the work of bringing about agreement; hence, they elicit concessions from Other. If you and I are approaching an intersection in our respective automobiles, and you believe (because I am staring straight ahead of me) that I am unaware of your presence, the responsibility for what happens to the two of us is not mine but yours; it is you who must do the work of jamming on your brakes to prevent a collision. Many a Boston driver has put this very tactic to good use in an effort to slip through a busy intersection (Rubin et al., 1974). More generally, it is clear that irrevocable commitment is a useful, if risky, tactic to employ in any negotiation.

A second virtue of irrevocable commitments is that they do not require Party to hold power that is equal to or greater than that of Other.[13] For a threat to work as intended, Party must be able to present itself as being in a position, even temporarily, of doling out costs that matter to Other. In this case, the basis for imposition of cost on Other is not Party's greater pool of resources but its ability to commit itself in ways that appear irreversible. Gandhi's power to compel the British to modify their policies in India stemmed not from superior physical resources but from his very weakness. Commitment of his frail body to a fast that it could not endure for very long was a powerful lever to force the mighty British to yield. Weakness can thus be a source of strength in irrevocable commitments—provided that this commitment is highly credible.

A third virtue of irrevocable commitments is that they often work without Party or Other ever witnessing the commitment's ultimate consequences. Gandhi did not actually have to fast to the death to prevail; it was sufficient for the British to believe that he would continue fasting as long as necessary. When Party has a history of "honoring" commitments of various kinds, this history may be sufficient for Party to prevail without carrying through to the bitter end.

Some Problems with Irrevocable Commitments

Precisely because of their irreversibility or apparent irreversibility, commitment tactics often entail considerable risk. Party's fate is placed in the hands of an Other who may *or may not* be ready to make the concessions

[13]Schelling (1960) has observed that, paradoxically, the weaker party is often in the stronger bargaining position because its very weakness gives it a commitment that would be taken away by strength. Its weakness makes its bargaining commitment irrevocable.

necessary to avoid disaster. If Other is not ready to make these concessions, the disaster is often mutual: both chicken players are killed, or Gandhi starves to death and India is thrown into massive communal disorder. This is a risky tactic indeed.

There are several reasons why Other may fail to make the concessions this tactic is designed to evoke. First, Other may have failed to understand or fully acknowledge the consequences of the commitment that has been made. If you cannot see me behind the wheel of my car and therefore do not know that I am unaware that we are both approaching the same intersection, the two of us have a serious problem. Similarly, if one chicken driver is unaware that the other driver has sent the steering wheel hurtling out the window, a genuine disaster is in the making.

Second, Other may want to comply with Party's wishes but may be unable to do so—as when the other driver in the chicken game has lost control of the brakes and is therefore unable to stop in time, or when a kidnap victim has no access to ransom money.

Third, and most important, Party may misjudge the relative value to Other of the options that it is forcing Other to choose between. Party may believe Other will prefer capitulation to mutual disaster, but Other may actually prefer disaster. In his fasts, Gandhi always ran the risk that the British would prefer massive communal disorder to the concessions he was asking them to make; they might decide that it was better to try to weather a political storm than to give in to yet another of Gandhi's demands. To minimize this latter danger, it is important for Party to have a thorough knowledge of Other's perceptions and values. For a newcomer to a relationship, making an irrevocable commitment can be playing with fire.[14]

Because of these three risks, it is desirable for Party's apparently irrevocable commitments to be reversible if necessary. Party would be well advised—before flinging its steering wheel out the window in a game of chicken—to engineer a second steering mechanism, unseen by Other, that can be used to avert a last-minute disaster in the event that the tactic fails to work. Similarly, perhaps a faster should arrange for a bit of sustenance to be squirreled in, unbeknownst to the other side. Under most circumstances it is better to be seen as a fool or a trickster than to die. The most effective unilateral commitment may be one that Other believes to be irreversible but that can be modified if absolutely necessary.

If a first general problem with irrevocable commitments is that they may prove too risky to actually implement, a second difficulty stems from the fact that they must be used preemptively. It is the *first* Party to strip itself of control in the game of chicken who is likely to prevail. For Party to

[14]This may help explain Kelley's (1966) experimental finding that irrevocable commitments tend to be made late in negotiations and that the greater the negotiator's experience, the later they are made.

throw its steering wheel out the window at the same moment as, or immediately after, Other does the same thing is to be both terribly brave and terribly foolhardy. It makes sense to surrender control over events only if Party can count on Other's retention of control. Unfortunately, it is precisely in those contentious encounters where irrevocable coercive commitments are most likely to occur that *both* sides are likely to resort to this tactic—often to their mutual detriment.

Because there are costs and uncertainties associated with the use of irrevocable commitments, Other may suspect Party of not wishing to carry such commitments through to completion. Therefore, a third major problem with this tactic is that of credibility: how to get Other to believe that Party means what it has said and should therefore be taken seriously. There are also risks involved with credibility. Party may think it is committed to take the stated action, but Other may doubt this commitment. Such a misunderstanding has the makings of tragedy.

Enhancing the Credibility of Irrevocable Commitments

There are several things that Party can do in an effort to bolster the credibility of an irrevocable commitment. First, Party may wish to employ the services of some third person who has been given instructions that are virtually impossible to change, such as a courier sent to deliver a message by a person who cannot subsequently be contacted in any way. Schelling (1960) observes in this general regard, "At many universities the faculty is protected by a rule that denies instructors the power to change a course grade once it has been recorded" (p. 38). This places the registrar in the position of a messenger conveying information that Party is now unable to change.

A second way to enhance the credibility of this tactic is to pledge commitment in public rather than in private, thereby laying on the line Party's reputation for consistency in word and deed. Writes Schelling, "If national representatives can arrange to be charged with appeasement for every small concession, they place concession visibly beyond their own reach" (p. 29).

A third way of enhancing credibility is to demonstrate that Party has a constituency looking on that will hold it responsible for anything surrendered. In effect, Party attempts to argue that its neck is in a noose that is about to be drawn tight by intransigent constituents who are watching every move that is made.

A fourth technique for enhancing the credibility of a seemingly irrevocable commitment involves confronting Other with evidence of Party's resolve. Such evidence contributes immeasurably to the effectiveness of nonviolent resistance. There is nothing like an eyeball-to-eyeball exchange for letting Other know the depth and intensity of Party's commitment to a position. In the absence of such direct interpersonal confrontation, Party's forcefulness cannot truly be grasped, and this tactic is less likely to work as intended. As Gandhi (1949) wrote, perhaps surprisingly, "Non-violence . . . does not mean meek submission to the will of the evil-doer, but it means putting one's whole soul against the will of the tyrant" (p. 4). In Gandhi's nonviolent resistance campaigns and Martin Luther King's civil rights movement, the forcefulness of the commitment was buttressed even further by the presence of ideology—a set of organizing beliefs that the resisters used to explain and justify their behavior.

We have seen that irrevocable commitments carry with them potential problems of risk and credibility. The most serious problem, however, stems from the contributions to escalation often made by such coercive commitments. These tactics tend to beget responses in kind that, instead of bringing an end to the contentious exchange, are likely to cause each side to dig in its heels, to take positions from which it feels it cannot budge without losing face, and thereby to exacerbate an already difficult situation.

CONCLUSIONS

In this chapter we have tried to outline several of the more important contentious tactics that Party uses in an effort to prevail. As reflected in the general organizational sequence of the topics presented, we believe there is a tendency for lighter contentious tactics to be utilized before Party resorts to their heavier counterparts. This light-to-heavy sequence is not always followed, as when Party moves away from an initially tough posture in order to seem cooperative by comparison, or when the ingroup eventually capitulates. But this sequence is very common, and it is a major source of escalation.

We have also portrayed Party as the initiator of contentious moves, and Other as their recipient and reactor. This portrayal is something of a distortion. The interactions of antagonists are often more like a minuet in which the steps of *each* side are matched quite precisely by corresponding moves on the part of the other. Each side takes, in turn, the stance of the aggressor and that of the defender, and escalation is as much (or more) the product of a vicious circle or conflict spiral as of a sequence of tactical initiatives on the part of only one side. Such conflict spirals will be closely examined in the next four chapters.

5

Escalation and Its Development

Development of the Cold War • Transformations that Occur During Escalation • *A Domestic Escalation* • Conflict Models • *The Aggressor-Defender Model* • *The Conflict Spiral Model* • *Psychological Forces in Conflict Spirals* • Conclusions

The term *escalation* brings the realm of international relations most prominently to mind. Hence, we start with an example from this realm, the development of the Cold War. However, escalation is not limited to this realm and can occur at all levels of society. Accordingly, we will present examples from several other realms as well.

DEVELOPMENT OF THE COLD WAR

The Cold War between the United States and the Soviet Union began to develop immediately after 1945 and persisted until the late 1980s. For most people now living, this harsh, often frightening conflict has been the dominant feature on the international landscape. Today the Soviet Union is gone, and the rivalry between these regions of the world has largely disappeared. But the Cold War has left a continuing legacy in many of our institutions and much of our literature.

The United States and the Soviet Union were allies during the Second World War, which ended in 1945 with high hopes for continued cooperation. But the

Soviets emerged from the war with deep suspicion of the West. This led them to seek control of the nations adjoining their territory, making it difficult to maintain East-West cooperation. The Soviets built a communist satellite system in Eastern Europe, supported communist guerrillas in Greece, and applied political pressure to Turkey. In 1947 the United States responded to these actions in three ways: It gave military aid to Greece and Turkey. It created the Marshall Plan, designed to revitalize the economy of Western Europe and weaken Communist parties in Western European countries. And (in conjunction with Britain and later with France) it began the slow process of unifying West Germany and rebuilding its economy, as a further bulwark against Soviet expansion.

The latter move was viewed with considerable alarm by the Soviet Union, which had been at war with Germany twice in the preceding 30 years. The Soviets responded at first with protests. Then, in 1948, they tried sporadically interrupting communications between Berlin (which was under joint control but was an enclave surrounded by the Russian-controlled portion of Germany) and West Germany. Finally, after the West introduced a unified currency in West Germany, the Soviets installed a full blockade of Berlin, claiming that they were repairing the routes to the city. The United States and its allies responded by launching a successful airlift between Berlin and West Germany. They also began negotiations that led to the formation of the North Atlantic Treaty Organization (NATO), a military alliance involving the United States and most of the Western European nations. This latter development led eventually to the rearmament of West Germany, which caused considerable further alarm in the Soviet Union.

This conflict continued until the late 1980s, but we interrupt the story at this point because we have said enough to give a dramatic example of conflict escalation.

TRANSFORMATIONS THAT OCCUR DURING ESCALATION

There are two related meanings of the term *escalation*. It may mean that one of the participants in conflict is using heavier tactics than before—is putting greater pressure on the other participant. Or it may mean that there is an increase in the intensity of a conflict *as a whole*. We use the term in both senses in this book, but mainly in the latter sense.

As conflicts escalate, they go through certain incremental transformations. Although these transformations occur separately on each side, they affect the conflict as a whole because they are usually mirrored by the other side. As a result of these transformations, the conflict is intensified in ways that are sometimes exceedingly difficult to undo. The aim of this chapter is to understand the nature of these transformations and some of the processes by which they take place.

At least five types of transformations commonly occur during escalation. All may not be found in a single conflict, but all are very common. The five transformations are as follows:

1. *Light→heavy.* As we observed in Chapter 4, Party's efforts to get its way in a contentious exchange typically begin with light influence attempts: ingratiation overtures, gamesmanship, persuasive arguments, guilt trips. In many cases, these gentle tactics are supplanted by their heavier counterparts: threats, irrevocable commitments, and so on. Eventually even violence may erupt. The events of 1948 illustrate this kind of transformation. The Soviet Union moved from protest to disrupting communication and eventually to blockading a city. The United States and its allies also moved decisively from strengthening a new ally to the formation of a full military alliance.
2. *Small→large.* As conflict escalates, there is a tendency for issues to proliferate.[1] There is also a tendency for Party and Other to become increasingly absorbed in the struggle and to commit additional resources to it in an effort to prevail. Both tendencies may be seen in the Cold War crisis. On the Soviet side, the initial general suspicion of the West mushroomed into a large number of specific complaints: the program to weaken Communist parties, the rebuilding of West Germany, the introduction of a separate West German currency, and finally the formation of a hostile military alliance. From the viewpoint of the United States, new issues appeared at every turn: the introduction of a communist dictatorship in Czechoslovakia, the support of guerrillas in Greece, the Berlin blockade. Both sides rapidly increased the resources allocated to the conflict, and the conflict developed into a national obsession on both sides.
3. *Specific→general.* In escalating conflict, specific issues tend to give way to general issues, and the overall relationship between Party and Other deteriorates. Over the painful history of an escalating exchange, small, concrete concerns tend to be supplanted by grandiose and all-encompassing positions and by a general intolerance of Other.

   These changes were very clear in the United States during the development of the Cold War. The concern about specific incidents that was seen in 1945 and 1946 changed rapidly into a gen-

[1]McEwen and Milburn (1993) have used the term *metaconflict* to describe a situation in which the initial issues around which a conflict begins are vastly outweighed by new issues produced by the conflict.

eral indictment of the Soviet Union and of communism as a whole. The Soviets were seen as new incarnations of Hitlerite Germany, a totally untrustworthy "evil empire" bent on conquering the world. This led to such excesses in the United States as McCarthyism, a refusal for many years to recognize the People's Republic of China, and participation in the Vietnam War. The relationship between the United States and the Soviet Union deteriorated so badly that at times there was practically no communication at all.

4. *Doing well→winning→hurting Other.* In the early stages of many conflicts, Party is simply out to do as well as it can for itself, without regard for how well or how poorly Other is doing. This outlook has been described by Deutsch (1958) as an "individualistic orientation," an outlook characterized by self-interest that is quite independent of Other's fate. As conflict escalates, however, Party's simple interest in doing well is supplanted by a clearly competitive objective. Now doing well means outdoing Other. Finally, as escalation continues and the costs for Party begin to mount, its goals tend to shift again. The objective now is to hurt Other and, if Party is experiencing cost, to hurt Other more than itself (Glasl, 1982). For every drop of blood that Party has shed, a far more terrible bloodletting must be forced on Other. This is competition in the extreme.

   Such transformations were apparent in Soviet-American relations after 1945. What began as a desire to reverse specific policies was transmogrified into a broad competition, in which the two parties sought the other's defeat in every corner of the globe. The importance of this competition in the United States was reflected in the widespread and politically explosive view that China had been "lost" as a result of its 1949 revolution. In the thinking of many on both sides, the logical solution to the problem was to weaken the other side—or even, for a few people, to destroy it.

5. *Few→many.* Conflicts that begin with the agitation of a small number of participants often grow, in the face of Party's failure to prevail, into collective efforts. If Other won't do as Party wants—and if Party is unable to get its way by threatening, promising, or in some other way manipulating Other—then it is in Party's best interest to find others who are willing to band together with it. What Party cannot accomplish on its own it may well be able to achieve with the increased support and muscle of its associates. An illustration of this is the development, during the Cold War, of two large military alliances: NATO and its Eastern counterpart, the Warsaw Pact.

A Domestic Escalation

The transformations just described are not limited to the international arena. Indeed, they are found just as often in domestic settings. Consider this example (Peterson, 1983) involving a young married couple, as recounted by the wife:

> We were in the car on the way to visit my parents. We had had a tough time getting ready for the trip and were both tired. Paul was in the back of the station wagon reading. I was driving. We were on the Turnpike, and I asked him to move to the side. I wanted to pass and I couldn't see through him. He told me to look out the side mirror or turn around and look. I'm accustomed to using the rear view mirror and I didn't feel I should have to change my driving habits when he could move to the side a little so I could see. A little later I said, "*Will* you move? I can't see through you." He just sat and glared. Twice more I asked him to move and finally he blew up and told me to pull over so he could drive. Then he told me he'd show me how he could pass without looking in either mirror by looking around. Paul kept on with some more nasty remarks. (p. 360)

This escalation ended a few minutes later with an apology from the husband, in reply to his wife's suggestion that he had overreacted. Thus, it was brief and by no means momentous. Nevertheless, three of the transformations we mentioned earlier occurred. The conflict went from *light to heavy,* with the wife making ever stronger demands and the husband first glaring, then showing anger, and finally becoming insulting. It went from *small to large,* with the wife reiterating her demands to the point that they overwhelmed the husband, and both of them become fixated on the quarrel. It went from *doing well to hurting Other,* with the husband first simply declining to move and eventually shifting to efforts to make his wife suffer. We are not told the nature of the husband's "nasty" remarks, but if they were a general indictment of his wife's driving skills, it would mean that a transformation from *specific to general* had also occurred.[2]

CONFLICT MODELS

To understand escalation, we must know what processes occur within and between Party and Other as their conflict intensifies. There are three

[2]For another domestic illustration of escalation, recall the Chapter 1 story of Ben and his father. There, light tactics were supplanted by heavier ones, the number of issues proliferated (starting with the car, then moving on to various other concerns), motivation shifted, and the number of parties to the conflict increased to the point of including the entire family. While the anecdote does not provide information about precisely what was said in the escalating exchange, one can imagine Dad shifting from a focus on the car to a focus on his son's laziness and selfishness—in which case the shift in focus from specific to general issues would be present as well.

broad models[3] of escalation (Pruitt & Gahagan, 1974): the aggressor-defender model, the conflict spiral model, and the structural change model. These models provide three accounts of what is happening when escalation takes place. All three have some value, accurately describing the developments in some kinds of escalation. None can be discarded in favor of another. We deal with the aggressor-defender and the conflict spiral models in this chapter, then turn to the structural change model in Chapters 6 and 7, which also deal with deteriorating relationships.

The Aggressor-Defender Model

The aggressor-defender model draws a distinction between Party and Other. Party, the aggressor, is viewed as having a goal of creating change that places it in conflict with Other, the defender. The aggressor's goal may be to take something from the defender, to alter reality at the defender's expense, or to stop the defender's annoying behavior. The aggressor (Party) ordinarily starts with mild contentious tactics, because this is the least risky approach. But if these do not work, Party moves on to heavier tactics, continuing to escalate until the goal is achieved or the cost of continued escalation is greater than the value of the goal sought. The defender (Other) merely reacts, escalating its efforts in response to Party's level of escalation. This process persists until Party either wins or gives up.

The aggressor-defender model helps understand one of the stages in the development of the Cold War. This is the point at which the Soviet Union adopted the goal of blocking the unification of West Germany. At first the Soviets employed the mild tactic of protest. When this did not work, they moved to a heavier tactic of sporadically interrupting communications between Berlin and West Germany. When this was unsuccessful, and the West introduced a unified West Ger-

[3]A model is an abstract pattern of thought from which explanations or predictions of particular events can be derived. It is quite common for alternative models to be available for explaining or predicting the same event, and more than one of these models may be correct. For instance, suppose we are trying to explain how a child has learned that 7 times 7 equals 49. If we derive an explanation from the reinforcement model of learning, we might conclude that the child acquired this knowledge because he or she was praised for correctly stating "Seven times seven is forty-nine." If we use instead a social learning model, we might conclude that the knowledge was formed because the child imitated people he or she respected, who were saying "Seven times seven is forty-nine." People often try to choose *between* two explanations of this kind, but it is frequently the case that *both* explanations are correct. The equation could first be acquired by imitation and then become a permanent part of memory by rewarded repetition.

man currency, the Soviets employed an extremely heavy tactic, a full blockade of Berlin.[4]

The aggressor-defender model fits some cases of escalation but is often given too much weight in everyday thinking. Typically, this is the only model that most people use in trying to understand escalation. Its popularity is probably due to the fact that it satisfies the natural urge to look for origins and people to blame.[5]

Many examples of escalation do not conform to the aggressor-defender model, including the broader Cold War escalation that included the Soviet efforts to block West German unification. This is because the aggressor-defender model postulates a *unidirectional* causal sequence, with the defender always reacting to the aggressor's behavior, whereas escalation is often a *circular* process, with Party reacting to Other's behavior and vice versa. To understand such circles, we need a different model: the conflict spiral.

The Conflict Spiral Model

The conflict spiral model[6] of escalation holds that escalation results from a vicious circle of action and reaction. Party's contentious tactics encourage a contentious reaction from Other, which provokes further contentious behavior from Party, completing the circle and starting it on its next iteration. Tactics move from light to heavy in this analysis, because each reaction is more severe and intense than the action that provoked it.

The conflict spiral model provides insight into the broader Cold War escalation, which involved a vicious circle. In response to Soviet moves in Eastern Europe and in Greece and Turkey, the United States and its allies began to establish a West German state. In response to this action, the Soviet Union instituted a blockade of Berlin. In response to that blockade, the United States and its allies formed NATO and began to arm West Germany. And so on.

In addition to explaining movement from light to heavy tactics, the conflict spiral model helps account for the fact that escalating conflicts

[4]The terms *aggressor* and *defender* in this model are not intended to be evaluative. They do not imply that the aggressor is wrong and the defender right. The aggressor is simply the side that seeks to change things and the defender the side that seeks to resist this change. In the marital example, the aggressor was the wife because she was trying to get her husband to move. It can be argued that her demands were reasonable, since her goal was safe driving, but she is still the aggressor in our terminology. The aggressor-defender model fits this case well, in the sense that Party escalated in an effort to change Other, who resisted by reciprocal escalation.

[5]In the popular use of this model, unlike ours, the person who is labeled the aggressor is usually blamed for the conflict. Social scientists try to understand how the world works rather than to allocate blame.

[6]This model is found in the writings of many theorists, including North et al. (1964), Osgood (1962, 1966), and Richardson (1967).

often move from small to large—that is, issues proliferate and the parties become more absorbed in these issues. This occurs because each retaliatory or defensive action in the spiral provides a new issue for the target of this action. Hence, each party's list of the other's transgressions grows longer and longer as the spiral continues, and each new grievance intensifies the sense of crisis. Recall the story of Ben and his father (Chapter 1) in this regard.

In addition to explaining the development of escalation, this model helps understand the *perpetuation* of high levels of escalation—that is, the fact that heavy tactics, once used, often continue to be employed. Consider a standard fistfight. If I hit you, you may well hit me back, which leads me to hit you again, and so on. At first, the blows become heavier and heavier and the conflict escalates. Then, because of limitations in human strength, the blows reach an asymptote beyond which they cannot grow heavier. Each of us is retaliating at about the level of provocation received. A conflict spiral is still going on, but it is now producing a highly escalated steady state rather than further escalation. The aggressor-defender and conflict spiral models are compared diagrammatically in Figure 5.1. In the aggressor-defender model, causation flows in only one direction; the aggressor (Party) acts and the defender (Other) reacts. In the conflict spiral model, causation flows in both directions; Other reacts to Party's actions and vice versa. The diagram of the conflict spiral involves an oversimplification, in that it pictures each party's action as a response only to the other's immediately preceding action. In reality, each action is a "result of the cumulative impression from all the previous actions by the

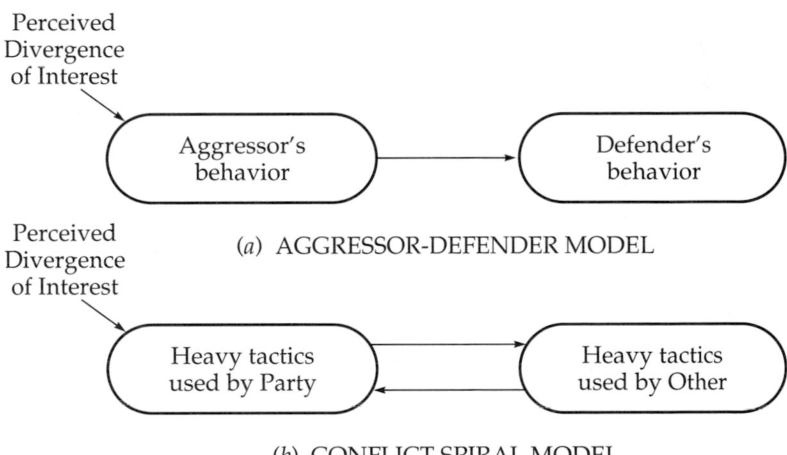

FIGURE 5.1
Aggressor-defender and conflict spiral models of conflict escalation.

other side" (White, 1984, p. 95), though more recent actions are usually given greater weight than earlier actions.

The conflict spiral model of escalation should *not* be viewed as an improved version of, or replacement for, the aggressor-defender model. The latter is useful whenever Party develops a goal that places it at odds with Other and pursues this goal by putting progressive pressure on Other. Many cases of escalation have this form. However, aggressor-defender sequences are often part of larger conflict spirals, as in the Soviet Union's reaction to the plan to unify West Germany. In such cases, the goal that impels the aggressor is, at least partly, a reaction to the defender's earlier actions.[7]

A further example of this point is the Nazi German effort to conquer Europe in the 1940s, an act of aggression by any definition of the term. This effort was partly a reaction to the humiliation of Germany after the First World War—the reparations Germany had to pay, the resulting inflation. Hence, the aggressor-defender sequence of the Second World War can be viewed as part of a larger conflict spiral that began before the First World War.

Psychological Forces in Conflict Spirals

From the viewpoint of a psychologist, the conflict spiral model in Figure 5.1 is incomplete, because it does not specify the motives and perceptions at work when Party and Other decide to use heavy tactics. An augmented conflict spiral model is shown in Figure 5.2. Here a cycle of escalation is seen, in which the heavy tactics used by Party produce *psychological states* in Other (segment A), which encourage a harsh reaction from Other (B), producing psychological states in Party (C), which encourage further heavy tactics from Party (D), and so on around and around. Four psychological states are particularly prominent in such a cycle: blame of Other, anger toward Other, fear of Other, and perceived threats to Party's image.

The value of the augmented conflict spiral model is that it allows us to derive hypotheses about the causes of escalation from our knowledge of these psychological states. Psychologists know a lot about the conditions that encourage the development of these states, in other words, the conditions that strengthen the causal sequences shown in segments A and C of Figure 5.2. There is also some knowledge about the conditions that encourage expression of these states, thus strengthening the causal sequences shown in segments B and D. By the logic of Figure 5.2, all of these

[7]This point is often missed by participants and observers, who attribute the cause of the conflict exclusively to Party's aggression. Participants usually view their adversary as the aggressor. They may be right with respect to the particular segment of the conflict at which they are looking, but they miss the broader picture.

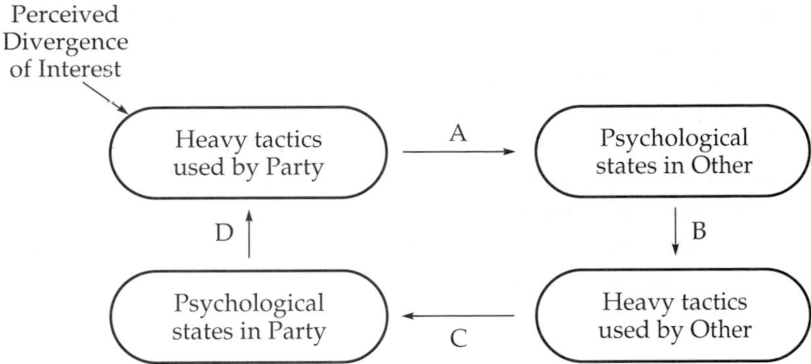

FIGURE 5.2
Augmented conflict spiral model, showing a cycle of escalation.

conditions should make conflict spirals more likely to go forward, thereby increasing the probability of escalation.[8]

Blame

Blame means faulting Other for its unpleasant behavior—holding Other responsible and hence accountable (Fiske & Taylor, 1991). Blame gives rise to a harsh reaction: if Other is responsible for provoking Party, Other must be punished. There are two reasons for this reaction: One is that blame produces a negative emotion, *anger* (Averill, 1983), which encourages aggression. The other is that blame produces a *rational desire to retaliate* against Other's provocation, in order to deter such behavior in the future. Research on distressed marriages suggests that such retaliation is particularly likely when Other's recent actions are seen as part of a broad, persistent pattern of behavior (Bradbury & Fincham, 1992). It seems important, in such cases, to "teach Other a lesson."

There are a number of perceptions that encourage blame when Other takes actions that harm Party's interests. Blame will be greater if it appears that Other could foresee that its actions would be harmful (Dyck & Rule, 1978). This makes the harm seem voluntary rather than accidental. Also, actions that seem freely taken are more likely to evoke blame than those that seem to result from heavy environmental pressures (Geen, 1990). Even the latter actions may evoke blame if Other is supposed to be

[8]The same conditions may also, at times, increase the likelihood of aggressor-defender sequences. When the goals of an "aggressor" are to stop the defender from annoying behavior or punish the defender for past provocative actions, the aggressor's level of escalation is likely to be a function of the extent of the aggressor's blame, anger, fear, or image threat. The defender's level of escalation may also be a function of the same psychological states. If the defender's actions in such a situation *do not* produce further escalation in the aggressor, we are dealing with a pure example of the aggressor-defender sequence. But if they *do* produce further escalation, the aggressor-defender sequence becomes an incident in a larger conflict spiral.

responsible for resisting such pressures. Actions that break social norms (Mallick & McCandless, 1966) or seem atypical of the way others behave (Dyck & Rule, 1978) are also viewed as especially blameworthy. Other must have a compelling excuse to avoid blame in such circumstance.

The implication of these points is that conflict is especially likely to escalate when Party sees Other's contentious behavior as illegitimate and not attributable to chance or extenuating circumstances (Ferguson & Rule, 1983). Under these conditions, Party is particularly likely to become angry or see a need to discipline Other, producing punitive behavior to which Other must then react.[9]

Anger

Most of the research on aggression (Baron, 1977; Berkowitz, 1993; Geen, 1990) can be interpreted as dealing with the sources and outcomes of anger. In the usual experiment on this topic, subjects are provoked by harsh actions from another person, and the effect of various environmental conditions on their level of retaliation is examined.[10]

Like other emotions, anger can be interpreted as resulting from cognitive labeling of an undifferentiated state of autonomic arousal. According to Schachter (1964), the first stage in emotional experience is arousal—activation of the autonomic nervous system. The second stage is interpretation of this arousal. To make this interpretation, Party employs whatever information is available. Not all interpretations lead to emotion; for example, if Party has recently taken a new medicine, it may assume that this is the cause. But there are certain standard interpretations that produce emotion. If Party sees danger, it is likely to interpret its arousal as fear and feel fear. If Party is aware of a recent aversive experience for which Other can be blamed, Party's reaction is instead likely to be one of anger. When such interpretations are made, greater arousal leads to stronger emotion and more extreme emotional behavior.

The last two points imply an *excitation transfer effect,* where Party becomes particularly angry when it is provoked in a situation that involves an additional source of arousal (Zillmann, 1979). For example, people who exercise and then are provoked aggress more vigorously against the source of the provocation than those who have not exercised (Zillmann et

[9]To forgive Other because of extenuating circumstances requires a high level of cognitive activity. Party must analyze Other's circumstances and motivation, and hold these up to standards of reasonable conduct. It is clear that this is socially learned behavior. Small children do not behave this way; children are much more likely than adults to hold people responsible for their actions, regardless of why these actions were taken (Shaw & Sulzer, 1964). Furthermore, Party pays less attention to extenuating circumstances when it is autonomically aroused, as might be expected with any complex cognitive behavior (Zillmann et al., 1975).

[10]Lazarus (1993), taking a cognitive perspective, argues that the provocation that produces anger is an injury to one's self-esteem, a "demeaning offensive against me and mine" (p. 13). A slightly different, but still cognitive, approach was taken by Aristotle, who argued that anger arises when we perceive that "we or our friends have been unfairly slighted" (1941, p. 1380). The latter acknowledges the importance of blame as an antecedent of anger.

al., 1974). This result is particularly apparent when the exercise comes somewhat earlier than the aversive experience, so that people lose track of why they are aroused and attribute it entirely to the aversive experience. The excitation transfer effect means that heavily contentious behavior and hence escalation are most likely to occur when Party approaches conflict in an aroused state.

In addition, it has been shown that angry reactions to provocation can be diminished by encouraging Party to misattribute the arousal resulting from the provocation to some other experience such as taking a pill, listening to loud noise, or conflict in the home (Loftis, 1974). Party's anger is diminished because it thinks something else is making it tense. This should reduce the likelihood of escalation.

The preferred target for Party's expression of aggression is Other, who is blamed for the aversive experience. However, it is not always possible to indulge this preference. The source of annoyance may be well protected, there may be extenuating circumstances that reduce Other's culpability, or it may be impossible to identify the source. Under these circumstances, Party's desire to punish is sometimes displaced onto another offending target. If one cannot hit an enraging boss, one overreacts to trivial frustration and yells at the spouse or kicks the cat.

Evidence of displacement may be seen in a study by Hovland and Sears (1940), who found an inverse correlation between the price of cotton in the South and the number of African Americans lynched over a 49-year period. The lower the price of cotton, the greater the number of lynchings. What presumably happened is that white farmers were frustrated by the decline in the cotton market but could not legitimately aggress against the cotton merchants who were paying them less. They took it out on a handy displacement object, an African American who had stepped out of line in some way.

Fear

Sometimes Other's harsh actions seem threatening and evoke fear instead of, or in addition to, blame and anger. Fear is another emotion; hence, we can speculate that it probably follows many of the same laws as anger. Unfortunately, research evidence is weak on this point.

Fear produces a different kind of conflict spiral than that produced by blame and anger. Blame and anger are prominent in *retaliatory spirals,* where each party punishes the other for actions it finds aversive. Examples are shouting matches, fistfights, and the like. Fear, on the other hand, is prominent in *defensive spirals,* in which each party is trying to protect itself from a threat it finds in the other's self-protective actions. An example is an arms race. In a defensive spiral, Party and Other may be thought of as alternating at being the aggressor and the defender. Escalation is often a combination of retaliatory and defensive spirals, the Cold War and the story of Ben and Dad being cases in point.

Image Threats

Threats to Party's image—the way Party appears—are an especially important source of escalation. Some image threats involve the way Other regards Party; others involve Party's own self-image. Escalation is particularly likely when there are threats to Party's image of power, status, forcefulness, adequacy, autonomy, loyalty, or integrity. Such threats produce both anger and fear.

Toch (1970) gives an example of an escalation that appears to have involved threats to Party's and Other's images of strength, status, and forcefulness. The incident took place in a state prison.

> We were watching these cats play cards, and we were standing behind this dude. He was one of these big iron lifters, you know. About ninety feet wide, you know, he was one of those. And he turned around and told us, "Don't stand behind me, punk, when I'm playing," you know. And I just looked at my partner and he looked at me, you know . . . and he turned around again and said, you know, "I told you not to stand behind me." And he said you know, "Bless you, man." And the dude got up, man, so I hit him on one side and the other dude hit him, and we were both on him, man. And we beat him to a pulp. . . . And after that I felt like a king, man. I felt like, you know, I'm the man; you're not going to mess with me. (pp. 164–165)

Image threats of this kind are as important to nations as they are to individuals.[11] Nations are often immensely concerned about their reputation for having power and being ready to use it. Many wars have been fought over these issues, an example being American involvement in the Vietnam War. Vietnam had no strategic importance to the United States, but American officials were concerned about the challenge to their image posed by the success of the communist movement there. They feared that the country would be seen as weak-willed if it did not fight, inviting communist aggression in other parts of the globe. This was part of a broader belief in interlocking commitments, which held, "If we aren't willing to fight them anywhere, we will have to fight them everywhere."

It is easy to belittle image-related concerns, to view them as senseless or even childish. But these concerns are a rational (though often shortsighted) reaction to many situations. In unregulated "jungles" such as the international arena and (probably to a lesser extent) a state prison, a reputation for strength and readiness to fight are seen as major deterrents against exploitation and assault by others. Environments of this kind lack adequate third party enforcement of norms against exploitation and the use of force. Hence, people feel they must defend themselves; they develop an image of toughness so others will believe that they are likely to do "whatever it takes." There are other, less violent ways to avoid exploitation and assault, but most people do not know or trust them.

[11]And of course image threats can, in theory at least, affect women as well as men—the all-male prison anecdote notwithstanding.

The usual motto, in Leo Durocher's words, is "Nice guys finish last."

The problem with this motto and with image-related concerns is that they often get people into serious trouble. In trying to look tough, people enrage or frighten others into a comparable reaction, starting a conflict spiral.[12] Paradoxically, people often end up as a target of the very assault they are trying to deter (Glasl, 1982).

CONCLUSIONS

We have described two conflict models that account for the processes by which escalation takes place: the aggressor-defender model and the conflict spiral model. We have also described an augmented conflict spiral model, which identifies the psychological conditions under which conflict spirals are especially likely to occur. In the next chapter, we turn to a third and more complicated model, the structural change model.

[12]In the resulting conflict spirals, power-related concerns become stronger and stronger, a phenomenon described by Winter (1987).

6

Structural Changes in Escalation

Psychological Changes • *Negative Attitudes and Perceptions* • Changes in Groups • *The Crisis at UB* • *The Nature, Source, and Impact of Group Changes* • Changes in Communities • Conclusions

The structural change model,[1] to which we turn in this chapter, provides further insight into the development of escalation. It also helps in understanding why escalation tends to persist and recur. Escalated conflict often lasts a long time, and it frequently leaves residues that make the next conflict between Party and Other more likely to escalate.

The structural change model is shown schematically in Figure 6.1. Considering only the dark arrows in the figure, it is clearly an extension of the conflict spiral model of Figure 5.2. These arrows also describe a cycle of escalation, in which heavy tactics used by Party tend to produce structural changes, which encourage similar heavy tactics from Other, provoking structural changes which start the cycle around again. What are these structural changes? Three varieties can be distinguished: changes in *psychological states*, changes in the structure and function of *groups*,[2] and changes in the nature of the *community* to which the parties belong.

[1]This model is implied by the writings of Burton (1962), Coleman (1957), and Schumpeter (1955, first published in 1919), among others.
[2]The reader will recall that the term *group* is being used to refer to collectives at all levels of society, from dyads to organizations to nations.

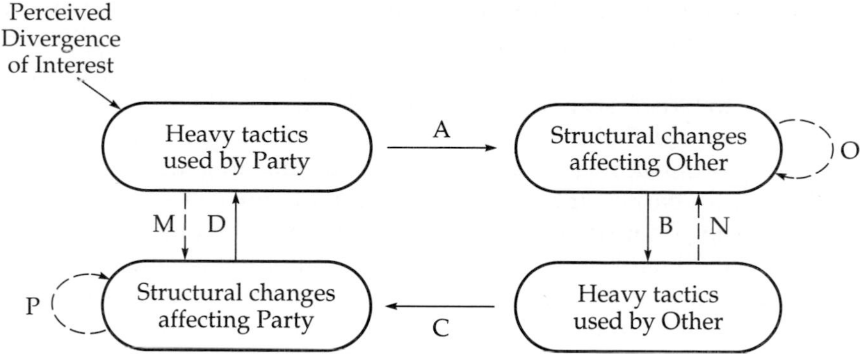

FIGURE 6.1
Structural change model. The circle of dark arrows represents a cycle of escalation. The dashed arrows represent several types of confirmatory mechanisms which cause structural changes to endure.

These three kinds of changes—their nature, origins, and impact—are discussed in the remainder of this chapter. The structural change model is more complicated than the other two models because it embodies *confirmatory mechanisms* that cause structural changes to endure. These mechanisms explain why escalation tends to persist and recur. They are shown schematically by the dashed arrows in Figure 6.1; they are discussed in detail in Chapter 7.

The arrow at the upper left in Figure 6.1 implies that the ultimate origin of escalation is a perceived divergence of interest, which provokes Party's initial contentious actions. Escalation often starts this way, but not always. Perceived divergence of interest can produce structural changes directly, and structural changes can have other origins as well.

PSYCHOLOGICAL CHANGES

In Chapter 5, we described four psychological states that are often part of conflict spirals and thus contribute to escalation: blame, anger, fear, and perceived threat to Party's (or Other's) image. We view these as temporary states, related to the events of the moment and persisting only so long as the conflict spiral persists. Once the conflict abates, these states tend to disappear.

We turn now to another class of psychological states: hostile and competitive goals, negative attitudes and perceptions, and deindividuation and dehumanization. These states have the same impact on conflict as blame, anger, fear, and image threat; hence, they could be placed in the boxes marked "Psychological states" in Figure 5.2. But they also have a quality of persistence which the other states lack.

It is common for negative attitudes and perceptions to develop in conflict. Other comes to be distrusted, in the sense of being seen as indifferent or even hostile to Party's welfare. Party tends to attribute uncomplimentary traits to Other, such as being self-centered, morally unfit, or (in extreme cases) a diabolical enemy. This causes a phenomenon noted in Chapter 5, a transformation of issues from specific to general; instead of dealing with a particular threat from Other, Party must now deal with the general issue of how to resist an immoral enemy. It becomes hard to empathize with Other because of deindividuation or dehumanization. And there is a tendency to break off contact—to be unwilling to communicate. Zero-sum thinking often develops—it's *either* victory for Other *or* victory for Party. As a result of these changes, hostile and competitive goals often develop: to look better than, punish, discredit, defeat, or even destroy Other. This is the transformation from doing well to hurting Other mentioned in Chapter 5. These changes typically occur on both sides of the dispute.

These psychological changes help to account for the escalation that led to the Cold War, and for the flinty persistence of this escalation. Profound distrust, enemy images, and an inability to empathize took root in the United States during the early period of the Cold War and persisted until recently. Zero-sum thinking was extremely common, producing an inordinate fear of any communist advance. This fear gripped every American president from Truman onward; none wanted to be in office when another country fell to communism. Most Americans became unable to empathize with the genuine Soviet security needs that underlay a large proportion of their actions. Most communication with the Soviet Union was broken off in the late 1940s and early 1950s, and it remained at a low level until the period of de-escalation under President Gorbachev.[3]

Negative Attitudes and Perceptions

An *attitude* is a positive or negative feeling toward some person or object. A *perception* is a belief about, or way of viewing, some person or object. Attitudes and perceptions tend to be consistent in valence. In other words, if Party has negative (positive) attitudes toward Other, Party also tends to have predominantly negative (positive) perceptions of Other.[4]

The following kinds of perceptions are particularly characteristic of

[3]As a reminder that zero-sum thinking continues unabated in the post–Cold War era, merely consider the ongoing debate in the Middle East over the future of Jerusalem. Palestinians and Israelis alike regard the Holy City as indivisible, and neither side appears willing to consider solutions that involve sharing control of Jerusalem. For a thoughtful analysis of conflicts over "indivisibles," see Albin (1993). Also see Chapter 10 on problem solving.

[4]There is an extensive social psychological literature on attitudes and perceptions. Less is known about deindividuation and dehumanization, so the section on them is brief. Little is known about hostile and competitive goals, so they are not discussed further.

escalated conflict: Other tends to be seen as deficient in moral virtue—as dishonest, unfriendly, or warlike. It tends to be seen as different from Party in basic values, and most particularly to be selfish and inhumane (Struch & Schwartz, 1989). Other also tends to be distrusted; Party believes Other to be hostile to Party's welfare and sometimes sees Other as an enemy. In addition, Other may be seen as lacking in ability or achievement (Blake & Mouton, 1962), though this kind of perceptual distortion is less likely because of the greater availability of sound evidence about these characteristics (Brewer, 1979). In contrast, Party usually sees itself as more moral, and sometimes as abler, than Other (White, 1984).

When groups are in conflict, a variant of these perceptions is sometimes found, which White (1984) has called the "evil-ruler enemy image." This is the perception that ordinary members of the other group feel neutral or even positive toward us but their leaders are hideous monsters. If there is hostility on the other side, it is because ordinary people are being misled by their leaders. During the Cold War, American views[5] of the Soviet Union and Soviet views of America reflected such images. The evil-ruler enemy image permits a decidedly negative view of Other while realistically acknowledging that not all members of any group can be evil.

Attitudes, and the perceptions that accompany them, tend to be similar on both sides of a controversy. This is known as the "mirror image" phenomenon (Bronfenbrenner, 1961; Frank, 1982; White, 1984). For example, the profound distrust felt by most Americans toward the Soviet Union had its counterpart in a somewhat less intense Soviet image of the United States. Unfortunately, the existence of a mirror image often goes unrecognized by Party and Other. Party tends to distrust Other without realizing that Other also distrusts Party.

Effects of Negative Attitudes and Perceptions

Negative attitudes and perceptions of Other encourage escalation and discourage the settlement of conflict in at least seven ways.

First, negative perceptions and attitudes make it easier to blame Other for Party's unpleasant experiences. Because people look for culprits to explain their unpleasant experiences, and because the evidence about whom to hold responsible is often ambiguous, a disliked and distrusted Other tends to be blamed—while a liked Other is given the benefit of the doubt. Since blame often leads to the adoption of harsh, escalative tactics (Sillars, 1981; Syna, 1984), this implies that negative attitudes tend to encourage escalation.

A finding by Blumenthal et al. (1972) illustrates the impact of attitudes on blame. During a period of political turmoil in the United States, in the summer of 1969, people were found to blame the conflict on groups whose views they did not like. Liberals blamed the police, whereas conservatives

[5]We use the terms *views* and *evaluations* to refer to attitudes and perceptions collectively.

blamed the demonstrators. Both tended to use the term *violence* to describe the behavior of groups they disliked and the term *justified force* to describe the behavior of groups whose views they favored. People were also more sympathetic to the use of force against the groups they blamed.

A second, related way in which negative attitudes and perceptions lead to escalation is when Other is distrusted and its ambiguous actions are seen as *threatening* (Pruitt, 1965). Other is given little benefit of the doubt or credit for good intentions. This encourages fear and defensive escalation. The tendency to misinterpret Other's behavior helps us understand one reason why escalation is so difficult to escape. Other, growing tired of escalation, often tries to escape it by making goodwill gestures.[6] But such gestures are usually highly ambiguous. They tend to be subtle and to seem like a drop in the bucket compared to the heavy tactics that Other has been using. If Other is distrusted, as is likely to be the case after heavy escalation, such gestures will often be misinterpreted, and the escalation will grind on.

A third way negative views of Other encourage escalation is by diminishing *inhibitions against retaliation* when Party has been provoked. Party is reluctant to aggress against an Other who is liked and respected, even when Other can clearly be blamed for unpleasant experiences. But Party is quite willing to aggress against an Other who is not liked or respected. The finding that southern white students (many of whom can be assumed to have been prejudiced) retaliated more vigorously when insulted by an African American than by a white (Rogers & Prentice-Dunn, 1981) supports these generalizations. Retaliation is, of course, a major part of the cycle of escalation.

A fourth way in which negative attitudes encourage escalation is by *interfering with communication.* People tend to avoid those toward whom they are hostile. The point is well put by Coleman (1957): "As controversy develops, associations . . . wither between persons on opposing sides" (p. 11). This contributes to misunderstandings and hence to the proliferation of conflictful issues. It also makes it difficult to reach a peaceful settlement of the controversy.

It is not altogether clear why this happens. Why stop meeting and talking when Party becomes hostile toward Other? A possible reason is that Party is afraid that associating with Other will be falsely interpreted as accepting Other's position. This is part of the reason for the long-term lack of contact between Israel and the Palestine Liberation Organization—an alienation which may finally be ending. This phenomenon may also have deeper emotional roots. According to balance theory (Heider, 1958), negative attitudes toward any object psychologically imply a negative relationship with that object—hence, a desire to put psychological distance between oneself and that object.

[6] Such gestures, technically called *unilateral initiatives,* are discussed in Chapter 9.

A fifth mechanism is that negative attitudes and perceptions tend to reduce *empathy* with Other (White, 1984). Other seems so different from Party that it is hard for Party to put itself in Other's shoes. Furthermore, there is an easy explanation that makes empathy seem unnecessary: Other's actions stem from evil motives. Absence of empathy is like absence of communication in that it fosters misunderstandings. It also encourages escalation by blocking insight into the conflict spiral. Awareness that Other's hostile behavior is a reaction to Party's own hostile behavior causes Party to limit escalation as a matter of self-protection. But if Party lacks empathy into Other's motives, Party is unaware of its own role in encouraging Other to aggress and is likely to escalate unthinkingly.

Sixth, negative attitudes and perceptions foster *zero-sum thinking*. Zero-sum thinking tends to make problem solving seem like an unworkable alternative. Positions become rigid, and creativity tends to disappear. This makes conflicts hard to resolve and encourages a sense that contentious behavior is the only way to succeed. Escalation is likely to be the result.

Seventh, and finally, when negative perceptions grow really severe, Other comes to be viewed as a *diabolical enemy* (White, 1984) and the conflict is seen as a war between light and darkness. We are the chosen people; they are the "evil empire" (to quote President Reagan's Cold War description of the Soviet Union).[7] In such circumstances, Party is ready to blame Other for all that goes wrong, communication often takes a nosedive, empathy is especially weak, and problem solving is extraordinarily hard to sustain. Heavily escalated tactics tend to become the rule; and new controversies regularly develop, confirming Party's view of Other, and vice versa.

Sources of Negative Attitudes and Perceptions

Like all structural changes, negative attitudes and perceptions are way stations in the cycle of escalation. These attitudes and perceptions are due, in part, to Party's experience of ill-treatment at the hands of Other. Such an experience tends to produce an initial reaction of anger, characterized by a state of autonomic arousal. This is followed by a cooler, longer-lasting residue: either an active goal to punish Other or a negative attitude toward Other, which acts in one or more of the ways just described.

Instead of blaming Other for an aversive experience, Party sometimes blames itself, reasoning that Other is reacting to Party's own behavior. This prevents the development of negative attitudes toward Other, and the conflict is often resolved by means of problem solving

[7]Charles Lane (1992), Berlin bureau chief of *Newsweek*, reported the following observation from Belgrade, in former Yugoslavia: "My favorite outrageous Belgrade T.V. report concerned the Serb babies whom Muslims fed to the lions at the Sarajevo Zoo. I was amused, until I heard the story repeated verbatim by a 55-year-old woman standing in line outside the Yugoskandic bank. `That's why the Serbs had to kill the animals,' she explained."

(Sillars, 1981; Syna, 1984). Party is likely to blame itself only when conflict is mild. When conflict is intense, blame almost always falls on Other (Sillars, 1981).

There are two main reasons for this (Brehm, 1992): One is ego-defensive, a product of the self-serving attributional bias. The larger the conflict, the more blame must be allocated. Since it is painful for Party to blame itself, it becomes increasingly hard to do so as conflict intensifies. The other reason is perceptual, a product of differences in perspective between actors and observers (Fiske & Taylor, 1991). In a conflict spiral, Party is more likely to perceive that it is reacting to Other's provocative behavior than that Other is reacting to Party's. This is because Party is well situated to see the sources of its own behavior but not so well situated to see the sources of Other's behavior. It is hard to peer into Other's head. Hence, as escalation develops and conflict becomes more intense, Party finds more and more evidence that this is through no fault of its own.

There is another way in which negative evaluations of Other can result from escalation. Party's efforts to rationalize its own escalated behavior can encourage negative views of Other that reinforce this escalated behavior. This causal sequence is shown by the dashed lines M and N in Figure 6.1. Party's feelings and beliefs tend to become consistent with its behavior through a process of rationalization (Bem, 1972; Festinger, 1957). Thus, the very fact that Party defends its nation against Other's nation is likely to create more negative attitudes toward Other, encouraging further defensive efforts.[8]

Deindividuation and Dehumanization

Other is *deindividuated* when it is perceived by Party as a member of a category or group rather than as an individual. This perception encourages escalated behavior, apparently by eroding inhibitions against acting aggressively. What may happen is that people who are deindividuated become dehumanized. They seem less human than those who are individuated; hence, the deindividuated are less protected by social norms against aggression.

Deindividuation was probably at work in an experiment by Milgram (1992) in which subjects in the role of "teacher" gave especially severe shocks to others in the role of "learner" when the latter were at a distance or out of sight. Deindividuation of the enemy may be what makes it easier for fliers to drop bombs than for foot soldiers to shoot an enemy they can see. Deindividuation is countered by receipt of information about Other that makes Other seem unique. For example, guards in Nazi prison camps

[8]Negative attitudes and perceptions can result from sources outside of the conflict as well. For example, Party may learn from role models. This is the main way in which racial and ethnic prejudice develops.

are said to have treated prisoners more leniently when they knew their names (Zimbardo, 1970).

Another way to discover that outgroup members are individuals is to have friendly relations with them over a period of time. It follows that residential settings that foster interracial friendships should diminish white prejudice against African Americans, an effect that has been demonstrated in two survey studies (Deutsch & Collins, 1951; Hamilton & Bishop, 1976). Before he led a protest demonstration, Gandhi would apparently ask for hospitality from the local English governor and thus make friends with him. This was a way of individuating himself and his movement in the eyes of the authorities, thereby reducing the aggressiveness of the tactics used by the government.[9]

Similar reasoning suggests that aggressive or discriminatory impulses should lead Party to deindividuate Other, by a process akin to rationalization. In this way, Party will feel more comfortable about its own hostile behavior. Evidence favoring this prediction emerges from a study by Worchel and Andreoli (1978). It was found that subjects who were angry with, or were expected to shock, another person were especially likely to forget individuating information about that person (such as his or her name) and to remember deindividuating information (such as his or her race).

This finding implies that deindividuation is another way station in the circle of conflict escalation. Party deindividuates Other in order to rationalize its own initial contentious moves. This then makes it easier to take more severe measures against Other, contributing to escalation.

In addition to viewing Other as deindividuated, it is possible for Party to see *itself* in this way—in other words, to lose awareness of its own distinct identity. This also facilitates aggression.[10] Among the sources of self-deindividuation are acting in concert with others, wearing nondistinctive clothing, emotional arousal, and lack of sleep. In a study of the effect of clothing on aggression, Zimbardo (1970) found that college women playing the role of punitive teachers were especially likely to give shocks when they were wearing a hood. Such apparel reduces Party's distinctiveness and inhibitions. Military and police uniforms probably have a similar effect.

There is also some direct evidence that *dehumanization* of Other—the

[9]During the Spanish Civil War, George Orwell was unable to shoot an enemy soldier who was running away while holding up his trousers with both hands. "I had come here to shoot at `Fascists'; but a man who is holding up his trousers isn't a `Fascist,' he is visibly a fellow creature, similar to yourself, and you don't feel like shooting at him" (1968, p. 254, cited in Brehm & Kassin, 1993).

[10]Research indicates that the bigger the group Party is a member of, the more Party is likely to lose self-awareness and engage in aggressive behavior. The phenomenon of deindividuation may partly explain the beating of Rodney King by Los Angeles police offers. It is reported that many other officers—besides the four who were actually involved in hitting Rodney King—watched the beating as it took place.

perception that Other is less than human—makes it easier to aggress against Other (Bandura, 1990; Kelman & Hamilton, 1989; Struch & Schwartz, 1989). This is probably because dehumanization makes the universal norm against harming other human beings seem irrelevant. If Other is less than human, the norm does not apply. Research suggests that Other is dehumanized when it seems to reject values that are important to Party (Schwartz & Struch, 1989).

Calling people names ("nigger," "idiot") has a dehumanizing effect. Name-calling strengthens the impression that Other is morally inadequate and dissimilar to Party. Some names[11] make Other seem particularly subhuman. Name-calling makes it easier for Party, and for those who hear Party's statements, to aggress against Other—since Other is thereby dehumanized.

CHANGES IN GROUPS

Psychological changes occur in all escalated conflicts, whether the actors are individuals or groups. But when groups (e.g., families, departments, nations) are involved, structural changes may also occur *in the group*. Hostile perceptions and goals are accentuated by group discussion and tend to become group norms. Group goals of defeating the enemy tend to develop, and subgroups are established to implement these goals. Increased cohesiveness, resulting from having an outside enemy, contributes to the force of these norms and to the dedication of group members to the newly found goals and the means of implementing them. New, more militant leadership often emerges, contributing further to the group's orientation toward struggle. Doves are replaced by hawks. If one of the parties is an unorganized set of individuals, conflict sometimes encourages the development of a struggle group—precipitated out of the mix of strong individual emotions—which then takes up the cudgel against the adversary.

Group changes of this kind were important in the Cold War escalation. In the United States, hostile norms became so strong that people who had a good word for the Soviet Union were made to feel uncomfortable and were sometimes hauled up before congressional committees. The country even flirted for a time in the 1950s with highly militant leadership, in the person of Senator Joseph McCarthy, a virulent anticommunist with a large political following. Fortunately for the nation, some of these collective excesses were overcome by the 1960s.

[11]Such as the epithet "pig," which was hurled at the police by student demonstrators in the 1960s and more recently during the riots that followed in the wake of the Rodney King beating.

The Crisis at UB

Before embarking on a detailed discussion of these group changes, we will describe a conflict that occurred at the State University of New York at Buffalo (or UB as it is known locally), where one of the authors (DGP) teaches. This narrative (based on a chronology provided by Pruitt & Gahagan, 1974), offers a striking illustration of a conflict spiral involving all three kinds of structural changes—particularly changes in groups.

The years from 1964 to 1969 saw the growth of a national student movement aroused about such issues as racial discrimination and U.S. involvement in the Vietnam War. This movement touched many campuses, including UB. As it began the 1969–1970 school year, UB had a large number of students who were concerned about such issues and a sizable contingent of campus radicals who were ready to provide any emerging student action with the necessary leadership.

The crisis began on a cold winter night in late February with the appearance of city police on campus at the time of a demonstration by African American athletes against the physical education department (the African American athletes played no further part in the demonstrations after this incident). The next night, forty to fifty white students, including many of the campus radicals, proceeded to the acting president's office to demand an explanation for the police appearance. The acting president, who was in a meeting about the African American athletes, refused to talk with the students, whereupon some of them threw rocks at his windows. The campus police arrived in riot gear, and the acting president instructed them to arrest the window breakers. Moving to the student union, the police apprehended two of the radicals, beating one of them in front of an excited crowd of student onlookers. The police officers were then chased across the campus by some members of this crowd, and one officer was badly injured when a metal trash barrel was thrown at him. Someone called for city police reinforcements, who confronted a crowd of about 500 enraged students and arrested several dozen of them.

During the next two days, the student government and the radical student leadership organized rallies to decide upon a student response to these incidents. The thousands of students who attended these rallies clearly rejected the student government proposal for communication with the administration and endorsed a plan developed by the radical leadership to organize a strike against class attendance. A set of nine demands was endorsed, including the barring of city police from campus, the resignation of the acting president, and the abolition of ROTC and of research supported by the Defense Department. During the first night, the library was firebombed by enraged students. By the end of the second evening, it had become clear that the student government was no longer respected by the bulk of the politically active students. As a result, this government collapsed. It was replaced by a radically led strike committee, which even took over the student government office suite.

The strike committee, consisting of about 400 active members, put together a well-organized campaign to discourage students from going to class. The strike was only partly successful, with class attendance being curtailed by about 30 to 40 percent. The strike committee then moved to heavier tactics, occupying the administration building and turning on its fire hoses. In an effort to defend itself, the administration suspended a group of radical leaders and eventually summoned the Buffalo police back onto the campus. Early on a Sunday morning, eleven days into the crisis, 400 Buffalo police officers quietly moved into position.

The student response was initially a series of symbolic events, such as a mock funeral for the university. Eventually an ultimatum was issued to the administration, and a "war council" was held to decide on appropriate action. The night of the war council, a large group of students began taunting and throwing objects at the police, who were massed in front of the administration building, presumably to defend it. The police finally broke ranks and charged into the crowd with clubs swinging, injuring and arresting a number of students.

The next day, forty-five faculty members held a sit-in at the acting president's office. The police removed them from the building and arrested them. No more student demonstrations were held after this time—but, angered by the arrest of their fellows, the faculty senate passed a motion of no confidence in the administration.

The rest of the semester witnessed a moderately successful effort to reunite the campus. As part of this effort, a committee made up of student, faculty, and administration representatives was organized to discuss the demands made by the strike committee and related matters. This committee made a number of recommendations that were adopted as campus policy, including the abolition of ROTC.[12]

The Nature, Source, and Impact of Group Changes

When small groups, organizations, or nations become involved in contentious conflict, these collectives (groups, as we call them) tend to change in at least six ways that contribute to the cycle of escalation.

First, group discussions often cause individual group members to become more extreme in their hostile attitudes and perceptions. This is due to *group polarization* (Moscovici & Zavalloni, 1969). When group members share any view and discuss it with one another, the view in question

[12]The reader can no doubt detect in the UB conflict a set of relatively predictable moves and countermoves. Those who want to understand the surprisingly consistent pattern of this pas de deux should read *The Rhetoric of Agitation and Control* by Bowers & Ochs (1971).

tends to become stronger. Two main mechanisms apparently account for this phenomenon (Isenberg, 1986). One is that group members hear one another's views and the arguments underlying them. Finding that others agree with them, they feel that their views are validated and they also learn new arguments favoring them. The other is that a sort of competition develops among the group members, in which each strives to hold an opinion that is at least as extreme in the direction favored by the group as that advocated by the average group member. As a result, members shift their opinions in the direction favored by the group.

In the context of social conflict, this means that psychological changes such as hostility and distrust are magnified when groups are involved. We see group polarization most clearly in mob action. A group of people who are upset about some incident gather and, through discussion, strengthen one another's sentiments to the point of angry action. Mob action by students occurred on the second night of the UB crisis, and mob action by police occurred on the night of the war council. But group polarization is not limited to mobs. It occurs in all groups, including perfectly stable and respected ones, such as the United States Senate and the board of directors of IBM.

A second kind of change is the development of *runaway norms* supporting a contentious approach to the controversy (Raven & Rubin, 1983). A norm is any attitude, perception, goal, or behavior pattern that is shared by the dominant segment of a group. Norms come to be seen as "right thinking" by most members of the group. They are taught to new members and imposed on old members who appear to question them. Most of the psychological changes mentioned earlier in this chapter—including negative attitudes, distrust, zero-sum thinking, and a reluctance to communicate with Other—can become the subject of norms. When this happens, they gain strength and stability. They become group traditions rather than the property of separate individuals. Hence, they are more likely to contribute to escalation.

The development of *contentious group goals* is a third common outcome of conflict. Examples are Party's ambition to defeat or even destroy Other. Such goals arise from the experience of conflict and further fan the flames. In addition, groups are capable of pursuing their goals in ways that are not available to individuals, because the activities of a number of individuals can be coordinated. A division of labor among group members adds to this capability, permitting highly complicated contentious routines such as the recruitment and training of an army. Hence, groups are particularly effective at conflict escalation if their members are so inclined. One group goal that resulted in a significant escalation during the UB crisis was the decision by the strike committee to try to close down all classes.

A fourth kind of change that can contribute to escalation is the development of *group cohesiveness*, or solidarity, as it is commonly called.

Groups are cohesive to the extent that their members find them attractive.

Cohesiveness affects group behavior in three important ways. It encourages conformity to group norms (Festinger et al., 1950). This conformity is due to enhanced communication within the group (Back, 1951); member fear of being ostracized (Festinger, 1950); and social pressure, which is especially strong in cohesive groups (Schachter, 1951). Cohesive groups are also capable of especially vigorous action in pursuit of their goals. And there is reason to believe that members of cohesive groups are particularly convinced of the rightness of their cause and the effectiveness of their intended actions (Janis, 1972; Kriesberg, 1982). The UB strike committee was a highly cohesive group that exhibited all of these characteristics.

For all these reasons, we can expect group cohesiveness to augment or multiply the effect of the psychological states discussed earlier in this chapter. If the attitudes toward an outgroup are generally negative, they should be particularly strong in a cohesive group. If the other group is distrusted or is seen as a threat, cohesiveness should strengthen these perceptions. If the goal of defeating Other is adopted and contentious tactics for achieving this goal are developed, a cohesive group will mount a particularly vigorous campaign in these directions.

Contentious conflict has been repeatedly shown to enhance group cohesiveness (Dion, 1979; Harvey, 1956; Ryen & Kahn, 1975; Worchel & Norvell, 1980).[13] It follows that enhanced cohesiveness is still another mechanism in the cycle of escalation, resulting from prior escalation and contributing to its continuation. In making this point, we do not intend to say that cohesiveness per se encourages antagonism or escalation. Research evidence (Dion, 1973) does not support such a position. The point is rather that contentious conflict encourages cohesiveness, and cohesive groups are particularly militant when involved in contentious conflict.

A fifth type of change that often occurs in groups engaged in heavy conflict is that *militant leaders* take over (Sherif et al., 1961). Most groups have leaders. Some are formally designated as such; others are highly influential people without titles. Leaders are usually chosen because they resonate with the dominant sentiments of group members and are good at the activities to which the group is dedicated (Hollander, 1978). This is as true of groups in conflict as of groups engaged in any other kind of activity. If conflict involves negotiation, people with bargaining skills are likely to come to the fore.[14] But if it involves heavy contentious activity, leader-

[13]Rabbie & Wilkens (1971) were not able to replicate this common finding, but it appears that the subjects in their study lacked faith in the ability of their group; hence, they may have expected to fail in the competition.

[14]See Kellerman & Rubin (1988) for a study of the relationship among leadership, conflict, and negotiation, using the Middle East (and its most prominent leaders) as a case in point.

ship is more likely to fall into the hands of militants, who can mirror the anger of the membership and build a fighting force. Such individuals have particularly strong negative attitudes and perceptions of the adversary and are especially rigid in the demands they make. Accordingly, once they take over, they tend to reinforce and augment the group's commitment to extreme tactics.

Leadership changes of this kind occurred on both sides in the UB crisis. The heaviest part of the controversy began when the campus police clubbed several demonstrators in the student union. At first, officers of the student government tried to exercise leadership over the campus, promising to negotiate with the university administration. But the students were so angry at the administration that they shunted these officers aside in favor of a group of radicals who had not previously exerted much influence. Similar changes occurred in the university administration. A vice president who wanted to mediate the controversy was excluded from decision making, while other officers who advocated sterner measures became very influential.

In addition to devising tactics for dealing with the opponent, leaders of groups that are in conflict often try to strengthen their members' dedication to the struggle by tarnishing the image of the adversary (Bowers & Ochs, 1971). An example is President Bush's comparison of Saddam Hussein with Hitler during the Persian Gulf crisis.

The sixth type of collective change that occurs in escalating conflict is the development of *militant subgroups*. Such a subgroup is sometimes part of a well-established organization, for example, a new department to deal with the emerging conflict. At other times, it is an entirely new struggle group.

As mentioned in Chapter 2, new struggle groups emerge when one of the parties is an unorganized or poorly organized collection of people. What often happens is that a number of people who have not had much contact with each other become aware that they have common interests and a collective identity (Kriesberg, 1982). They begin to communicate with each other, and a sense of ingroup-outgroup begins to develop, often in conjunction with growing pride about and favoritism toward the ingroup (Apfelbaum, 1979). Radical spokespersons now emerge, and their pronouncements help to crystallize the developing consciousness. The struggle group is then formed, at first in miniature but often growing to a sizable membership with a large following of sympathetic nonmembers. The main goals of such a group are to defeat the opponent and to foster its own further growth.

The organization of a struggle group is often a turning point toward rapid escalation (Coleman, 1957). An example is the formation of the strike committee during the UB crisis. There are two reasons for this: (1) the primary purpose of such groups is to prevail over the adversary, and (2) the people who organize and lead such groups tend to be highly militant. Often these organizers have been waiting a long time for a chance to challenge this particular adversary, as was true in the UB crisis.[15]

CHANGES IN COMMUNITIES

When two groups come into heavy conflict with each other, it is often hard for other community members to remain neutral. They tend to join one side or the other, a phenomenon called *community polarization*. Community polarization is another participant in the cycle of escalation—it is produced by earlier escalation and it contributes to later escalation.

Community polarization is produced by escalation in two ways. First, neutral community members are recruited by participants in the controversy, who demand that nonparticipants decide whether they are "with us or agin' us." Second, the use of escalated tactics is often annoying or frightening to the broader community. It is hard to remain indifferent when people are yelling at each other, damaging each other's property, or hurting each other. There is a tendency to cast blame in such circumstances and to support the side to which one is closer or the side that seems less blameworthy.[16]

Community polarization contributes to further escalation for two reasons. One is that new recruits give added support to the individuals or groups they join. They enhance the group's confidence in the validity of its position and its likelihood of winning and allow an easier justification for the use of heavy contentious tactics. The other reason is that polarization divides a community into two opposing camps. The bonds within each camp become stronger while those between camps deteriorate (Coleman, 1957). This causes a destruction of crosscutting group memberships[17] and a disappearance of neutral third parties who would otherwise urge moderation and mediate the controversy.

Community polarization underlies the transformation from few to many. It occurred during the Cold War in that many nations felt forced to choose sides between the United States and the Soviet Union. In addition, it occurred massively in the UB crisis. The student demonstrations began with a protest by forty or fifty radicals and ended with practically every

[15]At the end of the controversy, most struggle groups simply wither away. A few, however, go on to assume a permanent, legitimate place in the community as advocates of the interests of the people who organize them. Several American social movements have followed such a line of development, most notably the labor movement. At UB, a group that splintered from the strike committee near the end of the crisis formed the nucleus of a women's movement that survives to this day.

[16]Pruitt & Gahagan (1974) speculate that in trying to determine blame in a conflict, third parties sometimes compare the two parties on the amount they have escalated. The party that has escalated more is considered the more blameworthy and is less likely to be supported.

[17]Crosscutting group memberships are discussed in Chapter 8.

student on campus aligned with the activities of the strike committee. Large numbers of faculty members were also drawn to the student side, especially after the students were charged by the police and the "Faculty 45" were arrested. In contrast, a large part of the broader Buffalo community embraced the side of the university administration.

CONCLUSIONS

This chapter has introduced a third conflict model, the structural change model, which builds on the conflict spiral model. We have described a set of changes in the individuals and groups involved in conflict and the communities to which they belong. These changes are way stations in the cycle of escalation: they result from prior escalation *and* contribute to further escalation. In Chapter 7, we complete our discussion of this model by taking up the confirmatory mechanisms that cause structural changes to endure once established. These mechanisms underlie the tendency of escalation to persist and recur, and they help us to understand the deterioration of human relationships.

7

The Persistence of Escalation

The Tail of Cerberus: Residues that Change Things • The Persistence of Psychological Changes • *The Self-fulfilling Prophecy* • *Rationalization of Behavior* • *Selective Perception* • The Persistence of Changes in Groups • The Persistence of Community Polarization • Deteriorating Relationships • Overcommitment and Entrapment • Conclusions

Escalation occurs when Party's contentious tactics become heavier, putting more pressure on Other and often inflicting greater suffering. Escalation is accompanied by a series of incremental transformations, discussed in Chapter 5, where we described two conflict models that show how escalation develops: the aggressor-defender model and the conflict spiral model. In Chapter 6, we introduced a third conflict model: the structural change model. This model assumes a cycle of escalation: Party's heavy tactics produce structural changes that encourage reciprocal tactics from Other, provoking changes which encourage Party to employ further heavy tactics. We described the nature of these changes, as these occur in individuals, groups, and communities, and examined their sources and impact.

Chapter 7 completes the discussion by examining confirmatory mechanisms that cause structural changes to endure. These mechanisms explain why escalation often persists and sometimes recurs when new conflicts arise between the same parties.

THE TAIL OF CERBERUS: RESIDUES THAT CHANGE THINGS

According to Greek mythology, there stands near the entrance to Hades a three-headed dog named Cerberus. Cerberus has a scaly, spiked, powerful tail that allows the souls of the dead to pass into Hades with ease. Once a soul has passed the tail of Cerberus, however, the tail's spines and scales make it impossible to return. Many animal traps have similar properties, allowing the quarry to pass unimpeded into the trap, perhaps in search of bait, only to find that it is not possible to retreat. The treadles in parking garages, which allow cars to pass smoothly in but damage the tires of any car that tries to drive out, operate on the same principle.

So it is with structural changes. Once established, they are exceedingly difficult to eliminate. In this sense, escalation is like a rubber band. Up to a point, a rubber band may be stretched and, when released, still return to its original form and shape. Beyond that point, however, further stretching either breaks the rubber band or produces a change in its elasticity that prevents it from resuming its original dimensions. Like a rubber band stretched beyond its physical limits of tolerance, the relationship between individuals in an intensifying conflict may pass a psychological or collective threshold—a point of no return—that transforms the relationship into a new, conflict-intensified state.[1]

Consider this simple example of the crossing of a threshold. Party and Other are having an argument one day, and the exchange begins to heat up rather precipitously. Party is assailing and yelling at Other, and vice versa. At some point during the angry exchange of words, Party announces that it has never really respected or valued Other. Eventually the argument subsides, as most arguments do, but the relationship is likely to have changed—and not for the better. The words Party has uttered, perhaps primarily to goad Other and not out of deep-seated conviction, may have changed Other's attitude toward Party in ways that do not easily permit recovery. Party and Other may be able to continue transacting their interpersonal business, but those words of disrespect have introduced a *residue that changes things.*

Not all conflicts escalate. Moreover, many that do escalate produce residues that are either negligible or ephemeral. The latter conflicts may be understood in terms of the aggressor-defender and conflict spiral models. The purpose of this chapter is to examine the special and painful set of escalating conflicts that do manage to produce residues that endure. The question is *why* they endure, and our threefold answer focuses on the endurance of psychological changes, changes in group structure, and

[1]A geometric model that makes predictions about the location of points of no return is found in Pruitt (1969).

community polarization. The chapter ends with a closely related topic, the process of overcommitment to an escalating course of action.

THE PERSISTENCE OF PSYCHOLOGICAL CHANGES

Like all attitudes and perceptions, negative attitudes and perceptions[2] tend to endure once established. This is partly because they support each other: negative beliefs validate negative feelings, and negative feelings make negative beliefs seem right. In addition, there are six kinds of confirmatory mechanisms involving *self-reinforcement.* When these mechanisms are at work, negative views of Other have consequences that ultimately reinforce the views that gave rise to them. These mechanisms involve the self-fulfilling prophecy, rationalization of behavior, three kinds of selective perception, and autistic hostility.

The Self-fulfilling Prophecy

One mechanism of self-reinforcement is implicit in the cycle of escalation, which is traced out by the solid arrows in Figure 6.1. Party's negative views of Other encourage Party to behave in a way that is resented by Other, evoking a response from Other that confirms these views. A similar circular process can confirm Other's negative views of Party. Another name for this process is the *self-fulfilling prophecy.*

Consider the case of Ben and the family car, first mentioned in Chapter 1. Dad clearly perceives Ben as careless and inconsiderate, and presumably lets him know this from time to time. Dad's criticism, in turn, contributes to Ben behaving in ways that confirm Dad's perceptions, as when Ben fails to gas up the car.

The self-fulfilling prophecy is more than a hypothesis. It has been demonstrated experimentally, in both laboratory and natural settings. Whether we cite teachers' expectations about the performance of their pupils (Rosenthal & Jacobson, 1968), students' beliefs about the maze-learning abilities of their albino rats (Rosenthal & Fode, 1963), the effects of mental patients' admitting diagnoses, (Rosenhan, 1973), or platoon leaders' expectations about the potential of their trainees (Eden, 1990), it is clear that Party's expectations generate behavior that in turn prods Other to behave in ways that confirm Party's initial expectations.

[2]In Chapter 6, we described three kinds of psychological changes: the development of negative attitudes and perceptions, deindividuation and dehumanization, and the rise of hostile and competitive goals. Attitudes and perceptions occupy our attention here because little is known about persistence of the other two kinds of changes.

An Aside on the "Tar Baby" Effect

Most self-fulfilling prophecies are driven along by the things that Other *does,* which confirm Party's own worst suspicions. Occasionally, the prophecy is fulfilled because Other *does nothing* to *dis*confirm Party's expectations. In this variant of the mechanism, Party's preconceptions are confirmed by the absence of behavior by Other. For example, if I regard you as a cold and indifferent person and therefore avoid you at a social gathering, your very ignorance of the reasons for my behavior may lead you unwittingly to act in ways (such as paying no attention to me) that confirm my hypothesis and fulfill the prophecy.

In order to understand this paradoxical form of the self-fulfilling prophecy, let us examine the old tale of Brer Rabbit and the tar baby in one of Joel Chandler Harris's Uncle Remus stories (1955, first published in 1880). One day Brer Fox decided to trap his perennial adversary, Brer Rabbit, by fashioning a likeness of a baby out of tar. Brer Rabbit spotted this "tar baby" by the side of the road and tried to engage it in a bit of friendly conversation. The more Brer Rabbit talked to the tar baby, who of course had nothing to say in return, the angrier he got. "Mawnin! Nice wedder dis mawnin'," said old Brer Rabbit. No response. "Is you deaf? Kaze ef you is, I kin holler louder." No response. "Ef you don't take off dat hat and tell me howdy, I'm gwine ter bus' you wide open." No response. At last Brer Rabbit could stand it no longer. He punched the tar baby in the nose, only to get his fist stuck and find himself increasingly irate. So he hauled off and hit the tar baby with the other fist, and it too got stuck in the tar. Punch led to kick, and before long Brer Rabbit was completely entangled. The harder he tried to get loose, the more enmeshed he became.

Just as the tar baby knew nothing of Brer Rabbit's feelings or intentions, so Other is often unaware of Party's sensibilities. A common outcome of such a situation is for Party's worst expectations about Other to be confirmed by what Other *does not do.* Too many strikes have persisted, to the detriment of all concerned, because Party's (e.g., management's) inaction left Other (e.g., labor) oblivious to Party's true intentions. Ben and Dad may have been willing to make concessions to end their conflict, but each may have taken the other's *lack of initiative* as confirmation of the other's intransigence. If ever there were a situation in which communication would help conflicting parties, it is surely one like this.

Rationalization of Behavior

A second mechanism that encourages the persistence of attitudes and perceptions is the rationalization effect discussed in Chapter 6. Party's negative views lead to hostile actions against Other, which Party then rationalizes by reaffirming the views that gave rise to the actions.[3] This causal sequence, shown by the dashed lines M and N in Figure 6.1, is more common than it sounds. Consider the case of Ben again. Suppose that Ben's negative attitude toward Dad causes him to fail to get gasoline. The reasons for his behavior are likely to be at a fairly unconscious level, so that he must ask himself, "Why am I not getting gas?" He will then have to construct a rationalization. For example, he may come to believe that Dad is hostile to his interests. This will further reinforce Ben's negative attitude.[4]

Selective Perception

Once Party has formed a negative impression of Other—once the image of Other as an undesirable, unsavory, untrustworthy, unpleasant character has been shaped—the process of selective perception leads Party to search for and interpret information in ways that confirm the initial negative impression. Instead of gathering and evaluating data in scientific fashion, Party tends to locate information that supports these preconceptions. As a result, these preconceptions become stronger. An adversary who was first seen as rigid may now be regarded as stubborn, and eventually as hopelessly intransigent. Note that the structural changes supported by selective perception are self-reinforcing in a way that is quite independent of anything Other may say or do. Selective perception feeds on itself entirely, as represented by the circular loops O and P in Figure 6.1

Although the term *selective perception* has a negative ring (implying that Party develops a biased view of reality), the process is actually a hallmark of effective psychological functioning. The world is an immensely complex place, flooding everyone with far more social and nonsocial information than we can possibly hope to process. In response to this tendency toward "information overload," it is necessary to find ways to process information selectively, thereby reducing this input to manageable proportions.

Offsetting this virtue is the liability that stems from fitting impressions into a Procrustean bed—stripping away Other's rich individuality

[3]Many Serbs rationalize their aggression against Muslims as revenge for the suffering of their people at the hands of the Ottoman Empire of Turkey.

[4]Party will rationalize its behavior by changing attitudes only when it believes its behavior occurred freely and was not due to external pressures (Festinger, 1957). If I call a police officer a pig and believe I did so of my own free will, I shall probably develop a negative attitude toward that police officer or all police officers. But if I believe that I was coerced into taking this action or (and this is rare) acknowledge that I was trying to impress somebody, my attitude will not be affected. The issue is not whether the behavior is freely chosen (the authors of this volume take no stand on the question of whether people ultimately have free will) but whether the actor *believes* that it is. Because people believe that they are masters of their own actions, their behavior usually has a considerable impact on their attitudes.

in the service of developing a manageable stereotype. Moreover, in the midst of escalating conflict, selective perception is particularly dangerous. It can confirm Party's negative views of Other, thereby maintaining the existing level of escalation or even edging it upward.

The way in which selective perception operates in the service of escalating conflict has been addressed in a paper by Cooper and Fazio (1979). These authors discuss three interrelated forms that selective perception can take: distortion in the evaluation of behavior, the "discovery" of evidence that supports Party's expectations, and attributional distortion. Let us consider each in turn.

Selective Evaluation of Behavior

When there are strong views, an identical event can be judged quite differently depending on whether the source of this event is seen as a "good guy" or a "bad guy" (White, 1984). In an interesting study of student reactions to a Princeton-Dartmouth football game won by Princeton, Hastorf and Cantril (1954) found that the events of the game were judged very differently as a function of the viewer's allegiance. Princeton and Dartmouth students saw a film of the game and were asked to note all infractions. The Princeton students thought that the Dartmouth Indians had committed twice as many infractions as the Princeton Tigers, whereas the Dartmouth students saw no difference in the number of violations. In conflict, it appears, reality is too often in the eye of the beholder.

Similarly powerful results have been obtained in other social psychology experiments. For example, Oskamp (1965) presented American college students with two parallel lists of conciliatory and belligerent acts that had been undertaken by both the United States and the Soviet Union. The same acts (for example, "The government has provided military training and assistance to smaller nations") that were rated favorably when performed by the United States (the good guys) were rated extremely unfavorably when attributed to the Soviet Union (the bad guys). Sherif and Sherif (1953, 1969) and their colleagues (1961), in a series of field experiments in boys' camps, examined judgmental distortion among rival groups. The researchers sponsored a jelly bean hunt, then showed the boys a slide photograph of a partially filled jelly bean jar and told them that these beans had been collected either by a member of their own group or by a member of the other group. Then they asked the boys to judge the number of beans in the jar. The boys believed that the jar alleged to belong to their own group contained substantially more beans than the jar attributed to the enemy.

Supporting evidence is not confined to the experimental laboratory. For example, in a Boston suburb, a neighborhood church proposed to establish a social service program for less affluent, less fortunate members of society (a counseling program for the mentally retarded). This plan was seen by the church elders as an act of charity and love. It looked quite different to a set of neighbors (community residents and taxpayers who lived next to the church), who regarded the plan as a gross and inconsiderate violation of standards of neighborhood decency.[5]

The "Discovery" of Confirming Evidence

It is one thing for Party to attend selectively to those aspects of Other's manner or behavior that conform to Party's own preconceptions. It is quite another matter to "stack the deck" by gathering information in a way that encourages Other to behave in accordance with these preconceptions.

Mark Snyder and his colleagues have conducted several experiments that, although not directly related to the dynamics of conflict escalation, nevertheless shed light on the "discovery" of confirmatory evidence. In one of these studies, Snyder and Swann (1978) provided participants with hypotheses about other people and then allowed them to seek information about these people. Some participants were given the personality profile of an introvert while others were given a description of what an extrovert is like. All participants were then asked to choose twelve questions to be posed to the targets in an effort to test whether they had that personality profile.

Snyder and Swann found that people who were testing an "introvert" hypothesis (even though this hypothesis did not specifically apply to the target, about whom nothing yet was known) chose to pose interview questions that seemed to assume that the target was *already known* to be an introvert: "In what situations do you wish you could be more outgoing?"; "What things do you dislike about loud parties?" Those who were testing an "extrovert" hypothesis instead listed questions that presumed the target to be an extrovert: "What would you do if you wanted to liven up a party?"; "In what situations are you most talkative?" When, in a subsequent session, the participants were actually permitted to pose the respective questions they had formulated, the response of their targets was such that the interviewers concluded that the targets matched the profile they had been given at the outset.

It is clear that people selectively arrange for evidence to be available that confirms their hypotheses. If this phenomenon is fairly powerful in the world of everyday interaction, as Snyder and his colleagues have shown, we can expect it to be all the more powerful in an emotion-laden situation such as the conflict between the church and its neighbors. The neighbors in this example assumed that the church consisted of a bunch of inconsiderate territorial imperialists. If they had a chance to test this hypothesis by asking a few well-chosen questions, we might imagine the neighbors asking, "Why do you wish to ignore the views of the neighborhood in developing this plan?" or "How long have you been territorial

[5]Thanks to Lawrence Susskind for development of this case.

imperialists?" Representatives of the church, in turn, might ask their neighbors, "Why do you people always oppose efforts to take care of those who are in need of social assistance?" By framing questions in ways that could only confirm their hypotheses, both sides would be likely to discover only what they wanted to find. Their hypotheses would produce self-confirming evidence.[6]

Attributional Distortion

Information about Other that supports Party's private hypotheses about Other tends to be attributed to *dispositional* causes, whereas information that is discrepant with Party's hypotheses tends to be attributed to *situational* causes. That is, information in keeping with Party's expectations is seen as reflecting Other's enduring and stable characteristics, whereas information that violates Party's expectations is attributed to temporary environmental pressures on Other. This phenomenon, usually called *attributional distortion,* has been demonstrated in a number of experimental studies (Hayden & Mischel, 1976; Regan et al., 1974) and in studies of troubled married couples (Bradbury & Fincham, 1990; Holtzworth-Munroe & Jacobson, 1985).

The net effect of attributional distortion in escalating conflict is that there is virtually nothing that Other can do to dispel Party's negative expectations. If Other behaves in a nasty way, this is taken as a true indicator of Other's hostile intentions or belligerent disposition. If Other turns the other cheek and displays friendly behavior, this is explained as a temporary fluke.

Again, consider the community conflict between the church and its neighbors. Imagine that in a meeting between representatives of the two sides, the neighbors offer to be a bit more flexible on an issue of importance to the church (say, parking privileges on the street adjacent to the church). A concession such as this might be regarded as a Trojan horse or a gift with strings attached, or it might be seen as resulting from the church's own hard bargaining. In any event, it would not be viewed as evidence that the neighbors were any friendlier than the church elders had initially assumed. On the other hand, tough bargaining, the use of threats, and name-calling by the neighbors would probably confirm the elders' worst fears and expectations.

Given these three forms of selective perception—selective evaluation of information, distorted hypothesis testing, and attributional bias—it is small wonder that conflicts can more easily escalate than move back down the ladder. Once that genie emerges from the bottle, these three processes combine to make it exceedingly difficult to lure it back in. As represented

[6]This tendency diminishes when people are strongly motivated to develop accurate impressions (Neuberg, 1989) and when people are forewarned about the pitfalls of this phenomenon (Swann, 1987).

by the loops (O and P) of Figure 6.1, these are self-reinforcing processes. They feed on themselves in ways that lead escalation to persist.[7]

Selective Perception and Culture: An Aside

When individuals from different cultures[8] have reason to work together, as during international business or political negotiations, culture is likely to play a part in the process and outcome of the proceedings. Quite apart from the real and important differences in behavior that result from culture, however, we wish to develop the view that selective perception can go a long way toward determining how cross-cultural negotiations proceed.

We have already documented the pervasiveness of human tendencies to stereotype in the service of simplifying our cognitive environment. Imagine that Party enters into a negotiation with Other, proceeding from the stereotypic view that Other comes from a culture that is known, among other things, to be fair and trustworthy. If, during the ensuing negotiations, Other should insist that it can go no lower, make no further concessions, because it is close to its bottom line, Party (given its stereotypic views) is likely to accept Other's assertion as a simple statement of fact. Hence, Party is likely to yield a bit to close the gap between its own and Other's position. Similarly, assume that Other makes a series of concessions during the exchange. Party is likely to interpret these moves as signs of a genuine desire to converge upon some point of overlap, and Party is likely to reciprocate. Thus, given either concessions or intransigence by Other, Party is likely to respond with concessions, making it likely that agreement will be reached.

Now imagine that Other comes from a culture whose negotiators are stereotypically regarded, among other things, as sneaky and untrustworthy. Intransigence by Other, coupled with the assertion that Other is close to its bottom line and can go no further, is likely to lead Party to regard Other as disingenuous. Other's intransigence seems feigned in an effort to bully Party into yielding. Rather than yield, Party will therefore respond with intransigence of its own. Similarly, if Other at some point makes a series of concessions, Party is unlikely to view these as signs of genuine interest in moving toward agreement. Either Other is conceding because

[7]The same cognitive processes that operate in the service of conflict escalation sometimes also serve more positive ends. Two people who are wildly in love, for example, may be expected to see one another "through rose-colored glasses"—to continually find support for the hypothesis that the other is the most wonderful person in the world; to bias the explanations for their beloved's behavior in ways that discount negative information ("He was very grumpy this morning—must be the damp weather"); and to overstate the stability of positive information ("She just cracked another joke. What a wit she is!"). In other words, these processes are capable of reinforcing positive as well as negative impressions.

[8]In keeping with Faure & Rubin (1993), we define culture here as the set of shared and enduring meanings, values, and beliefs that characterize national, ethnic, or other groups and orient their behavior.

it is trying to pull the wool over Party's eyes or because it has no choice but to do so (in the face of Party's superior negotiating skill). Either way, Party's response is likely to be one of intransigence. So whether Other makes concessions or refuses to do so, Party's selective, stereotypic perceptions of Other are likely to lead Party to take a tough and resistant stance, reducing the likelihood that agreement will be reached.[9]

It is clear that cultural stereotypes are likely to structure Party's interpretations of Other's moves. This is another version of selective perception. Quite apart from the actual differences in negotiating style that result from the variable of culture, such selective perceptions may get in the way of effective negotiation (Breslin, 1989; Rubin, 1991; Rubin et al., 1974; Rubin & Sander, 1991).[10]

Autistic Hostility

As we mentioned in Chapter 6, there is a tendency to stop interacting and communicating with people we do not like or respect. An extreme example is the perhaps apocryphal case of two brothers who ran a store. One accused the other of stealing $1 from the cash register; the other denied it, whereupon the first brother stopped talking to the other. Thirty silent years later a stranger walked in, confessed to the theft (which had been preying on his conscience), and made restitution. Communication between the brothers was restored.

The problem with an interruption of communication—between two brothers, between a church and its neighbors, or between the aggrieved minority residents of Los Angeles and the city government—is that it makes it impossible to resolve the issue that fostered the initial breach. The parties are consigned to maintain their prior views of each other, including the ones that brought communication to a screeching halt. In effect, these views have initiated a process that perpetuates itself. This is called the phenomenon of *autistic hostility* (Newcomb, 1947). It is another self-reinforcing process, again represented by the two semicircular loops, O and P, in Figure 6.1.

[9]During the fall of 1990, as the Persian Gulf conflict was heating up, Iraq's Saddam Hussein released Western hostages (that he had no business taking in the first place). Their release was accompanied by Saddam's offer to begin negotiating an end to the crisis. U.S. President Bush refused to respond in kind, on two grounds: first, Saddam had released the hostages only as a ploy, to increase U.S. vulnerability to some subsequent act of duplicity; second, Saddam had been forced to concede by the growing threat of U.S. military intervention. The President deemed it preferable to pursue the path of conflict escalation—and eventual war. Given the death of an estimated 100,000 or more Iraqis during the Allied invasion of Iraq in the winter of 1991, and the fact that Saddam Hussein was still in power more than two years after the war, we wonder about the wisdom of the decision to move toward war rather than negotiation.

[10]The reader interested in understanding the rich interplay of culture and negotiation should begin by reading Faure's (1991) nuanced account of negotiating in the bazaar in Peshawar, Pakistan. Other treatments of culture and negotiation can be found in Binnendijk (1987), Cohen (1991), Faure & Rubin (1993), Salacuse (1991), and Shenkar & Ronen (1987).

A communication vacuum often provides a greenhouse in which rumors flourish. Facts are embellished or distorted, and personal attacks can be the rule—moving conflict along an escalatory path. Consider the confrontation between African Americans and Hasidic Jews in the Crown Heights section of New York City during the summer months of 1991. It was ignited by an incident in which a Hasidic Jewish driver hit two African American children, killing one and critically injuring the other. Following the accident, unsubstantiated rumors circulated widely in the community. One was that a Hatzolah ("rescue" in Hebrew) ambulance arrived before a city ambulance and drove the Hasidic driver away, abandoning the two critically wounded children at the scene. This rumor, found to be untrue according to police records and eyewitness testimony, triggered the violent murder of a Jewish man by a group of young African Americans.

THE PERSISTENCE OF CHANGES IN GROUPS

In Chapter 6 we described six kinds of group changes that result from and contribute to the escalation of conflict: group polarization, runaway norms, contentious group goals, cohesiveness, militant leadership, and militant subgroups. There are confirmatory mechanisms that encourage several of these changes to persist. As was true of the psychological changes, these mechanisms involve self-reinforcement or self-perpetuation. In other words, group changes often encourage new developments that confirm or strengthen these changes.

Some of these mechanisms involve the cycle of escalation represented by the progression of solid arrows in Figure 6.1. For example, Party's contentious group goals are likely to produce behavior that encourages Other to take actions that make these goals seem justified. Other mechanisms, entirely internal to the group, are modeled by loops O and P in the same figure.

Norms of all types tend to be self-perpetuating, including those that encourage competitive goals and aggressive behavior toward the outgroup. They often outlive the reasonable purpose for which they were first developed. This usually occurs because of *social pressure,* real and imagined. People who challenge a norm tend to be punished by the group. Others who doubt the validity of a norm remain silent for fear of being labeled deviates or, in the case of intergroup conflict, traitors. Still other group members then follow the norm because they do not realize that it is controversial.

Militant subgroups also become self-perpetuating because of *vested interests.* Group membership and participation in organized activities give some people status, others occupation and wealth, and still others a sense that life is meaningful. Such benefits are hard to surrender; hence, group members work hard to ensure that their group survives. If the raison d'être for a group is the conduct of contentious conflict, there are vested interests in the persistence of such conflict. This is another mechanism by which escalation tends to be self-perpetuating. The UB strike committee described in Chapter 6 is a case in point. This committee gave status and meaning to the lives of hundreds of students who would otherwise have been consigned to the routine of going to class and preparing for tests. These students had a vested interest in the perpetuation of the strike committee and thus a vested interest in the continuation of the crisis. Once formed, the strike committee could not easily be disbanded, and it continued to challenge the university administration.

Similar events have occurred many times in history (Schumpeter, 1955, first published in 1919), and the danger is not necessarily far from home. In his farewell address to the United States, President Eisenhower warned about the development of a built-in lobby for international conflict centered in what he called the "military-industrial complex."

Vested interests extend as well to *leaders*, who are almost always motivated to maintain their leadership positions. If they have gained these positions because of their militancy or skill at waging conflict, they have a vested interest in the perpetuation of conflict. Hence, they have incentives for resisting conflict resolution and for starting new conflicts. This is another mechanism by which escalation tends to be self-perpetuating.

Vested interests may have been at work in the Japanese attack on Pearl Harbor in 1941. According to Russett (1967), the Japanese leaders knew this attack was very risky. Indeed, in advocating the attack, one of them commented, "Sometimes it is necessary to close one's eyes and jump from the temple wall." But the alternative to the attack was apparently worse in their eyes. These leaders were military men who had gained high government positions in the late 1930s as a result of the great importance to the Japanese of the war they were waging in China and Indochina. In 1941 the United States began to block the shipment of oil from what is now Indonesia, which made it difficult to continue the war effort. Had the war effort stopped, these generals and admirals would almost surely have been demoted. Hence, they were willing to risk the future of their country in order to perpetuate the war effort and maintain their positions.

THE PERSISTENCE OF COMMUNITY POLARIZATION

We have already seen that escalating conflicts tend to polarize the communities around them. Formerly neutral parties gravitate or are pulled toward one side or the other. Fewer and fewer community members are left sitting on the fence or standing on the sidelines. Severely polarized communities become fractured into two large camps, with positive relations among the people in each camp and negative relations between the camps.

There are several mechanisms that cause community polarization, once established, to be perpetuated. Polarization means the disappearance of neutral third parties who would otherwise urge moderation and mediate the controversy. It also means reduction in loyalty to the community as a whole, and hence, reduction in the felt responsibility to be tolerant toward other community members (Coleman, 1957). As a result of these developments, the controversy tends to persist, maintaining the pressure on third parties to take sides.

In addition, community members who have joined one camp often have difficulty reestablishing their credentials with the other camp. They have become outsiders, forever distrusted because they have fraternized with the enemy. This means that polarization tends to persist even when the conflicts that gave rise to it have been resolved. Like Humpty Dumpty after his fall, it is hard to put polarized communities back together again.

DETERIORATING RELATIONSHIPS

It should be noted that most of the mechanisms just described affect the *broad relationship* between the parties in addition to the way in which conflict over a particular issue is handled. These mechanisms cause attitudes and perceptions, norms and types of leadership, and community polarization to persist as residues beyond the end of a particular conflict incident. These residues then encourage the development of further conflict and the use of escalated tactics when further conflict arises.

This point is illustrated by American reactions to the Soviet incursion into Afghanistan during the Cold War. As a result of the distrust that had built up in prior encounters, the United States concluded that the Soviet Union was ready to invade other Middle Eastern countries such as Saudi Arabia. This led the American government to invest billions of dollars in additional armaments. Yet evidence of this threat was highly ambiguous, in the sense that there were other plausible interpretations of the Soviet action. Most notable is the view that the Soviet Union was simply trying to protect a beleaguered communist government from disintegrating and being reabsorbed in the Western community of nations. Under the latter interpretation, the Soviet incursion would still be labeled aggression, as the term was used in Chapter 5. But it should not have been seen as evidence of a major threat to the West (White, 1984). The point of this example is that American distrust of the Soviet Union led many Americans to choose, from various possible interpretations, the one that threatened the greatest danger to the U.S. The result was renewed conflict and a new round of escalation.[11]

When structural changes have lasting influence, as in the case just described, it may be more proper to speak of the *escalation of a conflictful relationship* than to speak of the escalation of conflict. Relationships often deteriorate as a result of such escalation. For example, many marriages end in this way.[12]

OVERCOMMITMENT AND ENTRAPMENT

There is one other explanation for the persistence of escalation. This is that *commitments to contentious behavior* tend to be self-reinforcing. Such commitments produce changes in psychological and group processes which further strengthen the commitments. This type of causal loop is represented in Figure 6.1 by arrows M and D and by arrows N and B. One reason for this is the pervasive tendency for Party to rationalize its own behavior, which was mentioned earlier (see Festinger, 1957). Another reason is a process of overcommitment that has been studied in research on *entrapment*, a dysfunctional but pervasive human phenomenon.

An Aside on the Dollar Auction Game

In order to understand better the dynamics of overcommitment to an escalating course of action, consider a simple parlor game, first proposed by Shubik (1971) and extensively researched by Teger (1980). This game, known as the dollar auction, is played as follows: Several people are invited to participate in the auction of a dollar bill by calling out bids until a high bid has been reached. The high bidder is then awarded the dollar bill, in exchange for paying the amount that he or she bid. Thus, if the winning (high) bid were 15 cents, the winner would be awarded 85 cents (1 dollar minus 15 cents). The catch in this game is that the *second-highest bidder* is also required to pay the auctioneer the amount of his or her bid but does not receive a dollar bill in return. So, if the bidding for the dollar stopped with a high bid of 35 cents and a next-highest bid of 25 cents, the winner would receive a total of 65 cents and the next-highest bidder would have to pay the auctioneer 25 cents.

People typically start this game by calling out a small amount of

[11]In a strictly parallel fashion, increases in the American arms budget in response to the Afghan incursion were widely misunderstood in the Soviet Union as evidence of increased military threat. As in the case of the United States, distrust resulting from earlier incidents in the Cold War served to shape Soviet perceptions of this inherently ambiguous evidence.

[12]Escalation is not the only path to deteriorated relationships. In some cases, the parties simply lose importance to each other. For example, some marriages fail not because the partners cannot get along with each other but because the relationship has become empty (Levinger, 1983).

money. And why not? If the dollar bill can be won with a bid of 10, 20, or 30 cents, why not give it a try? Perhaps no one else will elect to play the game. Unfortunately, other people typically reason in much the same way, and the result is that several people begin to bid. Eventually the bidding approaches $1 (the objective value of the prize), and at this point two important things happen: the number of players typically decreases until only the two highest bidders remain in contention, and the motivation of each remaining bidder shifts from an initial concern about maximizing gain (doing as well for oneself as possible) to a concern with minimizing losses instead. As the bidding passes $1, the issue is no longer how much Party can win but how much it can keep from losing. Often the bidding goes much higher than $1.

Why does Party not quit at this point? Largely, it appears, because it is aware of how much time and money it has already spent and is reluctant to give up on this "investment." Moreover, Party continues to hold out hope that Other will stop bidding, lick its wounds, and depart from the scene—leaving victory to Party. "If I persist just a bit longer," Party reasons, "I can still snatch victory from the jaws of defeat." The problem is that if both Party and Other reason this way, neither is apt to quit and the conflict will continue to escalate.

As the conflict grows with each bidding increment, yet another transformation—one described in Chapter 5—takes place. Party's concern with maximizing winnings, which was first replaced by a concern with minimizing losses, is now supplanted by a determination to make certain that Other loses at least as much as Party. "I may go down in flames," Party reasons, "but in doing so I will take Other down with me." It is in this last stage of the dollar auction that concerns about looking foolish in the eyes of Other come to the fore. In other words, Party becomes increasingly preoccupied with threats to its image.

This illustration of Shubik's dollar auction game suggests that people in escalating conflicts may *overcommit* themselves in ways that appear quite irrational to most external observers. Shubik has reported, for example, that a dollar bill is often auctioned off for as much as $5 or $6.[13] Surely this is an illustration of commitment in the service of irrationality. How can this be explained? Why does Party sometimes commit itself and its resources above and beyond all reason? To develop a partial answer to this query, we must explore the topic of entrapment.

Defining Characteristics of Entrapment

Entrapment is a process in which Party, pursuing a goal over a period of time, expends more of its time, energy, money, or other resources than seems justifiable by external standards. According to Brockner and

[13]In a variation on this game, in which a $100 bill was auctioned off before a large group of business people, one of the authors (JZR) managed to sell the prize for $3,000!

Rubin (1985), situations that lead to entrapment have three defining characteristics.

First, it must be possible for Party to regard the same outflow of resources (be it in time, money, or human lives) as either an investment or an expense. In the dollar auction game, for example, the money Party spends on escalating its bidding may be regarded simultaneously as an investment (moving Party closer to its goal of winning the auction) and as an expense (money spent that cannot be retrieved, at least if Party is the second-highest bidder). As a result, Party is caught between two opposing forces, the desire to protect an investment and the desire to avoid an expense.

Second, as time passes or additional resources are invested, the cost associated with continuing increases, but so does the presumed proximity to the desired goal. This adds to Party's dilemma between commitment and withdrawal.

Third, of the two possible extreme decisions that can be made—total commitment and total withdrawal—the former is favored by the circumstances. The pressure restraining Party from continued involvement (represented by the total accumulated cost incurred) is *more* than offset by the pressures that drive Party to persist, such as the reward associated with obtaining the goal, the belief that the goal is just ahead, and the cost associated with giving up its investment. Although a player in the dollar auction game is continually restrained from further participation because of the amount of money that he or she has already committed, this restraint is offset by the desire to win the dollar bill, the hope or belief that such victory lies just a bid or two away, and the conviction that the money already spent needs to be justified by even more expenditure.

Some Examples of Entrapment

A great many situations have the characteristics leading to entrapment. Some of these situations (such as an individual trying to decide how much more money to sink into an old car, how much longer to wait for a bus or a friend, or how much longer to hold onto a failing stock investment) are *nonsocial* in nature. They pit Party against itself or nature—not against Other. However, the situations of greatest interest in this book are *social* in nature, entailing a competitive relationship between two or more individuals or groups. The dollar auction game is a quintessential illustration of an entrapping interpersonal conflict. At an intergroup level, consider the example of two sides persisting in a strike, partly because each has suffered so much already that to give up would be to have suffered in vain. Or recall our example of conflict between the church and the neighborhood. The longer each side has clung to an intransigent position, the more compelled it will probably feel to justify this position through continued intransigence.

Finally, at the level of international decision making, one can analyze the role and extended involvement of the United States in Vietnam as an illustration of entrapment. In his book *The Best and the Brightest,* Halberstam (1969) explains U.S. involvement in very much these terms. The "doves" argued time and again that the United States had embarked on a fool's journey (and an unethical one) and that we should withdraw our forces from Southeast Asia immediately before another American (or Vietnamese) life was lost. But this is exactly why we should remain in Vietnam, retorted the "hawks," exactly why we *should* persist. To withdraw now, they argued, would be to have sacrificed countless lives in vain, on an escapade that would be regarded as meaningless. And anyway, victory in Vietnam and the security of an anticommunist regime in Southeast Asia seemed just a battle or two away. A similar analysis is possible of the aftermath of Israel's 1982 invasion of Lebanon, the Argentine campaign in the Falkland/Malvinas Islands, Soviet intervention in Afghanistan, and the Persian Gulf conflict between Iraq and the United States and its allies in 1990–1991.

Combating Entrapment

In one form or another, both in the psychologist's laboratory and in the field, entrapment has been the object of investigation by a number of researchers over the last decade. The dollar auction game has been studied extensively by Teger (1980); Rubin, Brockner, and their associates have devised other laboratory paradigms in order to study very much the same phenomenon; and Staw (1981) and Lewicki (1980), among others, have studied entrapment in field settings. The results of these studies need not concern us here,[14] but it may be useful to conclude our discussion by mentioning a few strategies that can combat entrapment.

1. *Setting limits.* Research by Brockner et al. (1979) and by Teger (1980) indicates that when Party specifies a limit to its involvement before beginning a quest for a goal, Party is less likely to become entrapped. Moreover, when Party publicly commits itself to a limit, by announcing it to others, it is least likely to become entrapped.
2. *Chunking.* A particular problem arises when the resource expended in an entrapping situation is *time*—for example, when Party is placed "on hold" by a telephone receptionist. The problem is that there are no natural points of decision about whether to continue that line of investment. Party is passively involved in the expenditure and does not have to decide whether to commit further resources. Party is particularly vulnerable to entrapment in such situations.

   There is research evidence to support the view that entrap-

[14]See Brockner & Rubin (1985) for a detailed review of this literature.

ment can be avoided in such situations by encouraging Party to engage in periodic reappraisal of its commitment, a process called *chunking*. Findings by Brockner et al. (1979) suggest that even the minimal provision of opportunities for chunking can help. Participants in an entrapping task were stopped every three minutes by the experimenter, who inquired whether they wished to continue or quit. Merely considering this question led them to quit the task after waiting less than half as long as those who were not interrupted.

3. *Making costs salient.* The stopping points introduced by Brockner et al. (1979) not only allowed Party to chunk its involvement but also reminded Party of the costs associated with continued participation. In the absence of such reminders, entrapment is likely to increase. This point was demonstrated in a study by Brockner et al. (1981) in which participants were given a "payoff chart" that depicted their investment costs at each of a number of possible stopping points. Those who did not have access to this chart—that is, those for whom costs were not salient—became significantly more entrapped than their counterparts. Findings by Brockner et al. (1982) indicate that this effect is particularly striking when cost-salience information is either introduced or kept unavailable *early* in an entrapping task, before the pressures toward overcommitment come into play.
4. *Avoiding concern about Party's image.* In the last stages of the dollar auction, Party seems to persist largely in order to make sure that Other is forced to lose at least as much as Party does. It is in this last phase that Party becomes excessively concerned with the image of toughness that it projects to Other and to any observing audience.[15] As conflict continues to intensify between individuals or groups, Party becomes extraordinarily concerned that any conciliatory or friendly gesture will be taken to imply weakness and invite future exploitation. To the list of forces pressuring Party to persist in an entrapping situation (nearness to goal, value of the goal, amount invested already) may be added the concern that Party not be humiliated by Other (Brockner et al., 1981, 1982). It follows that keeping in mind the dangers associated with this concern may help to avoid entrapment.

We have seen that quite apart from the forces that cause structural changes to persist, there are important forces at work that prod Party not to give up on its tactical investments. Commitments that were made with an initial modicum of restraint too often become traps that produce a needless waste of precious re-

[15]Such image concerns were discussed in Chapter 5. They are found in virtually all forms of escalating conflict.

sources. And when Party *and* Other play the game of competition in this way, the results can be incendiary.[16]

CONCLUSIONS

In this chapter, we have described a number of mechanisms that maintain and sometimes augment the transformations that occur during conflict escalation. Some of these mechanisms perpetuate the changes in individual psychology, group process, and community structure that are both antecedent and consequent to contentious interaction. Others produce entrapment after an initial escalative phase.

Chapters 5 through 7 have been long on mechanisms that produce and perpetuate escalation, but somewhat short on conditions that encourage or discourage the development of these mechanisms and thus make escalation more or less likely. In Chapter 8 we turn to an exploration of such conditions.

[16]On the other hand, as we will argue in Chapter 9, entrapment can offer hope to parties stuck in a stalemate by helping them build commitment to a process of de-escalation.

8

Escalation and Stability

The Story of Michael Kohlhaas • Conditions that Encourage and Discourage Escalation • Stability and Environmental Conditions • Stability and Features of the Parties • *Psychological Features* • *Conflict Models Employed by the Parties* • *Features of Groups* • Stability and Relationships between Parties • *Social Bonds* • *Common Group Membership* • *Dependence* • *The Destruction of Bonds* • *The Fear of Escalation* • *Summary* • Stability and the Community • *Conflict-Limiting Norms* • *Conflict-Limiting Institutions* • *Audiences* • *The Geography of Social Bonds* • *Community Size and Social Geography* • *Summary* • Stability through Threats • *The Balance of Power* • *Balance of Power in the Nuclear Age* • *Problems with Basing Stability on Threats* • *Summary* • Conclusions

In Chapter 1, we defined conflict as perceived divergence of interest, involving two or more parties who believe that their aspirations cannot be achieved simultaneously. We pointed out that mild conflict is often benign, encouraging the parties to develop new ways of meshing their interests and producing needed social change. But heavy conflict can be destructive, and this is where escalation comes in. Escalation is what gives conflict its bad name. Though a little escalation may be part of a constructive process, heavy escalation is usually a problem for the parties involved and for the surrounding community.

To understand the difference between light and heavy escalation, compare the curves in Figure 8.1, which trace the course of escalation over time in two contrasting conflicts. Curve A represents a case of light escalation. Tactics and the

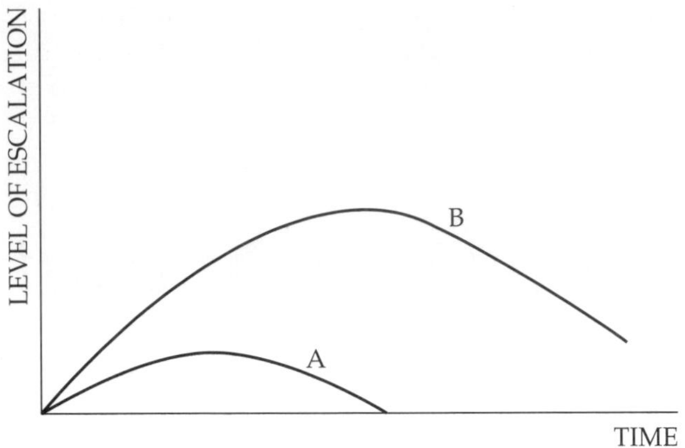

FIGURE 8.1
Course of escalation in two contrasting conflicts. Curve A represents a case of light escalation, and Curve B a case of heavy escalation.

feelings associated with them become harsher for a period of time. But they are limited in intensity and duration, and the situation quickly returns to normal. A good example of such a conflict is the husband-wife spat about driving the car, described in Chapter 5. The two parties argued briefly and then resolved their quarrel.

Curve B represents a case of heavy escalation. Tactics and feelings rapidly become more intense, moving to a higher level and lasting longer. In addition, because of the kinds of residues discussed in Chapter 7, the level of escalation may not return to the baseline from which it departed. Many of the conflicts in the Cold War and the UB crisis fit the pattern shown in curve B. So do the events in Heinrich von Kleist's (1967) novel, *Michael Kohlhaas*.

THE STORY OF MICHAEL KOHLHAAS

The main character in this novel is a kind, hardworking, and fair-minded man whose life is transformed by an incident that creates in him an unyielding desire for revenge. The incident begins when Kohlhaas, who is a well-respected horse dealer, is denied customary passage for his horses unless he pays a bribe to a local landowner, Junker von Tronka. He refuses to pay this bribe and is forced to leave two horses as security before he can pass through. Outraged by this incident, Kohlhaas appeals his case to the proper authorities. The authorities, however, take the side of the Junker, who has strong connections with the court.

Meanwhile, Kohlhaas's two horses, and the servant looking after them, are badly mistreated by the Junker's men. This mistreatment further infuriates Kohlhaas, who vigorously demands restitution for the abuse that he has received. The conflict spiral continues, and he suffers many additional insults and losses, including the death of his beloved wife, as he pursues revenge against the Junker.

Finally, Kohlhaas organizes an uprising, burning down the Junker's castle and killing many of the people who have mistreated him. He also wins in court when the intervention of impartial authorities results in the Junker's imprisonment and the return of Kohlhaas's two horses. His desire for revenge is finally fulfilled, but the victory is a Pyrrhic one. Kohlhaas is executed for his actions, an execution he readily accepts as his due.

The tale of Kohlhaas illustrates some of the issues being raised in this chapter. A seemingly minor divergence of interest, involving free passage, mushrooms into a heavily escalated conflict, which eventually produces substantial property loss and the deaths of many people, including the hero himself. What conditions could have driven the characters in this and similar stories to the actions they took and the fate they suffered?

CONDITIONS THAT ENCOURAGE AND DISCOURAGE ESCALATION

Heavy escalation has two kinds of antecedents: high perceived divergence of interest and low stability.

As we indicated in Chapter 2, high *perceived divergence of interest* is the product of lofty, rigid aspirations on both sides and little apparent common ground. In such circumstances, yielding is unthinkable and problem solving seems hopeless. Hence, contending looks like the only way for Party to succeed; it seems necessary to use pressure, politics, or trickery in order to achieve Party's goals. And the larger the perceived divergence of interest, the heavier the contentious tactics that seem to be needed. Seeing a need for harsh tactics does not always lead to action. But if action is taken, these tactics will produce escalation, which is likely to provoke a similar response from Other, starting a conflict spiral.

High perceived divergence of interest was part of the problem in the Kohlhaas story. The hero's fair-mindedness—a virtue in most other settings—appears to have made him so rigid about defending his rights that a seemingly unbridgeable gap developed between his aspirations and those of the Junker. As a result, both he and the Junker saw no alternative to escalation. We discussed the antecedents of perceived divergence of interest extensively in Chapter 2.

Here we will focus on *stability*, those aspects of the situation that discourage Party from acting harshly when it perceives a divergence of interest or is confronted with contentious behavior from Other. Situations are said to be highly stable if only the largest divergence of interest can push one or both parties into heavily escalated action. They are said to be highly unstable if minimal divergence of interest can have this effect.

There are three main sources of stability and instability. Some conditions encourage stability by *reducing the readiness to use harsh tactics.* An example would be bonds—of common group membership, friendship, or interdependence—between Party and Other. In Europe at the time of our story, there were usually no bonds between landed aristocrats like Junker von Tronka and merchants like Michael Kohlhaas; hence, bonds could not be a source of stability.

Other conditions encourage stability by *facilitating the development of solutions to a conflict.* An example would be the existence of third parties in the surrounding community who are ready to spring into action as mediators. Village elders and religious leaders in Somalia have been known to settle disputes by requiring the parties to promise, under oath, to set aside their differences (Lewis, 1961).[1] Again, such conditions were absent in the Kohlhaas case, where the surrounding community consisted almost exclusively of potential supporters for one side or the other.

Still other conditions encourage *in*stability by *producing* harsh reactions to provocation. For example, people who are in an aroused or tense state of mind are especially likely to retaliate in the face of provocation. Perhaps Kohlhaas was in such a state at the time of his first encounter with the Junker—due to a difficult journey, domestic problems, or whatever—making him prone to overreact to the Junker's contentious actions.

Harsh reactions to provocation are the basic events in the cycles of escalation that were shown in Figures 5.2 and 6.1 (the reader should turn back to one of these figures). They are the building blocks of these cycles. If the conditions encourage Party to respond harshly to provocation from Other (by energizing path C and/or path D in these figures), the cycle of escalation will turn more rapidly and generate faster and more extensive escalation. If the conditions also encourage Other to respond harshly to Party's provocations (by energizing path A and/or path B), the cycle will become a veritable flywheel. Party will react harshly to provocations from Other, producing provocations *for* Other, which will start the cycle around again. Such escalation may be really boundless if harsh responses become directed not only at Other but also at those identified with Other—family, associates, or ethnic group members—as exemplified by the Kohlhaas story, and by the tragic confrontations between Serbs and Muslims in Bosnia.

The chapter will examine these kinds of conditions under four headings—those pertaining to the *environment,* the *parties,* their *relationship,*

[1]It is reported that some American army officers made efforts to reinstate this tradition during the 1993 U.S. humanitarian intervention in Somalia.

and the *community* that surrounds them. At the end of the chapter, there will also be a special section on stability through threats, which will examine the so-called balance of power.

STABILITY AND ENVIRONMENTAL CONDITIONS

Research on aggression (see Berkowitz, 1993; Geen, 1990) has helped understand the environmental conditions that encourage harsh reactions to provocation from Other. Two kinds of conditions can be distinguished: those that affect the extent to which *anger develops* in response to Other's provocation, and those that affect the extent to which this *anger is expressed* in behavior.[2] Looking back at Figure 5.2, the first kind of condition can be viewed as influencing effect C (or its counterpart, effect A); the second kind, as influencing effect D (or its counterpart, effect B).

Autonomic arousal makes people get angrier when they are provoked, provided that they attribute this arousal to the provocation. This implies that conflict is more likely to escalate when Party has exercised recently, although not so recently as to be aware of the source of the arousal (Zillmann, Johnson, & Day, 1974). Folklore to the contrary, a fast game of basketball is more likely to exacerbate conflict than to cure it. Escalation is also more likely when Party is in a sexually excited state (Zillmann, 1971), or when there is considerable noise (Geen, 1978) or atmospheric pollution (Rotton & Frey, 1985).

The effect of autonomic arousal on anger tends to persist well after the arousal is gone (Bryant & Zillmann, 1979). For example, if Party exercises just before Other provokes it, Party's likelihood of aggressing against Other several months later will be strengthened. What probably happens is that the original anger, augmented by exercise, becomes translated into some form of negative attitude or goal which persists as a residue.

An angry reaction to provocation is also more likely when Party has been *recently angered in some other situation.* Pent-up anger can turn Party into a coiled spring, poised to displace its anger onto Other. For example, Berkowitz, Cochran, and Embree (1981) found that subjects who were forced to hold their hand in very cold water were more aggressive toward fellow subjects than those who held their hand in moderately cold water.

Pleasurable experiences, in contrast, tend to block an aggressive response to provocation. Humor (Baron, 1978); mildly erotic stimuli (Baron & Bell, 1977); and soft, sweet music (Konecni, 1975) tend to diminish aggressive expression, presumably by putting Party in a good mood. It is

[2]The common-sense view that anger is one source of aggression is not shared by all theorists. Berkowitz (1993), for instance, presents the view that "anger . . . does not directly instigate aggression but usually only accompanies the inclination to attack a target" (p. 20).

not altogether clear whether such experiences interfere with the development of anger or with the expression of anger in the form of an aggressive response.[3]

The ingestion of alcohol is probably the best-known antecedent of escalation. Barroom brawls are legendary, and alcohol is believed to have contributed to 64 percent of the homicide cases in Philadelphia between 1948 and 1953 (Wolfgang & Strohm, 1956). The effect of alcohol is to concentrate attention on the most salient stimuli in the situation (i.e., the provocation), making Party oblivious to the wider social context and the future impact of its actions (Steele & Josephs, 1990; Taylor & Leonard, 1983). This presumably produces an escalative effect in two ways: (1) by making the provocation seem larger; and (2) by reducing social and cognitive control over Party's behavior, thus increasing the likelihood that Party's anger will be released.

Interestingly, Party may use "the state of being drunk" as an opportunity to let Other know its complaints or grievances. This is particularly so when Party is in the presence of people (such as relatives or friends) who it knows will spring into action if things begin to get out of control. Dore (1978) has observed this sort of behavior in a small Japanese village where harmony is so heavily emphasized that the villagers have few opportunities to display their grievances openly:

> It's amazing, really, how some people change when they're drunk and surrounded by a lot of people. They seem to go out of their mind, sometimes, but they know really that they're safe, because if they provoke the other chap to violence there are enough people there to keep them apart. And the next morning they'll be all smiles and greet each other as if nothing happened. But the one who spoke his mind will know the other one will remember what he said. He'll have got his point home. In fact people—you could see it—often used to come to a party with the express intention of picking a quarrel and getting something off their chest! (p. 266)

Another anger-releasing experience is exposure to an *aggressive model*, somebody engaging in aggression. When Party is in such circumstances, it is especially likely to aggress (Baron & Kepner, 1970; Wheeler & Caggiula, 1966). Seeing an aggressive model on television has a similar effect, especially if the portrayal is realistic (Geen, 1975) and the model is engaged in retaliatory aggression (Geen & Stonner, 1973). A possible explanation for these effects is that the expression of anger is ordinarily under strong normative control. People have learned that society frowns on aggression. Hence, they tend to feel guilty or afraid of criticism about ag-

[3]A case can be made for either of these interpretations. However, the fact that humor and small gifts also reduce contentious behavior in negotiation (Carnevale & Isen, 1986; O'Quin & Aronoff, 1981) suggests that the effect is on the response production side. Anger is not usually prominent in negotiation; hence, the effect of pleasurable experience on negotiation behavior is not likely to be mediated by anger.

gression. As a result, they hold their anger in. But when an aggressive model appears, it places a temporary seal of social approval on aggression. The old norm suddenly seems less binding. If the model can do it, why not I? This allows the pent-up anger to be expressed.[4]

Aggression is also sometimes inhibited by *competing activities.* For example, moderate heat provokes aggression; but severe heat provokes flight if the situation allows it, a response that is incompatible with aggression (Bell & Baron, 1976). Similarly, a favorite way to stop children from angry crying is to divert them with a pleasurable competing activity.

We can summarize the points made in this section by examining their practical implications. For example, suppose you were traveling with a male companion who constantly got into arguments and fights along the way. What could you, as a third party who, for one reason or another, feels responsible, do to prevent further escalation? You could try to remove him from any situation in which conflict was brewing. In addition, you could try to keep his arousal level low by avoiding noise, pollution, or heavy physical exertion. You could avoid provoking him yourself to make him less of a coiled spring with others. You could keep him out of bars and away from violent movies and television shows. You could also conform your own behavior to the advice about problem solving given in Chapter 10, so as to provide him with a model of conciliatory behavior. Finally, you could try to keep him busy with all manner of pleasurable activities, so as to put him in a good mood and encourage responses incompatible with escalation.

STABILITY AND FEATURES OF THE PARTIES

Conflict is sometimes between individuals and sometimes between groups. When individuals are involved, psychological differences such as personality or male-female predispositions may be important. The behavior of individual participants may also be affected by the conflict models[5] they use for analyzing their dispute. Such variables are also important for understanding intergroup conflict; for example, male-female differences that apply to conflict between individuals will also help us understand conflict between groups that are homogeneous in gender. In addition, there are stable intergroup differences that affect the way conflict is handled by groups.

[4]Models have been shown to produce temporary release from normative strictures in two other settings. In the Asch (1956) conformity experiments, having a nonconforming "partner" in the group encouraged many subjects to reject a faulty group consensus. Similarly, Milgram (1992) found that subjects were less likely to take an unwelcome action required by an authority figure when confederates, posing as subjects, refused to conform.

[5]The term *model* in this context refers to a pattern of thought used in developing explanations rather than to a human being who is taking a particular kind of action.

Psychological Features

There is a built-in feature of human psychology that feeds into the cycle of escalation: Party tends to regard its own actions toward Other as more normative and less aggressive than the same actions from Other toward Party (Kim, 1991; Kim & Smith, 1993; Mummendey et al., 1984). This means that when Party is trying to retaliate in a measured fashion, matching its response to the extent of Other's provocation, it will often unwittingly "turn up the volume" and overreact.[6] By the logic of the cycle of escalation, the resulting provocation is likely to elicit an even more aggressive response from Other, completing the turn of the conflict spiral and starting it on another cycle at an even greater amplitude.

Research on aggression suggests that this perverse progression is particularly likely when certain kinds of personalities are involved. There is evidence of consistent individual differences in aggressive response to provocation (Geen, 1990). Some people are particularly *irritable,* reacting with anger to minor provocation (Berkowitz, 1993). Among these are the hard-driving, success-oriented "Type A" individuals, who tend to overreact when others get in their way (Carver & Glass, 1978). Other people are especially *impulsive,* easily expressing their anger when aroused (Hynan & Grush, 1986). Still other people are extremely vigilant for *threats to their image* of strength or adequacy (Toch, 1969). They are easily provoked and often respond aggressively in an effort to repair their image.[7] In addition, there are people who have learned a *personal code of retaliation*—an eye for an eye and a tooth for a tooth—because it has worked for them in the past or because they have been brought up with others who had such a code.[8] All four types of people are especially likely to get into escalative sequences and often end up hurting themselves and others.

Other personality traits contribute to stability in interpersonal relations. For example, people who are high in *need for social approval, fear of so-*

[6] The Carthaginian general Hannibal, in revenge for his slain grandfather at the city of Himera (in Sicily), destroyed all the houses and temples of Himera, distributed the captive women and children among his soldiers as prizes, and brought all 3,000 male captives to the very spot where his grandfather had been slain and killed them.

[7] Most people probably fall into such a vigilant stance during periods of low self-esteem, when their image of themselves becomes a little shaky.

[8] Note that in some cultures revenge is not a matter of personal choice but a matter of sacred obligation. Forgiving the enemy is regarded as a sign of weakness or lack of honor (Westermarck, 1912). Karsten (1935, cited by Daly & Wilson, 1988) illustrates the Jibaro Indian's obligation to avenge wrongs:

> The Jibaro Indian is wholly penetrated by the idea of retaliation. . . . The soul of the murdered Indian requires that his relatives shall avenge his death. The errant spirit, which gets no rest, visits his sons, his brothers, his father, in dreams, and weeping conjures them not to let the slayer escape but to wreak vengeance upon him for the life he has taken. . . . To avenge the blood of a murdered father, brother, or son, is therefore looked upon as one of the most sacred duties of a Jibaro Indian. . . . It may happen that a Jibaro keeps the thought of revenge in his mind for years, even for decades, waiting for the opportunity to carry it out, but he never gives it up. (pp. 271–272)

cial disapproval, or *guilt about aggression* tend to underreact when provoked (Dengerink, 1976). These findings suggest that aggressive responding, hence the likelihood of escalation, is reduced in those who are highly motivated to adhere to social norms. In addition, there is evidence that *empathy* with others diminishes the tendency to retaliate when provoked (Rusbult et al., 1991). Empathic people are sensitive to the needs of others, leading them to think twice about harming others' interests even when it seems justified. Hence, they are probably less likely to get involved in escalation.

What about *gender differences* in the propensity to escalate? There is considerable popular confusion about this issue. It is generally believed that women are the greater peacemakers; yet popular wisdom also holds that "hell has no fury like a woman scorned." The research literature on this topic is likewise mixed (Eagly & Steffen, 1986; Frodi et al., 1977), suggesting that the direction of gender differences depends on the circumstances and mode of response. One clear finding is that men are more likely than women to retaliate physically in response to physical provocation (Eagly & Steffen, 1986). There is also evidence that women protest more vigorously than men in response to persistent, illegitimate provocation (Da Gloria & De Ridder, 1979; Pruitt et al., 1993a). But more research is needed to sort out gender differences.

Conflict Models Employed by the Parties

We have presented three conflict models (aggressor-defender, conflict spiral, and structural change) as aids to a scholarly analysis of conflict. But they can also be seen as models of participant thought—concepts that describe the way Party understands what is happening to it in conflict. Each model has implications with respect to participant action and the extent to which conflict will escalate.

A firm belief in the *aggressor-defender* interpretation often serves to exacerbate a conflict spiral. When Party interprets the conflict in this way, it usually sees itself as the defender and Other as the aggressor. If surrender is out of the question, Party must redouble its efforts at defense or deterrence to prove to Other that aggression does not pay. Furthermore, Party's image of strength and forcefulness is at stake. Seeing this, Other is likely to redouble its efforts as well, spawning a new round of contentious activity. The result is a conflict spiral. The pace of the Cold War arms race between the United States and the Soviet Union was almost certainly accelerated by President Reagan's belief: "There is no arms race; they are racing and we are just trying to catch up."

On the other hand, the belief that Party is in danger of entering a *conflict spiral* can serve to dampen this spiral. Such an analysis is likely to lead Party to avoid overly contentious actions in order not to antagonize

Other, and to be conciliatory in the hope that Other will reciprocate (Tetlock, 1983). Party will behave like a dove, in contrast to the hawks, who make an aggressor-defender analysis.

If the doves are right about the nature of the conflict, as they often are, they can avoid escalation and even de-escalate their conflict. For example, in 1977 President Sadat of Egypt, concluding that his country was involved in a conflict spiral with Israel, made a gesture of goodwill in the form of a personal journey to Jerusalem. This started a de-escalative spiral in relations between these countries that resulted in the eventual resumption of diplomatic relations.

But if the hawks are right, as they sometimes are, a soft, conciliatory stance may encourage the adversary to redouble its efforts to force Party to yield. For example, after surrounding Indian outposts in 1961, Chinese forces withdrew in an effort to signal a desire to be conciliatory. Unfortunately, Indian leaders "interpreted the Chinese withdrawal as a sign of timidity [and] became even bolder in their efforts to occupy as much of the disputed territory, east and west, as was possible" (Lebow et al., 1984).[9]

A *structural change* analysis of the conflict Party is experiencing implies a third set of tactics. For example, Party may try to avoid structural changes in its own constituency that will contribute to further escalation of a conflict. A leader who fears that a permanent defense establishment will become a strong advocate for hawkish policies may insist that a temporary establishment be formed to meet a current threat. In addition, a structural change analysis implies the importance of *timing* in reversing or repudiating actions that are taken by Party and resented by Other (Pruitt & Gahagan, 1974). For example, it seems reasonable to assume that the UB campus crisis would have dissipated quickly if the administration had publicly apologized for the initial violence by the campus police, made restitution to the students who were assaulted, and arranged to drop the charges against those who were initially arrested. Such actions would probably have prevented the formation of the strike committee. Timing was important because once the strike committee had developed, and numerous students had taken leadership positions in it, the campus was consigned to an extended period of heavy conflict.

Features of Groups

Conflict between groups is more likely to escalate than conflict between individuals. The mere existence of an ingroup and an outgroup leads the

[9]Because both hawks and doves may have the right answer at times, it is wise for groups and organizations to cultivate both kinds of bird among their members and to allow them to engage in what is often an endless debate. However, it should be borne in mind that the hawkish analysis is the more common one and that, in deeper conflicts, it is often strengthened by a self-serving tendency for Party to think that Other must be the aggressor because Party's side cannot possibly be in the wrong in any way. Hence, cultivating doves is often the more elusive and challenging enterprise.

outgroup to become the object of negative perceptions and discrimination (Crocker et al., 1987; Tajfel, 1970) and produces more vigorous competition for scarce resources (Komorita & Lapworth, 1982). Furthermore, groups have been found to protest more adamantly than individuals in response to persistent, illegitimate provocation (Pruitt et al., 1993a) and to choose the noncooperative response more reliably in studies of behavior in the prisoner's dilemma (McCallum et al., 1985). There are a number of explanations for these effects, most prominently, *social identity theory.* This formulation holds that groups are more competitive than individuals because the self-respect of their members is tied to believing that their own group is better than other groups (Turner, 1981).

In Chapters 6 and 7, we discussed a number of changes that occur in groups during escalation and tend to augment and perpetuate the escalated state. The most important of these are the development of contentious group norms and goals, the establishment of subgroups that are dedicated to the struggle, and the ascendancy of militant leaders. Conflicts involving such changes do eventually die down or end, but the changes often persist as residues, making escalation more likely and more extensive the next time the group gets into conflict. In other words, when such changes take place, stability diminishes and the groups tend to overreact to divergence of interest or provocation.

STABILITY AND RELATIONSHIPS BETWEEN PARTIES

Social Bonds

Social bonds tend to encourage yielding and problem solving. They also discourage the use of contentious tactics, especially those of the harsher variety. Hence, social bonds are a source of stability in relationships; they reduce the likelihood of escalation. The bonds in question include positive attitudes, respect, friendship, kinship, perceived similarity, common group membership, and future dependence. As an example of the impact of friendship on social conflict, Ransford (1968) found that African Americans who had socialized with whites were less willing to endorse the use of violence in pursuit of racial justice than were those who had not. The importance of common group membership is reflected in Coleman's (1957) contention that identification with one's community tends to moderate the tactics used for pursuing disagreements with other community members.

Most bonds cut both ways. When Party feels bonded to Other, Other feels bonded to Party. This is inevitably true of kinship and common group membership and is usually true of perceived similarity. In addition, positive attitudes and respect are usually reciprocal (Berscheid & Walster, 1978) and friendship is usually a two-way street. The only kind of bond that is not typically reciprocal is dependence on the other party. Party is sometimes dependent on Other without Other being dependent on Party.

The stabilizing impact of bonding is often masked by the fact that people who are more securely bonded to each other feel less constrained by the canons of politeness. They are likely to raise more issues with one another and argue more vigorously, at least for a while. Still, if conflict persists, they are more likely to engage in problem solving and less likely to employ harsh contentious tactics. This paradox was observed in a laboratory study of cohesiveness (solidarity) in dyads (Back, 1951). When a difference of opinion arose, more cohesive dyads argued more vigorously but also eventually reached fuller agreement.[10]

Two types of bonds—common group membership and dependence—are particularly important.

Common Group Membership

One of the most important sources of bonding is *common group membership*—the perception that Other is a member of a group to which Party also belongs. The link between common group membership and stability has not yet been examined empirically. Nevertheless, it seems reasonable to assume that this phenomenon protects parties from escalation. Indirect evidence favoring this hypothesis comes from a study by Kramer and Brewer (1984), in which two groups were less likely to compete for common resources when their members saw themselves as coming from the same geographical community rather than two different communities. There is also evidence of a greater tendency toward escalation between groups whose members look or act very different and therefore cannot easily move from one group to the other (Struch & Schwartz, 1989).

Dependence

Dependence is the most complicated source of bonding. Party is dependent on Other to the extent that Other has control over certain of Party's outcomes and can reward Party for desired behavior and/or punish Party for undesired behavior. As mentioned in Chapter 3, dependence usually encourages yielding and problem solving and discourages the use of heavy contentious tactics (Ben-Yoav & Pruitt, 1984a, b; Heide & Miner, 1992). The more Other can help or harm Party, the more careful Party must be not to annoy Other by pressing petty claims or employing harsh

[10]The reader interested in an example of a cohesive dyad that argues vigorously need look no further than most happily married couples!

tactics. Hence, dependence ordinarily contributes to stability, especially if it is bilateral (i.e., if there is mutual dependence). An example is the high level of cooperation and absence of escalated conflict in relations between the United States and the Soviet Union during the Second World War, when they were dependent on each other for support in the common battle against Germany and her allies. This relationship deteriorated drastically as soon as the common battle was over, producing the Cold War.

Dependence is a two-edged sword. When Party depends on Other for rewards, there is the potential for divergence of interest. If Party depends on Other for rides to work and it is costly for Other to provide them, their interests are divergent. If Other is haphazard in providing this service and Party cannot find another source of rides, Party is likely to try to improve Other's performance by employing contentious tactics. The more dependent Party is on Other, the harsher the tactics Party is likely to employ in order to teach Other an enduring lesson. This is why friends and family members so often get into escalation, despite their bonds of affection and common group membership. Such people are highly interdependent and have a lot of potential divergence of interest. In short, dependence can both dampen and encourage escalation. Dependence on a reliable Other is a source of stability, but dependence on an unreliable Other can produce multiple conflicts and heavy escalation.

There is also a complicated association between *breadth* of dependence and stability. The greater the number of realms in which Party depends on Other, the less likely Party is to use harsh tactics in any one realm, for fear of losing Other's cooperation in alternative realms. Hence, the less likely is escalation.

Yet broader dependence also means more potential for conflict. If something goes wrong in the relationship between the United States and Ecuador, the United States is more likely to employ sanctions than if a comparable problem arises in the U.S. relationship with Britain. This is because the United States is more dependent on Britain. However, this very dependence means that there will be more frequent conflict with Britain than with Ecuador. Month after month, year after year, more issues arise in the relationship between the United States and Britain. Breadth of dependence increases the number of conflicts that take place but reduces the likelihood that any one conflict will escalate.

There are diminishing returns for stability when dependence becomes too broad. Extreme dependence can actually foster conflict escalation. The problem is that Party can never satisfy *all* of Other's needs. Suppose Party relies on Other for food, money, affection, respect, decisions about Party's clothes, haircuts, advice on presents to relatives, and so on. Unless Other is a Nietzschean superhero, some of Party's needs will go unfulfilled and Party will be frustrated. Party is likely to become angry and to employ harsh tactics in dealing with Other. This happens, for example, to some older people who become overdependent on a relative or nurse and, as a result, very crabby. Their relationships would be more stable, in the sense of producing fewer quarrels, if they had a wider circle of friends, so that they could rely on each person for the benefits that individual was most capable of providing.

There are two other ways in which involvement with people outside a relationship tends to protect the relationship from escalation. First, such involvement usually entails competing activity, which takes time and resources away from heavy conflict. People who are engaged in many outside pursuits ordinarily avoid escalation unless the issues are of considerable importance. Second, issues seem smaller when less attention is paid to them. When life is rich with many outside activities, people gain a certain perspective. It is unnecessary to win on every issue—we can afford to lose a few because we are winning on many more. The situation is more stable because it is easier to become reconciled to an occasional defeat.

The Destruction of Bonds

When conflict escalates, distrust develops and bonds disintegrate. Relationships are severed; love turns to hate; and people shift their dependencies to other, less difficult partners. As a result, new conflicts between the parties are even more likely to escalate. In short, prior escalation destroys interparty bonds, enhancing the likelihood of later escalation.

The opposite of bonding is antagonism. Antagonism encourages the use of harsh tactics, thereby encouraging escalation. Antagonism can take the form of anger or negative attitudes, and can result from grievances of all kinds, perceived dissimilarity, membership in an opposing group, or the expectation of frustration at Other's hands. Antagonism makes Party especially likely to overreact when new conflicts arises.

The Fear of Escalation

In his classic treatise on arms races, Richardson (1967) argued that conflict spirals, and hence escalation, are less likely to occur when Party is aware of the potential for such spirals and is concerned about the consequences of escalation. When such is the case, Party is likely to tone down its reactions to Other's aggressive actions. The fear of escalation may underlie in part the tendency noted in happy marriages (Gottman, 1979) and successful roommate relationships (Sillars, 1981) for people to respond in conciliatory fashion to contentious challenges from their partners. We find in such cases a stillborn spiral: Other is racing toward the brink—but Party is not trying to catch up.

Sometimes the fear of escalation arises because of a frightening prior episode of conflict between the parties (Zartman, 1989). If they manage to continue their relationship beyond such an incident, one or both of them is often chastened and wary of overreacting. This happened at the time of the Cuban missile crisis of 1962, when the United States and the Soviet Union came closer to a shooting war than at any other time during the Cold War. Shortly after this crisis, a period of détente emerged, in which both sides made efforts to de-escalate the controversy between them. The two nations looked over a precipice together, then drew back in an effort to avoid disaster. The fear of escalation resulting from this crisis wore off after a time, and escalative forces were once more in the ascendent.

What this means is that stability is sometimes encouraged by a fear of escalation. When a relationship is especially important to Party, or there has been an especially clear warning of trouble, Party will sometimes redouble its efforts to avoid escalation.

Summary

In our discussion about relationships, we emphasized that social bonding encourages stability. Two of the most important types of bonds are common group membership and dependence. The sense of common group membership can be produced by any classification scheme that divides people into two or more groups. Stability tends to be high within such groups, although there is a tendency toward escalation between them if conflict arises.

Dependence, on the other hand, is a two-edged sword. Ordinarily it contributes to stability, but it can flip-flop and contribute to escalation when Party depends on a grossly unreliable Other. Breadth of dependence has a curvilinear relationship with stability: stability increases with increasing dependence on Other until the point of overdependence is reached, where Other can no longer serve Party's needs adequately. Beyond this point, stability diminishes and the probability of escalation increases.

When a conflict escalates, bonds tend to disintegrate and to be replaced by antagonism, making the next conflict more likely to escalate. However, awareness of the potential for deterioration in a relationship can encourage fear of escalation, leading to measures to avoid this development.

STABILITY AND THE COMMUNITY

The stability of a relationship between Party and Other is very much a function of the broader community of which they are a part. What is meant by the term *community?* The community for two individuals might be their common family or office.[11] The community for two towns might be the county or state in which they are located. The community for two nations might be a regional association or the "family of nations" as a whole. Two parties may share membership in more than one community.

Conflict-Limiting Norms

Community norms often contribute to stability, prohibiting the use of harsh contentious tactics and prescribing problem solving as the proper approach to conflict between group members. "Don't let the sun set on your anger" and "Love thy neighbor as thyself" are but a few examples of maxims that may serve as guiding norms in the regulation of conflict.[12]

Like all norms, conflict-limiting norms are especially effective with parties who are well socialized and those who feel that the community has their interests at heart. They are effective with other types of parties to the extent that the community has the capacity for enforcement—that is, for learning about and punishing norm violation. Escalation is more likely when societies lack these elements.

In some cultures, norm violation evokes a strong sense of shame. For example, in many Japanese communities there is a strong preference for the settlement of disputes within one's own community; to seek outside help is to acknowledge failure at settling the conflict on one's own, thereby bringing shame on the entire community. Joy Hendry (1987) has cited a case that illustrates this point. A Japanese family filed a lawsuit against one of their neighbors because their young son had drowned while in the neighbor's care. The district court ordered the neighbor to pay a sum of money to the family as compensation.[13] This lawsuit apparently angered many people in the community. The family received hate mail condemning their legal action against their neighbor. Soon the father of the family was fired from his job, and the other children in the family were taunted and humiliated at school. Eventually the family yielded to the mounting community pressure to drop the lawsuit. However, by then it was too late to restore their damaged reputation, and they were forced to leave the community.

[11]For a helpful conceptual analysis of the ways an organizational community can function under conditions of conflict, see Kolb & Bartunek (1992) and Kolb & Faure (1994).

[12]Note that norms such as these must be distinguished from substantive norms and norms about who makes what decisions. As mentioned in Chapter 2, the latter types of norms tend to diminish the likelihood of conflict arising at all.

[13]In the West Bank, an equivalent dispute settlement mechanism is known as the *sulha*.

Conflict-Limiting Institutions

Most communities also provide forums and third party services for helping their members resolve conflict peacefully. Stability within the community depends on the availability and effectiveness of these institutions. Examples include legislative bodies (such as committees of representatives from different agencies), arbitral services (such as courts and formal arbitrators), and mediation services.

Formal judicial and mediation services are sometimes established by law, such as the services provided by the Public Employee Relations Board in the State of New York. This board provides a sequence of procedures for dealing with impasse in negotiations between public employee unions and government agencies. In police and firefighter disputes, a mediator is first sent to help the parties in their search for a mutually acceptable agreement. If mediation is unsuccessful, a fact finder is dispatched to look into the issues and render an advisory judgment. If fact-finding does not produce agreement, the controversy must go before an arbitrator, who renders a binding judgment.

More commonly, third party intervention is informal and relatively unstructured. A parent resolves an argument about a toy between two children, or a mutual friend helps two neighbors resolve a dispute about a noisy dog.

A middle ground between the formal and the informal is employed in many nonindustrial societies for dealing with controversies that might otherwise polarize and destroy a village or clan. As described by Gulliver (1979) and Merry (1989), certain high-ranking individuals in these societies gain a reputation as third parties. When conflict arises, community members summon one of these individuals, who talks with the disputants alone or in a larger group setting. If the disputants are willing to settle, the result is a mediated agreement. If not, the third party, often working with the rest of the community, imposes a settlement in the interest of community harmony.

Forums and third party institutions contribute to stability by giving people a nonviolent and face-saving way to resolve their disputes (Glasl, 1982). For such institutions to be effective, they must be seen as legitimate and as either unbiased—or biased in the direction of prevailing community norms. They must also be seen as giving a full hearing and careful consideration to user grievances, even if the ultimate decision or recommendation favors the opponent (Lind & Tyler, 1988; Thibaut & Walker, 1975).

In the absence of legitimate and trusted forums or third party institutions, people often "take the law into their own hands," employing harsh contentious tactics in an effort to settle conflicts in their own favor, thereby escalating these conflicts. An example is the final stage of Michael Kohlhaas's escalation, in which he joined with other disgruntled individuals in a frontal assault on the regional center of power. Such actions are common in frontier regions and in the more impoverished sections of many American cities, where the law is weak or not trusted. For instance, interviews with African American residents of Los Angeles after the Watts riots of 1965 showed that those who felt that it was not possible for the average citizen to influence government decisions were especially likely to endorse the use of violence in pursuit of racial justice (Ransford, 1968).[14]

Audiences

Few conflicts can be pursued without outsiders being aware of them. This means that communities usually provide audiences for conflict. In most of the examples we have given, these audiences are unhappy about conflict and try to stop it. But this is not always the case. Some audiences are amused by conflict and urge the participants to escalate, even to the point of threatening their images by calling them cowards if they do not fight. Such encouragement is legendary among schoolchildren and may have been present during the fight in the state prison described in Chapter 5. Heavy escalation is a frequent result of such encouragement (Brown, 1968).[15]

The Geography of Social Bonds

We already mentioned the stabilizing influence of bonds between conflicting parties. Among the most important bonds are those that link two parties to a third community member or group. Indeed, the entire configuration of bonding and antagonism in a community contributes to the stability or escalation potential between any two community members. We call such a configuration the *geography of social bonds.* To

[14]This attitude may explain why many residents of such regions exhibit an exaggerated vigilance for threats to their image of strength and resolve. In the absence of adequate third party protection, they become convinced that such an image is their first and most vital line of defense against exploitation and assault from others. Several people with this orientation are central to the movie *Boyz n the Hood,* which portrays a disastrous escalation between rival groups of young men in Los Angeles.

[15]Some years ago, in Albany, New York, a now legendary incident occurred, in which a man threatening to jump to his death from a downtown office building was scolded for not doing so by onlookers down below. Communities sometimes discourage their members from escalating and sometimes urge them on; this fact leaves us in a theoretical quandary. It appears that crowd size and physical anonymity play important roles in the "jumping" phenomenon. Leon Mann (1981) analyzed twenty-one cases in which crowds were present when someone threatened to jump from a building. He found that when the crowd was large or when the incident happened at night (where people could have anonymity under the cover of darkness), onlookers tended to bait the person to jump. Further theory and research is clearly needed to determine the circumstances that promote group-induced stability versus escalation.

understand how this geography works, we start with three-party systems and then move to larger configurations.

Three-Party Systems

In three-party systems, the critical question is how conflict between two parties (A and B) is affected by their relationship with a third party (X). Three situations or cases can be distinguished. These are shown schematically in Figure 8.2. In each case, the situation shown to the left of the arrow is assumed to lead to the situation shown to the right.

In case 1, parties A and B each have bonds to a third party, X; for example, husband and wife have a strong common friendship with the wife's father, or two nations have a common ally. This should strengthen the bonds between A and B—hence, the stability of their relationship—encouraging resolution rather than escalation of their conflict. There are two reasons for predicting this. One is perceived similarity; following balance theory (Heider, 1958), we can predict that A and B will have positive attitudes toward each other as a result of their similar relationship to X, an effect that has been demonstrated by Aronson and Cope (1968). The other reason is that X will often become active as an informal mediator, trying to reconcile any differences that develop between A and B, urging each side to avoid escalation, and providing an avenue of communication between the two sides.

Third parties often assume the role of mediator because they see conflict between friends, relatives, or allies as a threat. Such conflict disturbs the peace and endangers group unity and effectiveness. There is also an ever-present danger that both antagonists will press the third party to join their side and become resentful if the third party is reluctant to do so. Illustrative of these points are the constant efforts by the United States to mediate controversies between the nations in its orbit, such as those between Israel and the Arab states.

In case 2, parties A and B are antagonistic to party X—they share a common antipathy toward the third party. This should also increase the stability of the A-B relationship, for two reasons. One is the point made earlier that perceived similarity encourages the development of psychological bonds. The other is the need that may well arise for a common effort against X.

In case 3, there is a bond between parties A and X and antagonism between B and X. Here we can predict the development of antagonism and consequent instability in the A-B relationship. This is partly because A and B perceive dissimilarity in their attitudes toward X. It is also because X is likely to put pressure on A to join the campaign against B.

Four-Party Systems

Several more predictions are possible if we add a fourth party (Y) to the system just described. Excluding the relationship between A and B

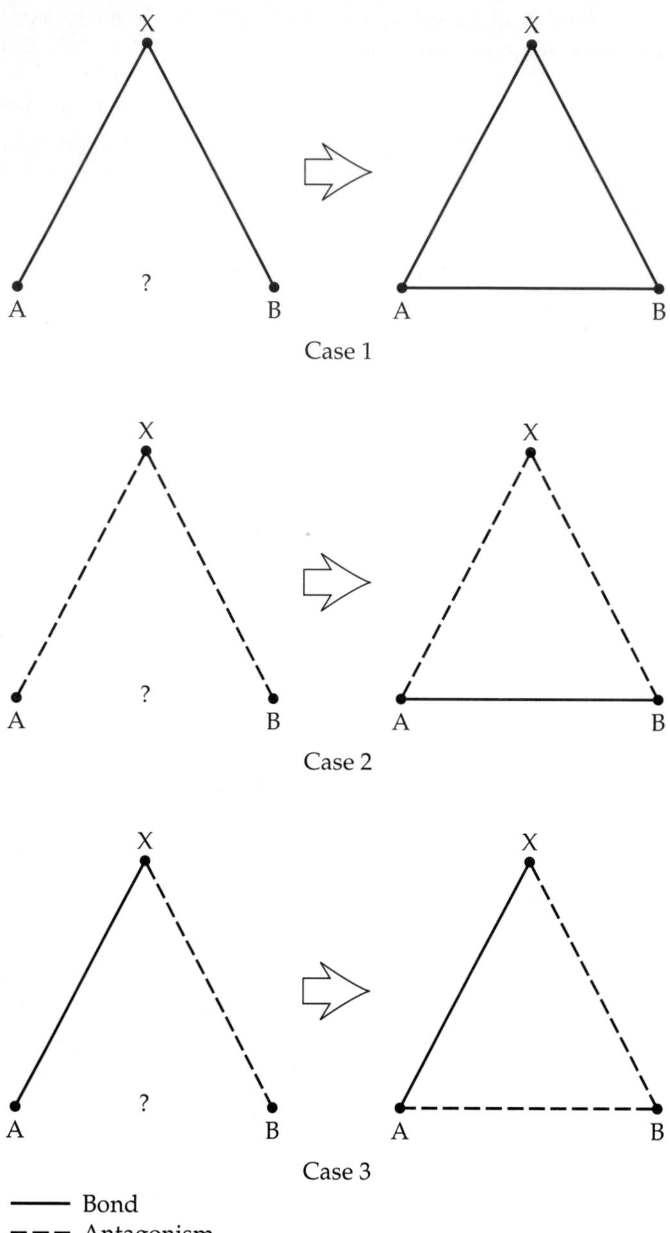

FIGURE 8.2
Predictions for some three-party systems. (In each case, the diagram on the right shows the bond or antagonism between parties A and B that is predicted from the diagram on the left.)

(whose nature is the item to be predicted), there are six possible configurations of bonds and antagonisms in such a four-party system. We shall examine only two of these configurations (shown in Figure 8.3), leaving the others for the reader to figure out. Both involve a bond between A and X and a similar bond between B and Y. In other words, A and X are friends or allies, as are B and Y. The question is how the X-Y relationship will affect the stability of the relationship between A and B.

In case 4, where X and Y are positively bonded, we can predict stability in the A-B relationship (Rubin, 1971). There are two reasons for this. One resides in the principle of balance: the friend of my friend is my friend. The other results from the activities of X and Y, who are likely to be motivated to try to solve problems between A and B *so as to protect their own relationship*. This relationship will be in jeopardy if conflict persists

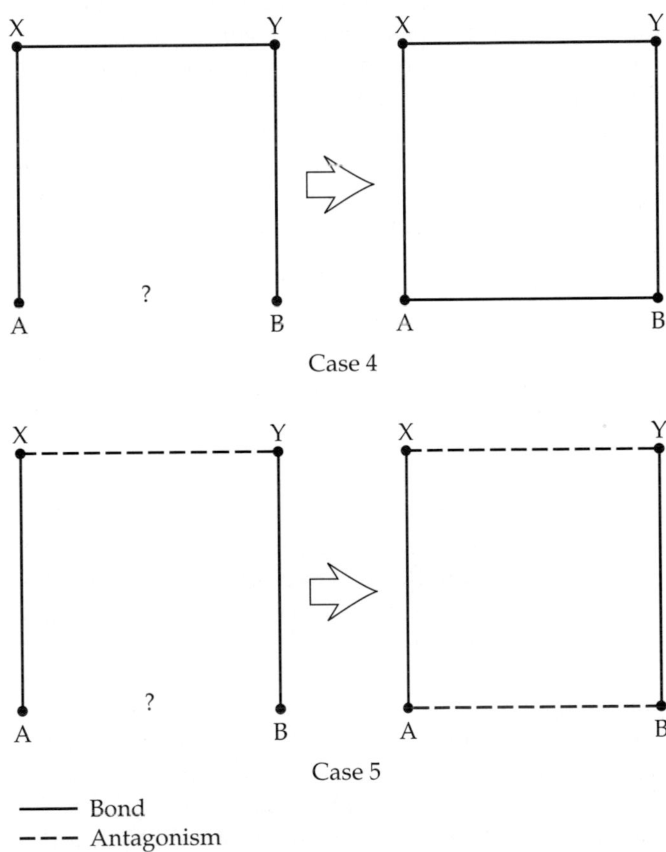

FIGURE 8.3
Predictions for some four-party systems. (In each case, the diagram on the right shows what is predicted from the diagram on the left.)

between A and B, because each of them is likely to experience pressure to join the side to which it is closer.

In case 5, where X and Y are antagonistic, we can predict instability in the A-B relationship and a tendency to escalate if conflicts develop. This is partly because of the principle of balance, and partly because X and Y can be expected to try to create antagonism between A and B in order to have more reliable allies in their struggle with each other.

Stability in Larger Communities

The points just made about three- and four-party systems can be used to explain stability in larger communities. Such communities may consist of two or more unrelated groups, or there may be varying degrees of cross-cutting memberships between groups.

Consider first the case of two groups (A and C) whose members have little or no relationship with each other. This is shown schematically as case 6 in Figure 8.4. There is considerable escalation potential in such a situation, for two reasons. First, the very existence of discriminable groups encourages the development of negative attitudes (Tajfel, 1970). Antagonism tends to develop between any two groups that are aware of, and lack bonds with, one another. The other reason is that a conflict between any two members of these rival groups is likely to polarize the situation. Because of case 5 dynamics, others from each group often join in the fray, producing a larger conflict. Barroom brawls sometimes develop this way. Two people get into an argument, then are joined by their friends, producing a large-scale struggle.[16] This process is more likely to occur when there have been earlier controversies between the groups—in other words, when there has been previous community polarization.

Coleman (1957) gives examples of two kinds of communities containing groups that have no bonds to each other but that interact often enough for conflicts to develop: (1) New England towns in which old Yankees are closely tied to one another but have few ties with Italian immigrants and (2) resort towns in which year-round residents view themselves as a group apart from seasonal transients. When conflict develops in such towns, the community tends to polarize, producing heavy escalation.

There are four methods for combating polarization in such communities. One is to try to strengthen *loyalty to the broader community*—that is, to forge sentimental bonds between the two groups by making them feel part of the same larger group. Flags and national anthems serve this function in the nation-state. The second is to install or strengthen a *central authority*. This is the conventional governmental approach to instability. If positive relations can be established between the central authority and each of the groups, this encourages stability via case 1 dynamics. If not,

[16]Or consider the battle between the Sharks and the Jets in Leonard Bernstein's musical, *West Side Story*.

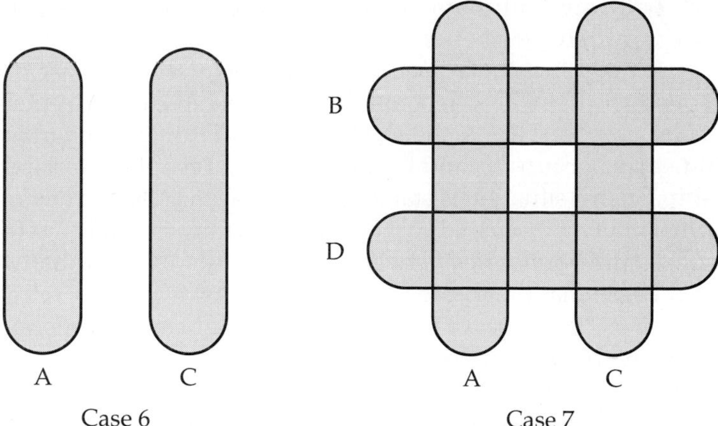

FIGURE 8.4.
Case 6 shows two unrelated groups; case 7, the same two groups (A and C) with crosscutting by two other groups (B and D).

the central authority may have to use force to prevent escalation. The third method is to foster *antagonism with an outside enemy*, making use of case 2 dynamics. An example is the Argentine occupation of the Falkland/Malvinas Islands in 1982, which appears to have been designed to unify a divided domestic polity around a patriotic issue.[17]

The fourth way to combat polarization in a divided community is to encourage the development of bonds between individuals on both sides, making use of case 4 dynamics. This method is used whenever ruling groups incorporate *(co-opt)* members of agitating factions into their decision making. Likert (1961) recommends the use of this method in organizations, urging that interdepartmental committees be formed involving representatives of conflicting departments. Membership in such committees will give these representatives a common group identity, and committee meetings will allow them to engage in problem solving about matters of common concern. Such representatives are called *linking pins.* A similar method was used by royal families in the past when they arranged for their sons and daughters to marry foreign princesses and princes in an effort to achieve peaceful relations with other countries.

Such procedures produce a small cadre of people in each group who oppose the use of heavy contentious tactics and are ready to serve as mediators when conflict arises between the groups. This solution moves in the direction of crosscutting group memberships. If one linking pin on

[17]Development of the disastrous escalation in Bosnia and Croatia can be partly explained by the reduced importance both of a central authority (the government of Yugoslavia) and an external enemy (the Soviet Union).

each side can contribute to community stability, two should be better and two hundred even better.

A diagram of a crosscutting system is shown as case 7 in Figure 8.4. Four groups are depicted, but the analysis can easily be extended to many more groups. Two of the groups (B and D) in the diagram crosscut the other two groups (A and C), in the sense of having overlapping membership. Such a situation is stable for two reasons. One is the familiar balance phenomenon discussed earlier: a friend of my friend is my friend. Balance fuzzes the boundaries between groups A and C (and between groups B and D), so that the members of these groups feel closer to each other than in case 6. The power of this mechanism has been demonstrated in a study that involved perceptual crosscutting but no real contact between the groups (Vanbeselaere, 1991). The other reason for the success of crosscutting has to do with efforts by people in the crosscutting groups (B and D) to resolve tensions when they arise between Groups A and C.

Crosscutting provides stability in both dimensions. Conflicts between groups A and C are held in check by crosscutting memberships in groups B and D, and conflicts between B and D are held in check by crosscutting memberships in A and C.

Gluckman (1955) provides two anthropological examples of crosscutting. He found that when a Nuer man moves away from his hometown, he becomes a mediator in quarrels between his relatives and residents of his new location. He probably has two motives for doing so. One is the fear of retribution from his new neighbors, causing him to urge caution on his kin. The other is that "he is likely to urge his kin to offer compensation, since he has many interests in the place where he resides" (p. 12). Gluckman also points out that marriage produces stability in those African societies in which the wife must move to her husband's village. Thereafter, she exerts a calming influence whenever there is conflict between her original village and that to which she has moved. Both examples illustrate crosscutting because the person who has moved becomes a member of both groups.

Closer to home, the United States today can be regarded as a heavily crosscutting system. For example, regional rivalries (e.g., northeast vs. southeast) are held in check by the fact that there are thousands of strong nationwide organizations, such as the Republican party and the Catholic church. There is also heavy crosscutting between social classes. And so on. In such a system, few subsets of people can form an unambivalent alliance against any other subset. A possible exception is the alignment of African Americans and whites in our society, because there are relatively few bonds between these groups. In this context, the civil rights movement, with its effort to introduce African Americans into every institution of our society, can be seen as a massive program to develop crosscutting bonds and the stability that goes with them, as well as to make our society more fair.

There is one other wrinkle to the theory of crosscutting group memberships—a paradoxical one. In a crosscutting situation, mild conflict between social groups can actually contribute to the overall stability of the community, making severe conflict less likely. Imagine a community of Yankees and Italians in which some people from each ethnic group are managers (and belong to management associations and clubs) and others are laborers (and belong to unions). A little conflict between management and labor should make it more difficult for Yankee-Italian antagonisms to escalate, because Yankees and Italians have served together on both sides of the industrial battle line and recognize that they may need to do so again. Likewise, a little conflict between Yankees and Italians tend to diminish the intensity of future conflict between labor and management. Hence—and this is the crucial point—if there has been a little conflict in both sets of groupings, severe controversy is likely to be avoided in both. Almost everybody in the community recognizes almost everybody else as a past or potential future ally.[18]

An example of this can be seen in the United States Congress. Coalitions change from issue to issue in this body, so antagonisms usually do not run very deep. Members maintain decorous relations with one another and observe many informal conflict-limiting norms in order to be able to work together in future coalitions. Today it may be the farm states against the manufacturing states, tomorrow north against south, the next day those who want to maintain military spending against those who want to cut it. One never knows whose help may be needed in a future conflict, so it is foolish to let current differences get out of hand.[19]

Crosscutting systems like those just described are highly resistant to escalation. But no system is completely escalation-proof. A really severe conflict of interest between two groups can break through any bonds, however secure, producing a runaway escalation and a set of antagonisms that may take years to repair.

Community Size and Social Geography

In the 1960s, at the height of the African American and student movements, statistical evidence showed that there were more racial blowups in large cities than in small, and more severe campus demonstrations on large campuses (such as UB) than on small. This can be explained in terms

[18]In addition, mild controversy sometimes contributes to the development of institutions (such as representative committees and mediation services) that stand ready to resolve more serious future controversies. This is a case of residues in the service of stability.

[19]Although crosscutting memberships reduce the likelihood of heavy contentious behavior between groups, they are not always beneficial to society as a whole. Society needs active competition between certain groups. For example, society must resist the development of interlocking directorates among corporations that produce the same kind of product, because of the need for competition between these corporations (Schoorman et al., 1981).

of social geography. More people know each other in small than in large communities, so bonds are closer and bond chains shorter. There is more opportunity for communication and problem solving, and less temptation to employ heavy contentious tactics.

Summary

Communities often provide conflict-limiting norms and institutions, which encourage disputants to avoid escalation. The concept of bonding can be extended to relationships between disputants and members of the community to which they belong. Stability in larger communities is encouraged by crosscutting group memberships, in which everyone is linked in some way to everyone else. Paradoxically, a certain amount of conflict in such a system can strengthen the stability of the system as a whole. Bonds tend to be weaker in larger communities, making such communities more vulnerable to escalated conflict.

STABILITY THROUGH THREATS

The mechanisms discussed so far (conflict-limiting norms and institutions, fear of escalation, social bonds, crosscutting group memberships) can have tremendous force, accounting for the quiet way in which most conflicts are pursued and the high rate of peaceful conflict resolution ordinarily found in human affairs. However, these mechanisms are not always strong enough to avert escalation. There may be danger of escalation for any of the following reasons:

- There may be so little perceived common ground, and the issues involved in a conflict may be so important, that the temptation to take harsh contentious action overwhelms all constraints.
- The people involved may be poorly socialized, or the norms governing them may be unclear or ineffective.
- The institutions for third party conflict resolution may be weak, as in frontier or center city areas where courts have little enforcement capability or are nonexistent.
- The people involved may have had no recent experience with a frightening crisis that would make them fear new escalation.
- The groups may be so large and self-sufficient, or at such a vast social distance, that the bonds between them are weak or nonexistent.

Under such circumstances, it may seem necessary for Party to use *threats and punitive action* to deter Other from employing harsh tactics.

Dramatic forms of threat and punishment can be seen in the apprehension and incarceration of violent criminals. Even more dramatic are the actions of nations to protect themselves against external aggression.

The circumstances just listed characterize much of international relations. Hence, most nations arm themselves against potential enemies, issue threats if there is apparent danger of attack, and go to war if they or their allies are attacked. Similar circumstances are sometimes found in fragmented domestic communities, such as frontier regions and dilapidated urban environments, where people arm themselves and sometimes engage in fierce battles.

Less obvious, but nevertheless of vast social significance, are the subtle threats and small penalties that all human interactions exhibit. All people have means of imposing costs on those around them. Children cry, workers move slowly, wives get angry, and husbands come home late. Most people are also adept at subtly signaling their discontent: the slow response to a statement, the lapse of attention, the lifted eyebrow, the frown, the sigh. These signals are tantamount to stating a full-blown threat, in that the recipients realize that punitive action will be forthcoming if they are not careful. In short, threats and penalties that are aimed at deterring others from taking bothersome actions are omnipresent in social relationships.

As we saw in Chapter 4, for a threat to be effective, the punishment threatened must be large enough to outweigh the benefits of noncompliance. The threat must also be credible—that is, believable. There are two kinds of credibility: credibility of capability and credibility of intent (Pruitt & Snyder, 1969). The former can be defined as the extent to which Party seems capable of carrying out its threats; the latter, as the extent to which it seems willing to carry them out. A threat need not always be 100 percent credible to be effective. The larger the damage threatened, the less credibility is needed, because Other will be less likely to take chances.

The Balance of Power

Several theories of threat-induced stability have been developed for international affairs, where other sources of stability are often at their weakest. The oldest and most famous of these theories is *balance of power*. This theory can be adapted so that it is broadly applicable to the use of threats in all social situations.

In one interpretation of this theory, a balance of power exists when all nations in a system are deterred for military reasons from attacking all others. Assuming conventional (nonnuclear) weapons, deterrence is a function of the existence of natural and artificial barriers to attack, the military capability of the target of a potential attack, and the assistance it can recruit from other nations. These are effective as deterrents either by making it impossible for aggression to succeed or by imposing unacceptable costs on an aggressor.

There are several mechanisms by which a balance of power can be achieved. Collective security, in which all other nations come to the rescue of a nation under attack, is often regarded as the ideal mechanism. Such a mechanism was built into the charter of the United Nations and was realized, to some extent, in the campaign against Iraq during the Gulf War. But collective security has been difficult to activate in most controversies, because some nations sympathize with one side and some with the other.

Barring collective security, nations that are faced with a militarily capable opponent try to maintain or restore the balance of power by arming themselves and seeking allies. Some analysts argue that the most stable situation is one in which all potential opponents are equal in military strength; others argue that the least aggressive nations must have a preponderance of military strength (Claude, 1962). The existence of a balancer nation contributes to both kinds of stability. Balancers are nations that change alliances from time to time in order to side with the underdog. In earlier times, England played the role of balancer in the European system of nations.

The following four conditions probably contribute to the international balance of power:

1. *Having a large number of nations in a system.* The argument usually given for this assertion (Deutsch & Singer, 1964; Kaplan, 1957) is that with more nations, a greater variety of coalitions can be formed. Hence, there are more ways to develop coalitions against would-be aggressors.
2. *Freedom of action among government leaders.* Leaders must have considerable autonomy to be able to execute the fine maneuvers involved in shifting alliances in order to restore the balance (Gulick, 1955). The greatest departure from freedom comes when the nations in a system are linked in two tight alliances, so that none of them can change sides and there are no potential mediators (Kaplan, 1957). This is a condition of severe community polarization.
3. *The absence of extreme hostility between nations.* If hostility is too great, it is not possible to join one's old adversaries in an alliance against an emerging aggressor.
4. *Measurability of military capacity.* When military capacity can be measured accurately in terms that are understood by all, it is possible to estimate the strength of arms and the size of a coalition that will deter a would-be aggressor (Lasswell, 1950). When this measurement is not possible, as when different sorts of weapons systems are found on each side, defensive coalitions may prove

inadequate, or potential aggressors may launch an attack on the basis of an erroneous assessment of their own strength.

Regardless of which mechanism is involved (collective security, equality, preponderance of peace-loving nations, or alliance shifts by balancers), a balance of power will be more effective when the military advantage lies with the defender rather than the aggressor. The greater the apparent military advantage of striking first, the more likely is escalation. Such situations are unstable for two reasons: (1) because of the temptation to strike first; and (2) because of fear that another nation is about to strike first, which can motivate a preemptive first strike.

A highly unstable situation of this kind existed in 1914, when it was believed that the first European nation to mobilize could gain a major advantage over its neighbor by loading its troops onto trains and rushing them to the border for a massive assault. The result of this instability was the First World War. This war began when Russia, attempting to deter an Austrian attack on Serbia, mobilized troops along its southern border. Germany, perceiving that this mobilization put it at a military disadvantage, launched a preemptive attack against Russia's ally, France, striking through Belgium.

Balance-of-power theory can be translated into other arenas of human interaction. For example, small groups, such as interdepartmental committees or families, must deter overly aggressive members who attack others or try to dominate discussions. Collective security is not uncommon in such situations, with all other group members forming a temporary coalition against the aggressor.[20] Barring this, smaller coalitions of like-minded individuals often form, and the members of each coalition support one another so that none can be overwhelmed. If two tight alliances form within such a group, the situation is likely to become quite unstable because even minor conflicts will produce rapid community polarization. The situation will be more stable if a few people act as balancers, forever shifting to the defense of the underdog. The role of balancer is frequently played by the group leader.

Balance of Power in the Nuclear Age

The development of nuclear weapons has forced some changes in thinking about the balance of power in international affairs. These weapons are fantastically destructive and there is no real defense against them. The only way to protect oneself militarily is to threaten to retaliate in the hope of deterring the other side from using these weapons. Such retaliation is called a *second strike*. It follows that a critical issue for stability is second-

[20]Recall that Mom and Sis took sides with Ben in the Chapter 1 story.

strike credibility: how believable it is that an aggressor will be destroyed.

According to *deterrence theory*, efforts to establish credibility must take somewhat different forms depending on whether the nation attacked has nuclear weapons or is the ally of a nuclear nation (Kahn, 1960). It is ordinarily assumed that nuclear nations under nuclear attack will retaliate in kind if they can. Hence, only second-strike capability is considered to be at issue—that is, whether the nation can retaliate after suffering a nuclear first strike. In contrast, in the deterrence of attack against a nonnuclear ally, intentions are the main issue. Will the nuclear nation run the risk of a devastating counterattack from the aggressor by actually retaliating? Willingness to come to the defense of an ally has always been an issue, even in strictly conventional contests; but it is more difficult to establish the credibility of intent in the age of nuclear weapons, because the cost of retaliation is so much greater.

Second-strike capability is believed to depend on the security of the carriers (missiles and planes) of nuclear weapons and on their capacity to penetrate the adversary's defenses. The security of weapons carriers can be achieved in a variety of ways, including increasing their numbers, dispersing them, moving them frequently, concealing them, and shielding them. For example, several major powers have nuclear weapons constantly on the move in submarines that are virtually impossible to locate and destroy.

Provided that its second-strike capability is secure, a nation can afford to have dramatically less capability than its adversary and still be secure within its borders. The United States is way "ahead" of Russia in destructive capacity, but there is little evidence that the Russians are worried about an attack. Despite the inequality, there is a stable nuclear "balance of terror."[21]

Problems with Basing Stability on Threats

There are many problems with efforts to base stability on threats, and hence with reliance on balance-of-power approaches. Such approaches assume that it is possible to clearly communicate Party's resolve to a potential aggressor. Yet history reveals many failures in this regard (Lebow et al., 1984). These approaches also assume that a would-be aggressor will be rational, able to predict accurately, and ready to avoid taking action if the risks are high or the probability of success is low.

It follows that threat-based deterrents are likely to fail and escalation to materialize in international relations when the responsible decision

[21]It can be argued that the credibility of Party's willingness to protect allies depends heavily on the strength of its bonds to these allies. Hence, trade, travel, and statements of friendship with allies may help to deter attacks against them.

makers (1) are mentally or emotionally incapacitated, and so unable to use the information available to them; (2) regard the military future as so bleak or the military balance as changing so fast against them that they feel they have little to lose by aggressing; or (3) are impelled by foreign or domestic political interests of such gravity that they are willing to take large risks in a military adventure. Lebow, Jervis, and Stein (1984) cite the Japanese attack on Pearl Harbor and two Egyptian attacks on Israel as examples of the latter condition. What happened, they contend, is that under the pressure of compelling political considerations, national leaders engaged in wishful thinking about the likelihood of winning a war.

The instability of threat-based systems can also be seen in domestic settings. Consider, for example, the impoverished section of Los Angeles portrayed in John Singleton's brilliant film *Boyz n the Hood* (mentioned earlier in the chapter). Intent on impressing local audiences and with little thought for the future, two young men get into a shoving and shouting match. The quarrel is continued by their friends and relatives—most prominently, by a man whose life and future are so empty that he seems unafraid of the consequences of violence. The local authorities are worse than useless, confining their activities to noisemaking and assaults that keep everyone in a high state of autonomic arousal. Eventually a series of shootings take place, eliminating most of the main characters in the movie.

Another problem with the use of threat-based deterrents is that they actually encourage escalation. They involve "fighting fire with fire"; hence, they run the risk of contributing to a conflict spiral. This means that threat-based deterrents are capable of producing the very problem they are designed to avoid. There are three reasons for this. One is that Party's threats tend to challenge Other's image of independence and strength, producing resentment. This problem is particularly acute when there is a moderate (as opposed to a large) difference in power between Party and Other, because the more powerful party often feels free to employ threats while the less powerful one refuses to acknowledge its inferiority and becomes resistant or belligerent (Pruitt & Carnevale, 1993). The problem is less acute when the threats are consistent with social norms and therefore at least moderately legitimate, as in the case of most threats of retaliation. Yet even such threats are likely to produce some resentment.

A second reason for escalation is that deterrent threats are often misinterpreted by Other (Jervis, 1976). An army mobilized to resist invasion may be misconstrued as an instrument of potential aggression. Missiles designed only for a second strike may be seen as a first-strike capability. A boys' gang organized to protect its members may seem to threaten another gang's "turf." Such perceptions produce defensive counterreactions that tend to start (or continue) a conflict spiral.

The third reason for escalation is that even if it is clear that Party's preparations have defensive motives, Other may still be cautious lest

Party later adopt aggressive motives. Hence, Other may feel the need to attack in order to diminish Party's capacity to do harm at a later time.

What can be done to avoid such interpretations and misinterpretations of defensive preparations? Party can carefully explain its behavior, trying to tie it action by action to Other's behavior so that Party is seen as essentially reactive. Furthermore, preparations that are clearly defensive and cannot be converted to offensive use should be favored, for example, building a wall or wearing a bulletproof vest. It may also be possible to couple the carrot with the stick, offering punishment for aggression and reward for cooperation. This works because the carrot both provides Other an avenue for goal achievement that does not require aggression and makes it harder for Other to believe that Party is preparing for aggression. Efforts to diminish tensions in other realms are also in order, so as to reduce the likelihood that Other will view Party's military efforts through the prism of anger and indignation (White, 1984).

Such procedures are sometimes effective, but threats are so often problematic that it seems preferable to avoid them altogether and to substitute other forms of conflict management, such as positive bonds, the building of social norms, and efforts to find solutions to the issues in dispute.

Summary

By threatening to retaliate, Party can sometimes deter Other from employing harsh contentious tactics, thereby reducing the likelihood of escalation. Part of the success of this tactic depends on the credibility of the threats used. Extending this notion, it can be argued that two or more parties are safe from conflict escalation when a balance of power exists, such that every party is defended or able to retaliate in the face of aggression. The problem with this reasoning is that it assumes that (1) threats will be adequately communicated; (2) decision makers will be perceptive and rational, and not so impelled by other considerations as to lose sight of the risks they are facing; and (3) threats will not produce the very escalation they are designed to avoid. Hence, other methods for discouraging escalation are preferable to the use of threats, if such methods are available.

CONCLUSIONS

Events as dramatic as the Cold War, the UB crisis, and the travail of Michael Kohlhaas are unusual. But escalation is all around us; any conflict can become intensified. A number of conditions increase or reduce stability, that is, the likelihood and extent of escalation during conflict. These include features of the individuals, groups, relationships, and communities involved. Many of the points in this chapter follow logically from the three process models described in Chapters 5 through 7, and we challenge the reader to come up with more derivations.

In escalating conflict, it is clearly easier to squeeze the toothpaste out of the tube than to put it back in. Once started, heavy escalation tends to be self-reinforcing. Yet we know that conflicts do not continue escalating forever. At some point (if the parties are still alive), the turmoil subsides and conflict begins to abate. Chapter 9 examines the transitional circumstances that make it possible for escalation to stop and for settlement of conflict to begin.

9

Stalemate and De-Escalation

Why Conflicts Stop Escalating • Why Stalemate Occurs • How De-Escalation Begins • *Stalemate and Negotiation in the Middle East* • *Negotiation and Face Saving* • Getting Unstuck • *Contact and Communication* • *Cooperation on Other Issues: Superordinate Goals* • *A Note on Third Party Intervention* • *Unilateral Conciliatory Initiatives* • *The Constructive Use of Entrapment* • Conclusions

In the last several chapters we have told the story of how and why conflicts escalate. We have seen some of the many ingenious ways in which Party manages to exploit Other in an effort to prevail in a competitive struggle, and we have charted the processes that drive and perpetuate conflict escalation. At some point, however, *escalation always ends.* Why and how this happens is the subject of this chapter. In addition, an important transition often occurs, bridging the end of escalation with the earliest moves toward conflict settlement. The nature of this transition is also of interest here.

To be sure, *not all* conflicts are addressed through contentious strategy and tactics. Many, perhaps most, conflicts move to solution through problem solving, outright yielding, or avoidance. Furthermore, *not all* conflicts in which contentious tactics are used lead to escalation. Party may give in or may realize that contentious tactics spell destructive consequences. And *not all* escalating conflict becomes severe or persists. The many powerful and effective pressures toward stability may restrain antagonists from excessive head bloodying, producing the light escalatory pathway represented by curve A in Figure 8.1.

Having said this, we turn our attention to the *other* curve in Figure 8.1, curve B. Here conflict continues to escalate despite the availability of more productive strategic alternatives. Even here, we will argue, there is room for hope. For if it is sadly the case that most good things eventually come to an end, it is happily true that most bad things come to an end as well. People in a heavily escalated exchange can do only so much damage to each other, and for only so long.

WHY CONFLICTS STOP ESCALATING

Imagine two children arguing about whose turn it is to use a shiny new bicycle. The argument continues back and forth as the conflict between the two children keeps escalating. At some point this escalation stops, typically for one of five possible reasons.[1]

First, Party succeeds in *overwhelming* Other, as when one child grabs the bicycle away from the other and fends off all efforts to take it back. As another example, recall the prison fight described in Chapter 5 (Toch, 1970). While the prisoner who lost the fight was undoubtedly most unhappy about the outcome, the two men who beat him up clearly felt otherwise. The conflict stopped escalating because Party had prevailed.

Second, Party is able to take *unilateral advantage* of Other. Suppose that one of the two children quarrelling over the bike (Party) simply ends the conflict by climbing onto the bike's leather seat and riding off into the sunset. Party is far happier with the outcome than Other, and the conflict stops escalating—not because Other is overwhelmed but because Party has taken advantage of the situation.

Third, Party *yields* to Other, giving Other what it wants, as when one child simply hands the bicycle over to the other. For one reason or another, Party no longer finds the conflict (or its escalation) acceptable and ends it through the mirror image of contending—namely, yielding.

Fourth, Party *avoids* the conflict—for example, by withdrawing from it. This would be the case if one of the children were simply to turn to some other activity, surrendering the bicycle by default (perhaps because of loss of interest, perhaps because of some other reason). As before, the conflict ends because Party finds it unacceptable.

Finally—and this is the reason we will want to explore in more detail—Party (and often Other) comes to regard the conflict as intolerable, as

[1]Note that the first four reasons correspond to the strategies of contending (the first and second reasons), yielding (the third reason), and avoiding (the fourth reason). Stalemate, the fifth reason, and the circumstances that bridge stalemate and problem solving, are the focus of this chapter.

something that should be ended as soon as possible. This is our definition of *stalemate.*

At the point of stalemate, Party cannot or will not escalate the conflict further, although Party may not yet be able or willing to take the actions that will eventually generate an agreement. The point of maximum conflict intensity has been reached. Stalemate is a high-water mark for the conflictual ark. The waters will probably rise no more, nor have they yet begun to subside in de-escalation.

Even in stalemate Party will probably continue to employ contentious tactics in an effort to prevail. Party's behavior, for a while at least, may appear unchanged. But what begins to change is Party's *outlook.* Though Party might like to "knock Other's block clean off," such an outcome is now seen as unattainable. Perhaps Other is refusing to yield. Perhaps Party's resources are flagging. Perhaps Party's costs or risks are becoming unacceptable. Whatever the reason, Party reaches the grudging realization that a stalemate has been reached and that it hurts more to continue the conflict than to settle it. Out of such a realization emerge the elements of conflict reduction or resolution, especially if Other comes to the same realization.

WHY STALEMATE OCCURS

There are four major reasons for the emergence of stalemate: failure of contentious tactics, exhaustion of necessary resources, loss of social support, and unacceptable costs. Contentious tactics that were used with some success in the past may begin to fail because they have lost their bite. Perhaps Party has tried once too often to ruffle feathers, threaten, or commit itself to some irreversible position, and Other no longer finds such moves believable or worth heeding. Another possibility is that, like two people who have lived together for many years, the adversaries have come to know each other's moves and gestures so well that it is no longer possible to seize the advantage. Each move has its properly orchestrated, well-learned countermove; thrust and parry fit neatly together.

Exhaustion of the resources necessary to continue the struggle is also related to the failure of contentious tactics to work as intended. Like two boxers, bloodied and weakened after many rounds of pounding each other against the ropes, one or both disputants in an escalating conflict simply run out of steam. There is no lack of determination to defeat Other, nor is there lack of insight into the necessary moves. Party would still like nothing more than to knock Other out and snatch a last-minute victory. But it just isn't possible. The verbal and tactical blows that once landed with such force and effect now have little impact on an adversary who is similarly weakened. Would that those arms could be raised once more to deliver a coup de grace, but by now they are heavy with fatigue.

There are several sorts of resources that may be exhausted as Party enters a stalemate. One, suggested by the prizefighter analogy, is *energy*—the physical and/or psychological stamina necessary to sustain continued struggle. Another important resource in many competitive struggles is *money*—the ability to sustain the continued financial costs incurred by investment in those tangibles used to wage competition. For example, in the dollar auction game (see Chapter 7), when bidders have no more funds to continue their struggle, the auction is over. When both combatants' supply lines are cut, the battle must come to an end. Finally, *time* in and of itself is often a limited resource which, once exhausted, forces the adversaries into stalemate. As the hands of the clock march toward midnight, the protagonists may feel uncomfortably close to a point of no return.[2]

Related to the exhaustion of resources is the possibility that Party is forced into stalemate because of diminishing social support. People in conflict often rely on the support of constituencies or backers in order to sustain a competitive struggle. Labor and management negotiators can persist in their bargaining only so long as they continue to have the endorsement—passive though it may be—of the organizations they represent. International diplomats, as the news media continually remind us, are limited and occasionally hamstrung by lack of support back home. Even prizefighters are best thought of not as individuals but as representatives of financial and social interests; and whether to continue fighting is typically not the fighter's decision alone. Thus, escalating conflicts often end in stalemate because Party is no longer able to secure the support of a necessary constituency.

Finally, there are important occasions when stalemate occurs because Party suspects that the costs associated with continued struggle will be so great that further escalation must be avoided. Perhaps constituents are complaining that wealth is being exhausted or protesting that lives are being lost. Possibly, new issues and people are about to become involved that will poison (or further poison) the broader relationship with Other.

One stalemate engendered by such cost estimates on both sides was the Cuban missile crisis of 1962. Several months prior to the crisis, the Soviet Union had begun to send shipments of medium-range missiles and nuclear warheads to the island of Cuba, with the clear and unmistakable intention of targeting these weapons, once assembled, at the major urban centers of the eastern United States. The crisis itself began

[2]Hostage taking often results in stalemate because of the exhaustion of resources. The kidnappers may have run out of supplies, the target government (subjected to media and public pressure) may have run out of time—and the result is a negotiation (Faure & Shakun, 1988; Friedland, 1986; Rubin & Friedland, 1986).

when incontrovertible photographic evidence of this activity was brought to the attention of President John F. Kennedy. The President responded by threatening to impose a naval blockade of all Soviet shipments to Cuba unless the Russians immediately stopped all further shipments and destroyed those weapons and sites already on the island. The response was Soviet silence. The stage was set for one of the most dramatic superpower confrontations in the history of either nation.

President Kennedy announced that the naval blockade would be put into effect on Wednesday, October 24. American cruisers and aircraft carriers were dispatched to the waters off Cuba. As 10 A.M. approached, two Russian ships were detected, proceeding toward the 500-mile quarantine barrier. The two ships, the *Gagarin* and the *Komiles,* neared the boundary; a Russian submarine had moved into position between them. The American carrier *Essex* was ordered to signal the submarine to surface and identify itself; if it refused, depth charges were to be used.

The President's brother, Robert F. Kennedy, who was at his side during these events, described them in some detail in his moving history, *Thirteen Days* (1969):

> I think these few minutes were the time of gravest concern for the President. Was the world on the brink of holocaust? Was it our error? A mistake? Was there something further that should have been done? Or not done? His hand went up to his face and covered his mouth. He opened and closed his fist. His face seemed drawn, his eyes pained, almost gray. . . . We had come to the time of final decision. (pp. 69–70)

At 10:25 came the message that the Russian ships had stopped dead in the water. The President immediately issued an order that no Russian ships were to be stopped or intercepted, giving the ships ample opportunity to turn back. RFK concludes:

> Then we were back to the details. The meeting droned on. But everyone looked like a different person. For a moment the world had stood still, and now it was going around again. (p. 72)

The United States and the Soviet Union had ample opportunity and ample resources to continue waging their contentious struggle off the shores of Cuba in October, 1962. The probable costs of doing so, however, were perceived by each to be so great that continued struggle was not possible. The result was a classic stalemate, in which each side had carried the escalation as far as it dared go. In the aftermath of this eyeball-to-eyeball confrontation, steps were set in motion that led to an agreement by which the United States promised not to invade Cuba, in exchange for a Soviet commitment to withdraw and/or destroy its missiles in Cuba.[3]

HOW DE-ESCALATION BEGINS

Thus far we have described the reasons for stalemate—that is, the reasons why Party might conclude that a conflict is intolerable and should be ended as soon as possible. But what happens next, once stalemate is reached?

At first, probably very little. Party has come to the grudging realization that it cannot prevail, yet it is also unwilling to cede victory to Other through yielding or withdrawal. Party is likely to be entrapped, feeling that it has invested too much energy and ego in the struggle to quit now. Yielding even a jot would be a blow to Party's pride and would run the risk of profound humiliation. Withdrawal, the other option, would be tantamount to capitulation; hence, it would also be unacceptable.

What's left is problem solving. The question is how to get there. Party is stuck, and probably blames Other for its misfortune. But Party has also come to understand that it cannot get what it wants without Other's consent. It is clear that such consent will be forthcoming *only* if Party can advance a proposal that Other will find acceptable.

The most important consequence of stalemate, then, is that Party is forced into a grudging acceptance of Other as an interdependent partner with whom some quid pro quo will have to be worked out. Other is not a friend with whom collaboration is a welcome opportunity but a despised enemy whose cooperation is nevertheless needed. (When asked about Great Britain's decision to form an alliance with the Soviet Union to defeat Nazi Germany, Winston Churchill responded, "To beat the Nazis I would form an alliance with the devil himself.") As Party takes the first tentative steps out of stalemate, it regards Other as the devil that is needed, the enemy who must be catered to and leaned on if the conflict is to be settled.

At the core of interdependence is the awareness that Party and Other have reached a point of relative parity. Sir Isaac Newton observed that for each action there is an equal and opposite reaction. In the language of an escalating conflict, this means that as stalemate is approached, Party's capacity to push Other any further is matched by a corresponding resistance to further yielding on the part of Other. Stalemate occurs because Party

[3]In a recent study of relations between the United States and the (erstwhile) Soviet Union, Patchen (1991) found that the two countries have tended to take cooperative actions and to reciprocate Other's cooperative actions under two conditions: first, when they lacked confidence in their ability to win advantage in competition; and second, when they were concerned about the costs of competition. This finding supports our contention that these conditions encourage impatience with escalation.

perceives that it can neither push Other further nor be pushed any further in return. Stalemate is the stopping point in this process of push and counterpush. Party may have been more powerful than Other at first. But if this power has caused Other to yield, Other's resistance to further yielding is likely to be sufficiently great to outweigh Party's initial advantage. Party and Other are now equal in *effective* power. This opens the door to *negotiation*.[4]

At the risk of oversimplification, we can state that negotiation tends to assume one of two forms in the extreme: Either Party competes eyeball to eyeball with Other, using the instruments of verbal exchange in order to best Other. Or Party makes an effort to work side by side with Other, to solve the problem jointly. Often, although not always, negotiation assumes the first form before moving to the second; that is, negotiation starts out as a contentious exchange and only subsequently evolves into a more collaborative arrangement. As Party tries to wriggle its way out of stalemate, it first uses negotiation for competitive advantage and shifts to problem solving only if contending fails to work.

For Party to become involved in negotiation requires not only a perception of interdependence, but also some faith in the chances of success. To echo a theme begun in Chapter 2, negotiation (including problem solving) seems more feasible to the extent that there is perceived common ground (PCG). Such perceived common ground, in turn, results either from the belief that Party's and Other's aspirations are not too high or too rigid, or from the view that there is potential for the development of integrative alternatives. Without some assurance along these lines, Party may prefer to withdraw rather than engage in a fruitless sequence of negotiating activities. Believing that Other is also in stalemate is often an element of perceived common ground. This means that Other is likely also to want to escape the conflict and may behave quite reasonably if given a chance.

Stalemate and Negotiation in the Middle East

The role of power equivalence and perceived common ground in the creation of stalemate and subsequent negotiation are perhaps nowhere better demonstrated than in the Middle East War of October, 1973. The war be-

[4]A great deal of material has been written about negotiation over the last several decades, ranging from theoretical treatises (see Douglas, 1962; Gulliver, 1979; Kochan, 1980; Lewicki & Litterer, 1985; Morley & Stephenson, 1977; Raiffa, 1982; Schelling, 1960; and Stevens, 1963) to summaries of research (see Carnevale & Pruitt, 1992; Faure, 1987; Kremenyuk, 1991; Mautner-Markhof, 1989; Pruitt, 1981; Pruitt & Carnevale, 1993; Rubin & Brown, 1975) to various efforts to bridge the divide between theory and practice (see Breslin & Rubin, 1991; Fisher & Brown, 1988; Fisher et al., 1991; Goldberg et al., 1992; Hall, 1993; Lax & Sebenius, 1986; Neale & Bazerman, 1991; Raiffa, 1982; Salacuse, 1991; Sjöstedt, 1993; Susskind et al., 1983; Ury, 1991; Zartman, 1994; Zartman & Berman, 1982). While this is not a book about negotiation per se, the topic is clearly pertinent to the de-escalation of conflict.

gan with a stunningly effective surprise attack launched simultaneously by the Egyptians and the Syrians against Israel while most Israelis were observing their religion's holiest day, Yom Kippur. Both the Egyptians and the Syrians made striking advances through territory that had been in Israeli possession since the so-called Six-Day War of 1967—a war in which Israel had seized control of the Sinai Peninsula, the West Bank of the Jordan River, and the strategically important Golan Heights.[5]

American Secretary of State Henry Kissinger seems to have understood the antecedents of negotiation, because he helped orchestrate an outcome to the October War that left Egypt and Israel in a position of relative power equality. In his history of American relations with Israel, Safran (1978) indicates that Kissinger systematically manipulated the flow of arms to Israel during the early days of the October War, deliberately timed American pressure to declare a cease-fire, and timed the American declaration of a worldwide alert (in response to the Soviets' stating their intention to enter the war)—all in order to create a stalemate that was characterized by relative equality and interdependence.

It appears that Kissinger believed the Israelis were so powerful in the wake of the 1967 campaign that they were unlikely to come to the bargaining table. Why should they consider yielding when the other side(s) had so little to offer in return? Egypt and Syria, in turn, had been so badly defeated in 1967 that they could not possibly hope to negotiate successfully with Israel, and they preferred to avoid such a process. The 1973 October War changed all of this. Israel now discovered that it could be defeated (at least temporarily) by a worthy adversary, while Egypt and Syria discovered that they had a few more "teeth" than they had realized. When a cease-fire was struck at the end of thirteen days of vicious fighting, the sense of stalemate on both sides was propitious for subsequent conflict resolution.

In his analysis of this period, Zartman (1981) points out that the Israelis, Egyptians, and Syrians were stalemated at the war's end in a number of ways. For one thing, an Israeli counterattack had completely encircled the Egyptian Third Army, whereas the Israelis themselves were encircled by other Egyptians. At another level, the Israelis had territory (the Sinai) but not the recognition and legitimacy that they desired from their Arab neighbors. For their part, the Egyptians and the Syrians lacked the territory but had the advantage of growing numbers on their side, as well as the ability to withhold recognition of Israel as a legitimate sovereign state. As Zartman writes,

> the 1973 war showed that the Israelis did not always win, nor did the Egyptians always lose. It reversed the fickle play of images under which each side

[5]The war was eventually turned around in Israel's favor, but not before giving the Israelis a bad scare.

> operated, so that even the resounding Israeli comeback and the short-lived quality of the Egyptian and Syrian advances could not destroy this new appreciation of capabilities and potentialities. (p. 150)

Kissinger helped to engineer a stalemate that set the stage for subsequent problem solving. As the hostilities ceased, he moved immediately into high gear, serving for several months as a mediator, shuttling back and forth between Israel and its adversaries. His constant argument was that neither side could hope to move further through force and that their relative equality of power made genuine trade-offs possible. He also chose easy issues to mediate first, thus fostering a sense of momentum in the negotiators. In these ways he kept alive the sense of stalemate and added to it an element of perceived common ground—a belief on the part of the principals that a mutually acceptable agreement could be reached if they would only stay the course with Henry. Zartman (1981) writes of Kissinger's skill in this regard as follows:

> Even as Kissinger was fostering the perception of stalemate, his real tactical skill came from an ability simultaneously to convince the parties that compromise was theoretically possible and that, wherever it lay, such compromise was preferable to the dire alternatives of unilateral action and inaction. (p. 152)[6]

Negotiation and Face Saving

We have been arguing that stalemate leads to de-escalation because Party is tired of escalation, acknowledges its interdependence with Other, and is searching for alternative ways of settling the conflict. Negotiation, particularly of a form that is rather contentious and adversarial, is likely to be a next step, as Party uses the verbal exchange of offers to try extracting concessions to its liking. This is not necessarily the most productive form of negotiation. Problem solving, which we analyze in Chapter 10, is usually a more effective way of moving toward agreement. But a concern about giving something up—about losing face—often stands in the way of more collaborative approaches to negotiation. Even proposing a meeting with Other, let alone offering a possible compromise, may be regarded by Party as conveying an impression of weakness. Party worries that if it seems too eager for settlement, it will be viewed as playing with a losing hand (Pruitt, 1971).

Consider this illustration from the world of championship chess. In

[6]As of this writing, the Middle East peace process has been rekindled yet again. Indeed, one of the reasons that it was possible to get this process under way, after a hiatus of more than a dozen years, is that George Bush's Secretary of State, James Baker, extracted a series of small concessions from the different sides to the conflict, thereby entrapping them in commitment to a conciliatory process.

the early 1970s Bobby Fischer of the United States and Boris Spassky of the Soviet Union participated in a series of classic confrontations in Reykjavik, Iceland, to determine the world chess champion.[7] As one of the early games in the match was drawing near a close, it became clear that neither Fischer nor Spassky had even the slightest chance of winning. Each had been reduced to a king and a pawn, and neither had the board position necessary to queen his pawn. Yet, despite the clear inevitability of a draw, neither player gave even the slightest sign of relenting. The two great chess experts stubbornly refused to show any awareness of each other's presence in the room, not to mention across the board. Instead, as chess commentator Shelby Lyman observed at the time, the two men continued to play "forehead to forehead" (that is, without any eye contact whatsoever).

The moves dragged on, the referee apparently becoming increasingly impatient about the behavior of the two players, whose game was so obviously headed for a draw. Why would neither propose the compromise solution under these circumstances? Apparently because to do so would have been to signal less self-assurance than was shown by one's adversary, thereby possibly weakening one's position in the games that were to come. How was a draw eventually reached? As Lyman tells the story, Fischer and Spassky stopped playing forehead to forehead at precisely the same instant, looked up and into the other's eyes, smiled, simultaneously nodded their heads, and agreed to a draw without saying a word!

The coordination process leading to calling this game a draw can be thought of as a very simple form of negotiation, resulting from the fact that neither party had the capacity to win and leading to a simple compromise agreement. The broader point is that because power equality is often very delicate, the parties to this arrangement are likely to go out of their way to avoid the appearance of having a strong interest in compromise. To show such interest may be to undermine the impression that Party is a tough and opportunistic opponent who cannot be forced into doing things against its will. Far better to wait a while in the hope that some way will emerge to escape from the stalemate than to suffer image loss in the eyes of Other and/or an interested third party.

GETTING UNSTUCK

Quite clearly, stalemate produces a quandary for Party. On the one hand, escaping the conflict seems essential. On the other hand, Party runs the danger of weakening its hand and suffering image loss by moving too vigorously in the direction of settlement. If Other can be induced to seek a

[7]Fischer and Spassky renewed their "clash of the titans" in 1992, albeit for stakes other than the world championship. After a long and uninteresting battle, Fischer prevailed.

solution to the conflict too, there will be much less danger of image loss. How can Party go about producing such changes in Other? Several different approaches are possible, which can be initiated by one or both parties or by a third party who is trying to render assistance.

Contact and Communication

Direct contact between antagonists and the communication that often goes with it can have a number of beneficial effects. First, contact and communication allow Party to explain actions and proposals that might otherwise elicit defensive reactions or retaliation. Second, they contribute to Party's understanding of Other's motives, sensitivities, and the like; this makes it easier to deflate concerns about image loss and to act in ways that will not upset Other. Third, contact and communication permit problem solving in which substantive and procedural issues can be resolved. Without such discussions, the search for a mutually acceptable formula must take the form of trial and error, which has many pitfalls. The surest way to achieve an integrative agreement is through discussion of needs and priorities. Finally, contact and communication contribute to interpersonal attraction, and hence to the development of positive bonds. Research (Festinger et al., 1950; Miller & Brewer, 1984; Miller & Davidson-Podgorny, 1987; Stephan, 1985; Zajonc, 1968) shows that contact encourages attraction more often than antagonism.

Despite their potential advantages, contact and communication should not be regarded as panaceas. Under some circumstances,[8] they tend to be useless or worse than useless (Rubin, 1980). In intense conflict, Party often will not use available communication channels (Deutsch, 1973). Party sees no point in doing so when it distrusts Other and is too angry to consider any solution that is acceptable to Other. When Party uses communication channels, it is often to threaten or try to trick Other rather than to engage in problem solving (Worchel, 1979). Indeed, when Party is severely at odds with Other, communication can be exceedingly explosive, with angry, insulting interchanges. This effect was observed in an experimental boys' camp run by Sherif and Sherif (1953, 1969; Sherif et al., 1961) and in couples locked in distressed relationships (Gottman & Levenson, 1988; Noller & Fitzpatrick, 1990). The boys were separated into cabins and encouraged to frustrate one another, producing considerable antagonism. Thereafter, contact between the cabins led to arguments and name-calling, which served to exacerbate the controversy.

These points qualify the value of contact and communication but do

[8]Among these circumstances is the condition when contacts are competitive and unequal (Aronson, 1988; Pettigrew, 1988; Stephan, 1987).

not completely invalidate these processes. They suggest, for example, that if Party is very angry with Other, a cooling-off period may be needed before communication is productive. Or a mediator may have to shuttle between Party and Other for a period of time, improving mutual images and laying the groundwork for agreement, before direct contact is of value.

Cooperation on Other Issues: Superordinate Goals

After experimenting with a number of unsuccessful approaches to conflict resolution, including the provision of opportunities for communication, Sherif and Sherif hit on a method that succeeded in breaking down the antagonism between the two cabins of boys in their camps. This was to have the boys cooperate on issues other than those involved in the controversy. For example, the counselors arranged for a breakdown in the water supply to the camp. The boys had to work together to disassemble the water tower and carry it to a truck that would take it into town for repair. Performance of these tasks reversed the prior escalation, building bonds between the groups.

The Sherifs call this the *method of superordinate goals,* because it involves development of an objective that is common to both Party and Other and beyond the capability of either alone.[9] Probably the most effective superordinate goals result from the emergence of a common enemy. Such a development was seen in the United States during the Second World War, when the negative sentiments toward the Soviet Union rapidly shifted to positive feelings in the face of the common enemy, Nazi Germany.

Some superordinate goals result from common opportunities for gain rather than common enemies. For example, some young married couples who quarrel decide to have a child so as to develop a common cause. This is seldom a good idea, because children can also put a strain on a relationship and can be the innocent losers if the tactic does not work, but it is a commonly applied "remedy" nevertheless (Rubin & Rubin, 1989).

Having and working on superordinate goals enhances bonds with Other (Johnson et al., 1984). This occurs in a number of ways. One is by the principle of psychological balance—my enemy's enemy is my friend (Aronson & Cope, 1968).[10] Another is by reducing the salience of group boundaries; people who are working toward common goals are in some sense members of the same group and hence are less likely to

[9]Robert Blake and Jane Mouton (1979) demonstrated that superordinate goals also ease conflict between adults and foster cooperation. They put company executives in a situation similar to the one experienced by the young boys in the Sherif experiments, obtaining similar results.

[10]This psychological machinery was analyzed in Chapter 8. See Figure 8.2, in particular.

be antagonistic toward one another (Bettencourt et al., 1992; Coombs, 1987; Turner, 1981).[11] A third is by a reinforcement mechanism; as we work together, each of us rewards the other and produces a sense of gratitude and warmth in the other. Pursuing superordinate goals also means that Party sees itself as working on behalf of Other, a view that is likely to foster positive attitudes toward Other and cut through the concerns with image loss that are often characteristic of stalemate.

The existence of superordinate goals is a powerful contributor to stability under most conditions—but not all. If cooperation toward these goals is unsuccessful (for example, if the common enemy wins), unity may disintegrate and an argument ensue about who is to blame for the loss. This is particularly likely to happen if there was prior tension in the relationship, because previously established images tend to leave residues, as we saw in Chapter 7 (Worchel et al., 1977; Worchel & Norvell, 1980).[12]

How can superordinate goals be developed in conflict situations? Sometimes circumstances force them on Party and Other, as when two nations are attacked by a third. Even a military crisis between two nations can have such an effect if it is sufficiently frightening to both sides. It was shortly after the Cuban missile crisis that the United States and the Soviet Union began to negotiate in earnest the terms of the détente that developed between them. The missile crisis had made nuclear war seem imminent in many people's thinking.

Because the principals in a conflict are so antagonistic toward one another, it is often hard for them to agree on common goals. People who are engaged in a struggle may have difficulty cooperating on anything, even on the development of superordinate goals to curb the struggle. Superordinate goals, like contact and communication, cannot be viewed as a cure-all. They can help, however, in the often painful process of moving from stalemate through de-escalation and into problem solving.

A Note on Third Party Intervention

Chapter 11 discusses the role of third parties, particularly mediators, in facilitating the settlement of conflict through problem solving. Here, in the context of a discussion of moves out of stalemate into de-escalation, it may be useful to comment on several of the things that a third party can do.

[11]This is recognition of superordinate identity—the perception that Other has a shared identity with Party by belonging to a larger group that encompasses both Party and Other. Superordinate identity fosters the attractiveness of outgroup members (Gaertner et al., 1989).

[12]More recent research on superordinate goals has continued to sort out other limiting conditions. These include the ambiguity of the intergroup task (Brown & Wade, 1987) and ambiguity of member roles in the conflicting groups (Deschamps & Brown, 1983).

Sometimes mediators can sponsor contact and communication or arrange superordinate goals, as the counselors did in the Sherifs' camps. It is also possible for one or both principals to arrange for the development of such goals. A classic example is the government that starts a conflict with another country in order to quell internal challenges to its legitimacy. This occurred in 1982, when the government of Argentina took over the Falkland/Malvinas Islands during a period of severe internal controversy. Married couples who try to resolve a blowup by planning a vacation trip are another case in point.

Another thing that mediators can do is help Party and Other to understand that the time to act is *now.* It is usually not sufficient for Party alone to perceive that a conflict has reached the point of stalemate. Other must also see the conflict this way, or efforts to move to de-escalation will probably fail. Mediators can help, since they may be able to approach a reluctant Other and persuade it that Party's readiness makes the time right for movement.[13]

Unilateral Conciliatory Initiatives

Even without the assistance of a third party, there are various things that Party can do on its own. We have already mentioned contact and communication, as well as efforts to work with Other on superordinate goals. These procedures have their value, but both of them require some acquiescence or collaboration by Other. Contact and communication require that Other be willing to associate with and talk with Party. For Party to work with Other on a superordinate goal requires that Other also work with Party. Sometimes the relationship is too escalated for Other to be willing to have anything to do with Party.

When this is the case, Party can simply reach out and take a unilateral conciliatory initiative on its own that requires no acquiescence from Other. The aim of such initiatives is to enhance Other's trust to the point where productive communication and cooperation can begin. Osgood (1962, 1966) has outlined a strategy of conciliatory initiatives that can be used at such times. This strategy, which is called graduated and reciprocated initiatives in tension reduction (GRIT), requires Party to take a se-

[13]Some theorists, such as Kriesberg (1982), Kriesberg Thorson (1991), and Zartman (1989), discuss the notion of "ripeness" in this connection. A conflict is considered ripe (like a Turkish fig that is about to drop from a tree) when both Party and Other are motivated to take it seriously and to do whatever it takes to settle the conflict through problem solving. Rather than wait for the fig to drop from the tree, third parties are often tempted to pluck the fruit and ripen it in a hothouse (like many tomatoes). This leads to the question of timing: should one wait for the disputants to be motivated, or should one try to create conditions of ripeness? Timing is an important issue, since to intervene too early in a conflict may be as costly as intervening too late (Rubin, 1991).

ries of trust-building initiatives within the framework of certain rules, summarized by Lindskold (1978) as follows:

1. Party's series of initiatives should be announced ahead of time in an effort to reduce tension.
2. Each initiative should be labeled as part of this series.
3. The announced timetable should be observed.
4. Other should be invited to reciprocate each initiative.
5. The series of initiatives should be continued for a while even if Other does not reciprocate.
6. The initiatives should be clear-cut and susceptible to verification.
7. Party should retain a capacity to retaliate should Other respond by becoming more contentious.
8. Party should retaliate if the Other becomes contentious.
9. The initiatives should be of various kinds, so that all they have in common is their cooperative nature.
10. Other should be rewarded for cooperating, the level of reward being pegged to the level of cooperation.

One example of a unilateral initiative was Egyptian President Sadat's dramatic 1977 flight to Jerusalem. Sadat said that his trip was designed to reduce tensions (that is, to improve Israeli trust in Egypt) so as to pave the way for negotiations. He apparently viewed the prior escalation between the two countries as mainly due to a conflict spiral in which the countries were alternately antagonizing each other. Not all of the Osgood rules were followed, but Sadat did announce his peaceful intentions ahead of time (rule 1), and he called for reciprocity (rule 4). The success of his trip can probably also be explained as due to the operation of some of the principles of attribution theory (Kelley, 1973). By making his trip, Sadat clearly suffered severe costs in terms of alienation from the rest of the Arab world and from some of his own citizens. Hence, it was hard to doubt the genuineness of his interest in peace. Furthermore, it must have been hard for the Israelis to develop a rationale for explaining his trip in any other way. For example, it could not be seen as an act of obeisance, because Egypt was not in a militarily weak position compared to Israel. His trip appears to have engendered considerable trust among Israelis (Kelman, 1985). The development of this trust did not guarantee solution to all problems, but it contributed to the initiation and success of the subsequent negotiation.

It is important to note that Sadat made his trip to Jerusalem after the 1973 war. If he had done so before that war, it is questionable whether Israel would have responded in a conciliatory way. Before the war Egypt seemed militarily weak, so Israel did not see itself as in a stalemate. Israel was "top dog" in the Middle East and had little reason to seek a jointly acceptable solution to its Egyptian problem. Furthermore, Sadat's initiatives might well have been interpreted in Israel as a sign of weakness rather than as evidence of a change of heart. But after Egypt's attack, Israel was ready for problems and could hardly misperceive Sadat as weak.

The point is that Sadat's conciliatory initiative was part of a broader "firm but conciliatory" strategy (discussed in Chapter 10). He first sent a message of firmness about defending Egypt's basic interests by going to war against Israel. Within the context of this earlier message, the later conciliatory message embodied in his trip to Jerusalem probably had a greater chance of working than if it had been sent alone.[14]

Of course, in such a highly escalated relationship, conciliatory messages are often quite hard to get across because of the suspicions that have been generated by the escalation. Hence, it is usually necessary to employ a dramatic and concerted tension-reduction program that involves striking unilateral initiatives, such as Sadat's trip to Jerusalem.

A special form of unilateral conciliatory initiative is the *apology*, where Party conveys to Other its regret over some prior behavior or the conflictual state in which Party and Other have found themselves. A sincere "I am sorry" by Party often appeases Other's desire for revenge, thereby preventing an escalatory counterresponse (Kim & Smith, 1993).

As Goldberg, Green, and Sander (1987) point out, saying you're sorry can help to repair a frayed relationship. Most importantly, an apology can serve as a double line of sorts, a temporal divide separating events that have taken place in the past from those that are yet to come. An apology is a way of helping bygones to be bygones, to distinguish a period of heavy escalation from a new, more generous problem-solving phase. To be sure, an apology is no panacea. If improperly timed or meant insincerely, an apology can arouse suspicion on the part of Other. Moreover, an apology is a public admission of responsibility for causing harm to Other (Ohbuchi et al., 1989). For Party, bearing this public disgrace may be worse and more painful than remaining in the dispute. Nevertheless, this simple but powerful tool can and should be used more often to alter the climate of a conflictual relationship.[15]

[14]For a fascinating analysis of the costs associated with dramatic unilateral rewarding initiatives (such as Sadat's visit to Jerusalem), see Kelman (1985). These costs derive from the possibility that the object of influence (e.g., the Israelis) may fail to reciprocate in kind, thereby creating a backlash effect.

[15]One example that demonstrates the effectiveness of apology comes from the resolution of a lengthy conflict between Henry Kissinger and Morton Halperin, who was a White House aide during Kissinger's years as President Nixon's national security advisor. In the fall of 1992, Mr. Halperin dropped a 19-year-old lawsuit stemming from a 1969 telephone tap that Kissinger had approved. Mr. Halperin dropped the suit because Kissinger "accepted moral responsibility for what happened" (*New York Times*, Nov. 13, 1992).

The Constructive Use of Entrapment

In Chapter 7 we described the dysfunctional role that entrapment can play in conflict escalation, as Party finds itself increasingly committed to a course of action it cannot escape. The more resources Party commits to this course of action without having reached a goal, the more likely Party is to come to feel that it has "too much invested to quit"—the sine qua non of entrapment. Given entrapment's usual pathological nature, then, can it also be used constructively?

A number of years ago, Sid Caesar (an early television comedian) wrote a book about his successful struggle to overcome alcoholism. It is not clear whether he became an alcoholic because his program *(Your Show of Shows)* went off the air or the program was taken off because of his problem with alcoholism. What is clear is that Sid Caesar was an alcoholic. In his book, he wrote something that can be crudely paraphrased as follows: "I'd gone an hour without a drink. Then another hour. Then one more. 'Click.' I heard a click go off in my head for that interval of time that I'd gone without a drink. Then another 'click.' And another. Soon I had so many clicks going off that I began to feel committed to not giving up on *that*."

Notice that what Sid Caesar was describing was entrapment, not in some conflict-escalating cause but in the service of self-improvement. He created a psychological process that committed him to a course of action designed to allow him to change a difficult personal habit—indeed, an addiction. The same technology could obviously be applied to all forms of self-improvement, whether Party is trying to lose weight, stop gambling, quit smoking, or change an undesirable or unacceptable interpersonal style.

The point is that Party can take actions that get Party and Other entrapped in a process that overcomes stalemate and moves toward de-escalation. Party can make a small unilateral concession, coupled with a request that Other make a similarly small concession. The smaller these concessions, the better; the purpose of these concessions is not to weaken Party and Other but to set in motion a process to which both come to feel committed. Party then makes a second symbolic concession, requesting similar movement from Other. In this way the process of concession and counterconcession continues until momentum has been established in the relationship, and both Party and Other have come to feel that they have too much invested in the process of de-escalation to give up on that!

A good illustration of entrapment in de-escalation was the 1992 Madrid Conference, which was designed to convene many of the parties to the ongoing Middle East conflict. President Bush and Secretary of State Baker seem to have understood (without ever having read this book!) the importance of extracting a series of small symbolic commitments from the various sides. Thus, Baker's first request was not for concessions on territory or security but simply for attendance at a series of meetings, beginning with one in Madrid, Spain. This meeting was followed by others, and at least some of the parties have advanced measurably toward agreement. What Bush and Baker were probably trying to do, like Dr. Henry Kissinger almost fifteen years earlier, was create *commitment to a process* of moving forward. It remains to be seen what kinds of agreements will come from this round of creative international diplomacy.

CONCLUSIONS

We began this chapter by observing that not all conflicts escalate—but many do. Moreover, not all escalating conflicts end in stalemate—but many do. Once both sides come to believe that they are stuck in a situation that is unacceptable—that is, when they find themselves in a stalemate—the stage is set for the hard work of getting unstuck. The ideas presented in this and earlier chapters help explain why conflict so often goes through these stages. Intent on fostering its own interests, with little or no concern about Other's interests, Party initially gravitates toward contentious tactics. Some of these tactics prove effective, and Other yields on certain issues. But there comes a time of diminishing returns at which "all of the threats, commitments and debating points that can be made have been made; and the opponent, while duly impressed, is unwilling to make further concessions" (Pruitt, 1971, p. 210). This is the point of stalemate. It is tempting to allow the stalemate to continue, but this is often infeasible or unacceptable. Costs are mounting—negotiators must be paid, customers are being lost, there is a danger of further alienating the opponent—and a deadline is sometimes approaching at which agreement must be reached or dire consequences (such as a strike) will result. Hence, assuming that Party is ready to withdraw, it must turn to the only remaining strategy, problem solving. This is the focus of the next chapter.

10

Problem Solving

The theme of Chapter 9 was that escalating conflict often reaches the point where both parties find the further use of contentious tactics either unworkable or unwise. If yielding is also ruled out, as it frequently is, the solution to stalemate must eventually be found in problem solving, the only remaining one of the three basic strategies. Problem solving can be defined as any effort to develop a mutually acceptable solution to a conflict.

Problem solving is by no means always the last step in a controversy. It is often the approach taken first, especially when Party values its relations with Other and there is perceived common ground (PCG). Thus, many conflicts are resolved through initial problem solving and never escalate. Other conflicts display a different, albeit consistent, progression of events: problem solving is tried first, but fails; the parties then turn to contentious behavior; the conflict escalates for a while; and eventually, a stalemate is reached and problem solving is reasserted.

At its best, problem solving involves a joint effort to find a mutually acceptable solution. The parties or their representatives talk freely to one another. They exchange information about their interests and priorities, work together to identify the true issues dividing them, brainstorm in search of alternatives that bridge their opposing interests, and collectively evaluate these alternatives from the viewpoint of their mutual welfare.

However, a full problem-solving discussion of this kind is not always practical because of the realities of divergent interests. Party may fear that such openness will deny it an opportunity for competitive gain or will give Other such an opportunity. When these fears exist, individual problem solving is a practical alternative. A single person or small partisan group can perform all the functions just described: seeking insight into Other's interests, identifying the true issues, devising mutually beneficial alternatives, and evaluating these alternatives from a joint perspective. Another approach, described in Chapter 11, is for a mediator to do the problem solving.

One of the arguments for engaging in problem solving is that the strategy reduces the likelihood of runaway escalation. Problem solving does not pose a threat to Other and is psychologically incompatible with the use of heavy contentious tactics. As the saying goes, "It is better to jaw-jaw than to war-war." Problem solving also encourages the discovery of compromises and integrative options that serve both parties' interests.

Problem solving is not without its risks. Individual efforts to find a mutually acceptable solution tend to weaken Party's own resolve and, if there is ambiguity about Party's strength, may telegraph weakness to Other. Also, problem-solving discussions may be more advantageous to one party than the other. For example, they are likely to provide greater benefit to the more verbal of the two parties, the one who is often better armed with statistics and other persuasive devices (Pruitt & Syna, 1983).

These are real risks, but they are not insuperable. It is often possible to engage in problem solving and at the same time cope directly with these risks by means of various devices. These include communicating covertly with Other, combining problem solving with contentious behavior, equalizing the parties in verbal ability, or paying greater attention to the needs of the party with greater threat capacity so as to discourage it from resorting to a contentious approach. The first two of these devices are discussed in greater detail later in this chapter.

The next section deals with the impact of problem solving on the outcome of conflict. We emphasize one possible outcome, the development of an integrative solution. In the following section we examine five types of integrative solutions, along with the refocusing questions that make it possible to devise these solutions. Next we examine methods that can be used to analyze Party's interests, and we give some theoretically based advice about how to get the most out of problem solving. We outline four steps in formulating the problem; we advocate a firm but conciliatory strategy; and we suggest ways to structure the agenda, search for an overarching formula, and break rigidifying linkages. Then we describe some covert methods to use when overt problem-solving approaches seem too risky. We close the chapter with a discussion of tactics that Party can use to persuade Other to join it in problem solving.

OUTCOMES OF PROBLEM SOLVING

Successful problem solving can lead to three broad classes of outcomes: compromise, agreement on a procedure for deciding who will win, or integrative solution.

Compromise

A *compromise* is an agreement reached when both Party and Other concede to some middle ground along an obvious dimension. For examples, the parties to a wage dispute can split the difference between their proposals; Sales and Production (described in Chapter 1) can agree to a production schedule halfway between their respective positions; or a couple can resolve a dispute about whether to vacation in Maine or Florida by going to a beach in North Carolina.[1]

Compromises can sometimes be very good for both parties and sometimes very bad. Most commonly they provide both parties with a middling outcome—by no means as good as what they had hoped for or as bad as what they might have gotten. Where it can be achieved, an integrative solution is usually much better for both parties than a compromise. Yet many conflicts end in compromise. Among the reasons for this are aspirations that are not sufficiently high, time pressure that makes it hard to embark on a search for new options (Yukl et al., 1976), fear of prolonged conflict, and a societally endorsed fetish for "fairness" that often attracts unwarranted attention to the fifty-fifty division. In addition, compromises sometimes grow out of an unduly escalated episode. Party has devoted so much energy to trying to beat Other, and so much attention is focused on partisan options, that the parties cannot engage in creative efforts to de-

[1]The popular use of the term *compromise* is somewhat broader; it often means any agreement in which the parties abandon their initial demands. Following the lead of Follett (1940), we have adopted a narrower definition in order to distinguish compromises from integrative solutions.

vise new alternatives. Hence, when they finally see that they are in a hurting stalemate, they reach out for an obvious compromise.

Agreement on a Procedure for Deciding Who Will Win

Compromise is not the only kind of solution that seems fair. Sometimes the outcome of problem solving is a procedure for deciding who will win—that is, a rule for awarding Party all it is asking while Other gets little or nothing. A number of these procedures are commonly employed:

- Tossing a coin, with victory for the winner
- Comparing needs, with victory for the party who feels most strongly about the issue under consideration
- Submitting to a third party decision, with victory for the disputant whose position seems most cogent to a judge or arbitrator
- Voting, with victory to the party who can command a majority of some deliberative body.

It is sometimes essential to use one of these procedures—for example, when there are only two possible outcomes (such as I go first or you go first). In most cases, more integrative solutions are available if the parties will only seek them out. This means that legitimate procedures like voting can sometimes be "snakes in the grass," undermining the parties' will to look for more integrative solutions and the benefits that come with such solutions.

Integrative Solutions

An integrative solution is one that reconciles (that is, integrates) the interests of Party and Other.[2] Integrative solutions produce the highest joint outcomes of the three types of agreement. Consider, for example, the story of two sisters who are quarreling over an orange, which was mentioned in Chapter 2. The sisters could reach a compromise agreement to split the fruit in half—the first sister can squeeze her half for juice while the other uses the peel from her half to bake a cake. But both would clearly profit more from the integrative solution of giving the first sister all the juice and the second all the peel. If they are intent on compromise, the sisters will never find the best solution.

In this story, it is possible for a *fully* integrative solution to be reached, one that totally satisfies both parties' aspirations. However,

[2]Integrative solutions are also sometimes called win-win solutions (see Pruitt & Carnevale, 1993).

most integrative solutions are not so successful. They *partially* reconcile the parties' interests, leaving them fairly content but not quite so happy as if they had achieved all they had hoped for.

Integrative solutions sometimes entail known alternatives, but more often they involve the development of novel alternatives and require some creativity and imagination. For this reason, it is proper to say that they usually emerge from a process of creative thinking. Integrative solutions can be devised by Party and Other acting separately, by the two of them in joint session, or by a third party such as a mediator.

Situations that allow for the development of integrative solutions are said to be high in *integrative potential* (Walton & McKersie, 1965). Not all situations have such potential. For example, there is little integrative potential when a tourist dickers with a North African merchant about the price of a rug; Party's gain is almost surely Other's loss. But there is more integrative potential in most situations than is usually assumed. Hence, a skilled and sustained problem-solving effort is often richly rewarded.

Integrative solutions are often advantageous to the parties, both collectively and individually, so they are worth pursuing if at all possible. This is so for four main reasons:

1. If aspirations are high and there is resistance to yielding on both sides, it may be impossible to resolve the conflict unless a way can be found to join the two parties' interests.
2. Agreements involving higher joint benefit are likely to be more stable. Compromises, coin tosses, and other mechanical agreements are often unsatisfying to one or both parties, so the issue is likely to come up again later (Thomas, 1976).
3. Because they are mutually rewarding, integrative solutions tend to strengthen the relationship between the parties. Strengthened relationships usually have inherent value and also facilitate the development of integrative solutions in subsequent situations.
4. Integrative solutions ordinarily contribute to the welfare of the broader community of which the two parties are members. For example, a firm usually benefits as a whole when its departments are able to reconcile their differences creatively.

The discovery of an integrative solution diminishes, and can even abolish, perceived divergence of interest. This point is demonstrated in Figure 2.2*d*, which shows a fairly severe perceived divergence of interest. There is a possible compromise with the center alternative, but it comes nowhere near satisfying the two parties' aspirations (which are shown by the dashed lines). This divergence of interest disappears in Figure 2.2*a* as a result of developing an integrative solution (shown at the upper right). It follows that if an integrative solution is known at the outset of concern about an issue, conflict can be avoided. Had the sisters in our example thought immediately about exchanging peel for pulp, there would have been no conflict.

We can see that of the three outcomes that can result from problem solving, integrative solutions are almost always the most desirable. They tend to last longer and to contribute more to the relationship between the parties and the welfare of the broader community than do compromises and agreements about how to choose the winner. In addition, they tend to diminish the sense of conflict. Integrative solutions are not always available, but there is more integrative potential in most situations than people often realize. Problem solving is especially likely to lead to integrative solutions when aspirations are high, time pressure is low, fear of conflict is low, and the parties are not overly impressed by the importance of fairness.

TYPES OF INTEGRATIVE SOLUTIONS

If integrative solutions are so important to achieve, how do they emerge? What are the routes for moving from opposing demands to an alternative that reconciles the interests of Party and Other? We have identified five such routes, leading to five types of integrative solutions: expanding the pie, nonspecific compensation, logrolling, cost cutting, and bridging. In addition to its theoretical value, this typology should be useful as a checklist for any negotiator or mediator seeking a way to settle a conflict.

To increase the theoretical and practical value of our presentation, we mention the kind of information needed in order to formulate each type of solution and pose several refocusing questions that can aid in the search for such a solution. The types of solutions are listed according to the difficulty of getting the necessary information—with the least difficult listed first.[3]

Our typology of integrative solutions is illustrated by a running example concerning a husband and wife (or any two people) who are trying to decide where to go on a two-week vacation. The husband wants to go to the mountains, the wife to the seashore. They have considered the compromise of spending one week in each location but are hoping for something better. What approach should they take?

Expanding the Pie

Some conflicts hinge on a resource shortage. Time, money, space, automobiles, handsome men, or what have you—all are in long demand but

[3]The reader interested in learning more about theoretical assumptions underlying the development of integrative solutions can do no better than read chapter 5 of Lax & Sebenius' (1986) excellent book, *The Manager as Negotiator*. The chapter presents a succinct overview of the process by which value is created in negotiation. The reader interested in learning more about specific techniques for advancing integrative solutions in negotiation should read Fisher et al.'s (1991) *Getting to YES*.

short supply. In such circumstances, integrative solutions can be devised by expanding the pie, which means increasing the available resources. For example, our couple might solve the problem by persuading their employers to give them two additional weeks of vacation so that they can spend two weeks in the mountains *and* two weeks at the seashore. Follett (1940) cited another example—two milk companies, vying to be first to unload cans on a creamery platform, resolved their controversy when somebody thought of widening the platform.

Expanding the pie is a useful formula when Party finds Other's proposals inherently acceptable but rejects them because they pose opportunity costs. For example, the husband rejects the seashore because it keeps him away from the mountains, and the wife rejects the mountains because they deny her the pleasures of the seashore. However, expanding the pie is by no means a universal remedy. If there are inherent costs, as opposed to opportunity costs, in Other's proposal (the husband cannot stand the seashore or the wife the mountains), broadening the pie may yield strikingly poor results. Other types of integrative solutions are better in such cases.

The information requirements for expanding the pie are very small. All that is required is knowledge of the parties' demands. No analysis of the interests underlying these demands is needed. This does not mean that such a solution is always easy to find. There may be no resource shortage, or it may be expensive to enlarge the pool of resources. Furthermore, it may not be apparent that the problem hinges on a resource shortage. In an argument over who goes first on the loading platform, it may not be clear that the real issue is the size of the platform.

Several refocusing questions can be useful in seeking a solution by expanding the pie. How can Party and Other get what they want? Does the conflict hinge on a resource shortage? How can the critical resource be expanded?

Nonspecific Compensation

In nonspecific compensation, Party gets what it wants and Other is repaid in some unrelated coin. Compensation is nonspecific when it does not deal with the precise costs incurred by Other. For example, the wife in our example might agree to go to the mountains—even though she finds them boring—if her husband agrees that some of the family resources can be spent on buying her a new car. Another example is a supervisor giving an employee a bonus for going without dinner in order to meet a deadline.

Compensation usually comes from the party whose demands are granted, because Party is "buying" concessions from Other. But it can also originate with a third party or even with the party who is compensated. An example of the latter is an employee who pampers himself or herself by finding a nice office to work in while going without dinner.

Two kinds of information are useful for devising a solution via nonspecific compensation: (1) information about one or more realms of value to Other, for example, knowledge that it values love or attention or is money-mad; and (2) information about how badly Other is hurt by making the concessions. Such information is useful for devising adequate compensation. If only one of these kinds of information (or neither) is available, it may be possible to conduct an "auction" for Other's acquiescence, changing the sort of benefit offered or raising Party's offer in trial-and-error fashion until a formula is found to which Other can agree.

Refocusing questions can help locate a means of compensation. For example, what does Other value that Party can supply? How valuable is this to Other? How much is Other hurt by conceding to Party?[4]

Though it is often useful, nonspecific compensation has its limitations. These are mainly due to normative constraints. For example, it is not proper to pay a government employee for food stamps. When there are normative constraints against a compensatory scheme that is desired by the parties, three strategies are available for avoiding community awareness of the transaction: making a secret agreement, secretly transferring one or both benefits, and delayed sequential enactment of the benefits (separating the actions of Party and Other in time so that outsiders do not see the connection). A traveler who places a $20 bill in his or her passport at a foreign airport is making a secret transfer. Another secret agreement that was sequentially enacted was the American pledge to withdraw missiles from Turkey during the 1962 Cuban missile crisis. This withdrawal was delayed for four months after the Soviets took their missiles out of Cuba, presumably so that the connection would not be obvious. One can only assume that the American president feared that if this agreement became known, he would be criticized by opposition politicians or nervous allies.[5]

[4]Foa & Foa (1975) have developed a general theory about the kinds of compensation that are considered appropriate as repayment for certain kinds of concessions. They classify resources on two dimensions: concreteness (tangibility) and particularism (the extent to which the value of the resource depends on the identity of the person delivering it). Status and love are abstract, particularistic resources; goods and money are concrete, nonparticularistic resources. These authors have shown, in a series of studies, that a form of compensation appears more appropriate the closer it is in this dimensional space to the resource received. Thus goods can properly be exchanged for money and status for love. But money cannot properly be exchanged for love.

[5]Compensatory schemes often take the form of promises—guarantees of later benefit in exchange for present compliance. Promises were alluded to in Chapter 4 in the context of an analysis of their conceptual cousin, threats. As Schelling (1960) has pointed out, promises are at the heart of all contractual relations. For a broad conceptual analysis of promises, read Schelling's (1960) *The Strategy of Conflict*. For a comparison of promises and threats, see Chapter 4 of the first edition of this book. And for a summary of research on the credibility and effectiveness of promises, see Pruitt (1981), Pruitt & Carnevale (1993), and Rubin & Brown (1975).

Logrolling

In a solution by logrolling, each party concedes on issues that are of low priority to itself and high priority to the other party. In this way, each gets that part of its demands that it deems most important. Like the other types of solutions, logrolling is not a universal route to integrative solutions. It is possible only when several issues are under consideration and the parties have different priorities among these issues. Suppose that in addition to disagreeing about where to go on vacation, the wife in our example prefers a first-class hotel and the husband wants to go to a tourist home. If accommodations are most important to the wife and location is most important to the husband, they can reach a fairly integrative solution by agreeing to go to a first-class hotel in the mountains.

Another example is a hypothetical case of bargaining between labor and management in which labor initially demands a 20 percent increase in overtime rate and 20 more minutes of rest breaks, and management indicates unwillingness to provide either concession. If the overtime rate is especially important for labor and if long rest breaks are particularly abhorrent to management, a reasonably integrative solution can be achieved if labor drops its demands for more rest breaks in exchange for management giving in on the overtime rate. This sort of solution is typically better for both parties than a compromise on the two issues, such as a 10 percent increase in overtime rate and 10 more minutes of rest time.

Logrolling can be viewed as a variant of nonspecific compensation in which Party is compensated for making concessions desired by Other, and vice versa. More generally, both logrolling and nonspecific compensation rely for their effectiveness on what Lax and Sebenius (1986) describe as "the trading of differences."[6]

To develop solutions by logrolling, it is useful to have information about the two parties' priorities among the issues so that concessions can be matched up, but it is not necessary to have information about the nature of the interests (goals and values) underlying these priorities. Information about priorities is not always easy to get. One reason for this is that people often try to conceal their priorities for fear that they will be forced to concede on issues of lesser importance to themselves without receiving compensation. Another reason is that people often erroneously

[6]Lax & Sebenius (1986) offer the following quaint example: "If a vegetarian with some meat bargains with a carnivore who owns some vegetables, it is precisely the *difference* in their known preferences that can facilitate reaching an agreement" (p. 92). Jack Sprat (who could eat no fat) and his wife (who could eat no lean) worked out a similar arrangement. These authors identify six kinds of differences that can be exploited in conflict in order to help create (negotiated) agreements. These are differences of relative value (as in the preceding examples), expectation, capacity, risk-taking propensity, and time preference. For more detailed analysis of these forms of difference, see pp. 90–105 of Lax & Sebenius (1986).

project their own priorities onto others, assuming that what they want is what the other also wants.

Solutions by logrolling can also be developed by a process of trial and error: Party offers a series of possible packages, keeping its own aspirations as high as possible, until an alternative is found that is acceptable to Other (Kelley & Schenitzki, 1972; Pruitt & Carnevale, 1982).

Several refocusing questions can be useful for developing solutions by logrolling: Which issues are of higher priority and which of lower priority to Party? Which issues are of higher priority and which of lower priority to Other? Are some of Party's high-priority issues of lower priority to Other, and vice versa?

Cost Cutting

In solutions by cost cutting, Party gets what it wants and Other's costs are reduced or eliminated. The result is high joint benefit, not because Party has changed its position but because Other suffers less. For instance, suppose that the husband in our example dislikes the beach because of the hustle and bustle. He may be willing to go there on vacation if his costs are cut by renting a house with a quiet inner courtyard where he can read while his wife goes out among the crowds.[7]

Cost cutting often takes the form of specific compensation, in which the party who concedes receives something in return that satisfies the precise values frustrated. For example, if the wife's main objection to the mountains is the absence of seafood, it may be possible to reach agreement by locating a mountain hotel that serves seafood. Specific compensation differs from nonspecific compensation in that it deals with the precise costs incurred rather than providing repayment in an unrelated coin. The costs are actually canceled out rather than being overbalanced by benefits achieved in some other realm.

Information about the nature of Other's costs is, of course, helpful for developing solutions by cost cutting. This is a deeper kind of information than knowledge of Other's priorities. It involves knowing something about the interests—the values and needs—underlying Other's overt position.

Refocusing questions can help in developing solutions by cost cutting: What costs are posed for Other by Party's proposal? How can these costs be mitigated or eliminated?

[7]A variation in which costs are cut on *both* sides is offered by Lax & Sebenius (1986) in their discussion of economies of scale: Two health care institutions are interested in setting up a new clinic in an underserved area. Instead of each organization building its own clinic, they might agree to establish one facility, thereby sharing the various expenses incurred while making their services available to a larger clientele. Thus, instead of expanding the pie, this proposal calls for reducing the costs for Party and Other of baking a pie of fixed size.

Bridging

In bridging, neither Party nor Other achieves its initial demands, but a new option is devised that satisfies the most important interests underlying those demands. For example, suppose the husband in our vacation example is mainly interested in fishing, and the wife wants mainly to swim. These high-priority interests might be bridged by finding an inland resort with a lake that is close to woods and streams. Follett (1940) gives another example of two women reading in a library room. One wants to open the window for ventilation, the other to keep it closed in order not to catch cold. The ultimate solution involves opening a window in the next room, thereby letting in the fresh air while avoiding a draft.

Bridging typically stems from a reformulation of the issue(s) on the basis of analysis of underlying interests. For example, a critical turning point in our vacation example is likely to come when the initial formulation "Shall we go to the mountains or the seashore?" is replaced by "Where can we find opportunities for fishing and swimming?" This new formulation becomes the basis for a search model (Simon, 1957) that is employed in an effort to find a new alternative.[8]

It is rare that a solution can be found that bridges all interests of Party and Other, as the window in the next room of the library does. More often, higher-priority interests are served while lower-priority interests are discarded. For example, the wife who agrees to go to an inland lake may have foregone the lesser value of smelling the sea air, whereas the husband may have given up his predilection for spectacular mountain vistas.

It follows that people who seek to develop bridging solutions must usually have information about the nature of the two parties' interests and about their priorities among these interests. Information about priorities among interests is different from information about priorities among issues (which is useful for developing solutions by logrolling). Issues are the concrete matters under discussion now; interests are the hidden concerns that underlie preferences with respect to issues.

To achieve an optimal solution by bridging, the information just described should be used as follows: In an initial phase, one's search model should include all of the interests on both sides. But if this does not generate a mutually acceptable alternative, some of the lower-priority interests should be discarded from the model and the search begun anew. The result will not be an ideal solution, but it is likely to be one that is mutually acceptable. Dropping low-priority values in the development of bridging solutions is analogous to dropping low-priority demands in the search for a solution by logrolling. But the latter is in the realm of concrete

[8]A number of practice-oriented books on negotiation have focused further on the process by which bridging alternatives can be found. Relevant work in this regard includes Fisher et al. (1991); Lax & Sebenius (1986); Raiffa (1982); and Susskind & Cruikshank (1987).

proposals, while the former is in the realm of the interests underlying these proposals.

A number of refocusing questions can be raised in searching for a solution by bridging: What are the two parties' basic interests? What are the priorities among these interests? How can both sets of high-priority interests be achieved?

THE ANALYSIS OF UNDERLYING INTERESTS

To devise an integrative solution involving cost cutting or bridging, we usually need to know something about the interests underlying Party's position (in the case of cost cutting) or both parties' positions (in the case of bridging). The most obvious way to get this information is to persuade the parties to talk about their interests. However, there are two problems with this method. One is that Party does not always understand the precise nature of the interest underlying its preferences. Party's position in a controversy is often a matter of what "feels" best; Party feels good about its own proposal or uneasy about Other's proposal without knowing precisely why. For example, the wife may feel comfortable at the seashore and uncomfortable in the woods but not be sure why she feels this way. The other problem is that Party is often unwilling to reveal its interests for fear that Other will use this information to personal advantage—for example, for constructing threats. This problem arises when distrust exists. An example is unwillingness to tell one's spouse that one is greatly in need of affection for fear that the spouse will later threaten to withdraw affection whenever he or she wants a concession.

Fortunately, there are other approaches to gathering information about Other's interests besides getting Other to talk about them directly. These include listening "with a third ear"—that is, being attentive to the points Other emphasizes, the places where it becomes emotional, and the issues it neglects to mention (Fisher et al., 1991); drawing inferences from Other's behavior outside the conflict situation; and finally, asking third parties about Other's values and standards.

Interests Underlying Interests

Learning about the first-level interests that underlie Other's proposals is often not enough. Party must seek the interests underlying these interests, or the interests underlying the interests underlying these interests, and so on. The point is that interests are often organized into hierarchical trees, with more basic interests underpinning more superficial ones. If Party moves along the tree far enough, it may locate an interest that can be easily bridged with an interest of Other.

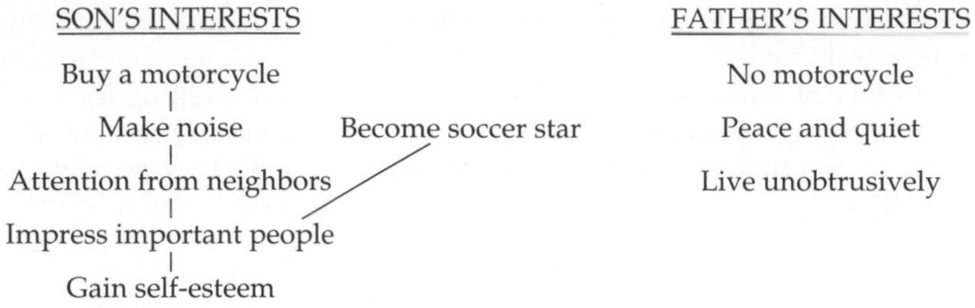

SON'S INTERESTS		FATHER'S INTERESTS
Buy a motorcycle		No motorcycle
Make noise	Become soccer star	Peace and quiet
Attention from neighbors		Live unobtrusively
Impress important people		
Gain self-esteem		

FIGURE 10.1
Son's interest tree in a controversy with his father.

An example of an interest tree appears on the left of Figure 10.1. It is that of a boy trying to persuade his father to let him buy a motorcycle. At the right are listed those of the father's interests that conflict with the son's. At the top of the tree is the boy's initial position (buy a motorcycle), which is hopelessly opposed to his father's position (no motorcycle). Analysis of the boy's proposal yields a first-level underlying interest: to make noise in the neighborhood. But this is opposed to his dad's interest in maintaining peace and quiet. Further analysis of the boy's position reveals a second-level interest underlying the first level: to gain attention from the neighbors. But again this conflicts with one of his father's interests, to live unobtrusively. The controversy is resolved only when someone (the father, the boy, the boy's mother, or someone else) discovers an even more basic interest underlying the boy's desire for a motorcycle: the desire to impress important people. This discovery is significant because there are other ways of impressing important people that do not contradict the father's interests—for example, the bridging solution of going out for the high school soccer team. At the bottom of the boy's preference tree is a fourth-level interest, self-esteem. But it is unnecessary to go down this far, because the controversy can be resolved at the third level.

Same Issue—Different Meaning

When Party seeks the interests underlying divergent positions with Other, it often finds that the issue under consideration has a different meaning to each of the two. Though there appears to be disagreement, there is no fundamental opposition in what they are really asking. Figure 10.2 shows some dimensions that leave room for bridging.

One controversy was resolved when a mediator discovered that one party was seeking substance while the other was seeking appearance (Golan, 1976). A cease-fire in the 1973 October War found the Egyptian Third Army surrounded by Israeli forces. A dispute arose about the control of the only road available for bringing food and medicine to this

ONE PARTY CARES MORE ABOUT	THE OTHER PARTY CARES MORE ABOUT
Substance	Form, appearance
Economic considerations	Political considerations
Internal considerations	External considerations
Symbolic considerations	Practical considerations
Immediate future	More distant future
Ad hoc results	The relationship
Hardware	Ideology
Progress	Respect for tradition
Precedent	This case
Prestige, reputation	Results
Political points	Group welfare

FIGURE 10.2
Polar opposites that are not necessarily in conflict (from Fisher, Ury, & Patton, 1991, p. 74).

army, and the two parties appeared to be at loggerheads. After careful analysis, the mediator (Henry Kissinger) concluded that Israel wanted actual control of the road, whereas Egypt wanted only the appearance that Israel did not control it (in order to avoid embarrassment back home). A bridging solution was found that involved stationing Israeli soldiers unobtrusively on the sides of the road (so that they actually controlled it) and having United Nations checkpoints on the road itself (to give the impression of international control).

Another conflict was resolved when it was discovered that Party had immediate concerns but Other's concerns were more distant. This situation involved a strike by public transit workers in Buffalo. The mayor of the city, who was asked to mediate the dispute, found that the bus company's refusal to pay stemmed from budget problems, whereas the workers' main concern was their salary in future years. Hence, the mediator recommended that the workers get half of what they were asking immediately and the other half a year later, after the company had a chance to petition the city for an increase in the fare. This was another bridging solution.

We have described five types of integrative solutions: expanding the pie, nonspecific compensation, logrolling, cost cutting, and bridging. These, and the refocusing questions that make them possible, provide five routes along which the disputants or a third party can move from an apparent divergence of interest to an agreement that satisfies both parties' major interests. These solutions require different information to attain them. Expanding the pie requires only knowledge of Party's and Other's current demands. Nonspecific compensation requires information about a realm of value to Other outside the current controversy. Logrolling requires knowledge of both sides' priorities among the issues under discussion. And cost cutting and bridging require information about the interests that are served by each side's current demands. Interests are often organized hierarchically; hence, it is frequently productive to seek the interests underlying the interests that are served by current demands, the interests further underlying those interests, and so on. Quite often, when Party digs down into underlying interests, it turns out that the issue in dispute has a different meaning to Party and to Other, which makes agreement easier to reach.

HOW TO GO ABOUT PROBLEM SOLVING

It clearly makes sense to search for integrative solutions in most conflicts. How should Party go about this search—how should it be organized? This is the question of creative problem solving.

Steps in Creative Problem Solving

The following sequence of steps makes most sense in the search for creative solutions to apparent conflicts of interest:

Step 1: Ask Whether There Really Is a Conflict of Interest. An apparent conflict of interest may be *illusory* if there is a misunderstanding about the circumstances, or if Party misconstrues Other's proposals or interests.[9] If the parties can grasp this point, the conflict will go away and problem solving will be unnecessary. Hence, asking whether there is a real conflict of interest is the logical first step.

Illusory conflict can arise in at least three ways. Party may have a false impression about Other's intentions or aspirations. For example, a carpenter who came to look at a job in the home of one of the authors (DGP) said that the estimate would cost $50. When asked why he expected a fee, he indicated that he feared homeowners would file for an insurance payment on the basis of his estimate, then do the repairs themselves. When assured that this homeowner was all thumbs with tools, he withdrew the request for a fee. Second, Party may think Other's intended actions will create costs that they actually will not create. For example, parents may oppose a teenage party because of the anticipated noise until they learn that the proposed party will take place while they are away.[10] Third, Party may view Other's intentions as arbitrary or illegitimate when they really are not. For example, a university department chair thought she

[9]Thompson (1990b) and Thompson & Hastie (1990) have demonstrated that negotiators often fall into illusory conflict, thereby failing to see the same preferences.
[10]Of course, a tree *has* fallen in the forest even if *you* don't hear it. And the parents being away won't make the party any quieter. Just ask the neighbors.

was in conflict with the dean of continuing education over the division of some student fees. At the "showdown" meeting between these two administrators, the dean argued that continuing education should get the larger share because more of its budget depended on "soft money." Once this argument had been presented, the dean's claims seemed nonarbitrary, and there no longer seemed to be a conflict in the eyes of the chair.

Step 2: Analyze Party's Own Interests, Set Reasonably High Aspirations, and Be Ready to Stick to Them. If Party concludes that a conflict really exists, the next step is to examine carefully its own interests—Party's basic goals and values. This avoids the danger of going off half-cocked and getting involved in controversy over nonessential issues. The methods for analyzing interests described earlier can be useful in this enterprise. Having done so, Party must set reasonably high aspirations regarding these interests and be ready to stick to them. In short, Party must be both ambitious and stubborn about its basic interests.

We acknowledge that by endorsing ambition and stubbornness we are saying that protracted conflict is often necessary for the development of truly integrative solutions (Filley, 1975). Party must maintain high aspirations, fully cognizant of the fact that they may not be compatible with Other's aspirations. This seems paradoxical, but we hasten to add that we are not talking about heavily competitive conflict. Creative conflicts are in the category of vigorous discussions or mild arguments, in which both parties state their preferences and stick to their goals while remaining flexible about the means of attaining them.[11]

Step 3: Seek a Way to Reconcile Both Parties' Aspirations. Having set high aspirations, Party should seek a way to reconcile these aspirations with those held by Other. In other words, Party should engage in problem solving—in a search for integrative solutions. The various refocusing questions discussed in the prior section should be posed, and one or more search models should be developed in an effort to achieve the goals that both parties find most important.

It is not clear that any one of the five kinds of integrative solutions is better or easier to achieve than the others. Hence, we do not recommend starting the search with any particular type of solution in mind. The right kind of solution depends in part on the kind of information available. If Party cannot fathom Other's reasons for making its demands, cost cutting and bridging are not possible, and Party must be content with the other three approaches. On the other hand, if this information *is* available, it may make sense for Party to pursue several kinds of solutions at once—

[11]We are also not endorsing bullheadedness. Aspirations should start and stay high, but not so high as to outrun any reasonable integrative potential. If they remain too high, time will be lost and Other may withdraw because the conflict seems hopeless or because it has found a better alternative.

for example, to seek a way to expand the pie at the same time that it seeks a bridging solution.

Sometimes there is too little information about Other's situation to permit a thoughtful approach to the development of integrative solutions. For example, Other may reject Party's proposals but refuse to give reasons or make a counterproposal. When this happens, a policy of trial and error must be adopted (Kelley & Schenitzki, 1972; Pruitt & Carnevale, 1982), in which Party proposes a sequence of alternatives that satisfy its aspirations in the hope of finding one that appeals to Other as well.

Step 4: Lower Aspirations and Search Some More. If agreement is not reached at step 3, a choice should be made between two further options. Party can reduce its aspirations somewhat—that is, concede on low-priority issues or discard low-priority interests—and try again. Alternatively, if Party's search model includes Other's aspirations as well as its own, Party can lower its conception of Other's aspirations and then, if a solution is found, try to persuade Other that such a reduction is desirable.

Step 4 should be repeated until an agreement is reached or withdrawal becomes inevitable.

Being Firm but Conciliatory

The policy described in steps 2 and 3 of the sequence just given can be viewed as *firm but conciliatory*. Party should be firm about its basic interests—yielding only when it is clear that they cannot be attained—but conciliatory toward Other in the sense of being responsive to Other's basic interests also. An important aspect of being conciliatory is for Party to be flexible about how its interests are achieved, in order to be open to new ideas about how to reconcile its interests with Other's. Hence, this policy can also be described as involving *firm flexibility;* Party should be firm with regard to ends, but flexible with regard to the means used to reach these ends. A quotation from Fisher et al. (1991) captures the essence of firm flexibility: "It may not be wise to commit yourself to your position, but it is wise to commit yourself to your interests. This is the place . . . to spend your aggressive energies" (p. 54).

A firm but conciliatory strategy is often employed with success in child rearing. Wise parents are strict about ethical standards and such minimal goals as cleanliness, safety, and parental peace of mind. They urge their children to live within the framework of these values and discipline a child who moves outside of them. Yet the same parents are concerned about their children's welfare, so they are flexible about the means by which their values are achieved, allowing and even helping their children to accomplish the children's own goals within the framework of the parents' values. For example, a father may be firm with his son about straightening up his room yet be flexible about when and how this work will be done. The result of such an approach is likely to be conformity to parental values, high joint benefit, and a good relationship between parent and child.

Structuring the Agenda

The firm but conciliatory approach and the step model to which it is related are useful for dealing with either a single issue or a small group of related issues. But when many issues are being discussed in a joint problem-solving session, an agenda must be developed specifying the order in which the issues are to be taken up. Three guidelines for constructing such an agenda can be stated.

First, it often makes sense to put easier issues earlier in an agenda. This is because the success of problem solving is to some extent cumulative, in that earlier achievement establishes the impression that later achievement is possible—that there is integrative potential.[12]

If solutions involving logrolling are to emerge from a problem-solving discussion, it is necessary to consider several issues at the same time, so that concessions on one issue can be traded for concessions on another. This implies the second guideline, that it is often desirable to expand the agenda to include seemingly extraneous matters. In doing so, problem solvers must be careful not to slip into the error of insisting that all new issues put on the table for this purpose necessarily be resolved in order for agreement to be reached. We are advocating discussing a number of issues in the same session, not trying to resolve them all.

The third guideline is useful when the agenda contains such a large number of items that logrolling opportunities may be missed because the issues on which it is possible to trade concessions are considered at different times. To avoid settling for a less attractive solution in such a situation, it may be possible at the beginning of problem solving to adopt the ground rule that no element of the agreement can be finally approved until all issues have been thoroughly discussed. This allows earlier issues to be reconsidered in light of later ones.

Searching for a Formula

When complex issues are under consideration, a twofold approach is often essential. The early stages of problem solving must be devoted to devising an overarching formula—a brief statement of common objectives

[12]In Chapter 9 we discussed the role of entrapment in building commitment to a process of de-escalation. The same perspective applies to the development of a burgeoning commitment to problem solving.

that can serve as a road map to the eventual agreement. Only then is it possible to devise an efficient agenda for working out the details of the agreement (Zartman, 1977). If a formula is not developed, the proceedings are likely to get so mired in details that momentum is lost and the parties withdraw or resort to a contentious approach.

An example of such a formula is the basic agreement in the Camp David talks between Israel and Egypt. In essence, Israel agreed to withdraw from the Sinai and begin talks about Palestinian autonomy in exchange for a peace treaty with Egypt. This formula was somewhat expanded in the Camp David accords and became the basis for many years of further negotiation.

Breaking Linkages

Totally integrative solutions, in which both parties get all they were seeking, occasionally occur, but such agreements are quite rare. It is usually necessary for one or both parties to make selective concessions in search of a partially integrative solution. They must give up certain demands, diminish certain aspirations, or compromise certain values, while firmly adhering to others.

Demands, goals, aspirations, and values often come in a bundle—that is, they are psychologically linked to other demands, goals, aspirations, and values. Hence, in order to make a concession, a process of unlinking must take place in which some items in a bundle are psychologically separated from others. For example, consider the conflict between the son who wants a motorcycle and the father who opposes this purchase. There may be a close link in the son's thinking between making noise and making an impression on other people. To resolve the controversy, someone (such as his mother) must tell him, "It's not necessary to make noise to get attention." Another example concerns the married couple who disagree about where to go on vacation. If they cannot find a solution like those discussed earlier, unlinking may be helpful. Most couples assume that they must take a vacation together; that is, they link the concept of vacation to that of togetherness. Separating these concepts may yield the most integrative solution possible for some couples. It is not always necessary to go on vacation together.

The following four-step sequence of moves is suggested for problem solvers who are seeking integrative agreements: (1) Examine the situation to be sure that there is a conflict of interest. (2) Set reasonably high aspirations and be ready to stick to them. (3) Search for alternatives that satisfy both parties' aspirations. (4) If step 3 fails to achieve a settlement, Party should lower its own aspirations or its conception of Other's aspirations, and search some more. These recommendations imply a firm but conciliatory policy, in which Party works hard to satisfy its own and Other's aspirations. In addition, Party may wish to put easier issues early on the agenda, and to expand the agenda to include issues that permit the exchange of concessions. When many issues are under consideration, Party should search for an overarching formula and should adopt the ground rule of not reaching an agreement on any issue until all issues have been discussed. To reach an integrative agreement, it is often necessary to break psychological linkages that make things seem to go together naturally.[13]

COVERT PROBLEM SOLVING

Problem-solving behavior obviously makes a lot of sense in many situations. But what if Other has adopted a contentious approach and is unwilling to engage in problem solving? Might Party's problem-solving efforts be misinterpreted or exploited?

The answer is yes. There are three risks in problem solving. All problem-solving behavior poses the risk of *image loss*—that is, a perception that Party is weak and irresolute, hence, willing to make extensive concessions. This perception can actually undermine problem solving by encouraging Other to adopt contentious behavior in an effort to persuade Party to make those concessions. There is also some risk of *position loss* if Party, in pursuing a solution to the problem, makes tentative suggestions of possible options. Position loss is a perception by Other that Party has conceded from a previous position. A third risk is *information loss*, which can occur if Party talks about its interests or reveals information about its limit. The danger of providing such information is that Other may be able to use it to fashion threats or noncontingent commitments.

One solution to the problem of image loss, position loss, and information loss is to employ covert forms of problem solving. It is possible to conceive of a continuum of problem-solving tactics, ranging from the highly overt to the highly covert. At the overt end are such moves as openly engaging in a discussion of possible alternatives, making a concession on one issue in the hope of receiving a reciprocal concession on another issue, and proposing a compromise or integrative solution. At the covert end are three basic kinds of tactics: back-channel contacts, the use of third parties, and efforts to send signals to Other. Such tactics allow Party to explore possible problem solutions or to move toward overt

[13]We are reminded of a *New Yorker* cartoon some years ago, which showed a man with a puzzled look on his face, studying a wall chart that described a ten-step procedure for opening a door! Much of what we are describing here is done rather effortlessly and intuitively by people who problem solve. Being a problem solver, and being a wise and effective problem solver, however, are often two different things. The reader interested in improving problem-solving effectiveness should read Fisher et al's. (1991) *Getting to Yes* and get as much practice as possible.

problem solving without prematurely tipping its hand. If Party discovers through such exploration that Other is ready to accept a solution that is also acceptable to Party or to join in a problem-solving process, Party can then become more overt—confident that there is no need to worry about image loss, position loss, or information loss.

Another value of covert problem solving is its compatibility with contentious behavior. If Party wants to explore the feasibility of problem solving or of certain problem solutions while maintaining an overtly contentious stance, covert problem solving is the answer. The point is that there are psychological contradictions between overt problem solving and highly contentious behavior. The attitudes required for these two kinds of performance are different. Covert problem solving is easier to reconcile with contentious behavior because it involves less commitment to cooperation. It is also less jarring for constituents if they are dedicated to a belligerent campaign. It is hard for Party to rally its forces around the battle cry that Other is partly right. Hence, leaders are often overtly contentious while engaging in covert problem solving—out of sight of their constituents.

Covert problem solving is commonly found after a period of escalation when the conflicting parties have moved into stalemate. Each is groping separately for a different approach, but neither is fully clear about the other's frame of mind. Is Other ready for problem solving? If Party makes conciliatory moves, will Other reciprocate or simply exploit Party's initiatives and turn them to competitive advantage? By employing covert initiatives, Party can test Other's interest in problem solving without taking undue risks. If Other passes the test, Party can then turn with confidence to more overt forms of problem solving.

If covert approaches were not available, stalemates would often be insoluble despite both parties' desire for problem solving, because Party would not have a low-risk way of checking out Other's readiness to cooperate.

Let us now examine three types of covert approaches in greater detail.

Back-Channel Contacts

Back-channel contacts consist of informal problem-solving discussions behind the scenes. Such discussions usually involve a small number of people and often take place in relaxed and neutral settings, such as over a shared meal. Back-channel contacts commonly occur during negotiation while seemingly rigid, contentious posturing is taking place on the official level. Reports of such contacts are found in accounts of negotiation in the international (Alger, 1961), industrial (Douglas, 1962), and domestic commercial (Pruitt, 1971) arenas. They were especially important during the Iranian hostage negotiations. Such contacts provide a more flexible arena for the development of integrative solutions than is usually available at the negotiating table. Back-channel contacts are also found outside the context of formal negotiation. For example, secret meetings between Secretary of State Henry Kissinger and Premier Chou En-lai laid the groundwork for President Nixon's trip to China, which was the watershed for improved Sino-American relations in the 1970s.

Back-channel contacts reduce the three risks mentioned earlier. Position loss is seldom a problem, because both parties ordinarily understand that ideas mentioned in a private discussion are not official positions unless or until they are formally labeled as such. Image loss and information loss cannot be completely averted, but they can be minimized by arranging for the participants to speak for themselves as individuals rather than for their organizations. This reduces the likelihood that their problem-solving activities will be seen as a sign that their constituents are ready to capitulate, or that information about the needs and values of their constituents will be derived from what the informal representatives say. Additional insurance against these latter losses can be achieved by assigning to back-channel meetings lower-status members of the organizations (such as technical experts) who are capable of problem solving but cannot be assumed to speak definitively for their superiors.

There are certain trade-offs in assigning low-level personnel to such meetings and allowing participants to speak for themselves. Image loss and information loss are indeed minimized, but there is also a danger that these people will be less capable of engaging in effective problem solving because they are not fully acquainted with their organization's perspective or are not fully believed when they speak about this matter. This danger can be minimized by a two-step progression in which informal problem-solving discussions are followed by more formal meetings where actual commitments can be made. The informal discussions make their contribution by increasing Party's assurance that Other is genuinely interested in problem solving, and by identifying possible directions in which the final agreement can go. The formal discussions put the finishing touches, and the official stamp of approval, on the agreement.

Back-channel meetings also have the virtue of being out of the public eye. Participants can reveal information and take positions without worrying about the reactions of allies, third parties, and (to some extent) constituents. This allows a degree of flexibility that may not be possible in more open contexts.

Use of Intermediaries

When the risks seem too great for back-channel meetings, or when it is impossible for the parties to make direct contact, third parties can sometimes be used for problem solving. An American newsman, John Scali, carried messages back and forth between the governments of the United States and the Soviet Union during the Cuban missile crisis (Young, 1968). A similar function was served by Christian Bourguet and Hector Villalon, a French lawyer and an Argentine businessman, respectively, during the negotiations that freed the American hostages in Iran (ABC News, 1981). Extended chains of intermediaries are sometimes necessary when the parties have very poor relations with each other. During the Vietnam War, a chain went from the United States government through officials in Great Britain to officials in Eastern Europe and finally to the government of North Vietnam (Kraslow & Loory, 1968). The relations between the parties at each link of this chain were better than the relations between the United States and North Vietnam.

Intermediaries provide greater protection against image loss and information loss than is found in back-channel meetings, because it is even less clear whether they represent the thinking of the people who sent them. If they seem soft, Party cannot be sure that Other is ready to make deep concessions; if they reveal information about underlying interests, Party cannot be sure that this information is accurate, so it it is not useful for constructing threats. Yet intermediaries are often able to find enough common ground and provide enough assurance of Other's commitment to problem solving to make it seem worthwhile to launch more direct contacts.

Sending Conciliatory Signals

Conciliatory signals (also called tacit communication or sign language) are hints of a willingness to make a particular concession or to take some other cooperative action. Recall our description in Chapter 9 of Fischer and Spassky negotiating a draw in their chess match. Or consider Peters's (1952) account of an exchange between negotiators for labor and management—after a mediator had just suggested a compromise raise of 9 cents per hour:

> Frazier and Turner looked each other in the eye. Somewhere a communication established itself without a word between them. The question in each other's eye was, "If I move to 9 cents will you move to 9 cents?" Frazier said, "Well, we are willing to give it some consideration for the sake of averting a strike." Turner nodded his acquiescence. The tension was gone as he buzzed his secretary to come in and take down a memorandum of agreement. (p. 18)

Both the glances and the tentative statement by Frazier can be regarded as signals. The latter signal was less ambiguous than the former, presumably because the glances convinced Frazier that the risks were small enough so that he could afford to gamble on a tentative endorsement of the mediator's suggestions. Ping-Pong–like sequences such as this, advancing to greater and greater clarity, are very common in conversations by signaling.

An effective signal must be both noticeable and disavowable. The latter is necessary so that image loss and position loss are minimized in the event that Other is not ready to accept the proposal implied by the signal. Party must be ready and able to deny it intended to send a signal if Other turns out to be uninterested in exchanging concessions. Otherwise Party's negotiation position may be weakened.

Conciliatory signals are useful for sending up trial balloons about proposed compromises or integrative solutions. They are also useful for proposing that joint problem solving begin while minimizing image loss if Other is not interested. However, unlike back-channel contacts and the activities of intermediaries, signals cannot contribute directly to the development of new ideas for integrative solutions.

We have determined that covert problem solving is often employed where there is fear of image loss, position loss, or information loss. This kind of activity takes three forms: back-channel contacts, sending messages through third parties, and sending conciliatory signals.

STRATEGIES FOR PERSUADING OTHER TO ENGAGE IN PROBLEM SOLVING

When Party is ready for problem solving (whether because of being in a perceived stalemate or because of feeling a genuine interest in Other's welfare), it is helpful if Other is also ready for problem solving. This is so for two reasons. First, Party can now employ more overt forms of problem-solving tactics, confident that Other will not take advantage of them. Such tactics are usually more effective. Second, joint problem solving—wherein the two parties exchange information about their values and perceptions and work together in search of a jointly acceptable solution—is usually more efficient than individual problem solving. If the two parties can talk things over, they can develop a search model that will represent a true melding of their separate interests.

As mentioned earlier, if Party is uncertain about Other's readiness for problem solving, it often adopts covert moves to explore this readiness. However, this is not the only possible approach. Party can sometimes take the initiative and try to convert Other to problem solving.

A key to success in the latter enterprise is for Party to adopt *overtly* a firm but conciliatory stance (Komorita & Esser, 1975; McGillicuddy et al., 1984). Earlier we argued that a firm but conciliatory stance is efficient in generating creative solutions. What we are arguing now is that such a stance, *if clearly telegraphed to Other*, encourages Other to follow Party into problem solving.

Our reasoning is as follows: The firm part of this strategy is needed in order to persuade Other that contentious tactics are infeasible, because Party is unalterably committed to achieving its basic interests, and to prevent Other from misinterpreting the conciliatory parts of Party's message as signs of weakness. The conciliatory part of this strategy is needed in order to convince Other that there is integrative potential in the situation—that Party can be trusted to help find a reasonable solution to the problems at hand and not to revert to contentious behavior if Other decides to initiate problem solving. There is a bumper sticker that says "Courtesy is catching." Good problem solving, we believe, is catching too.

An example of a firm but conciliatory stance can be seen in the statements made and actions taken by President John F. Kennedy in 1961 during the second Berlin crisis. The Soviet Union, under Premier Nikita Khrushchev, had been trying to end American occupation of West Berlin—and hence to end the rapid flight of skilled personnel from East Germany—by threatening to sign a separate peace treaty with East Germany and buzzing planes in the Berlin Corridor. Recognizing that some concessions had to be made, Kennedy "decided to be firm on essentials but negotiate on non-essentials" (Snyder & Diesing, 1977, p. 566). In a speech delivered on July 25, he announced three fundamental principles that ensured the integrity and continued American occupation of West Berlin. The firmness of these principles was underscored by a pledge to defend them by force and a concomitant military buildup. Kennedy also indicated flexibility and a concern about Russian sensitivities by calling for negotiations to remove "actual irritants" to the Soviet Union and its allies.

Two results were achieved. One was the building of the Berlin Wall. At the time, this action was seen in the West as a contentious move by the Soviet Union. In retrospect, it can be viewed as an outcome of problem solving, because it was the culmination of a sequence of public statements on both sides hinting at the desirability of building a wall (Pruitt & Holland, 1972). It solved both parties' problems, stopping the population loss from East Germany without disturbing American rights in West Berlin. The second result was eventual negotiations, which made these American rights explicit in writing.

Specific guidelines for demonstrating that one has adopted the two sides of the firm but conciliatory stance are explored in the next several subsections.

Signaling Firmness

Our analysis suggests a variety of ways in which Party can signal firm commitment to its basic interests. One is to make a vigorous verbal defense of these interests. A second is to be unwilling to make unilateral concessions (Komorita & Esser, 1975). A third is to arrange for Party's constituents to make tough statements and to make it clear to Other that Party is accountable to these constituents (Wall, 1977). A fourth is to develop a moderate amount of threat capacity (Lindskold & Bennett, 1973) sufficient to impress Other with Party's firmness, but not so formidable as to provoke Other into adopting fear-based countermeasures.[14]

It may also be necessary to employ contentious tactics in order to underscore firmness with respect to basic principles. This can be particularly important when Party has recently yielded ground. Otherwise, Other may interpret Party's flexibility as a sign of weakness, maintain or raise its aspirations, and redouble its dedication to a contentious approach. Again, Kennedy's performance is a good example. His pledge to use force if necessary to defend Western rights in Berlin and the concomitant American military buildup served this function. Contentious tactics are also sometimes needed in conjunction with problem-solving overtures to motivate Other to take enough of an interest in Party's welfare to engage in problem solving.

In recommending the use of contentious tactics, we are mindful of their many problems. Using these tactics can undermine problem solving by encouraging both the user and the target to become more rigid in their positions. These tactics also tend to alienate the target, hence, to encourage the development of conflict spirals. In short, contentious tactics have the capacity of both contributing to and detracting from the development of mutually acceptable solutions. How can one obtain the advantages of these tactics while avoiding the pitfalls? There are at least four answers to this question:

1. Use contentious tactics to defend basic interests rather than as a particular solution to the conflict. Thus, Kennedy defended the American presence in Berlin without prejudging particular arrangements.
2. Send signals of flexibility and of concern about Other's interests in conjunction with contentious displays. Kennedy did this by offering to negotiate about "actual irritants." Such maneuvers are designed to make the integrative potential appear great enough to Other that problem solving seems warranted.
3. Insulate contentious behavior from conciliatory behavior so that neither part of the strategy undermines the other. The most common form of insulation is the "bad cop/good cop" routine, in which contentious behavior is assigned to one team member (the bad cop) and problem-solving behavior to another (the good cop). In the context of the bad cop's threats, the good cop's offer of cooperation is more likely to be reciprocated by the target. In the

[14]Experimental evidence shows that if agreement is reached, firmer negotiators tend to achieve better outcomes (Bartos, 1974; Donohue, 1981; Siegel & Fouraker, 1960; Weingart et al., 1990).

context of the good cop's blandishments, the bad cop's escalation is less likely to produce a reciprocal escalation by the target. An example is the collection agent who indicates to a laggard creditor that his or her principal will sue unless the two of them can reach a mutually acceptable agreement.

4. Employ deterrent rather than compellent threats. Compellent threats require Other to adopt a specific option. Deterrent threats rule out an action or solution favored by Other but do not comment on the adequacy of other options, allowing Other to choose among them. In short, deterrent threats involve saying no to Other without demanding that Other say yes.

Signaling Conciliatory Intentions

Flexibility about the shape of the final agreement and concern about Other's outcomes can be signaled in a number of ways:

- Party should openly express concern about Other's welfare and "acknowledge its interests as part of the problem" (Fisher et al., 1991, p. 51).
- Party should indicate a willingness to change its proposals if a way can be found to bridge the interests of Party and Other.
- Party should demonstrate problem-solving capacity—for example, by assembling an expert negotiating team so that it is obvious to Other that Party has the capacity to develop useful new ideas.
- Party should maintain open communication channels to show Other that it is ready for cooperation.
- Party should reward Other for taking any cooperative initiatives (Deutsch, 1973).
- Party should reexamine any elements of its supposed interests that are clearly unacceptable to Other to be sure that they are essential to Party's welfare. If these turn out to be low in priority to Party, it may be possible to drop them. If they turn out to be high in priority, it may be possible for Party to discover interests underlying these interests that are not incompatible with Other's stance.

CONCLUSIONS: THE DEBATE BETWEEN THE HAWKS AND THE DOVES

Most communities (small groups, organizations, and nations) contain subgroups of hawks and doves who take opposing positions with respect to external relations. The hawks favor a tough, contentious defense of collective interests; the doves favor negotiation and problem solving with the outgroup in question. Our analysis of the importance of being firm but conciliatory suggests that both factions are needed to conduct external relations sanely: doves to work out agreements and hawks to avoid giving away the store.[15]

Groups in conflict usually try to conceal the hawk-dove debate in an effort to present a united front to the adversary. Research suggests that revealing such internal divisions is more likely than concealing them to encourage the outgroup to make a cooperative response (Jacobson, 1981). The presence of hawks sends a message of firmness and determination, while the presence of doves sends a message of readiness for conciliation. The convergence of these two messages encourages the outgroup to cooperate, so it is wise to show that the ingroup consists of both kinds of birds. This effect should be even stronger if one can demonstrate that these two factions are about equal in political strength. If so, contentious behavior from the outgroup will backfire by leading to the ascendancy of the hawks, whereas cooperative behavior will be rewarded by encouraging political triumph by the doves. This effect is closely related to that produced by the bad cop/good cop routine.

In this chapter we have demonstrated the importance of problem solving as a technique for settling conflict. It is not always possible for the parties to a conflict to take this approach. Escalation may have made them too rigid and suspicious of one another to embark on such a course, or they may have little faith in the integrative potential of their situation. In such circumstances, it is often necessary to involve third parties in the controversy, a topic to which we now turn.

[15]Lax and Sebenius (1986) develop a parallel, and more fundamental, distinction in negotiation theory between "creating value" and "claiming value."

11

The Intervention of Third Parties: Mediation

What Is a Third Party? • The Range and Variety of Third Party Roles • *Formal vs. Informal Roles* • *Individual vs. Representative Roles* • *Invited vs. Noninvited Roles* • *Impartial vs. Partial Roles* • *Advisory vs. Directive Roles* • *Interpersonal vs. Intergroup Roles* • *Resolution-oriented vs. Relationship-oriented Roles* • Effective Mediation • *Modification of Physical and Social Structure* • *Modification of Issue Structure* • *Increasing the Disputants' Motivation to Reach Agreement* • An Aside on the Limits of Third Party Intervention • The Evolution of Third Party Intervention • *Other New Developments in Third Party Intervention* • *Determinants of Third Party Behavior* • Conclusions

In the course of this book, we have seen that people in the throes of escalation become heavily invested in waging conflict. Positions tend toward rigidity because the protagonists are reluctant to budge lest any conciliatory gesture be misconstrued as a sign of weakness. Moreover, the parties may lack the imagination, creativity, and/or experience necessary to work their way out of the pit they have jointly engineered—not because they don't want to, but because they don't know how. Thus, for a variety of reasons, disputants are sometimes either unable or unwilling to move toward agreement of their own accord. Under these circumstances, third parties often become involved at the behest of one or more of the disputants,[1] on their own initiative, or by institutional arrangement. The form of third party intervention that has received the most attention—in research, theory, and practice—is *mediation*. For that reason, mediation will command much of our attention here.

In this chapter, we examine more closely the important role played by third parties.[2] We begin by considering what is meant by a third party and what it is about a third party's very existence and inclusion in a conflict that has transforming implications. Next we review the range and variety of third party roles that exist in interpersonal, intergroup, and international settings.[3] Then we take a closer look at the kinds of things that mediators can do to bring about more effective dispute settlement. In other words, we address the important question of exactly how mediation can help. We then examine some of the limits of third party intervention more generally—the circumstances in which such outside intervention is likely to prove ineffectual or even destructive. We discuss third party intervention as an ongoing and continually evolving process, and we close the chapter by introducing a new, emerging area of third party intervention, focusing on the design of dispute resolution systems.

WHAT IS A THIRD PARTY?

Stated most simply, a third party is an individual or collective that is external to a dispute between two or more people and that tries to help them reach agreement. Intervention by a third party may be classified broadly into two types: contractual and emergent (Kressel & Pruitt, 1989; Pruitt & Carnevale, 1993). Contractual intervention is performed by a conflict management specialist (e.g., a professional mediator or judge) who has expertise and experience with the issues under discussion. The third party usually has no prior relationship with the disputants, and its primary focus is on settling the dispute rather than improving the relationship between Party and Other.

Emergent intervention is performed by a nonspecialist who has an interest in resolving the conflict. The third party typically has an ongoing

[1]There are a variety of other reasons why Party contacts a third party, including seeking its advice or sympathy; hoping the third party will denounce or pressure Other (Averill, 1983; Keating et al., 1993); and "scoring points" with Other by being the first to seek outside assistance.

[2]Reviews of the theoretical and research literature on third party functions may be found in Bercovitch (1984), Bercovitch & Rubin (1992), Kolb (1994), Kressel & Pruitt (1989), Pruitt & Carnevale (1993), Rubin (1980, 1981), Smith (1987), and Wall & Lynn (1993).

[3]Third party intervention, mediation in particular, has been applied in recent years to such diverse areas as community conflict, school disputes, civil and criminal litigation, divorce and child custody cases, sexual harassment cases, public sector disputes, environmental regulation, labor-management conflict, and international disputes.

relationship with the disputants and often has a stake in the outcome of the dispute. A parent's intervention in a quarrel between two siblings, a manager's mediation of a disagreement between two workers, a nation's intervention in a land dispute between two of its neighbors—all are examples of emergent intervention. A third party in emergent intervention tends to work not only for settlement of the substantive issues under discussion but also to improve the disputants' perhaps damaged relationship. The bluffs, threats, and irrevocable commitments that characterize Party's efforts to prevail in an escalating struggle are apt to be interrupted by the third party's presence. This can help to shift the disputants in the direction of settlement.

The mere presence of a third party, either in contractual or emergent intervention, is likely to profoundly change the interactions between Party and Other. Under most circumstances, such change is likely to be beneficial. The destructive path of the escalating conflict is diverted, at least momentarily, by the third party's inclusion. Merely introducing a third person into a dyadic system dramatically changes the relational possibilities and has a profoundly disruptive effect (Simmel, 1902). The effect of such disruption can be highly beneficial, but it can also prove problematic.[4]

Thus, inclusion of the third party may occur in the midst of efforts by the disputants to work directly toward settlement. Involvement in a conflictual relationship that is characterized by genuine and effective movement toward settlement may have the costly effect of breaking a newly established—and possibly quite fragile—momentum toward agreement. Indeed, research shows that third party intervention, particularly active and forceful intervention, is counterproductive when the disputants are able to move toward settlement by themselves (Hiltrop, 1985, 1989; Lim & Carnevale, 1990; Zubek et al., 1992). For example, a mediator's active intervention in a divorce mediation has been found to be harmful when couples are already engaging in constructive conversation (Donohue, 1989).

The more general point is that *third party intervention is not a panacea in conflict resolution.* Throughout this chapter we shall continue to hammer away at this important point. Third party intervention is like a strong medicine that may have undesirable side effects, and that should therefore be employed with caution and some reluctance. The best, most effective third parties become involved only when needed and are so successful at helping the principals find a settlement and develop a good working relationship with each other that their intervention is no longer necessary.

[4]See Sartre's (1955) magnificent play *No Exit* for a dramatic illustration of a three-way relationship in danger of running amok.

THE RANGE AND VARIETY OF THIRD PARTY ROLES

Third parties have probably been in business since the dawn of humanity; their various roles are well documented in such sources as the *Bible,* the *Iliad,* and the *Odyssey.* In examining the range and variety of these roles, it may be useful to distinguish among a set of dimensions. The seven we discuss next are but a few of the many possibilities.

Formal vs. Informal Roles

The roles of many third parties are defined on the basis of some formal understanding among the disputants or on the basis of legal precedent or licensing/certification procedures. Some third party roles are *mediator* (someone who helps the principals reach a voluntary agreement—for example, United Nations Secretary General Perez de Cuellar during the months leading up to the 1991 Gulf War), *arbitrator* (someone empowered to make binding recommendations for the settlement of a dispute), and *ombudsperson* (someone charged with the resolution of conflicts that arise between individuals and institutions). The effectiveness of such formal third party roles stems from their legitimacy—these third parties have the right to be in the business of resolving conflicts.

In contrast are those more informal third party roles, such as *intermediary* (whose job it is to communicate messages between the principals)[5] and *special envoy* (someone dispatched to convey a particular message on behalf of Party). Unlike their more formal counterparts, informal third parties typically function behind the scenes, out of the glare of the spotlight. During the 1979–1980 Iranian hostage crisis, Hector Villalon and Christian Bourguet played two of the more important informal third party roles: they served as behind-the-scenes conduits between Iran and the United States at a time when all formal communication between the two nations had ground to a halt. Informal third parties can thus be enormously helpful in the shaping of a settlement, especially when more formal roles have been discounted because the conflict is so intense that direct, public communication is deemed unacceptable.

Individual vs. Representative Roles

Third parties usually act as individuals, reflecting their own idiosyncratic points of view. On occasion, particularly in complex disputes involving multiple parties, such as labor-management negotiations or international

[5]This role was described in Chapter 10 in the discussion of ways of initiating problem solving.

affairs, third parties occupy representative roles instead. As representatives, such third party intervenors speak for the interests of a constituency and can convey all the clout and legitimacy attendant on being the spokesperson for a potentially vast organization. Part of U.S. Secretary of State James Baker's effectiveness in convening a Middle East peace conference in Madrid in 1992 was surely attributable to his position as representative of an extremely powerful state with many resources.

As this illustration makes clear, a representative third party role is likely to prove effective—even more effective than an individual role—only so long as the constituency represented is seen by the principals as having legitimate rights and interests. To the extent that such perceived legitimacy is absent, the representative role may prove quite ineffective. During the Iranian hostage crisis, for example, United Nations Secretary General Kurt Waldheim was ineffective in his intervention attempts precisely because he was regarded by the Iranians as a representative of an illegitimate organization.[6]

Invited vs. Noninvited Roles

It often happens that a third party intervenes at the request of one or both of the principals, as when the members of a divorcing couple agree to seek out the services of a divorce mediator. When this happens, the third party's recommendations are likely to prove quite effective, for two reasons: First, the invitation to intervene suggests that at least one of the parties is motivated to address the dispute in question. Second, the fact that the third party has been invited increases its legitimacy, thereby making its intervention more likely to gain acceptance.

In contrast are those uninvited roles, in which a third party (such as a person witnessing a dispute between two mutual friends) spontaneously intervenes or does so by virtue of a legal requirement. Such uninvited third parties have none of the automatic benefit accruing to their invited counterparts, but they may nevertheless prove effective. This is especially likely when the disputants regard the uninvited third party as impartial and genuinely motivated to help.

Impartial vs. Partial Roles

A third party who is seen as impartial is generally more likely to be successful than one who is not. When disputants believe that a mediator is bi-

[6]See Bercovitch & Rubin (1992) for further analysis of individual vs. representative mediation roles in international relations.

ased against them, they are likely to be less receptive to mediation (Welton & Pruitt, 1987). However, impartiality is by no means an absolute requirement for effectiveness—and fortunately so, because impartiality in a third party may prove impossible to obtain.[7]

As Fisher (1981) points out, people in conflict often expect a third party to be some sort of "eunuch from Mars." Such pure, dispassionate, and disinterested individuals rarely exist. Indeed, it is often the case that a partial mediator is the only readily available alternative (Faure, 1989; Kressel, 1972; Touval & Zartman, 1985, 1989),[8] and this partiality may even prove to be of some benefit in the dispute settlement process (Wittmer et al., 1991). Since disputants usually have as their main concern the mediator's ability to get them what they want, they may be receptive to a partial third party in such circumstances (Touval & Zartman, 1989).

In addition, it is not unusual for mediators to take sides in order to offset a power disparity. As we saw in our discussion of stalemate (Chapter 9), before disputants can be motivated to work toward settlement, they need to feel that they are relatively equal in power. This causes them to view the situation as a stalemate and encourages them to employ problem-solving tactics, including collaboration with the third party. Knowing this, a mediator who is confronted with a situation of power disparity often sides with the less powerful disputant.[9] For example, by suggesting that discussions take place on the home turf of the weaker party, or even by appearing to favor the interests and positions of this less powerful disputant, a mediator may be able to create more nearly ideal conditions for joint problem solving.

Advisory vs. Directive Roles

Sometimes third parties are placed in the position of giving advice only (mediators); on other occasions they are allowed to be directive (arbitrators). Third party directiveness is sometimes needed, as when the principals are so hostile or have such opposed interests that they are incapable of reaching agreement. But third party directiveness also has its drawbacks. Solutions devised by arbitrators are less likely to be integrative, in the sense of synthesizing the two parties' interests, than are those devised by the principals with the aid of a mediator. This is because the principals

[7]See Kressel & Pruitt (1989), Smith (1991), and Touval & Zartman (1985) for more detailed discussions of mediator impartiality.

[8]In international relations, for example, it is impossible find a third party who doesn't come from some country of origin; any mediator can be suspected of partiality.

[9]An interesting finding is that mediators are not perceived as biased even when they have attempted to equalize power between the disputants (Ippolito & Pruitt, 1990). These authors reason that the parties somehow regard balancing attempts as justifiable or simply do not understand that such attempts are being made.

usually know their own interests better than any third party can. Also, the principals are more likely to identify with and become committed to agreements of their own devising than those imposed by the third party.[10] Both because the solutions tend to be integrative and because the parties tend to make a stronger commitment, agreements reached through mediation tend to last longer than those reached through arbitration.

Interpersonal vs. Intergroup Roles

Third parties, such as couple therapists, divorce mediators, and judges, typically intervene in disputes between individuals. Just as important, and far more complex, are instances of third party intervention in disputes between groups and between nations. Sometimes these disputes appear to be between individuals. However, when these individuals are accountable to (or represent) a constituency, the conflict is more accurately understood as one between *groups.* Only a foolish labor mediator would assume that a strike can be resolved simply by meeting with the representatives of each side, without taking into account the constituency pressures to which each is subject.

Resolution-oriented vs. Relationship-oriented Roles

Some third parties focus primarily on settling the dispute at hand. Others focus more on improving or repairing the relationship between the disputants. Arbitrators and some types of mediators typically assume a resolution orientation; other mediators (such as marriage counselors and couple therapists) assume more of a relationship focus. Whereas a resolution-oriented third party is likely to focus on the content of a dispute and try to push the dispute toward substantive settlement, a relationship-oriented third party is likely instead to focus on the process of decision making, the way in which the disputants are discussing the issues.

EFFECTIVE MEDIATION

In this section, we develop the view that there are three kinds of things a mediator can do to intervene effectively: modify the physical and social structure of the dispute, alter the issue structure of the dispute, and

[10]In this general regard, Kolb (1983) makes a useful and interesting distinction between "deal makers" and "orchestrators." Mediators who function as deal makers are active, intrusive, and eager to put together a deal. Orchestrators are more interested in the interplay (orchestration) of elements that allow the disputants to work out an agreement for themselves.

act in ways that increase the parties' motivation to take their dispute seriously.[11]

Modification of Physical and Social Structure

A mediator who wishes to move the disputants closer to settlement can modify the physical and/or social structure of the conflict in many ways. The possibilities for such modification include structuring communication between the principals, opening and neutralizing the site in which problem solving takes place, imposing time limits, and infusing additional resources. Let us now consider each of these forms of physical and social modification in turn.

Direct Contact

At first blush it might appear that a mediator should always encourage direct contact[12] between the disputants. What better way for parties to work through a conflict than by openly airing their differences? However, social psychological research does not fully support this advice. Experiments by Krauss and Deutsch (1966) and others indicate that direct contact between people in conflict helps only when the intensity of the conflict is relatively small—in other words, when hostility is low and perceived common ground is large. Under these circumstances, disputants who are given an opportunity for direct contact are likely to use it for joint problem solving in order to work through those few differences that separate them.

Quite the opposite is likely to occur when conflict is intense or highly escalated. When Party is required or encouraged to talk with Other, Party (in an intense conflict) uses this opportunity to heap abuse on Other, to make an already bad interpersonal situation even worse. Under such circumstances, a mediator would be well advised to *prevent* direct contact between the principals until a point is reached where it appears that such contact will improve the situation rather than exacerbate it.

When direct communication is ill advised, there are two things a mediator can do that will allow the disputants to make better use of later opportunities for direct contact. One is to "caucus" with the two parties separately and thus control the communication between them. Caucusing is a favorite mediator tactic when hostility runs high and disputants will not

[11]Actually, there are *lots* of things a third party can do. Here we have identified the most important general approaches that an effective mediator can take. For more information on third party tactics, see Fisher & Ury (1978), Kressel & Pruitt (1989), Wall (1981), and Wall & Lynn (1993).

[12]In the first edition of *Social Conflict*, we discussed "communication" instead of "direct contact." As our students have correctly observed, communication entails not only talking but, more importantly, effective listening. The research described here focuses primarily on the effects of talking.

engage in joint problem solving (Welton et al., 1992). Through caucusing, the mediator can obtain insight into Party's underlying concerns and interests in ways that would be impossible in the presence of Other. Furthermore, the mediator can improve Party's image of Other by encouraging Party to put itself in Other's shoes and by presenting Other's position in a sympathetic way. Evidence indicates that caucus use tends to reduce hostility between the disputants and increase problem solving between the mediator and each of the disputants (Welton et al., 1988, 1992). Moreover, caucusing tends to enhance perceptions that the mediator is empathic (Bethel & Singer, 1982).[13]

Another thing a mediator can do is teach the disputants effective and constructive communication skills. In their classic research on the effects of communication in conflict-intensified relationships, Krauss and Deutsch (1966) found that conflict abated only when a third party (the experimenter in this case) actively tutored the disputants in the effective use of communication. In particular, the competitive struggle ended only when the experimenter taught Party how to take the role of Other, to place itself in Other's shoes, and to understand the issues as Other might.[14]

In general, when conflict is mild it makes sense for a mediator to bring the disputants together so that direct communication can take place. But when conflict is severe it often makes better sense to keep them separate and to act as an intermediary who conveys messages back and forth, improves the parties' images of each other, and trains them in communication skills.

Site Openness

Quite apart from encouraging or restricting communication, an effective mediator may be able to generate movement toward agreement by systematically varying the openness of the site in which discussions between the principals take place. An open site is one that can be readily observed and influenced by a variety of audiences, including constituents and the media. A closed site is characterized by limited access on the part of external observers to the discussions that take place.

An effective mediator would do well to recommend that all early discussions between the disputants take place under closed-site condi-

[13]Caucusing may have negative consequences as well, as when Party's suspicions are aroused by a private meeting between the mediator and Other. These and other issues concerning the impact of caucusing are discussed by Jones (1989), Pruitt et al. (1989a), and Welton et al. (1988, 1992).

[14]The same sort of effect has been observed in research by Herbert C. Kelman and his colleagues (Cohen et al., 1977; Kelman, 1972, 1982; Kelman & Cohen, 1976, 1986). In one study, for example, four Israeli, four Egyptian, and four Palestinian participants were brought together for a meeting to discuss the ongoing Middle East conflict. By providing the three groups of participants with separate prenegotiation training in communication skills and perspective taking, the participants were better able to engage in a constructive discussion of the many differences among them.

tions. Only when an agreement has been struck, or is virtually certain to be struck, should the doors to the site be thrown open to the external world. The line of reasoning behind this conclusion is that site openness has the effect of "setting in concrete" whatever moves, gestures, or offers have just occurred. In the presence of an observing audience, including the media, disputants are likely to take far more seriously the image of strength or weakness that they project. As a result, premature site openness is apt to encourage the adoption of tough and intransigent bargaining positions, which make it difficult to reach agreement.

Paradoxically, site openness makes sense at a later time, when settlement has been, or is about to be, reached. This is because the presence of external observers is likely to commit the parties to their agreement in a way that does not permit reversal.

During the 1978 Camp David negotiations between Israel and Egypt (described in Chapter 1), U.S. President Carter apparently incorporated into the discussions virtually all aspects of the preceding analysis. Throughout the thirteen days of negotiations, Carter went out of his way to shield Prime Minister Begin of Israel and Egyptian President Sadat from public view. Virtually nothing was made known to the public other than the fact that Begin was watching particular television programs at night while Sadat was enjoying his stay in a particular cabin in the woods. Only at the conclusion of the meetings, when an agreement had been reached in principle, did the parties surface. At the very end of the negotiations, they appeared on the lawn of the White House, where they signed multiple documents in full view of a world of onlookers.

Site Neutrality

Systematically varying site neutrality is another useful tactic. It is often advantageous for negotiation to take place at a neutral site—one that is not on the home turf of either disputant, but on neutral territory. This helps the third party control the access of observers to the negotiations and also prevents either side from gaining a tactical advantage by virtue of site location. Research supports the importance of site neutrality: international mediations that take place in neutral sites have higher success rates than those that take place in the territory of one of the disputants (Bercovitch & Lamare, 1992). However, when one party is much weaker than the other, the effective third party may do well to offset this power discrepancy by deliberately staging discussions on the home turf of the less powerful party.[15]

Time Limits

A third party can sometimes get the principals moving by unilaterally suggesting or imposing deadlines. In the face of such time pressure, the disputants are forced to come to grips with the costs that will result if

[15]For further analysis of the pros and cons of site location, see Salacuse & Rubin (1990).

agreement is not reached in time. This makes them more likely to move toward settlement. Moreover, if time is more costly to the more powerful disputant, the mediator can further the cause of power equalization by imposing a deadline. As an example of the effectiveness of time limits, consider the deadline imposed by President Carter on Begin and Sadat toward the end of the Camp David talks. Carter indicated that he would have to abandon his mediation and turn to other pressing activities in Washington if they were unable to reach agreement by a certain date. Agreement was reached shortly thereafter.

When imposing a deadline, mediators must be careful not to move too soon. Principals need to be given enough time to reduce their aspirations or to engage in the creative thinking necessary to develop an integrative solution.[16] Research evidence indicates that time pressure makes joint problem solving less likely (Carnevale & Lawler, 1986; Yukl et al., 1976). Thus, the best advice for third parties is to wait to impose a deadline until a solution is just around the corner. The effect of such a judiciously timed deadline is to inspire Party to finish the process rather than waiting endlessly for Other to make the next move. Carter adhered to this principle at Camp David, announcing a deadline only after the negotiators had made considerable progress toward agreement.

Additional Resources

Effective mediators can manipulate at least three kinds of resources in an effort to generate pressure toward agreement. The first is their own time. As we have mentioned, by setting a limit to their participation, mediators can sometimes encourage the principals to move off the dead center of stalemate.

A second resource available is related to our earlier discussion of site openness. Mediators often have access to the domain of public sentiment and can unleash the "mad dogs of the media" in an effort to present information about the ongoing discussion in ways that apply pressure for settlement. Thus, a mediator can reward Party for conceding by lavishing public praise (Wall, 1979). Alternatively, it can punish intransigence by judicious public criticism. Mediators worth their salt know the power of a timely press release.

Finally, a mediator may be able to engender movement toward settlement by compensating the principals for their concessions. A good example is the role the United States has played as mediator between Egypt and Israel over the past several decades. Again and again the United States has promised military and economic assistance in exchange for flexibility in the negotiations between the two countries. Increasing the size of the pie in this way transforms a zero-sum game into a non-zero-

[16]There is another danger. The threat of deadline imposition may encourage Party to play a game of chicken (Schelling, 1960) in which Party digs in and refuses to concede, in the hope that Other will yield first.

sum game in which both disputants can do well. Of course, only a wealthy mediator with a large stake in solution of the controversy will be willing and able to play such a role.[17] This kind of role brings the mediator into active negotiation with the two principals so that they often become "actors with interests, or 'full participants' (to use current diplomatic language), not just neutral intermediaries" (Touval & Zartman, 1989, p. 128), and this level of mediator involvement of third parties produces a triangular (or "three-cornered") relationship.

Triangular arrangements, of course, can lead to triangulation, where two people gang up against the third. This can increase the mediator's leverage by allowing it to threaten to side with Other unless Party agrees to a concession (Touval & Zartman, 1989). But it can also cause the mediator to become trapped in a tug-of-war between the disputants.

A successful mediator always runs the risk of becoming too important to the principals. Its actions increase movement toward settlement but also may invite the principals' continued dependence on the mediator. If agreement this time was possible because of third party assistance, then why not lean on the mediator for similar help next time?[18] Moreover, to the extent that the mediator compensates the principals for reaching agreement, the infusion of third party resources may actually encourage a sort of blackmail. In this regard, Harris and Carnevale (1990) have found that when disputants realize that a mediator can compensate them for their concession making, and also has high concern for their aspirations, they make fewer concessions and send more contentious messages in order to elicit compensation. The mediator comes to be seen as wanting agreement so badly that it can be bullied into providing increased assistance.

The history of American mediation in the Middle East illustrates these points. Beginning with Kissinger's intervention between 1973 and 1975, and continuing through Carter's assistance at Camp David in 1978, the United States has made it clear that it will facilitate the settlement process by providing military and economic assistance as needed. Needs have a way of becoming demands (Zartman, 1981), and the Israelis and Arab states have both proved quite adept at delaying concessions to each other until American aid is promised. American interest in developing Middle East agreements may have created a condition that can be viewed as excessive dependence on the third party.

Modification of Issue Structure

People in the throes of escalating conflict often lose sight of the issues with which they began their struggle. They experience a lack of creativity and

[17]This role has been described aptly by Straus (1981) as "mediation with muscle."
[18]Dependence on the third party is called the "narcotic" effect (Chelius & Extejt, 1985; Kochan & Baderschneider, 1978).

imagination that deprives them of the opportunity to work their way out of the hole they have dug for themselves. An effective mediator can be helpful in this regard, assisting the disputants in the identification of existing issues and alternatives, helping them to package and sequence issues in ways that lead toward agreement, and introducing new issues and alternatives that did not occur to the disputants themselves. Let us consider each of these three forms of intervention.

Issue Identification

Research indicates that one of the most useful things a mediator can do is help the principals identify the several issues in dispute (Carnevale et al., 1989; Hiltrop, 1989; Pruitt et al., 1989b; Zubek et al., 1992). Because escalating conflict is often characterized by Party's distorted perceptions of Other and the issues in question, accurate information about preferences, expectations, and intentions should move the disputants closer to agreement. One useful tactic that a third party can employ is to have preliminary separate meetings with each of the parties to identify the issues.

Unfortunately, there are also some dangers in issue identification. If the disputants differ substantially on basic values or hold decidedly uncomplimentary views of one another, the mediator must be very careful *not* to allow certain issues to come to the fore—lest the result be an unproductive explosion. Unearthing issues that are rooted in values tends to harden the disputants' position and foster hostile behavior.

Closely akin to the matter of issue identification, but less fraught with the danger of a backfire, is third party education of the disputants about the dynamics of conflict. Kochan and Jick (1978) have observed that third parties can teach bargainers about the general nature of the process in which they are involved, thereby helping them to move toward a mutually acceptable agreement. Similarly, Burton (1969), who has developed a workshop method for studying and resolving international disputes, points to the importance of instruction regarding conflict dynamics. Finally, Fisher et al. (1991) observe that one of the most useful things a mediator can do is help disputants understand key negotiation concepts—such as the difference between the positions one takes in public and the interests one holds in private—and the way in which these concepts may be applied to facilitate dispute settlement.

Issue Packaging and Sequencing

Although disputants are occasionally required to address a single, monolithic issue, more often there are multiple issues to address. Under these conditions, the principals—often with the assistance of a skillful mediator—must decide whether to address these multiple issues all at once or sequentially.

Social psychological research on the bargaining process (Froman & Cohen, 1970; Kelley, 1966; Mannix et al., 1989) has consistently indicated that bargainers do better, in terms of the quality of the agreements reached, when they negotiate multiple issues as a package rather than sequentially. Such holistic negotiating allows the principals to explore all possible types of concession exchange and come up with wiser solutions.

Unfortunately, as issues proliferate, it becomes more difficult to deal with them as a package. In such cases, Party needs a sequential agenda to keep its sanity. Two principles should probably govern a mediator's efforts to structure such an agenda. One is that the sequence should run from more general to more specific issues if at all possible—or from formula to detail, in Zartman's (1977) terminology. This allows the parties to develop a "road map" before setting out on the difficult trip through the welter of specific issues. The other principle is that when there is a choice, easier issues should be tackled earlier in the agenda. The research evidence just cited favors the strategy of starting negotiation with easy issues. Neale and Bazerman (1991) have questioned this strategy, however, arguing that easy issues should be settled late, when concessions on them can be traded for concessions on more difficult issues. Success on these easy issues generates a kind of momentum that should carry over to the more intractable later issues and make them seem more amenable to problem solving (Donohue et al., 1984; Huber et al., 1986).

New Issues and Alternatives

Perhaps the most creative thing a mediator can do is introduce new issues and alternatives, thereby broadening the disputants' horizons and providing them with ideas for achieving integrative agreements. Using a variety of tactics such as caucusing, a mediator is often able to discern the parties' underlying interests and use this information to come up with new issues that might lead to resolving the dispute (Kolb & Rubin, 1991; Lax & Sebenius, 1986).

Although a mediator can introduce new issues and alternatives in many ways, several methods are particularly important. First, Fisher (1964) has pointed out that a mediator may attempt to break a conflictual stalemate by dividing large, all-encompassing issues into smaller, more manageable pieces; Fisher refers to this technique as *fractionation.* The 1962 Cuban missile crisis appeared, at first glance, to be comprised of a single issue: the relative toughness or weakness of the United States and the Soviet Union. Over the course of the thirteen days of the conflict, however, this monolithic, zero-sum issue was fractionated by the disputants themselves into a number of sub-issues (timing of missile removal, American compensation for this removal, and so on) that could be negotiated and that led eventually to a peaceful conclusion of the crisis.[19]

Second, a mediator may be able to introduce superordinate goals that help the disputants transcend the existing conflict (Brown & Wade, 1987; Deschamps & Brown, 1983; Sherif & Sherif, 1969). As mentioned in Chapter 9, superordinate goals have the capacity to transform a competitive struggle into a cooperative opportunity. The nations of the Middle East, for example, although they have been at one another's throats for years and are clearly in the throes of an intense competitive struggle, share several concerns that are potentially superordinate in nature. These include a harsh climate, drought, shared economic concerns, and a number of common enemies. At some point, a skillful mediator may be able to help the principals in this region to bridge at least a portion of their ongoing conflict by getting them to work on common objectives that offer possibilities for mutual cooperation.

Third, as we have already seen in our Chapter 7 discussion of the entrapment process, people in conflict may find themselves overcommitted to a course of action that privately makes no sense but from which they feel unable to escape. A skillful mediator may be able to help disputants escape from such entrapment by introducing a formula that allows them to circumvent the commitment. There are three ways in which this can be done. One is by dividing a concept into two or more subconcepts that can coexist. For example, when the state of Texas was ready to join the Union, it was committed to retaining a navy—a commitment that was incompatible with statehood. This was circumvented by dividing the concept of navy into two subconcepts, naval personnel and naval vessels. This allowed Texas to have all the naval personnel it wanted, but no ships!

A second way of circumventing a commitment is by relabeling an object or event so that it no longer falls within the scope of the commitment. Instead of demanding that the Israelis meet with the PLO, the United States, in devising the Madrid Conference, encouraged preliminary discussions by Israel with an entity identified simply as Palestinians, thereby allowing the Israelis a face-saving way to meet with spokespersons for a group that has not yet recognized the right of Israel to exist as a sovereign nation.

Finally, a mediator can help the disputants circumvent commitments through an "agreement to disagree." The United States and the People's Republic of China appear to have agreed to disagree about the status of Taiwan, thereby allowing the two nations to develop talks on a number of other topics. Agreeing to disagree permits the disputants to circumvent prior commitments to a competitive struggle by compartmentalizing

[19]By breaking large issues into smaller ones, the mediator can also elicit reciprocal cooperation from the disputants even if they do not trust each other (Pruitt & Carnevale, 1993). It is less risky for each party to make concessions on smaller issues than on large issues. Small concessions enhance the likelihood of further concessions.

those areas of disagreement in such a way that the remaining areas are available for work and discourse.

Increasing the Disputants' Motivation to Reach Agreement

A mediator's effectiveness hinges on its ability to move the disputants out of stalemate, in the direction of concession making and problem solving. A mediator can sometimes goad the disputants into such movement, but it is far better if the disputants themselves are motivated to take their conflict seriously. Only then will a solution be engineered that is apt to last. How can a mediator induce the disputants to move toward settlement? The answer entails work on five fundamental motivational concerns: concession making without loss of face, trust, emotions, momentum, and autonomy.

Encouraging Face Saving

People in the throes of escalating conflict tend to develop a distorted sense of the importance of looking tough and unyielding in the eyes of their adversaries and various constituencies. They also go out of their way to avoid doing things that might be construed as signs of weakness or image loss. All too often, the making of concessions—no matter how trivial or superfluous these concessions may be—is construed by each side as just such a sign. An effective mediator can be helpful in this regard, by allowing concession making without loss of face. By explicitly or implicitly requesting concessions, the mediator can deflect the responsibility for compromise from the shoulders of the disputants onto its own shoulders. A concession that each side was unwilling to grant before, lest it be seen as a chink in the armor that invites exploitation in the future, can now be made with the understanding that it has been suggested by the mediator (Pruitt & Johnson, 1970). In effect, Party can now say to Other that it has given something up not because it had to (because Other forced it to do so) but because Party chose to. In the spirit of being an obliging, cooperative, fair-minded individual, Party has gone along with the mediator's request for concessions and, in so doing, has moved closer to agreement.

Encouraging Trust

For disputants to be motivated to engage in problem solving, they must have some modicum of trust in each other; otherwise they will be too fearful of image loss, position loss, and information loss to proceed. For example, the level of trust that one spouse has for the other has been found to be a strong predictor of joint problem solving (Haun & Stinnett, 1974; Indvik & Fitzpatrick, 1982).

There are several things that a mediator can do to engender trust. First, it can encourage Party and Other to each make irrevocable concessions, no matter how small, in an effort to create tangible evidence of a willingness to give something up and to build commitment to a conciliatory process. The important consideration here resides in the concession's irrevocability, not in its magnitude.

At another level, a mediator can engender trust by pointing out areas of overlapping interests while downplaying areas of disagreement and conflict. By drawing the principals' attention to the interests they have in common, the mediator may be able to focus attention more on the possibilities of mutual gain than on the potential Party has for exploiting Other.

Defusing Emotions

Escalating struggles typically generate heavy emotions such as anger, resentment, and frustration. These emotions sometimes reflect deep-seated concerns that are not easily brushed away. In such cases, a mediator needs to train Party to identify emotions in itself and in Other and to deal with them sympathetically and realistically rather than in a punitive fashion. This is called "emotion-focused therapy" by Johnson and Greenberg (1985), who have developed and validated procedures for accomplishing such training.[20]

At other times, such emotions constitute only "hot steam," the venting of which permits the principals to work more effectively toward a settlement of their differences (Russell & Drees, 1989).[21] While disputants are venting their emotions, the mediator can listen carefully and sympathetically. Such active listening alone can help cool off the parties' high-running emotions. Consider the account of a female student at Bryant High School in Astoria, New York,[22] who participated in the school's mediation program:

> I came into a mediation session as a disputant with four girls on the other side. I thought, "Who needs this? What am I doing here?" I just wanted to punch these girls out. I figured that the mediator would tell me what I was going to have to do. But she didn't. Instead she drew me out, listened to me. It felt so good to let it all out: then I wasn't angry anymore. (Davis, 1986, p. 289)

By encouraging the venting of emotions, ideally in private caucus with Party rather than in the presence of Other, the mediator serves as a substitute target for the principals' emotional displays, thereby deflecting anger away from Other. The mediator's role here is analogous to a psy-

[20]Helping Party understand why Other behaves as it does often helps to cool off high-running emotions (Bies, 1989; Weiner et al., 1987).

[21]This is very much what Fisher et al. (1991) have in mind when they call for "separating the people from the problem" in negotiation.

[22]Trivia item: the first author's hometown.

chotherapist dealing with negative transference. Serving as a substitute target for the client's anger and emotion, the therapist allows the client to experience catharsis and to adopt a more realistic outlook. Henry Kissinger's intervention in the Middle East was repeatedly characterized by just such a willingness to absorb the angry sentiments that each side intended for the other but that were directed toward him instead (Rubin, 1981).

A final, important way in which a mediator can help the disputants come to grips with their angry feelings is through the timely infusion of humor. Humor can help to create a good mood in the midst of angry displays. In doing so, it may place the disputants in a state of mind that makes them more amenable to reaching agreement. As mentioned in Chapter 3, a good mood fosters genuine concern for Other, which can reduce retaliatory behavior (Baron, 1984, 1990; Baron & Ball, 1974), encourage concession making (O'Quin & Aronoff, 1981), and facilitate creative problem solving (Carnevale & Isen, 1986; Hollingshead & Carnevale, 1990). Humor also contributes to a willingness to trust the mediator (Kressel, 1972). Many professional mediators are keenly aware of the effectiveness of humor in defusing a hostile climate and eliciting cooperation (Kressel & Pruitt, 1989). In short, the judicious use of humor may actually facilitate movement toward settlement.

Encouraging Momentum

For the principals to be motivated to engage in problem solving, each must believe that there is common ground—that agreement is ultimately possible. There is nothing more desperate or hopeless than the sense that Party is working to no avail and that its best, most conciliatory efforts have little chance of bearing the fruit of agreement. A mediator can create the sense that agreement is possible by initiating and sustaining momentum in the negotiations.

As evidenced by Kissinger's form of "step-by-step" diplomacy in the Middle East, one way of establishing momentum is by engineering a series of small agreements linked to one another in chainlike fashion. Fed on a diet of small agreements, the principals in the Middle East moved from one disengagement arrangement to another, thereby establishing and maintaining a sense of movement and keeping the lines of communication and negotiation open at all times. As discussed earlier, to get such momentum going, it is often useful to arrange the issues so that the parties can work on the easier issues first.

Overcoming Autonomy Needs

Students of conflict, as well as third parties themselves, too often have assumed that people in conflict automatically welcome the assistance of outside intervenors. The model applied likens the conflict scenario to a town in the old American west, beset by discord and violence. Into this troubled picture rides the squeaky-clean third party, bringing peace and justice to the beleaguered citizens. At the conclusion, the third party rides off into the sunset, basking in the gratitude of the humble townsfolk, and on into the next troubled community. A comfortable Panglossian view of conflict, perhaps, but not a picture of reality.

A more accurate view of life in conflict, we suspect, is that people wish to manage their own affairs without the intrusion of an outsider. People typically want to mend their own fences and restore order to their own affairs. Hence, they are apt to turn to a third party only (or primarily) in desperation. People do not like to ask for help if they don't need it. To do so involves putting their fate in somebody else's hands and running the risk of being seen as needy, helpless, or unduly dependent on others. Disputants, like people in general, are guided by an intense need for autonomy. Third parties who wish to be effective would do well to keep this in mind.

Social psychological research on the effects of anticipated third party intervention has generally supported the preceding analysis of autonomy, particularly when the intensity of conflict is moderate or low. As research by various scholars (Bigoness, 1976; Hiltrop & Rubin, 1982; Johnson & Pruitt, 1972; LaTour et al., 1976; Pruitt et al., 1989b) has indicated, when disputants are in the midst of a conflict of relatively low intensity and are confronted with the possible intervention of a highly directive third party, they are more likely to come to agreement than when they anticipate less directive intervention. These results suggest that when disputants anticipate the intervention of a third party who will take over (like the old-time western hero), they move to avert such intervention by reaching agreement themselves—sooner and more readily the bossier the third party seems likely to be.

This is the situation that seems to prevail under conditions of low conflict intensity. When conflict intensity is large, however—when Party sees little common ground and/or is hostile toward Other—the effects of anticipated third party intervention look rather different. Party often sees itself as in stalemate. It despairs of solving the conflict on its own. Furthermore, as observed earlier, Party often has face-saving concerns that make it reluctant to make concessions, lest these concessions be construed by Other as a sign of weakness.

Under these circumstances, the intervention of a third party (particularly a directive third party) is often a welcome event. If the third party takes over and imposes a settlement, neither side will have been made to look foolish by giving in. These observations are supported by the finding that forceful third party intervention is effective when conflict intensity is high but is not effective when conflict intensity is low (Lim & Carnevale, 1990; Zubek et al., 1992).

Autonomy needs are often important under conditions of mild conflict, reducing receptivity to third party intervention. When conflict is intense, these autonomy needs may be swamped by an even greater concern with face saving, which encourages disputants to work with third parties.

AN ASIDE ON THE LIMITS OF THIRD PARTY INTERVENTION

We began this chapter by observing that third party intervention is no panacea. Mediators, for example, can help enormously, but they can also hamper efforts by the principals to develop an agreement. A truly effective third party, we believe, intervenes in such a way that disputants do not become dependent on it for help in the future. Like the dodo, an effective third party should be able to render itself obsolete and extinct. It should help instill in the disputants a sense of autonomy and self-sufficiency. Beware the third party who lingers and loiters about the scene of conflict indefinitely; such a person is either intervening ineffectively or has a vested interest in keeping the third party role alive.

There are several conditions under which third party intervention is likely to prove ineffective.[23] As but one example, consider the situation in which hostility between disputants is running high. Even when a third party offers well-intentioned, unbiased proposals for settlement under these conditions, the disputants tend to perceive these proposals as biased and unfavorable to their side (Vallone et al., 1985). Third party attempts to intervene in hostile conflict meet only with suspicion from each side. The discouraged third party may eventually give up its efforts at intervention.

Consider again the confrontation between African Americans and Hasidic Jews mentioned in Chapter 7. The conflict was ignited by an incident in which a Hasidic Jewish driver hit two African American children, killing one and critically injuring the other. When David Dinkins, mayor of New York City, went to the dead boy's house and pleaded for peace and harmony, his plea was answered with cries of "Traitor" from the African American community. Some time later, a group of Hasidic Jews beat an African American man who allegedly burglarized community property. When Dinkins made a statement denouncing this beating, he

[23]Such conditions include (1) a high level of hostility between the disputants (Bercovitch, 1989; Hiltrop, 1989; Pruitt et al., 1989b); (2) distrust of the third party (Hiltrop, 1989); (3) lack of resources (Carnevale & Pegnetter, 1985; Kochan & Jick, 1978; Pearson et al., 1982); (4) the existence of issues involving general principles (Bercovitch, 1989; Pruitt et al., 1989b); (5) low commitment to intervention (Carnevale et al., 1989; Hiltrop, 1989); (6) unequal power between the disputants (Bercovitch, 1989); (7) a high level of internal conflict (Bercovitch, 1989—but see Carnevale et al., 1989, for a failure to confirm this effect; Bingham, 1986; Pearson & Thoennes, 1982); and (8) the existence of a distressed relationship between the disputants, where stronger forms of intervention, such as psychotherapy, may be required. See Kressel & Pruitt (1989) and Pruitt & Carnevale (1993) for a more thorough discussion of this topic.

was severely criticized by the Hasidic Jews for taking sides with the African American group. Both groups appeared convinced that Dinkins favored the other side.

THE EVOLUTION OF THIRD PARTY INTERVENTION

Third party intervention has clear limitations; it is by no means an all-purpose cure for conflict. However, it is our view that third parties can be enormously helpful and important in the reduction and resolution of differences. At a time when so many conflicts—between individuals and among and between groups and nations—continue to plague us, at a time when our technological skills have dramatically outstripped our collective social skills, it is all the more important that alternatives be found to competitive, destructive conflict escalation. Third party intervention is a prominent example of such an alternative.

Third party intervention is not a fixed, stable set of nostrums, tools, and techniques. Rather, it is a set of procedures that change and grow in relation to the needs and adjustments of the disputants—and in response to creative thinking. A particular drug may be a powerful remedy at first, then become less effective as the organism against which it is directed begins to adapt to it. Similarly, a third party tool or technique that proves useful at first may lead disputants to accommodate and adjust in ways that weaken its effectiveness. Just as new drugs must be introduced when old ones become ineffective, new methods of third party intervention require invention in response to disputant accommodations.

Conventional Arbitration

This evolutionary process can be illustrated most clearly in some of the transformations that have taken place in third party methods of dealing with public employment disputes. Third parties started with mediation and have increasingly turned to conventional arbitration. To be sure, mediation has been an extremely influential and important intervention device. When used effectively, mediation can lead disputants to devise an agreement that makes good sense to them—and that is therefore likely to endure. The major problem with mediation, especially in public employee disputes in which it is essential that agreement be reached (for instance, with police officers and fire fighters, without whose services the lives or well-being of thousands of citizens might be threatened), is that mediation lacks the teeth of third party enforcement. There are times when disputants simply choose to ignore the advice of the mediator, to the detriment of the disputants and the public.

It is for this reason that, over the years, third parties in public employee disputes have resorted to the use of conventional arbitration when possible. Under the rules of this form of intervention, the third party is empowered to impose any agreement that it sees as proper to resolve the issues under consideration. Such action in itself provides a settlement of the controversy. Furthermore, the anticipation of such action—with its implication that control will be wrested from the hands of the disputants—is capable of goading the disputants into working out their own agreements.

Unfortunately, conventional arbitration has several weaknesses. Many arbitrators, when confronted with the last demands of each side, tend to split the difference, thereby creating an apparently fair and equitable agreement. As disputants have come increasingly to expect an arbitrator to split the difference, the anticipation of conventional arbitration, instead of facilitating agreement, has often led each side to adopt a tough and extreme position (Feuille, 1977; Magenau, 1983; Stern et al., 1975). By refusing to budge beyond a set of intransigent demands, each disputant tries to incline the halfway point between the two positions in its own direction. Hence, if the arbitrator splits the difference, it will favor that disputant's welfare. This process, which has been called the *chilling effect,* can stop negotiation in its tracks.

Final-offer Arbitration

The problem of the chilling effect has led to yet another third party innovation: a procedure known as final-offer arbitration, first proposed by Stevens (1966). In this procedure, if disputants are unable to come to an agreement, they are required to submit to the arbitrator their best, most conciliatory offer. Unlike conventional arbitration—in which the third party can decide on any final, binding settlement that it chooses—final-offer arbitration requires the third party to choose *one* of the two final offers *or* the other. Improvisation is not permitted.

Final-offer arbitration places Party in the following bind: It wants its own final offer to be the one selected by the third party. The only way to guarantee that this will happen is for Party to figure out what the Other is likely to offer and then submit a proposal that seems slightly more reasonable. This is a tricky business. It is hard to guess what Other will offer, and Party may lose its shirt if Other's offer is chosen. Hence, Party often prefers to reach agreement directly with Other rather than take a chance on the third Party's judgment. Final-offer arbitration is a procedure designed to create so risky a situation that disputants prefer to settle the issues on their own without involving a third party.

Most experimental evidence has lent support to the foregoing reasoning, and to the generally greater effectiveness of final-offer arbitration than its conventional counterpart (Bazerman & Neale, 1982; DeNisi & Dworkin, 1979; Magenau, 1983; Neale & Bazerman, 1983; Notz & Starke, 1978; Starke & Notz, 1989; Subbarao, 1978). For example, final-offer arbitration has been found to produce more concession making in negotiation, and greater commitment to the outcome reached, than conventional arbitration (Starke & Notz, 1989). Final-offer arbitration, which has been used to settle the salary disputes of major league baseball players and public sector contract disputes, has been required by law in a number of U.S. states and Canadian provinces.

Third party intervention is an evolving process. Consider the following problem with final-offer arbitration that might necessitate still a further change in third party strategy. It is in the interest of Party to mislead Other into thinking that Party is totally nonconciliatory so that Other does not believe it is necessary to make a truly reasonable final offer. Hence, there is some temptation for both disputants faced with final-offer arbitration to maintain extremely rigid offers during the negotiation and become reasonable only in the final offer that is privately submitted to the arbitrator. The problem with this strategy is that if it is practiced on both sides, it creates more conflictual impasses than might have been necessary if the final-offer procedure had not been in effect.

Other New Developments in Third Party Intervention

The rapid evolution of new third party techniques can be seen in three other developments: mediation/arbitration (med/arb), problem-solving intervention, and the design of dispute resolution systems.

Mediation/Arbitration (Med/Arb)

In this hybrid process of mediation and arbitration, arbitration is imposed if the disputants fail to reach agreement through mediation. There are two forms of med/arb: med/arb (same), in which the same mediator serves as the arbitrator if mediation fails, and med/arb (diff), in which the mediator and the arbitrator are different people. Med/arb has a number of advantages over either mediation or arbitration alone. One advantage is that the disputants may be motivated to reach agreement during mediation because of fear that they will lose control over the final outcomes if mediation fails and the conflict is settled through arbitration (Pruitt et al., 1989b). A second advantage is that a referral agency using med/arb will not have to deal with the same dispute again; a final settlement, whether negotiated or imposed, will surely be achieved (Pruitt et al., 1989b). A third advantage, which applies only to med/arb (same), is that another third party need not be informed of the dispute all over again (Ury et al., 1988). A fourth advantage, which also applies to med/arb (same), is that it enhances the mediator's power, making disputants more attentive to the third party's recommendations (Pruitt et al., 1989b).

There is some evidence that med/arb is more effective than either mediation or arbitration alone (Kochan & Jick, 1978; McGillicuddy et al., 1987). For example, McGillicuddy et al. (1987), in a field experiment conducted at a community mediation center, assigned dispute cases to three conditions: mediation, med/arb (same), and med/arb (diff). Med/arb (same) produced the highest levels of problem solving, med/arb (diff) the next highest levels, and mediation the least problem solving.

Med/arb also has its share of disadvantages. It may decrease the disputants' satisfaction and commitment, since they may feel they have been forced into settlement by the threat of arbitration hanging over their head (Ury et al., 1988). Another disadvantage is that the mediator in med/arb (same), by having power to impose a settlement, may become too forceful during the mediation session and prematurely shift to arbitration (Pruitt et al., 1989b).

Problem-Solving Intervention

As noted earlier, third party intervention may prove ineffective in repairing a damaged relationship. However, a procedure commonly known as the problem-solving workshop can address this problem. Using this procedure, scholar/practitioners rely on their stature and expertise on conflict to change the parties' perceptions of their dispute from that of a battle to be won to that of a problem to be solved together. Furthermore, these third parties educate the disputants on how to deal with new issues in a constructive way and encourage them to take each other's perspective, thereby enhancing their understanding of each other.

This mode of intervention has been applied to various conflict situations, including border disputes in the Horn of Africa (Doob, 1970, 1971); religious conflict in Northern Ireland (Doob & Foltz, 1973); Arab-Israeli relations (Benjamin & Levi, 1979; Cohen et al., 1977; Kelman, 1982); organizational disputes (Bennis, 1969; Muench, 1963); community disputes (Fisher & White, 1976); and marital conflicts (Baucom, 1984; Jacobson, 1984; Johnson & Greenberg, 1985).

Research evidence shows that problem-solving intervention produces higher joint outcomes and greater satisfaction with the agreement than does mediation (Keashly, 1988). Furthermore, problem-solving intervention improves the relationship between the disputants which, in turn, can increase joint problem solving when new issues arise (Fisher, 1983, 1990; Jacobson, 1984; Johnson & Greenberg, 1985; Pruitt et al., 1993b; Wedge, 1970).

Designing Dispute Resolution Systems

The third party roles described so far involve officiating at hearings and workshops. But third parties are by no means confined to these settings. A newly evolved role for third parties involves designing dispute resolution systems which are available to help people settle their conflicts effectively and efficiently whenever they arise.

Ury, Brett, and Goldberg (1988), the major innovators in this new field, emphasize the importance of developing dispute resolution systems that encourage the parties to reconcile their underlying interests. They argue that an interests-oriented approach to resolving conflict is usually preferable to an approach that is rights-oriented (determining who is right—e.g., courtroom procedures) or power-oriented (determining who is more powerful—e.g., strikes). An interests-oriented approach tends to produce more satisfying, lasting outcomes that contribute to the development of better working relationships. Better relationships, in turn, are likely to prevent the recurrence of the dispute.[24]

Ury et al. (1988) offer the following basic guidelines for designing interests-oriented dispute resolution systems:

1. Establish negotiation procedures that specify the participants in the negotiation, the timetable, and the procedures to use if negotiations fail.
2. Build in "loop-backs" to negotiation that encourage disputants to move away from issues of who is right or power contests to an interests approach. For example, a procedure that can help to avoid rights contests is *advisory arbitration,* in which a third party provides an opinion about how the dispute would probably be settled in court.[25] This information should narrow the differences between disputants regarding the likely outcome of a rights contest, thereby encouraging them to adopt a more interests-oriented approach. One procedure that can help avoid power contests is the *cooling-off period*—a requirement that disputants take no action for a period of time. This allows the disputants to vent their emotional steam.
3. Teach the disputants negotiation skills, motivate them to use low-cost procedures, and provide them with necessary resources—such as easy access to third parties who can encourage interests-based negotiation.
4. Provide low-cost rights-oriented and power-oriented procedures that disputants can fall back on in case an interests-oriented approach fails. There are a variety of such procedures, including med/arb, voting, and rules of prudence (which restrict the use of certain costly, destructive tactics in power contests).
5. Arrange procedures in such a way that disputants start with low-cost procedures, then turn to high-cost procedures only if the low-cost arrangements fail to resolve disputes.

[24]The authors acknowledge that an interests-oriented approach may be either unfeasible or undesirable under conditions where (1) the interests are opposed, (2) the disputants have very different perceptions of who is right or who is more powerful, or (3) settlement through adjudication is necessary to resolve a matter of public policy. In cases such as these, a dispute resolution system should also contain low-cost procedures that determine who is right and who is more powerful.

[25]In a closely related procedure, the minitrial, disputants have a chance to see what might happen if their conflict were to go to trial.

Dispute resolution system designers may have to occupy more diverse roles than more traditional mediators or arbitrators. As Brett et al. (1990) note, designers should play the roles of ". . . coach, evaluator, and evangelist, in addition to those of expert, mediator, and negotiator" (p. 169).

It should be clear from the discussion in this section that the field of third party intervention is in a period of rapid evolution. There is no such thing as a perfect or ideal intervention procedure. Each has its virtues and liabilities. Moreover, some of the procedures have given rise to clever adjustments and modifications on the part of resourceful disputants, necessitating the development of new and still more ingenious intervention techniques. This should prove to be no problem, in the ultimate analysis. Party is infinitely resourceful, always trying to find ways to beat Other and/or the system—but the people who are in the business of bringing about mutually acceptable agreements are infinitely resourceful too. Conflict may be a growth industry, but so too is the business of dispute settlement.

Determinants of Third Party Behavior

So far, we have largely focused on what a third party can do to intervene effectively. We now turn to the factors that influence a third party's choices among the procedures and tactics that are available. Most of the research on this issue has been conducted with mediators.[26]

The Concern-likelihood Model

This model, developed by Carnevale (1986), postulates two variables that interact to determine mediator behavior: (1) the mediator's likelihood estimate of a win-win agreement ("perceived common ground"); and (2) the mediator's level of concern that the parties achieve their aspirations. Both likelihood and concern range from low to high. These two antecedents predict the mediator's choice among four basic strategies: *problem solving*, also referred to as integration (which involves efforts to discover a win-win solution that satisfies both parties' aspirations); *compensation* (which uses the promise of reward to induce the parties into concessions or agreements); *pressure* (which involves efforts to force the parties into concessions or agreements by punishment or the threat of punishment); and *inaction* (which involves conscious efforts to let the parties handle the conflict by themselves).

The concern-likelihood model makes the following predictions about

[26]There are many other determinants of mediator behavior, such as mediator goals, cognitive biases, and conflict intensity—to name just a few. See Carnevale & Pruitt (1992), Kressel & Pruitt (1989), Pruitt & Carnevale (1993), and Wall & Lynn (1993) for a more detailed discussion of this topic.

mediator behavior: Mediators adopt a problem-solving strategy when they have high concern for the parties' achieving their aspirations and perceive the likelihood of a win-win agreement to be high. Mediators employ a compensation strategy when they have high concern for the parties' achieving their aspirations and perceive the likelihood of a win-win agreement to be low. They use a pressure strategy when they have low concern for the parties' achieving their aspirations and perceive the likelihood of a win-win agreement to be low. And mediators adopt an inaction strategy when they have low concern for the parties' achieving their aspirations and perceive the likelihood of a win-win agreement to be high. Research has supported and extended parts of this model (Carnevale & Conlon, 1988; Carnevale & Henry, 1989; Chaudhry & Ross, 1989; Harris & Carnevale, 1990).

Mediator Power

Mediator power often comes from authority, status, reputation, and the capacity to reward or punish the disputants (Bercovitch & Rubin, 1992; Carnevale, 1986; Kressel & Pruitt, 1989; Touval & Zartman, 1985). Mediators with power over the disputants tends to use more forceful tactics (Conlon et al., 1994; McGillicuddy et al., 1987; Pruitt et al., 1989b; Sheppard et al., 1989; Wall & Rude, 1989). For example, community mediators with the power to arbitrate use heavier pressure tactics than those who do not have such power (McGillicuddy et al., 1987).

Mediation Stages

Mediator behavior is often influenced by the stages of mediation. Pruitt and colleagues (1989a) have developed a three-phase model. According to this model, phase 1 consists of setting the stage, which includes clarifying the ground rules and gathering information about the conflict. Phase 2 is problem solving, which includes posing issues and generating alternatives. And phase 3 is achieving a workable agreement, which includes pressing the parties to reach agreement.[27] Several studies report findings consistent with this model (Carnevale & Conlon, 1988; Wall & Rude, 1991). For example, Carnevale and Conlon have found that mediators are less assertive at first but come to use pressure and compensation tactics as time passes and time pressure increases.

CONCLUSIONS

In this concluding chapter, we have examined various third party roles, the things that a third party can do to intervene effectively, and some of the limits of third party intervention. We have also described third party

[27]Similar models have been proposed by Landsberger (1955) and Shaw et al. (1973).

intervention as an evolving process and have reviewed some of the recent developments in this field.

In this book we have outlined a simple framework for understanding why conflicts escalate, reach a point of stalemate, then move to de-escalate. Not all conflicts follow this three-stage sequence. And certainly, not all escalated conflicts require outside intervention if they are to be settled. Many do, however, and this chapter has indicated some of the approaches and elements that contribute to third party effectiveness.

It is fitting that our book conclude right about here, in the transition from theory to practice, between the sometimes rarefied world of research and the often messy problems that arise when the parties to real and pressing social conflicts require assistance if settlement is to be achieved. But we cannot resist one last story . . .

Anthropologist William Ury likes to tell the apocryphal tale of an old gentleman who, anticipating the day of his death, announced that his estate would be divided among his three sons as follows: one-half to the oldest, one-third to the middle son, and one-ninth to the youngest. The old gentleman eventually died, and his estate consisted of seventeen camels. The three sons attempted to divide up the estate according to their father's wishes but quickly found that they couldn't—at least not without doing violence to the camels. They argued and argued, to no avail.

Around this time, a village elder rode up on her own dusty camel, dismounted, and asked what the problem seemed to be. After listening to the three brothers, she offered to make her own camel available if that might help. And it did. With the addition of an eighteenth camel, the problem suddenly seemed soluble. The oldest son took his *nine* camels (one-half of eighteen), the middle son pried loose *six* more (one-third of eighteen), and the youngest son extracted *two* camels (one-ninth of eighteen). Nine plus six plus two equals seventeen. Almost before the three brothers knew what had happened, the old wise woman climbed back onto her own camel and rode off into the setting desert sun.

We have told this story for two reasons: First, to illustrate, yet again, what creative third parties can do. And second, so that we could convey to you, the reader, our sincere hope that—in the form of a new idea—you have found an eighteenth camel (or two) in the pages of this book.

References

ABC NEWS. (1981). America held hostage: The secret negotiations. New York, January 22, 1981.

ABELES, R. P. (1976). Relative deprivation, rising expectations and black militancy. *Journal of Social Issues, 32,* 119–137.

ADAMS, J. S. (1965). Inequity in social exchange. In L. Berkowitz (Ed.), *Advances in experimental social psychology* (Vol. 2, pp. 267–299). New York: Academic Press.

ALBIN, C. (1993). *Resolving conflicts over indivisibles through negotiation: The case of Jerusalem.* Doctoral dissertation, Johns Hopkins University.

ALGER, C. F. (1961). Non-resolution consequences of the United Nations and their effect on international conflict. *Journal of Conflict Resolution, 5,* 128–145.

ALLEN, V. L., & WILDER, D. A. (1975). Categorization, belief similarity and intergroup discrimination. *Journal of Personality and Social Psychology, 32,* 971–977.

APFELBAUM, E. (1979). Relations of domination and movements for liberation: An analysis of power between groups. In W. G. Austin & S. Worchel (Eds.), *The social psychology of intergroup relations* (pp. 188–204). Monterey, CA: Brooks/Cole.

ARISTOTLE (1941). *The basic works of Aristotle* (R. McKeon, Ed.). New York: Random House.

ARONSON, E. (1988). *The social animal.* San Francisco, CA: Freeman.

ARONSON, E., & COPE, V. (1968). My enemy's enemy is my friend. *Journal of Personality and Social Psychology, 8,* 8–12.

ASCH, S. E. (1956). Studies on independence and conformity: A minority of one against a unanimous majority. *Psychological Monographs, 70,* 416.

AVERILL, J. R. (1982). *Anger and aggression.* New York: Springer-Verlag.

AVERILL, J. R. (1983). Studies on anger and aggression: Implications for theories of emotion. *American Psychologist, 38,* 1145–1160.

BACK, K. W. (1951). Influence through social communication. *Journal of Abnormal and Social Psychology, 46,* 9–23.

BANDURA, A. (1990). Selective activation and disengagement of moral control. *Journal of Social Issues, 46,* 27–46.

BARON, R. A. (1977). *Human aggression.* New York: Plenum.

BARON, R. A. (1978). Aggression-inhibiting influence of sexual humor. *Journal of Personality and Social Psychology, 36,* 189–197.

BARON, R. A. (1984). Reducing organizational conflict: An incompatible response approach. *Journal of Applied Psychology, 69,* 272–279.

BARON, R. A. (1990). Environmentally induced positive affect: Its impact on self-efficacy, task performance, negotiation, and conflict. *Journal of Applied Social Psychology, 20,* 368–384.

BARON, R. A., & BALL, R. L. (1974). The aggression-inhibiting influence of non-hostile humor. *Journal of Experimental Social Psychology, 10,* 23–33.

BARON, R. A., & BELL, P. A. (1977). Sexual arousal and aggression by males: Effects of type of erotic stimuli and prior provocation. *Journal of Personality and Social Psychology, 35,* 79–87.

BARON, R. A., & KEPNER, C. R. (1970). Model's behavior and attraction toward the model as determinants of adult aggressive behavior. *Journal of Personality and Social Psychology, 14,* 335–344.

BARTOS, O. J. (1974). *Process and outcome in negotiation.* New York: Columbia University Press.

BARTUNEK, J. M., BENTON, A. A., & Keys, C. B. (1975). Third-party intervention and the bargaining of group representatives. *Journal of Conflict Resolution, 19,* 532–557.

BAUCOM, O. H. (1984). The active ingredients of behavioral marital therapy: The effectiveness of problem-solving/communication training, contingency, contracting, and their combination. In K. Hahlweg & N. S. Jacobson (Eds.), *Marital interaction: Analysis and modification* (pp. 73–88). New York: Guilford.

BAZERMAN, M. H., & NEALE, M. A. (1982). Improving negotiator effectiveness under final-offer arbitration: The role of selection and training. *Journal of Applied Psychology, 67,* 543–548.

BELL, P. A., & BARON, R. A. (1976). Aggression and heat: The mediating role of negative affect. *Journal of Applied Social Psychology, 6,* 18–30.

BEM, D. J. (1972). Self-perception theory. In L. Berkowitz (Ed.), *Advances in experimental social psychology* (Vol. 6, pp. 1–62). New York: Academic Press.

BENJAMIN, A. J., & LEVI, A. M. (1979). Process minefields in intergroup conflict resolution: The Sdot Yam Workshop. *Journal of Applied Behavioral Science, 15,* 507–519.

BENNIS, W. G. (1969). *Organization development: Its nature, origins and prospects.* Reading, MA: Addison-Wesley.

BENTON, A. A., & DRUCKMAN, D. (1973). Salient solutions and the bargaining behavior of representatives and nonrepresentatives. *International Journal of Group Tensions, 3,* 28–39.

BENTON, A. A., & DRUCKMAN, D. (1974). Constituent's bargaining orientation and intergroup negotiations. *Journal of Applied Social Psychology, 4,* 141–150.

BEN-YOAV, O., & PRUITT, D. G. (1984a). Resistance to yielding and the expectation of cooperative future interaction in negotiation. *Journal of Experimental Social Psychology, 20,* 323–353.

BEN-YOAV, O., & PRUITT, D. G. (1984b). Accountability to constituents: A two-edged sword. *Organizational Behavior and Human Performance, 34,* 282–295.

BERCOVITCH, J. (1984). *Social conflicts and third parties: Strategies of conflict resolution.* Boulder, CO: Westview.

BERCOVITCH, J. (1989). Mediation in international disputes. In K. Kressel & D. G. Pruitt (Eds.), *Mediation research* (pp. 284–299). San Francisco: Jossey-Bass.

BERCOVITCH, J., & LAMARE, J. (1992). Understanding international mediation: Some notes toward a causal model. Paper presented at the Annual Conference of the International Society of Political Psychology, San Francisco.

BERCOVITCH, J., & RUBIN, J. Z. (1992). *Mediation in international relations: Multiple approaches to conflict management*. London: Macmillan.

BERKOWITZ, L. (1993). *Aggression: Its causes, consequences, and control*. New York: McGraw-Hill.

BERKOWITZ, L., COCHRAN, S. T., & EMBREE, M. C. (1981). Physical pain and the goal of aversively stimulated aggression. *Journal of Personality and Social Psychology, 40,* 687–700.

BERSCHEID, E. (1983). Emotion. In H. H. Kelley, E. Berscheid, A. Christensen, et al. (Eds.), *Close relationships* (pp. 110–168). New York: Freeman.

BERSCHEID, E., & WALSTER, E. (1978). *Interpersonal attraction*. Reading, MA: Addison-Wesley.

BETHEL, C., & SINGER, L. (1982). Mediation: A new remedy for cases of domestic violence. *Vermont Law Review, 7,* 15–32.

BETTENCOURT, B. A., BREWER, M. B., CROAK, M. R., & MILLER, N. (1992). Cooperation and the reduction of intergroup bias: The role of reward structure and social orientation. *Journal of Experimental Social Psychology, 28,* 301–319.

BIES, R. J. (1989). Managing conflict before it happens: The role of accounts. In M. A. Rahim (Ed.), *Managing conflict: An interdisciplinary approach* (pp. 83–91). New York: Praeger.

BIGONESS, W. J. (1976). The impact of initial bargaining position and alternative modes of third-party intervention in resolving bargaining impasses. *Organizational Behavior and Human Performance, 17,* 185–198.

BINGHAM, G. (1986). *Resolving environmental disputes: A decade of experience*. Washington, DC: Conservation Foundation.

BINNENDIJK, H. (1987). *National negotiating styles.* Washington, DC: Foreign Service Institute, U.S. Department of State.

BLACK, T. E., & HIGBEE, K. L. (1973). Effects of power, threat, and sex on exploitation. *Journal of Personality and Social Psychology, 27,* 382–388.

BLAKE, R. R., & MOUTON, J. S. (1962). Overevaluation of own group's product in intergroup competition. *Journal of Abnormal and Social Psychology, 64,* 237–238.

BLAKE, R. R., & MOUTON, J. S. (1964). *The managerial grid.* Houston, TX: Gulf.

BLAKE, R. R., & MOUTON, J. S. (1979). Intergroup problem solving in organizations: From theory to practice. In W. G. Austin & S. Worchel (Eds.), *The social psychology of intergroup relations* (pp. 19–23). Monterey, CA: Brooks/Cole.

BLALOCK, H. M. (1989). *Power and conflict: Toward a general theory.* Newbury Park, CA: Sage.

BLUMENTHAL, M. D., KAHN, R. L., ANDREWS, F. M., & HEAD, K. B. (1972). *Justifying violence: Attitudes of American men.* Ann Arbor, MI: Institute for Social Research.

BONOMA, T. V., SCHLENKER, B. R., SMITH, R., & TEDESCHI, J. (1970). Source prestige and target reactions to threats. *Psychonomic Science, 19,* 111–113.

BONOMA, T. V., & TEDESCHI, J. T. (1973). Some effects of source behavior on target's compliance to threats. *Behavioral Science, 18,* 34–41.

BOWERS, J. W., & OCHS, D. J. (1971). *The rhetoric of agitation and control.* Reading, MA: Addison-Wesley.

BRADBURY, T. N., & FINCHAM, F. D. (1990). Attributions in marriage: Review and critique. *Psychological Bulletin, 107,* 3–33.

BRADBURY, T. N., & FINCHAM, F. D. (1992). Attributions and behavior in marital interaction. *Journal of Personality and Social Psychology, 63,* 613–628.

BREHM, J. W., & COLE, A. H. (1966). Effect of a favor which reduces freedom. *Journal of Personality and Social Psychology, 3,* 420–426.

BREHM, S. S. (1992). *Intimate relationships* (2nd ed.). New York: McGraw-Hill.

BREHM, S. S., & KASSIN, S. M. (1993). *Social psychology* (2nd ed.). Boston: Houghton Mifflin.

BRESLIN, J. W. (1989). Breaking away from subtle biases. *Negotiation Journal, 5,* 219–222.

BRESLIN, J. W., & RUBIN, J. Z. (Eds.). (1991). *Negotiation theory and practice.* Boston: Program on Negotiation Books at Harvard Law School.

BRETT, J. M., GOLDBERG, S. B., & URY, W. L. (1990). Designing systems for resolving disputes in organizations. *American Psychologist, 45,* 162–170.

BREWER, M. B. (1979). Ingroup bias in the minimal intergroup situation: A cognitive motivational analysis. *Psychological Bulletin, 86,* 307–324.

BREWER, M. B. (1986). The role of ethnocentrism in intergroup conflict. In S. Worchel and W. G. Austin (Eds.), *Psychology of intergroup relations* (pp. 88–102). Chicago: Nelson-Hall.

BREWER, M. B., & KRAMER, R. M. (1986). Choice behavior in social dilemmas: Effects of social identity, group size, and decision framing. *Journal of Personality and Social Psychology, 50,* 543–549.

BROCK, T. C., & BECKER, L. A. (1966). "Debriefing" and susceptibility to subsequent experimental manipulations. *Journal of Experimental Social Psychology, 2,* 314–323.

BROCKNER, J., & RUBIN, J. Z. (1985). *The social psychology of conflict escalation and entrapment.* New York: Springer-Verlag.

BROCKNER, J., RUBIN, J. Z., FINE, J., HAMILTON, T. P., THOMAS, B., & TURETSKY, B. (1982). Factors affecting entrapment in escalating conflicts: The importance of timing. *Journal of Research in Personality, 16,* 247–266.

BROCKNER, J., RUBIN, J. Z., & LANG, E. (1981). Face-saving and entrapment. *Journal of Experimental Social Psychology, 17,* 68–79.

BROCKNER, J., SHAW, M. C., & RUBIN, J. Z. (1979). Factors affecting withdrawal from an escalating conflict: Quitting before it's too late. *Journal of Experimental Social Psychology, 15,* 492–503.

BRONFENBRENNER, U. (1961). The mirror-image in Soviet-American relations. *Journal of Social Issues, 17,* 45–56.

BROWN, B. R. (1968). The effects of need to maintain face on interpersonal bargaining. *Journal of Experimental Social Psychology, 4,* 107–122.

BROWN, R. J., & WADE, G. (1987). Superordinate goals and intergroup behavior: The effect of role ambiguity and status on intergroup attitudes and task performance. *European Journal of Social Psychology, 17,* 131–142.

BRYANT, J., & ZILLMANN, D. (1979). Effect of intensification of annoyance through unrelated residual excitation on substantially delayed hostile behavior. *Journal of Experimental Social Psychology, 15,* 470–480.

BURTON, J. W. (1962). *Peace theory.* New York: Knopf.

BURTON, J. W. (1969). *Conflict and communication.* New York: Macmillan.

BURTON, J. W. (1979). *Deviance, terrorism & war: The process of solving unsolved social and political problems.* New York: St. Martin's Press.

BYRNE, D. (1971). *The attraction paradigm.* New York: Academic Press.

BYRNE, D., RASCHE, L., & KELLEY, K. (1974). When "I like you" indicates disagreement. *Journal of Research in Personality, 8,* 207–217.

CARLSMITH, J. M., & GROSS, A. E. (1969). Some effects of guilt on compliance. *Journal of Personality and Social Psychology, 11,* 232–239.

CARLSON, M., & MILLER, N. (1987). Explanation of the relation between negative mood and helping. *Psychological Bulletin, 102,* 92–108.

CARNEVALE, P. J. (1986). Strategic choice in mediation. *Negotiation Journal, 2,* 41–56.

CARNEVALE, P. J., & CONLON, D. E. (1988). Time pressure and strategic choice in mediation. *Organizational Behavior and Human Decision Processes, 42,* 111–133.

CARNEVALE, P. J., & HENRY, R. (1989). Determinants of mediator behavior: A test of the strategic choice model. *Journal of Applied Social Psychology, 19,* 481–498.

CARNEVALE, P. J., & ISEN, A. M. (1986). The influence of positive affect and visual access on the discovery of integrative solutions in bilateral negotiation. *Organizational Behavior and Human Decision Processes, 37,* 1–13.

CARNEVALE, P. J., & KEENAN, P. A. (1990). Frame and motive in integrative bargaining: The likelihood and the quality of agreement. Paper presented at the Third Annual Meeting of the International Association for Conflict Management, Vancouver, British Columbia.

CARNEVALE, P. J., & LAWLER, E. J. (1986). Time pressure and the development of integrative agreements in bilateral negotiation. *Journal of Conflict Resolution, 30,* 636–659.

CARNEVALE, P. J., LIM, R. G., & MCLAUGHLIN, M. E. (1989). Contingent mediator behavior and its effectiveness. In K. Kressel & D. G. Pruitt (Eds.), *Mediation research* (pp. 213–240). San Francisco: Jossey-Bass.

CARNEVALE, P. J., & PEGNETTER, R. (1985). The selection of mediation tactics in public-sector disputes: A contingency analysis. *Journal of Social Issues, 41,* 65–81.

CARNEVALE, P. J., & PRUITT, D. G. (1992). Negotiation and mediation. *Annual Review of Psychology, 43,* 531–582.

CARVER, C. S., & GLASS, D. C. (1978). Coronary-prone behavior pattern and interpersonal aggression. *Journal of Personality and Social Psychology, 36,* 361–366.

CHAUDHRY, S. S., & ROSS, W. P. (1989). Relevance trees and mediation. *Negotiation Journal, 5,* 63–73.

CHELIUS, J. R., & EXTEJT, M. R. (1985). The narcotic effect of impasse-resolution procedures. *Industrial and Labor Relations Review, 38,* 629–637.

CIALDINI, R. B., & KENRICK, D. T. (1976). Altruism as hedonism: A social development perspective on the relationship of negative mood state and helping. *Journal of Personality and Social Psychology, 34,* 907–914.

CIALDINI, R. B., & RICHARDSON, K. D. (1980). Two indirect tactics of image management: Basking and blasting. *Journal of Personality and Social Psychology, 39,* 406–415.

CLARK, M. S., & MILLS, J. (1979). Interpersonal attraction in exchange and communal relationships. *Journal of Personality and Social Psychology, 37,* 12–24.

CLARK, M. S., & REIS, H. (1988). Interpersonal processes in close relationships. *Annual Review of Psychology, 39,* 609–672.

CLAUDE, I. L. (1962). *Power and international relations.* New York: Random House.

CLORE, G. L., & BYRNE, D. (1974). A reinforcement-affect model of attraction. In T. L. Huston (Ed.), *Foundations of interpersonal attraction* (pp. 143–170). New York: Academic Press.

COHEN, R. (1991). *Negotiating across cultures: Communication obstacles in international diplomacy.* Washington, DC: United States Institute of Peace Press.

COHEN, S. P., KELMAN, H. C., MILLER, F. D., & SMITH, B. L. (1977). Evolving intergroup techniques for conflict resolution: An Israeli-Palestinian pilot workshop. *Journal of Social Issues, 33,* 165–189.

COLEMAN, J. S. (1957). *Community conflict.* New York: Free Press.

CONLON, D. E., CARNEVALE, P. J., & MURNIGHAN, J. K. (1994). Intravention: Third-party intervention with clout. *Organizational Behavior and Human Decision Processes.*

COOMBS, C. H. (1987). The structure of conflict. *American Psychologist, 42,* 355–363.

COOPER, J., & FAZIO, R. H. (1979). The formation and persistence of attitudes that support intergroup conflict. In W. G. Austin & S. Worchel (Eds.), *The Social Psychology of Intergroup Relations* (pp. 149–159). Monterey, CA: Brooks/Cole.

COSER, L. A. (1956). *The functions of social conflict.* New York: Free Press.

CROCKER, J., THOMPSON, L., MCGRAW, K. M., & INGERMAN, C. (1987). Downward comparison, prejudice, and evaluations of others: Effects of self-esteem and threat. *Journal of Personality and Social Psychology, 52,* 907–916.

CUNNINGHAM, M. R., SHAFFER, D. R., BARBEE, A. P., WOLFF, P.L., & KELLEY, D. J. (1990). Separate processes in the relation of elation and depression to helping: Social versus personal concerns. *Journal of Experimental Social Psychology, 26,* 13–33.

DA GLORIA, J., & DE RIDDER, R. (1979). Sex differences in aggression: Are current notions misleading? *European Journal of Social Psychology, 9,* 49–66.

DAHRENDORF, R. (1959). *Class and class conflict in industrial society.* Stanford, CA: Stanford University Press.

DALY, M., & WILSON, M. (1988). *Homicide.* New York: Aldine de Gruyter.

DAVIES, J. C. (1962). Toward a theory of revolution. *Sociological Review, 27,* 5–19.

DAVIS, A. M. (1986). Dispute resolution at an early age. *Negotiation Journal, 2,* 287–297.

DENGERINK, H. A. (1976). Personality variables as mediators of attack-instigated aggression. In R. G. Geen & E. C. O'Neal (Eds.), *Perspectives on aggression* (pp. 61–98). New York: Academic Press.

DENISI, A. A., & DWORKIN, J. B. (1979). Final-offer arbitration. Unpublished manuscript.

DESCHAMPS, J. C., & BROWN, R. (1983). Superordinate goals and intergroup conflict. *British Journal of Social Psychology, 22,* 189–195.

DEUTSCH, K. W., & SINGER, J. D. (1964). Multipolar power systems and international stability. *World Politics, 16,* 390–406.

DEUTSCH, M. (1958). Trust and suspicion. *Journal of Conflict Resolution, 2,* 265–279.

DEUTSCH, M. (1973). *The resolution of conflict: Constructive and destructive processes.* New Haven, CT: Yale University Press.

DEUTSCH, M., & COLLINS, M. (1951). *Interracial housing: A psychological evaluation of a social experiment.* Minneapolis: University of Minnesota Press.

DEUTSCH, M., & KRAUSS, R. M. (1960). The effect of threat upon interpersonal bargaining. *Journal of Abnormal and Social Psychology, 61,* 181–189.

DEUTSCH, M., & LEWICKI, R. J. (1970). "Locking in" effects during a game of chicken. *Journal of Conflict Resolution, 14,* 367–378.

DICKOFF, H. (1961). Reactions to evaluations by another person as a function of self-evaluations and the interaction context. Unpublished manuscript, Duke University.

DION, K. L. (1973). Cohesiveness as a determinant of ingroup-outgroup bias. *Journal of Personality and Social Psychology, 28,* 163–171.

DION, K. L. (1979). Intergroup conflict and intragroup cohesiveness. In W. G. Austin & S. Worchel (Eds.), *The social psychology of intergroup relations* (pp. 211–224). Belmont, CA: Wadsworth.

DIPBOYE, R. L., & WILEY, J. W. (1977). Reactions of college recruiters to interviewee sex and self-presentation style. *Journal of Vocational Behavior, 10,* 1–12.

DIPBOYE, R. L., & WILEY, J. W. (1978). Reactions of male raters to interviewee self-presentation style and sex: Extensions of previous research. *Journal of Vocational Behavior, 13,* 192–203.

DONOHUE, W. A. (1981). Analyzing negotiation tactics: Development of a negotiation interact system. *Human Communication Research, 7,* 273–287.

DONOHUE, W. A. (1989). Communicative competence in mediators. In K. Kressel & D. G. Pruitt (Eds.), *Mediation research* (pp. 322–343). San Francisco: Jossey-Bass.

DONOHUE, W. A., DIEZ, M. E., & WEIDER-HATFIELD, D. (1984). Skills for successful bargainers: A valence theory of competent mediation. In R. Bostrom (Ed.), *Competence in communication* (pp. 219–258). Beverly Hills, CA: Sage.

DOOB, L. W. (Ed.). (1970). *Resolving conflict in Africa: The Fermeda workshop.* New Haven, CT: Yale University Press.

DOOB, L. W. (1971). The impact of the Fermeda workshop on the conflicts in the Horn of Africa. *International Journal of Group Tensions, 1,* 91–101.

DOOB, L. W., & FOLTZ, W. J. (1973). The Belfast Workshop: An application of group techniques to a destructive conflict. *Journal of Conflict Resolution, 17,* 489–512.

DORE, R. P. (1978). *Shinohata: A portrait of a Japanese village.* New York: Pantheon Books.

DOUGLAS, A. (1962). *Industrial peacemaking.* New York: Columbia University Press.

DRACHMAN, D., DECARUFEL, A., & INSKO, C. A. (1978). The extra credit effect in interpersonal attraction. *Journal of Experimental Social Psychology, 14,* 458–465.

DRIGOTAS, S. M., & RUSBULT, C. E. (1992). Shall I stay or should I go? A dependence model of breakups. *Journal of Personality and Social Psychology, 62,* 62–87.

DYCK, R. J., & RULE, B. G. (1978). Effect on retaliation of causal attributions concerning attack. *Journal of Personality and Social Psychology, 36,* 521–529.

EAGLY, A. H., & STEFFEN, V. J. (1986). Gender and aggressive behavior: A meta-analytic review of the social psychological literature. *Psychological Bulletin, 100,* 309–330.

EDEN, D. (1990). Pygmalion without interpersonal contrast effects: Whole groups gain from raising manager expectations. *Journal of Applied Psychology, 75,* 394–398.

ENZLE, M. E., HARVEY, M. D., & WRIGHT, E. F. (1992). Implicit role of obligations versus social responsibility in constituency representation. *Journal of Personality and Social Psychology, 62,* 238–245.

FALBO, T. (1977). Multidimensional scaling of power strategies. *Journal of Personality and Social Psychology, 35,* 537–547.

FALBO, T., & PEPLAU, L. A. (1980). Power strategies in intimate relationships. *Journal of Personality and Social Psychology, 38,* 618–628.

FAURE, G. O. (1987). Les théories de la négociations. In P. Messerlin and F. Vellas

(Eds.), *Conflits et négociations dans le commerce international: l'Uruguay Round.* Paris: Economica.

FAURE, G. O. (1989). The mediator as a third negotiator. In F. Mautner-Markhof (Ed.), *Processes of international negotiations.* Boulder, CO: Westview Press.

FAURE, G. O. (1991). Negotiating in the Orient: Encounters in the Peshawar Bazaar, Pakistan. *Negotiation Journal, 7,* 279–290.

FAURE, G. O., & RUBIN, J. Z. (1993). *Culture and negotiation.* Newbury Park, CA: Sage.

FAURE, G. O., & SHAKUN, M. (1988). Negotiating to free hostages. In M. Shakun (Ed.), *Evolutionary systems design: Policy-making under complexity.* San Francisco, CA: Holden-Day.

FERGUSON, T. J., & RULE, B. G. (1983). An attributional perspective on anger and aggression. In R. G. Geen & E. Donnerstein (Eds.), *Aggression: Theoretical and empirical reviews* (Vol. 1, pp. 41–74). New York: Academic Press.

FESTINGER, L. (1950). Informal social communication. *Psychological Review, 57,* 271–292.

FESTINGER, L. (1957). *A theory of cognitive dissonance.* Stanford, CA: Stanford University Press.

FESTINGER, L., SCHACHTER, S., & BACK, K. (1950). *Social pressures in informal groups: A study of human factors in housing.* New York: Harper & Row.

FEUILLE, P. (1977). Final-offer arbitration and negotiating incentives. *Arbitration Journal, 32,* 203–220.

FILLEY, A. C. (1975). *Interpersonal conflict resolution.* Glenview, IL: Scott, Foresman.

FISHER, R. (1964). Fractionating conflict. In R. Fisher (Ed.), *International conflict and behavioral science: The Craigville papers.* New York: Basic Books.

FISHER, R. (1981). Playing the wrong game. In J. Z. Rubin (Ed.), *Dynamics of third-party intervention: Kissinger in the Middle East* (pp. 95–121). New York: Praeger.

FISHER, R., & BROWN, S. (1988). *Getting together: Building a relationship that gets to YES.* Boston: Houghton Mifflin.

FISHER, R., & URY, W. L. (1978). *International mediation: A working guide.* New York: International Peace Academy.

FISHER, R., URY, W. L., & PATTON, B. (1991). *Getting to YES: Negotiating agreement without giving in* (2nd ed.). Boston: Houghton Mifflin.

FISHER, R. J. (1983). Third-party consultation as a method of intergroup conflict resolution. *Journal of Conflict Resolution, 27,* 301–334.

FISHER, R. J. (1990). *The social psychology of intergroup and international conflict resolution.* New York: Springer-Verlag.

FISHER, R. J., & WHITE, J. H. (1976). Reducing tensions between neighbourhood housing groups: A pilot study in third party consultation. *International Journal of Group Tensions, 6,* 41–52.

FISKE, S. T., & TAYLOR, S. E. (1991). *Social Cognition* (2nd ed.). New York: McGraw-Hill.

FOA, U. G., & FOA, E. B. (1975). *Resource theory of social exchange.* Morristown, NJ: General Learning Press.

FOLLETT, M. P. (1940). Constructive conflict. In H. C. Metcalf & L. Urwick (Eds.), *Dynamic administration: The collected papers of Mary Parker Follett* (pp. 30–49). New York: Harper.

FRANK, J. (1982). *Sanity and survival* (rev. ed.). New York: Vintage Books.

FREEDMAN, J. L., WALLINGTON, S. A., & BLESS, E. (1967). Compliance without pressure: The effects of guilt. *Journal of Personality and Social Psychology, 7,* 117–124.

FREEDMAN, S. C. (1981). Threats, promises, and coalitions: A study of compliance and retaliation in a simulated organizational setting. *Journal of Applied Social Psychology, 11,* 114–136.

FRENCH, J. R. P., & RAVEN, B. H. (1959). The bases of social power. In D. Cartwright (Ed.), *Studies in Social Power* (pp. 150–167). Ann Arbor, MI: Institute for Social Research.

FRIEDLAND, N. (1986). Hostage negotiations: Types, processes, outcomes. *Negotiation Journal, 2,* 57–72.

FRODI, A., MACAULAY, J., & THOME, P. R. (1977). Are women always less aggressive than men? A review of the experimental literature. *Psychological Bulletin, 84,* 634–660.

FROMAN, L. A., Jr., & COHEN, M. D. (1970). Compromise and logroll: Comparing the efficiency of two bargaining processes. *Behavioral Science, 15,* 180–183.

FRY, W. R., FIRESTONE, I. J., & WILLIAMS, D. L. (1983). Negotiation process and outcome of stranger dyads and dating couples: Do lovers lose? *Basic and Applied Social Psychology, 4,* 1–16.

GAERTNER, S. L., MANN, J. A., MURRELL, A. J., & DOVIDIO, J. F. (1989). Reducing intergroup bias: The benefits of recategorization. *Journal of Personality and Social Psychology, 57,* 239–249.

GAHAGAN, J. P., TEDESCHI, J. T., FALEY, T., & LINDSKOLD, S. (1970). Patterns of punishment and reactions to threats. *Journal of Social Psychology, 80,* 115–116.

GANDHI, M. K. (1949). *For pacifists.* Ahmedabad, India: Navajivan Publishing House.

GEEN, R. G. (1975). The meaning of observed violence: Real vs. fictional violence and consequent effects on aggression. *Journal of Research in Personality, 12,* 15–29.

GEEN, R. G. (1978). Effects of attack and uncontrollable noise on aggression. *Journal of Research in Personality, 12,* 15–29.

GEEN, R. G. (1990). *Human aggression.* Pacific Grove, CA: Brooks/Cole.

GEEN, R. G., & STONNER, D. (1973). Context effects in observed violence. *Journal of Personality and Social Psychology, 25,* 145–150.

GERARD, H. B., & GREENBAUM, C. W. (1962). Attitudes toward an agent of uncertainty reduction. *Journal of Personality, 30,* 483–495.

GERHART, B., & RYNES, S. (1991). Determinants and consequences of salary negotiations by male and female MBA graduates. *Journal of Applied Psychology, 76,* 256–262.

GLADWIN, T. N., & WALTER, I. (1980). *Multinationals under fire: Lessons in the management of conflict.* New York: Wiley.

GLASL, F. (1982). The process of conflict escalation and roles of third parties. In G. B. J. Bomers & R. B. Peterson (Eds.), *Conflict management and industrial relations* (pp. 119–140). Boston: Kluwer-Nijhoff.

GLUCKMAN, M. (1955). *Custom and conflict in Africa.* Glencoe, IL: Free Press.

GODFREY, D. K., JONES, E. E., & LORD, C. G. (1986). Self-promotion is not ingratiating. *Journal of Personality and Social Psychology, 50,* 106–115.

GOLAN, M. (1976). *The secret conversations of Henry Kissinger.* New York: Quadrangle.

GOLDBERG, S. B., GREEN, E. D., & SANDER, F. E. A. (1987). Saying you're sorry. *Negotiation Journal, 3,* 221–224.

GOLDBERG, S. B., SANDER, F. E. A., & ROGERS, N. H. (1992). *Dispute resolution: Negotiation, mediation, and other processes* (2nd ed.). Boston: Little, Brown.

GOTTMAN, J. M. (1979). *Marital interaction: Experimental investigations.* New York: Academic Press.

GOTTMAN, J. M., & LEVENSON, R. L. (1988). The social psycho-physiology of marriage. In P. Noller & M. A. Fitzpatrick (Eds.), *Perspectives on marital interaction* (pp. 182–200). Clevendon, England: Multilingual Matters.

GREENBERG, M. S., & FRISCH, D. M. (1972). Effect of intentionality on willingness to reciprocate a favor. *Journal of Experimental Social Psychology, 8,* 302–311.

GREENHALGH, L., & GILKEY, R. W. (1984). Effects of sex-role differences on approaches to interpersonal and interorganizational negotiations. Paper presented at the Academy of Management Annual Meeting, Boston.

GRUDER, C. L. (1971). Relationship with opponent and partner in mixed-motive bargaining. *Journal of Conflict Resolution, 15,* 403–416.

GULICK, E. V. (1955). *Europe's classical balance of power.* Ithaca, NY: Cornell University Press.

GULLIVER, P. H. (1979). *Disputes and negotiations: A cross-cultural perspective.* New York: Academic Press.

GURR, T. R. (1970). *Why men rebel.* Princeton, NJ: Princeton University Press.

HALBERSTAM, D. (1969). *The best and the brightest.* New York: Random House.

HALL, J. (1969). *Conflict management survey: A survey of one's characteristic reaction to and handling of conflict between himself and others.* Monroe, TX: Telemetrics International.

HALL, L. (1993). *Negotiation: Strategies for mutual gain.* Newbury Park, CA: Sage.

HAMILTON, D. L., & BISHOP, G. D. (1976). Attitudinal and behavioral effects of initial integration of white suburban neighborhoods. *Journal of Social Issues, 32,* 47–67.

HAMNER, W. C. (1974). Effects of bargaining strategy and pressure to reach agreement in a stalemated negotiation. *Journal of Personality and Social Psychology, 30,* 458–467.

HANCOCK, R. D., & Sorrentino, R. N. (1980). The effects of expected future interaction and prior group support on the conformity process. *Journal of Experimental Social Psychology, 16,* 261–269.

HARFORD, T., & SOLOMON, L. (1967). "Reformed sinner" and "lapsed saint" strategies in the prisoner's dilemma game. *Journal of Conflict Resolution, 11,* 104–109.

HARRIS, J. C. (1955). *The complete tales of Uncle Remus.* Boston: Houghton Mifflin.

HARRIS, K. L., & CARNEVALE, P. J. (1990). Chiling and hastening: The influence of third-party power and interests on negotiation. *Organizational Behavior and Human Decision Processes, 47,* 138–160.

HARVEY, O. J. (1956). An experimental investigation of negative and positive relations between small groups through judgmental indices. *Sociometry, 14,* 201–209.

HASTORF, A. H., & CANTRIL, C. (1954). They saw a game: A case study. *Journal of Abnormal and Social Psychology, 49,* 129–134.

HAUN, D. L., & STINNETT, N. (1974). Does psychological comfortableness between engaged couples affect their probability of successful marriage adjustment? *Family Perspectives, 9,* 11–18.

Hayden, T., & Mischel, W. (1976). Maintaining trait consistency in the resolution of behavioral inconsistency: The wolf in sheep's clothing? *Journal of Personality, 44,* 109–132.

Heide, J. B., & Miner, A. S. (1992). The shadow of the future: Effects of anticipated interaction and frequency of contact on buyer-seller cooperation. *Academy of Management Journal, 35,* 265–291.

Heider, F. (1958). *The psychology of interpersonal relations.* New York: Wiley.

Hendry, J. (1987). *Understanding Japanese society.* London: Croom Helm.

Hiltrop, J. M. (1985). Mediator behavior and the settlement of collective bargaining disputes in Britain. *Journal of Social Issues, 41,* 83–99.

Hiltrop, J. M. (1989). Factors associated with successful labor mediation. In K. Kressel & D. G. Pruitt (Eds.), *Mediation research* (pp. 241–262). San Francisco: Jossey-Bass.

Hiltrop, J. M., & Rubin, J. Z. (1982). Effects of intervention mode and conflict of interest on dispute resolution. *Journal of Personality and Social Psychology, 42,* 665–672.

Hilty, J., & Carnevale, P. J. (1994). Black-hat/white-hat strategy in bilateral negotiation. *Organizational Behavior and Human Decision Processes.*

Hofstede, G. (1980). *Culture's consequences: International differences in work-related values.* Beverly Hills, CA: Sage.

Hollander, E. P. (1978). *Leadership dynamics: A practical guide to effective relationships.* New York: Free Press.

Hollingshead, A. B., & Carnevale, P. J. (1990). Positive affect and decision frame in integrative bargaining: A reversal of the frame effect. *Proceedings of the Fiftieth Annual Conference of the Academy of Management* (pp. 385–389), San Francisco.

Holtzworth-Munroe, A., & Jacobson, N. S. (1985). Causal attributions of married couples: When do they search for causes? What do they conclude when they do? *Journal of Personality and Social Psychology, 48,* 1398–1412.

Hornstein, H. A. (1976). *Cruelty and kindness: A new look at aggression and altruism.* Englewood Cliffs, NJ: Prentice-Hall.

Hovland, C. I., & Sears, R. R. (1940). Minor studies of aggression. VI: Correlation of lynchings with economic indices. *Journal of Psychology, 9,* 301–310.

Huber, E. L., Pruitt, D. G., & Welton, G. L. (1986). The effect of prior negotiation experience on the process and outcome of later negotiation. Poster presented at the annual meeting of the Eastern Psychological Association, New York.

Hynan, D. J., & Grush, J. E. (1986). Effects of impulsivity, depression, provocation, and time on aggressive behavior. *Journal of Research in Personality, 20,* 158–171.

Indvik, J., & Fitzpatrick, M. A. (1982). "If you could read my mind, love . . . ," understanding and misunderstanding in the marital dyad. *Family Relations, 31,* 43–51.

Ippolito, C. A., & Pruitt, D. G. (1990). Power balancing in mediation: Outcomes and implications of mediator intervention. *International Journal of Conflict Management, 1,* 341–356.

Isen, A. M., & Levin, P. F. (1972). Effect of feeling good on helping: Cookies and kindness. *Journal of Personality and Social Psychology, 21,* 384–388.

ISENBERG, D. J. (1986). Group polarization: A critical review and meta-analysis. *Journal of Personality and Social Psychology, 50,* 1141–1151.

IZARD, C. E. (1977). *Human emotions.* New York: Plenum.

JACOBSON, D. (1981). Intraparty dissensus and interparty conflict resolution. *Journal of Conflict Resolution, 25,* 471–494.

JACOBSON, N. S. (1984). The modification of cognitive processes in behavioral marital therapy: Integrating cognitive and behavioral intervention strategies. In K. Hahlweg & N. S. Jacobson (Eds.), *Marital interaction: Analysis and modification* (pp. 285–308). New York: Guilford Press.

JANIS, I. L. (1972). *Victims of groupthink: A psychological study of foreign-policy decisions and fiascos.* Boston: Houghton Mifflin.

JERVIS, R. (1976). *Perception and misperception in international politics.* Princeton, NJ: Princeton University Press.

JOHNSON, D. F., & PRUITT, D. G. (1972). Preintervention effects of mediation versus arbitration. *Journal of Applied Psychology, 56,* 1–10.

JOHNSON, D. W., JOHNSON, R., & MARUYAMA, G. (1984). Goal interdependence and interpersonal attraction in heterogenous classrooms: A meta-analysis. In N. Miller & M. B. Brewer (Eds.), *Groups in contact: The psychology of desegregation* (pp. 187–212). New York: Academic Press.

JOHNSON, S. M., & GREENBERG, L. C. (1985). Differential effects of experiential and problem-solving interventions in resolving marital conflict. *Journal of Consulting and Clinical Psychology, 53,* 175–184.

JONES, E. E., & DAVIS, K. E. (1965). From acts to dispositions: The attribution process in person perception. In L. Berkowitz (Ed.), *Advances in Experimental Social Psychology* (Vol. 2, pp. 219–266). New York: Academic Press.

JONES, E. E., & GORDON, E. M. (1972). Timing of self-disclosure and its effects on personal attraction. *Journal of Personality and Social Psychology, 24,* 358–365.

JONES, E. E., JONES, R. G., & GERGEN, K. J. (1963). Some conditions affecting the evaluation of a conformist. *Journal of Personality, 31,* 270–288.

JONES, E. E., RHODEWALT, F., BERGLAS, S., & SKELTON, J. A. (1981). Effects of strategic self-presentation on subsequent self-esteem. *Journal of Personality and Social Psychology, 41,* 407–421.

JONES, E. E., & WEIN, G. (1972). Attitude similarity, expectancy violation, and attraction. *Journal of Experimental Social Psychology, 8,* 222–235.

JONES, E. E., & WORTMAN, C. (1973). *Ingratiation: An attributional approach.* Morristown, NJ: General Learning Press.

JONES, T. S. (1989). A taxonomy of effective mediator strategies and tactics for nonlabor-management mediation. In M. A. Rahim (Ed.), *Managing conflict: An interdisciplinary approach* (pp. 221–229). New York: Praeger.

KABANOFF, B. (1987). Predictive validity of the MODE conflict instrument. *Journal of Applied Psychology, 72,* 160–163.

KAHN, H. (1960). *On thermonuclear war.* Princeton, NJ: Princeton University Press.

KAPLAN, M. (1957). *System and process in international politics.* New York: Wiley.

KARSTEN, R. (1935). *The head-hunters of western Amazonus.* Helsingfors: Societas Scientiarum Fennica.

KEASHLY, L. (1988). A comparative analysis of third party interventions in intergroup conflict. Doctoral dissertation, University of Saskatchewan, Canada.

KEATING, M. E., PRUITT, D. G., EBERLE, R., & MIKOLIC, J. M. (1993). Strategic choice in everyday disputes. Unpublished manuscript, State University of New York at Buffalo.

KELLERMAN, B., & RUBIN, J. Z. (1988). *Leadership and negotiation in the Middle East.* New York: Praeger.

KELLEY, H. H. (1966). A classroom study of the dilemmas in interpersonal negotiations. In K. Archibald (Ed.), *Strategic interaction and conflict: Original papers and discussion* (pp. 49–73). Berkeley, CA: Institute of International Studies.

KELLEY, H. H. (1973). The process of causal attribution. *American Psychologist, 28,* 107–128.

KELLEY, H. H., BECKMAN, L. L., & FISCHER, C. S. (1967). Negotiating the division of reward under incomplete information. *Journal of Experimental Social Psychology, 3,* 361–398.

KELLEY, H. H., & SCHENITZKI, D. P. (1972). Bargaining. In C. G. McClintock (Ed.), *Experimental social psychology* (pp. 298–337). New York: Holt.

KELLEY, H. H., & STAHELSKI, A. J. (1970). Social interaction basis of cooperators' and competitors' beliefs about others. *Journal of Personality and Social Psychology, 16,* 66–91.

KELMAN, H. C. (1972). The problem-solving workshop in conflict resolution. In R. L. Merritt (Ed.), *Communication in international politics* (pp. 168–204). Urbana, IL: University of Illinois Press.

KELMAN, H. C. (1982). Creating the conditions for Israeli-Palestinian negotiations. *Journal of Conflict Resolution, 26,* 39–75.

KELMAN, H. C. (1985). Overcoming the psychological barrier: An analysis of the Egyptian-Israeli peace process. *Negotiation Journal, 1,* 213–234.

KELMAN, H. C., & COHEN, S. P. (1976). The problem-solving workshop: A social psychological contribution to the resolution of international conflicts. *Journal of Peace Research, 13,* 79–90.

KELMAN, H. C., & COHEN, S. P. (1986). Resolution of international conflict: An interactional approach. In S. Worchel & W. G. Austin (Eds.), *Psychology of intergroup relations* (pp. 323–342). Chicago: Nelson-Hall.

KELMAN, H. C., & HAMILTON, V. L. (1989). *Crimes of obedience: Toward a social psychology of authority and responsibility.* New Haven, CT: Yale University Press.

KENNEDY, R. F. (1969). *Thirteen days: A memoir of the Cuban missile crisis.* New York: Norton.

KILMANN, R. H., & THOMAS, K. W. (1977). Developing a forced-choice measure of conflict handling behavior: The "Mode" instrument. *Educational and Psychological Measurement, 37,* 309–325.

KIM, S. H. (1991). Revenge and conflict escalation: The effects of power and audience. Doctoral dissertation, Tufts University.

KIM, S. H., & SMITH, R. H. (1993). Revenge and conflict escalation. *Negotiation Journal, 9,* 37–43.

KIMMEL, M. J., PRUITT, D. G., MAGENAU, J. M., KONAR-GOLDBAND, E., & CARNEVALE, P. J. (1980). Effects of trust, aspiration and gender on negotiation tactics. *Journal of Personality and Social Psychology, 38,* 9–23.

KLEINKE, C. L., STANESKI, R. A., & WEAVER, P. (1972). Evaluation of a person who uses another's name in ingratiating and noningratiating situations. *Journal of Experimental Social Psychology, 8,* 457–466.

KLEIST, H. V. (1967). *Michael Kohlhaas* (J. Kirkup, Trans.). London: Blackie & Son.

KLIMOSKI, R. J. (1972). The effects of intragroup forces on intergroup conflict resolution. *Organizational Behavior and Human Performance, 8,* 363–383.

KOCHAN, T. A. (1980). *Collective bargaining and industrial relations.* Homewood, IL: Irwin.

KOCHAN, T. A., & BADERSCHNEIDER, J. (1978). Dependence on impasse procedures: Police and firefighters in New York State. *Industrial and Labor Relations Review, 31,* 431–449.

KOCHAN, T. A., & Jick, T. (1978). The public sector mediation process: A theory and empirical examination. *Journal of Conflict Resolution, 22,* 209–240.

KOGAN, N., LAMM, H., & TROMMSDORFF, G. (1972). Negotiation constraints in the risk-taking domain: Effects of being observed by partners of higher or lower status. *Journal of Personality and Social Psychology, 23,* 143–156.

KOLB, D. M. (1983). *The mediators.* Cambridge, MA: M.I.T. Press.

KOLB, D. M., & Bartunek, J. M. (Eds.) (1992). *Hidden conflict in organizations: Uncovering behind-the-scenes disputes.* Newbury Park, CA: Sage.

KOLB, D. M. (1994). *When talk works: Profiles of working mediators.* San Francisco, CA: Jossey-Bass.

KOLB, D. M., & COOLIDGE, G. C. (1991). Her place at the table: A consideration of gender issues in negotiation. In J. W. Breslin & J. Z. Rubin (Eds.), *Negotiation theory and practice* (pp. 261–277). Boston: Program on Negotiation Books at Harvard Law School.

KOLB, D. M., & FAURE, G. O. (1994). Organization theory. In I. W. Zartman (Ed.), *Multilateral negotiation.* San Francisco, CA: Jossey-Bass.

KOLB, D. M., & RUBIN, J. Z. (1991). Mediation from a disciplinary perspective. In M. H. Bazerman, R. J. Lewicki, & B. H. Sheppard (Eds.), *Research on negotiation in organizations* (Vol. 3, pp. 231–258). Greenwich, CT: JAI.

KOMORITA, S. S. (1973). Concession making and conflict resolution. *Journal of Conflict Resolution, 17,* 745–762.

KOMORITA, S. S., & ESSER, J. K. (1975). Frequency of reciprocated concessions in bargaining. *Journal of Personality and Social Psychology, 32,* 699–705.

KOMORITA, S. S., & LAPWORTH, C. W. (1982). Cooperative choice among individuals vs. groups in an *n*-person dilemma situation. *Journal of Personality and Social Psychology, 42,* 487–496.

KONECNI, V. J. (1975). The mediation of aggressive behavior: Arousal level vs. anger and cognitive labeling. *Journal of Personality and Social Psychology, 32,* 706–712.

KRAMER, R. M., & BREWER, M. B. (1984). Effects of group identity on resource use in a simulated commons dilemma. *Journal of Personality and Social Psychology, 46,* 1044–1057.

KRASLOW, D., & LOORY, S. H. (1968). *The secret search for peace in Vietnam.* New York: Vintage Books.

KRAUSS, R. M., & DEUTSCH, M. (1966). Communication in interpersonal bargaining. *Journal of Personality and Social Psychology, 4,* 572–577.

KREMENYUK, V. A. (Ed.) (1991). *International negotiation: Analysis, approaches, issues.* San Francisco, CA: Jossey-Bass.

KRESSEL, K. (1972). *Labor mediation: An exploratory survey.* Albany, NY: Association of Labor Mediation Agencies.

KRESSEL, K., & PRUITT, D. G. (1989). Conclusion: A research perspective on the mediation of social conflict. In K. Kressel & D. G. Pruitt (Eds.), *Mediation research* (pp. 394–435). San Francisco: Jossey-Bass.

KRIESBERG, L. (1982). *Social conflicts* (2nd ed.). Englewood Cliffs, NJ: Prentice-Hall.

KRIESBERG, L., & THORSON, S. J. (Eds.) (1991). *Timing the de-escalation of international conflicts*. Syracuse, NY: Syracuse University Press.

LANDSBERGER, H. A. (1955). Interaction process analysis of the mediation of labor-management disputes. *Journal of Abnormal and Social Psychology, 51,* 552–559.

LANE, C. (1992, December 28). Mob rule. *The New Republic,* pp. 22–23.

LASSWELL, H. D. (1950). *A study of power*. New York: Free Press.

LATOUR, S., HOULDEN, P., WALKER, L., & THIBAUT, J. (1976). Some determinants of preference for modes of conflict resolution. *Journal of Conflict Resolution, 20,* 319–356.

LAWRENCE, P. R., & LORSCH, J. W. (1967). *Organizational and environment*. Cambridge, MA: Harvard University Press.

LAX, D. A., & SEBENIUS, J. K. (1986). *The manager as negotiator: Bargaining for cooperation and competitive gain.* New York: Free Press.

LAZARUS, R. L. (1993). From psychological stress to the emotions: A history of changing outlooks. *Annual Review of Psychology, 44,* 1–21.

LEBOW, R. N., JERVIS, R., & STEIN, J. G. (1984). *Psychology and deterrence.* Baltimore, MD: Johns Hopkins University Press.

LEVINGER, G. (1983). Development and change. In H. H. Kelley, E. Berscheid, A. Christensen, J. H. Harvey, T. L. Huston, G. Levinger, E. McClintock, L. A. Peplau, & D. R. Peterson, (Eds.), *Close relationships* (pp. 315–359). New York: Freeman.

LEVINGER, G. (1987). The limits of deterrence: An introduction. *Journal of Social Issues, 43,* 1–4.

LEWICKI, R. J. (1980). *Bad loan psychology: Entrapment and commitment in financial lending* (Working Paper 80-25). Durham, NC: Duke University Graduate School of Business Administration.

LEWICKI, R. J., & LITTERER, J. (1985). *Negotiation.* Homewood, IL: Irwin.

LEWICKI, R. J., & RUBIN, J. Z. (1973). Effects of variations in the informational clarity of promises and threats upon interpersonal bargaining. *Proceedings of the 81st Annual Convention of the American Psychological Association, 8,* 137–138.

LEWIS, I. M. (1961). *A pastoral democracy: A study of pastoralism and politics among the Northern Somali of the Horn of Africa.* London: Oxford University Press.

LIDEN, R. C., & MITCHELL, T. R. (1988). Ingratiating behaviors in organizational settings. *Academy of Management Review, 13,* 527–587.

LIKERT, R. (1961). *New patterns of management.* New York: McGraw-Hill.

LIM, R. G., & CARNEVALE, P. J. (1990). Contingencies in the mediation of disputes. *Journal of Personality and Social Psychology, 58,* 259–272.

LIND, E. A. and TYLER, T. R. (1988). *The social psychology of procedural justice.* New York: Plenum.

LINDSKOLD, S. (1978). Trust development, the GRIT proposal, and the effects of conciliatory acts on conflict and cooperation. *Psychological Bulletin, 85,* 772–793.

LINDSKOLD, S., & BENNETT, R. (1973). Attributing trust and conciliatory intent from coercive power capability. *Journal of Personality and Social Psychology, 28,* 180–186.

LINDSKOLD, S., BONOMA, T., & TEDESCHI, J. T. (1969). Relative costs and reactions to threats. *Psychonomic Science, 15,* 303–304.

LOFTIS, J. E. (1974). *Anger, aggression and attribution of arousal.* Doctoral dissertation, Stanford University.

LONGLEY, J., & PRUITT, D. G. (1980). A critique of Janis's theory of groupthink. In L. Wheeler (Ed.), *Review of personality and social psychology* (Vol. 1, pp. 74–93). Beverly Hills, CA: Sage.

LOOMIS, J. L. (1959). Communication, the development of trust, and cooperative behavior. *Human Relations, 12,* 305–315.

LOWE, C. A., & GOLDSTEIN, J. W. (1970). Reciprocal liking and attributions of ability: Mediating effects of perceived intent and personal involvement. *Journal of Personality and Social Psychology, 16,* 291–298.

MAGENAU, J. M. (1983). The impact of alternative impasse procedures on bargaining: A laboratory experiment. *Industrial and Labor Relations Review, 36,* 361–377.

MAJOR, B., & FORCEY, B. (1985). Social comparisons and pay evaluations: Preferences for same-sex and same-job wage comparisons. *Journal of Experimental Social Psychology, 21,* 393–405.

MALLICK, S. K., & MCCANDLESS, B. R. (1966). A study of catharsis of aggression. *Journal of Personality and Social Psychology, 4,* 591–596.

MANN, L. (1981). The baiting crowd in episodes of threatened suicide. *Journal of Personality and Social Psychology, 41,* 703–709.

MANNIX, E. A., THOMPSON, L. L., & BAZERMAN, M. H. (1989). Negotiation in small groups. *Journal of Applied Psychology, 74,* 508–517.

MAUTNER-MARKHOF, F. (1989). *Processes of international negotiations.* Boulder, CO: Westview.

MCCALLUM, D. M., HARRING, K., GILMORE, R., DRENAN, S., CHASE, J. P., INSKO, C. A., & THIBAUT, J. (1985). Competition and cooperation between groups and between individuals. *Journal of Experimental Social Psychology, 21,* 301–320.

MCCLINTOCK, C. G. (1988). Evolution, systems of interdependence, and social values. *Behavioral Science, 33,* 59–76.

MCCLINTOCK, C. G., STECH, F. J., & BEGGAN, J. K. (1987). The effects of commitment to threats and promises upon bargaining behaviour and outcomes. *European Journal of Social Psychology, 17,* 447–464.

MCEWEN, C. A., & MILBURN, T. W. (1993). Explaining a paradox of mediation. *Negotiation Journal, 9,* 23–36.

MCGILLICUDDY, N. B., PRUITT, D. G., & SYNA, H. (1984). Perceptions of firmness and strength in negotiation. *Personality and Social Psychology Bulletin, 10,* 402–409.

MCGILLICUDDY, N. B., WELTON, G. L., & PRUITT, D. G. (1987). Third party intervention: A field experiment comparing three different models. *Journal of Personality and Social Psychology, 53,* 104–112.

MERRY, S. E. (1989). Mediation in nonindustrial societies. In K. Kressel & D. G. Pruitt (Eds.), *Mediation research* (pp. 68–90). San Francisco: Jossey-Bass.

MESSICK, D. M., & MACKIE, D. M. (1989). Intergroup relations. *Annual Review of Psychology, 40,* 51–81.

MICHENER, H. A., VASKE, J. J., SCHLEIFER, S. L., PLAZEWSKI, J. G., & CHAPMAN, L. J. (1975). Factors affecting concession rate and threat usage in bilateral conflict. *Sociometry, 38,* 62–80.

MILGRAM, S. (1992). *The individual in a social world: Essays and experiments* (2nd ed.). New York: McGraw-Hill.

MILLER, N., & BREWER, M. B. (Eds.). (1984). *Groups in contact: The psychology of desegregation*. New York: Academic Press.

MILLER, N., & DAVIDSON-PODGORNY, G. (1987). Theoretical models of intergroup relations and the use of cooperative teams as an intervention for desegregated settings. In C. Hendrick (Ed.), *Group processes and intergroup relations*. Newbury Park, CA: Sage.

MOGY, R. B., & PRUITT, D. G. (1974). Effects of a threatener's enforcement costs on threat credibility and compliance. *Journal of Personality and Social Psychology, 29,* 173–180.

MORGENTHAU, H. J. (1967). *Politics among nations*. New York: Knopf.

MORLEY, I. E., & STEPHENSON, G. M. (1977). *The social psychology of bargaining*. London: Allen and Unwin.

MOSCOVICI, S., & ZAVALLONI, M. (1969). The group as a polarizer of attitudes. *Journal of Personality and Social Psychology, 12,* 125–135.

MUENCH, G. A. (1963). A clinical psychologist's treatment of labor-management conflicts: a four-year study. *Journal of Humanistic Psychology, 3,* 92–97.

MUMMENDEY, A., LINNEWEBER, V., & LOSCHPER, G. (1984). Actor or victim of aggression: Divergent perspectives—divergent evaluations. *European Journal of Social Psychology, 14,* 297–311.

MUSSER, S. J. (1982). A model for predicting the choice of conflict management strategies by subordinates in high stakes conflict. *Organizational Behavior and Human Performance, 29,* 257–269.

NADLER, L. B., & NADLER, M. K. (1984). Communication, gender, and negotiation: Theory and findings. Unpublished paper. Eastern Communication Association Convention, Philadelphia.

NEALE, M. A. (1984). The effect of negotiation and arbitration cost salience on bargaining behavior: The role of arbitrator and constituency in negotiator judgment. *Organizational Behavior and Human Performance, 34,* 97–111.

NEALE, M. A., & BAZERMAN, M. H. (1983). The role of perspective-taking ability in negotiating under different forms of arbitration. *Industrial and Labor Relations Review, 36,* 378–388.

NEALE, M. A., & BAZERMAN, M. H. (1985). The effects of framing and negotiator overconfidence on bargaining behaviors and outcomes. *Academy of Management Journal, 28,* 34–39.

NEALE, M. A., & BAZERMAN, M. H. (1991). *Negotiator cognition and rationality*. Free Press: New York.

NEMETH, C. (1970). Effects of free versus constrained behavior on attraction between people. *Journal of Personality and Social Psychology, 15,* 302–311.

NEUBERG, S. L. (1989). The goal of forming accurate impressions during social interactions: Attenuating the impact of negative expectancies. *Journal of Personality and Social Psychology, 56,* 374–386.

NEWCOMB, T. M. (1947). Autistic hostility and social reality. *Human Relations, 1,* 69–86.

New York Times, November 13, 1992.

NOLLER, P., & FITZPATRICK, M. A. (1990). Marital communication in the eighties. *Journal of Marriage and the Family, 52,* 832–843.

NORTH, R. C., BRODY, R. A., & HOLSTI, O. R. (1964). Some empirical data on the conflict spiral. *Peace Research Society (International) Papers, 1,* 1–14.

NOTZ, W. W., & STARKE, F. A. (1978). Final-offer vs. conventional arbitration as modes of conflict management. *Administrative Science Quarterly, 23,* 189–203.

OHBUCHI, K., KAMEDA, M., & AGARIE, N. (1989). Apology as aggression control: Its role in mediating appraisal of and response to harm. *Journal of Personality and Social Psychology, 56,* 219–227.

O'QUIN, K., & ARONOFF, J. (1981). Humor as a technique of social influence. *Social Psychology Quarterly, 44,* 349–357.

ORWELL, G. (1968). Looking back on the Spanish War. In S. Orwell & I. Angus (Eds.), *The collected essays, journalism and letters of George Orwell: Vol. 2. My country right or left, 1940–1943* (pp. 249–267). New York: Harcourt, Brace & World.

OSGOOD, C. E. (1962). *An alternative to war or surrender.* Urbana; University of Illinois Press.

OSGOOD, C. E. (1966). *Perspective in foreign policy* (2nd ed.). Palo Alto, CA: Pacific Books.

OSKAMP, S. (1965). Attitudes toward U. S. and Russian actions—A double standard. *Psychological Reports, 16,* 43–46.

PATCHEN, M. (1991). Conflict and cooperation in American-Soviet relations: What have we learned from quantitative research? *International Interactions, 17,* 127–143.

PEARSON, J., & THOENNES, N. (1982). Mediation and divorce: The benefits outweigh the costs. *The Family Advocate, 4,* 26–32.

PEARSON, J., THOENNES, N., & VANDERKOOI, L. (1982). The decision to mediate: Profiles of individuals who accept and reject the opportunity to mediate contested child custody and visitation issues. *Journal of Divorce, 6,* 17–35.

PETERS, E. (1952). *Conciliation in action.* New London, CT: National Foremen's Institute.

PETERSON, D. R. (1983). Conflict. In H. H. Kelley, E. Berscheid, A. Christensen, J. H. Harvey, T. L. Huston, G. Levinger, E. McClintock, L. A. Peplau, & D. R. Peterson (Eds.), *Close relationships* (pp. 360–396). New York: Freeman.

PETTIGREW, T. F. (1988). Advancing racial justice: Past lessons for future use. Paper presented at *Opening Doors: An Appraisal of Race Relations in America,* University of Alabama Conference.

POTTER, S. (1948). *The theory and practice of gamesmanship: The art of winning games without actually cheating.* New York: Holt.

PRATKANIS, A. P., & ARONSON, E. (1992). *Age of propaganda: The everyday use and abuse of persuasion.* New York: Freeman.

PRUITT, D. G. (1965). Definition of the situation as a determinant of international action. In H. C. Kelman (Ed.), *International behavior: A social-psychological analysis* (pp. 391–432). New York: Holt, Rinehart and Winston.

PRUITT, D. G. (1969). Stability and sudden change in interpersonal and international affairs. *Journal of Conflict Resolution, 13,* 18–38.

PRUITT, D. G. (1971). Indirect communication and the search for agreement in negotiation. *Journal of Applied Social Psychology, 1,* 205–239.

PRUITT, D. G. (1981). *Negotiation behavior.* New York: Academic Press.

PRUITT, D. G., & CARNEVALE, P. J. (1982). The development of integrative agreements in social conflict. In V. J. Derlega & J. Grzelak (Eds.), *Living with other people.* New York: Academic Press.

PRUITT, D. G., & CARNEVALE, P. J. (1993). *Negotiation in social conflict.* Buckingham: Open University Press.

PRUITT, D. G., CARNEVALE, P. J. D., BEN-YOAV, O., NOCHAJSKI, T. H., & VAN SLYCK, M. R. (1983). Incentives for cooperation in integrative bargaining. In R. Tietz (Ed.), *Aspiration levels in bargaining and economic decision making* (pp. 22–34). Berlin: Springer-Verlag.

PRUITT, D. G., CARNEVALE, P. J., FORCEY, B., & VAN SLYCK, M. (1986). Gender effects in negotiation: Constituent surveillance and contentious behavior. *Journal of Experimental Social Psychology, 22,* 264–275.

PRUITT, D. G., & DREWS, J. L. (1969). The effect of time pressure, time elapsed, and the opponent's concession rate on behavior in negotiation. *Journal of Experimental Social Psychology, 5,* 43–60.

PRUITT, D. G., FRY, W. R., CASTRIANNO, L., ZUBEK, J., WELTON, G. L., MCGILLICUDDY, N. B., & Ippolito, C. (1989a). The process of mediation: Caucusing, control, and problem solving. In M. A. Rahim (Ed.), *Managing conflict: An interdisciplinary approach* (pp. 201–208). New York: Praeger.

PRUITT, D. G., & GAHAGAN, J. P. (1974). Campus crisis: The search for power. In J. T. Tedeschi (Ed.), *Perspectives on social power* (pp. 349–392). Chicago: Aldine.

PRUITT, D. G., & HOLLAND, J. (1972). *Settlement in the Berlin Crisis, 1958–62.* Buffalo, NY: Council on International Studies, State University of New York at Buffalo.

PRUITT, D. G., & JOHNSON, D. F. (1970). Mediation as an aid to face saving in negotiation. *Journal of Personality and Social Psychology, 14,* 239–246.

PRUITT, D. G., MCGILLICUDDY, N. B., WELTON, G. L., & FRY, W. R. (1989b). Process of mediation in dispute settlement centers. In K. Kressel & D. G. Pruitt (Eds.), *Mediation research* (pp. 368–393). San Francisco: Jossey-Bass.

PRUITT, D. G., MIKOLIC, J. M., EBERLE, R., PARKER, J. C., & PEIRCE, R. S. (1993a). The escalation of conflict: Group vs. individual response to persistent annoyance. Paper presented at the Sixth Annual Conference of the International Association for Conflict Management, Houthalen, Belgium, June 14–17.

PRUITT, D. G., PEIRCE, R. S., MCGILLICUDDY, N. B., WELTON, G. L., & CASTRIANNO, L. M. (1993b). Long-term success in mediation. *Law and Human Behavior, 17,* 313–330.

PRUITT, D. G., & SNYDER, R. C. (Eds.) (1969). *Theory and research on the causes of war.* Englewood Cliffs, NJ: Prentice-Hall.

PRUITT, D. G., & SYNA, H. (1983). Successful problem solving. In D. Tjosvold & D. W. Johnson (Eds.), *Conflicts in Organization* (pp. 62–81). New York: Irvington.

PUTNAM, L. L., & POOLE, M. E. (1987). Conflict and negotiation. In F. M. Jablin, L. L. Putnam, K. H. Roberts, & L. W. Porter (Eds.), *Handbook of organizational communication: An interdisciplinary perspective* (pp. 549–599). Newbury Park, CA: Sage.

RABBIE, J. M., & WILKENS, C. (1971). Intergroup competition and its effect on intra- and intergroup relations. *European Journal of Social Psychology, 1,* 215–234.

RAHIM, M. A. (1983). A measure of styles of handling interpersonal conflict. *Academy of Management Journal, 26,* 368–376.

RAHIM, M. A. (1986). Referent role and styles of handling interpersonal conflict. *Journal of Social Psychology, 126,* 79–86.

RAHIM, M. A., & BONOMA, T. V. (1979). Managing organizational conflict: A model for diagnosis and intervention. *Psychological Reports, 44,* 1323–1344.

RAIFFA, H. (1982). *The art and science of negotiation.* Cambridge, MA: Harvard University Press.

RALSTON, D. A. (1985). Employee ingratiation: The role of management. *Academy of Management, 10,* 477–487.

RANSFORD, H. E. (1968). Isolation, powerlessness and violence: A study of attitudes and participation in the Watts riot. *American Journal of Sociology, 73,* 581–591.

RAVEN, B. H., & RUBIN, J. Z. (1983). *Social psychology* (2nd ed.). New York: Wiley.

REGAN, D. T. (1971). Effects of a favor and liking on compliance. *Journal of Experimental Social Psychology, 7,* 627–639.

REGAN, D. T., STRAUS, E., & FAZIO, R. H. (1974). Liking and the attribution process. *Journal of Experimental Social Psychology, 10,* 385–397.

REGAN, D. T., WILLIAMS, M., & SPARLING, S. (1972). Voluntary expiation of guilt: A field experiment. *Journal of Personality and Social Psychology, 24,* 42–45.

RHODEWALT, F., & AGUSTSDOTTIR, S. (1986). Effects of self-presentation on the phenomenal self. *Journal of Personality and Social Psychology, 50,* 47–55.

RICHARDSON, L. F. (1967). *Arms and insecurity.* Chicago: Quadrangle.

RIFKIN, J. (1984). Mediation from a feminist perspective: Problems and promise. *Law and Inequality, 21,* 2.

ROGERS, R. W., & PRENTICE-DUNN, S. (1981). Deindividuation and anger-mediated aggression: Unmasking regressive racism. *Journal of Personality and Social Psychology, 41,* 63–73.

ROSENHAN, D. L. (1973). On being sane in insane places. *Science, 179,* 250–258.

ROSENTHAL, R., & FODE, K. (1963). The effect of experimental bias on the performance of the albino rat. *Behavioral Science, 8,* 183–189.

ROSENTHAL, R., & JACOBSON, L. F. (1968). *Pygmalion in the classroom.* New York: Holt, Rinehart and Winston.

ROTTON, J., & FREY, J. (1985). Air pollution, weather, and violent crime: Concomitant time-series analysis of archival data. *Journal of Personality and Social Psychology, 49,* 1207–1220.

RUBIN, J. Z. (1971). The nature and success of influence attempts in a four-party bargaining relationship. *Journal of Experimental Social Psychology, 7,* 17–35.

RUBIN, J. Z. (1980). Experimental research on third-party intervention in conflict: Toward some generalizations. *Psychological Bulletin, 87,* 379–391.

RUBIN, J. Z. (1981). *Dynamics of third-party intervention: Kissinger in the Middle East.* New York: Praeger.

RUBIN, J. Z. (1991). The timing of ripeness and the ripeness of timing. In L. Kriesberg & S. J. Thorson (Eds.), *Timing the de-escalation of international conflicts* (pp. 237–246). Syracuse, NY: Syracuse University Press.

RUBIN, J. Z., & BROWN B. R. (1975). *The social psychology of bargaining and negotiation.* New York: Academic Press.

RUBIN, J. Z., & FRIEDLAND, N. (1986). Theater of terror. *Psychology Today,* March, 20–28.

RUBIN, J. Z., & LEWICKI, R. J. (1973). A three-factor experimental analysis of promises and threats. *Journal of Applied Social Psychology, 3,* 240–257.

RUBIN, J. Z., LEWICKI, R. J., & DUNN, L. (1973). Perception of promisors and threateners. *Proceedings, 81st Annual Convention of the American Psychological Association* (pp. 141–142).

RUBIN, J. Z., PROVENZANO, F. J., & LURIA, Z. (1974). The eye of the beholder: Parents' views on sex of newborns. *American Journal of Orthopsychiatry, 44,* 512–519.

RUBIN, J. Z., & RUBIN, C. (1989). *When families fight: How to handle conflict with those you love.* New York: Ballantine Books.

RUBIN, J. Z., & SANDER, F. E. A. (1991). Culture, negotiation, and the eye of the beholder. *Negotiation Journal, 7,* 249–254.

RUBIN, J. Z., STEINBERG, B. D., & GERREIN, J. R. (1974). How to obtain the right of way: An experimental analysis of behavior at intersections. *Perceptual and Motor Skills, 39,* 1263–1274.

RUBLE, T. L., & THOMAS, K. W. (1976). Support for a two-dimensional model of conflict behavior. *Organizational Behavior and Human Performance, 16,* 143–155.

RUSBULT, C. E., VERETTE, J., WHITNEY, G. A., SLOVIK, L. F., & LIPKUS, G. A. (1991). Accommodation processes in close relationships: Theory and preliminary empirical evidence. *Journal of Personality and Social Psychology, 60,* 53–78.

RUSSELL, C. S., & DREES, C. M. (1989). What's the rush?—A negotiated slowdown. In J. F. Crosby (Ed.), *When one wants out and the other doesn't: Doing therapy with polarized couples* (pp. 93–117). New York: Brunner/Mazel.

RUSSETT, B. M. (1967). Pearl Harbor: Deterrence theory and decision theory. *Journal of Peace Research, 2,* 89–106.

RYEN, A. H., & KAHN, A. (1975). The effects of intergroup orientation on group attitudes and proxemic behavior: A test of two models. *Journal of Personality and Social Psychology, 31,* 302–310.

SAFRAN, N. (1978). *Israel: The embattled ally.* Cambridge, MA: Harvard University Press.

SALACUSE, J. W. (1991). *Making global deals: Negotiating in the international marketplace.* Boston: Houghton Mifflin.

SALACUSE, J. W., & Rubin, J. Z. (1990). Your place or mine? *Negotiation Journal, 6,* 5–10.

SALOVEY, P., Mayer, J. D., & ROSENHAN, D. L. (1991). Mood and helping: Mood as a motivator of helping and helping as a regulator of mood. In M. S. Clark (Ed.), *Review of personality and social psychology: Vol. 12. Prosocial behavior* (pp. 215–237). Newbury Park, CA: Sage.

SARTRE, J.-P. (1955). *No exit and three other plays.* New York: Random House.

SCHACHTER, S. (1951). Deviation, rejection, and communication. *Journal of Abnormal and Social Psychology, 46,* 190–207.

SCHACHTER, S. (1964). The interaction of cognitive and physiological determinants of emotional state. In L. Berkowitz (Ed.), *Advances in experimental social psychology* (Vol. 1, pp. 49–80). New York: Academic Press.

SCHELLING, T. C. (1960). *The strategy of conflict.* Cambridge, MA: Harvard University Press.

SCHELLING, T. C. (1966). *Arms and influence.* New Haven, CT: Yale University Press.

SCHELLING, T. C. (1978). *Micromotives and macrobehavior.* New York: Norton.

SCHLENKER, B. R. (1980). *Impression management: The self-concept, social identity, and interpersonal relations.* Belmont, CA: Brooks/Cole.

SCHOORMAN, F. D., BAZERMAN, M. H., & ATKIN, R. S. (1981). Interlocking directorates: A strategy for reducing environmental uncertainty. *Academy of Management Review, 6,* 243–251.

SCHUMPETER, J. (1955). *The sociology of imperialism.* New York: Meridian Books.

SCHWARTZ, S. H., & STRUCH, N. (1989). Values, stereotypes, and intergroup antagonism. In D. Bar-Tal, C. R. Grauman, A. W. Kruglanski, & W. Stroebe (Eds.), *Stereotypes and prejudice: Changing conceptions* (pp. 151–167). New York: Springer-Verlag.

SHARP, G. (1971). The technique of nonviolent action. In J. V. Bondurant (Ed.), *Conflict: Violence and nonviolence* (pp. 151–171). Chicago: Aldine.

SHAW, J. L., FISCHER, C. S., & KELLEY, H. H. (1973). Decision making by third parties in settling disputes. *Journal of Applied Social Psychology, 3,* 197–218.

SHAW, M. E., & SULZER, J. L. (1964). An empirical test of Heider's levels in attribution of responsibility. *Journal of Abnormal and Social Psychology, 69,* 39–46.

SHENKAR, O., & RONEN, S. (1987). The cultural context of negotiations: The implications of Chinese interpersonal norms. *The Journal of Applied Behavioral Science, 23,* 263–275.

SHEPPARD, B. H., BLUMENFELD-JONES, K., & ROTH, J. (1989). Informal thirdpartyship: Studies of everyday conflict intervention. In K. Kressel & D. G. Pruitt (Eds.), *Mediation research* (pp. 166–189). San Francisco: Jossey-Bass.

SHERIF, M., HARVEY, O. J., WHITE, B. J., HOOD, W. R., & SHERIF, C. W. (1961). *Intergroup cooperation and competition: The Robbers Cave experiment.* Norman, OK: University Book Exchange.

SHERIF, M., & SHERIF, C. W. (1953). *Groups in harmony and tension.* New York: Harper & Row.

SHERIF, M., & SHERIF, C. W. (1969). *Social psychology.* New York: Harper & Row.

SHUBIK, M. (1971). The dollar auction game: A paradox in noncooperative behavior and escalation. *Journal of Conflict Resolution, 15,* 109–111.

SIEGEL, S., & FOURAKER, L. E. (1960). *Bargaining and group decision making: Experiments in bilateral monopoly.* New York: McGraw-Hill.

SILLARS, A. L. (1981). Attributions and interpersonal conflict resolution. In J. H. Harvey, W. J. Ickes, & R. F. Kidd (Eds.), *New directions in attribution research* (Vol. 3, pp. 279–305). Hillsdale, NJ: Erlbaum.

SIMMEL, G. (1902). The number of members as determining the sociological form of the group. *American Journal of Sociology, 8,* 158–196.

SIMON, H. A. (1957). *Models of man: Social and rational.* New York: Wiley.

SJÖSTEDT, G. (1993). *International environmental negotiation.* Newbury Park, CA: Sage.

SMITH, D. L., PRUITT, D. G., & CARNEVALE, P. J. (1982). Matching and mismatching: The effect of own limit, other's toughness, and time pressure on concession rate in negotiation. *Journal of Personality and Social Psychology, 42,* 876–883.

SMITH, W. P. (1987). Conflict and negotiation: Trends and emerging issues. *Journal of Applied Social Psychology, 17,* 641–677.

SMITH, W. P. (1991). Effectiveness of the biased mediator. In J. W. Breslin & J. Z. Rubin (Eds.), *Negotiation theory and practice* (pp. 419–428). Cambridge, MA: The Program on Negotiation at Harvard Law School.

SMITH, W. P., & ANDERSON, A. J. (1975). Threats, communication, and bargaining. *Journal of Personality and Social Psychology, 32,* 76–82.

SNYDER, G. H., & DIESING, P. (1977). *Conflict among nations.* Princeton, NJ: Princeton University Press.

SNYDER, M., & SWANN, W. B., JR. (1978). Behavioral confirmation in social interaction: From social perception to social reality. *Journal of Experimental Social Psychology, 14,* 148–162.

SOLOMON, L. (1960). The influence of some types of power relationships and game strategies upon the development of interpersonal trust. *Journal of Abnormal and Social Psychology, 61,* 223–230.

SOMMERS, S. (1984). Adults evaluating their emotions: A cross-cultural perspective. In C. Z. Malatesta & C. E. Izard (Eds.), *Emotions in adult development* (pp. 319–338). Beverly Hills, CA: Sage.

STARKE, F. A., & NOTZ, W. W. (1989). The impact of managerial arbitration and subunit power on bargainer behavior and commitment. In M. A. Rahim (Ed.), *Managing conflict: An interdisciplinary approach* (pp. 171–183). New York: Praeger.

STAW, B. M. (1981). The escalation of commitment to a course of action. *Academy of Management Review, 6,* 577–587.

STEELE, C. M., & JOSEPHS, R. A. (1990). Alcohol myopia: Its prized and dangerous effects. *American Psychologist, 45,* 921–933.

STEPHAN, W. G. (1985). Intergroup relations. In G. Lindzey & E. Aronson (Eds.), *Handbook of social psychology* (Vol. 2, pp. 599–658). New York: Random House.

STEPHAN, W. G. (1987). The contact hypothesis in intergroup relations. In C. Hendrick (Ed.), *Group processes and intergroup relations.* Newbury Park, CA: Sage.

STERN, J. L., REHMUS, C. M., LOWENBERG, J. J., KASPER, H., & DENNIS, B. D. (1975). *Final-offer arbitration.* Lexington, MA: Health.

STERNBERG, R. J., & DOBSON, D. M. (1987). Resolving interpersonal conflicts: An analysis of stylistic consistency. *Journal of Personality and Social Psychology, 52,* 794–812.

STERNBERG, R. J., & SORIANO, L. J. (1984). Styles of conflict resolution. *Journal of Personality and Social Psychology, 47,* 115–126.

STEVENS, C. M. (1963). *Strategy and collective bargaining negotiation.* New York: McGraw-Hill.

STEVENS, C. M. (1966). Is compulsory arbitration compatible with bargaining? *Industrial Relations, 65,* 38–52.

STRAUS, D. B. (1981). Kissinger and management of complexity: An attempt that failed. In J. Z. Rubin (Ed.), *Dynamics of third party intervention: Kissinger in the Middle East* (pp. 253–270). New York: Praeger.

STROEBE, W., LENKERT, A., & JONAS, K. (1988). Familiarity may breed contempt: The impact of student exchange on national stereotypes and attitudes. In W. Stroebe, A. W. Kruglanski, D. Bar-Tal, & M. Hewstone (Eds.), *The social psychology of intergroup conflict: Theory, research and applications* (pp. 167–187). New York: Springer-Verlag.

STRUCH, N., & SCHWARTZ, S. H. (1989). Intergroup aggression: Its predictors and distinctness from in-group bias. *Journal of Personality and Social Psychology, 56,* 364–373.

SUBBARAO, A. V. (1978). The impact of binding arbitration. *Journal of Conflict Resolution, 22,* 70–104.

SUMNER, W. G. (1906). *Folkways.* Boston: Ginn.

SUSSKIND, L., BACOW, L., & WHEELER, M. (1983). *Resolving environmental regulatory disputes.* Rochester, VT: Schenkman.

SUSSKIND, L., & CRUIKSHANK, J. (1987). *Breaking the impasse: Consensual approaches to resolving public disputes.* New York: Basic Books.

SWANN, W. B., JR. (1987). Identity negotiation: Where two roads meet. *Journal of Personality and Social Psychology, 53,* 1038–1051.

SWAP, W. C., & RUBIN, J. Z. (1983). Measurement of interpersonal orientation. *Journal of Personality and Social Psychology, 44,* 208–219.

SYNA, H. (1984). Couples in conflict: Conflict resolution strategies, perceptions about sources of conflict and relationship adjustment. Doctoral dissertation, State University of New York at Buffalo.

TAJFEL, H. (1970). Experiments in intergroup discrimination. *Scientific American, 223,* 96–102.

TAJFEL, H., BILLIG, M. G., BUNDY, R. P., & FLAMENT, C. (1971). Social categorization and intergroup behavior. *European Journal of Social Psychology, 1,* 149–178.

Taylor, S. E. (1991). Asymmetrical effects of positive and negative events: The mobilization-minimization hypothesis. *Psychological Bulletin, 110,* 67–85.

TAYLOR, S. P., & LEONARD, K. E. (1983). Alcohol and human physical aggression. In R. G. Geen & E. Donnerstein (Eds.), *Aggression: Theoretical and empirical reviews, Vol. 2: Issues in research* (pp. 77–101). New York: Academic Press.

TEDESCHI, J. T., & MELBURG, V. (1984). Impression management and influence in the organization. In S. B. Bacharach & E. J. Lawler (Eds.), *Research in the sociology of organizations* (Vol. 3, pp. 31–58). Greenwich, CT: JAI Press.

TEGER, A. I. (1980). *Too much invested to quit.* New York: Pergamon.

TETLOCK, P. E. (1983). Policymakers' images of international conflict. *Journal of Social Issues, 39,* 67–86.

THIBAUT, J. W., & KELLEY, H. H. (1959). *The social psychology of groups.* New York: Wiley.

THIBAUT, J. W., & WALKER, L. (1975). *Procedural justice: A psychological analysis.* Hillsdale, NJ: Erlbaum.

THOMAS, K. (1976). Conflict and conflict management. In M. D. Dunnette (Ed.), *Handbook of industrial and organizational psychology* (pp. 889–935). Chicago: Rand McNally.

THOMPSON, L. L. (1990a). Negotiation behavior and outcomes: Empirical evidence and theoretical issues. *Psychological Bulletin, 108,* 515–532.

THOMPSON, L. L. (1990b). An examination of naive and experienced negotiators. *Journal of Personality and Social Psychology, 59,* 82–90.

THOMPSON, L. L., & HASTIE, R. (1990). Social perception in negotiation. *Organizational Behavior and Human Decision Processes, 47,* 98–123.

Tjosvold, D. (1977). Commitment to justice in conflict between unequal persons. *Journal of Applied Social Psychology, 7,* 149–162.

TJOSVOLD, D., & OKUN, M. A. (1976). Corrupting effects of unequal power: Cognitive perspective-taking and cooperation. Paper presented at the American Psychological Association Annual Convention, Washington, D.C.

TOCH, H. (1969). *Violent men: An inquiry into the psychology of violence.* Chicago: Aldine.

TOCH, H. (1970). The social psychology of violence. In E. I. Megargee & J. E. Hokanson (Eds.), *The dynamics of aggression* (pp. 160–169). New York: Harper & Row.

TOUVAL, S., & ZARTMAN, I. W. (1985). *International mediation in theory and practice.* Boulder, CO: Westview.

TOUVAL, S., & ZARTMAN, I. W. (1989). Mediation in international conflicts. In K. Kressel & D. G. Pruitt (Eds.), *Mediation research* (pp. 115–137). San Francisco: Jossey-Bass.

TRIANDIS, H. C. (1989). The self and social behavior in differing cultural contexts. *Psychological Review, 96,* 506–520.

TRIANDIS, H. C., BONTEMPO, R., VILLAREAL, M. J., ASAI, M., & LUCCA, N. (1988). Individualism and collectivism: Cross-cultural perspectives on self-ingroup relationships. *Journal of Personality and Social Psychology, 54,* 323–338.

TURNER, J. C. (1981). The experimental social psychology of intergroup behavior. In J. C. Turner & H. Giles (Eds.), *Intergroup behaviour* (pp. 66–101). Oxford, UK: Basil Blackwell.

URY, W. L. (1991). *Getting past no: Negotiating with difficult people.* New York: Bantam.

URY, W. L., BRETT, J. M., & GOLDBERG, S. (1988). *Getting disputes resolved.* San Francisco: Jossey-Bass.

VALLONE, R. P., ROSS, L., & LEPPER, M. R. (1985). The hostile media phenomenon: Biased perception and perceptions of media bias in coverage of the "Beirut Massacre." *Journal of Personality and Social Psychology, 49,* 577–585.

VANBESELAERE, N. (1991). The different effects of simple and crossed categorization: A result of the category differentiation process or of differential category salience? In W. Stroebe & M. Hewstone (Eds.), *European Review of Social Psychology* (Vol. 2, pp. 247–279). Chichester, England: Wiley.

VAN DE VLIERT, E. (1990). Positive effects of conflict: A field assessment. *The International Journal of Conflict Management, 1,* 69–80.

VAN DE VLIERT, E., & PREIN, H. C. M. (1989). The difference in the meaning of forcing in the conflict management of actors and observers. In M. A. Rahim (Ed.), *Managing conflict: An interdisciplinary approach* (pp. 51–63). New York: Praeger.

VANGELISTI, A. L., DALY, J. A., & RUDNICK, J. R. (1991). Making people feel guilty in conversations: Techniques and correlates. *Human Communication Research, 18,* 3–39.

WALKER, I., & MANN, L. (1987). Unemployment, relative deprivation, and social protest. *Personality and Social Psychology Bulletin, 13,* 275–283.

WALL, J. A., JR. (1975). Effects of constituent trust and representative bargaining orientation on intergroup bargaining. *Journal of Personality and Social Psychology, 31,* 1004–1012.

WALL, J. A., JR. (1977). Intergroup bargaining: Effects of opposing constituent's stance, opposing representative's bargaining, and representative's locus of control. *Journal of Conflict Resolution, 21,* 459–474.

WALL, J. A., JR. (1979). The effects of mediator rewards and suggestions upon negotiations. *Journal of Personality and Social Psychology, 37,* 1554–1560.

WALL, J. A., JR. (1981). Mediation: An analysis, review and proposed research. *Journal of Conflict Resolution, 25,* 157–180.

WALL, J. A., JR., & LYNN, A. (1993). Mediation; A current review. *Journal of Conflict Resolution, 37,* 160–194.

WALL, J. A., JR., & RUDE, D. E. (1989). Judicial mediation of settlement negotiations. In K. Kressel & D. G. Pruitt (Eds.), *Mediation research* (pp. 190–212). San Francisco: Jossey-Bass.

WALL, J. A., JR., & RUDE, D. E. (1991). The judge as mediator. *Journal of Applied Psychology, 76,* 54–59.

WALLACE, J., & SADALLA, E. (1966). Behavioral consequences of transgressions: II. The effects of social recognition. *Journal of Experimental Research in Personality, 14,* 187–194.

WALSTER, E. H., WALSTER, G. W., & BERSCHEID, E. (1978). *Equity: Theory and research.* Boston: Allyn and Bacon.

WALTON, R. E. (1969). *Interpersonal peacemaking: Confrontations and third-party consultation.* Reading, MA: Addison-Wesley.

WALTON, R. E., & MCKERSIE, R. B. (1965). *A behavioral theory of labor negotiations: An analysis of a social interaction system.* New York: McGraw-Hill.

WEBSTER, N. (1983). *New Twentieth Century Dictionary* (2nd ed.). New York: Simon & Schuster.

WEDGE, B. (1970). A psychiatric model for intercession in intergroup conflict. *Journal of Applied Behavioral Science, 6,* 733–761.

WEINER, B., AMIRKHAN, J., FOLKES, V. S., & VERETTE, J. A. (1987). An attributional analysis of excuse giving: Studies of a naive theory of emotion. *Journal of Personality and Social Psychology, 52,* 316–324.

WEINGART, L. R., THOMPSON, L. L., BAZERMAN, M. H., & CARROLL, J. S. (1990). Tactical behavior and negotiation outcomes. *International Journal of Conflict Management, 1,* 7–31.

WELTON, G. L., & PRUITT, D. G. (1987). The mediation process: The effects of mediator bias and disputant power. *Personality and Social Psychology Bulletin, 13,* 123–133.

WELTON, G. L., PRUITT, D. G., & MCGILLICUDDY, N. B. (1988). The role of caucusing in community mediation. *Journal of Conflict Resolution, 32,* 181–202.

WELTON, G. L., PRUITT, D. G., MCGILLICUDDY, N. B., IPPOLITO, C. A., & ZUBEK, J. M. (1992). Antecedents and characteristics of caucusing in community mediation. *International Journal of Conflict Management, 3,* 303–318.

WESTERMARCK, E. (1912). *The origin and development of moral ideas* (Vol. 1). London: Macmillan.

WHEELER, L., & CAGGIULA, A. R. (1966). The contagion of aggression. *Journal of Experimental Social Psychology, 2,* 1–10.

WHITE, R. K. (1984). *Fearful warriors: A psychological profile of U.S.-Soviet relations.* New York: Free Press.

WILDER, D. A. (1984). Predictions of belief homogeneity and similarity following social categorization. *British Journal of Social Psychology, 23,* 323–333.

WINTER, D. G. (1987). Enhancement of an enemy's power motivation as a dynamic of conflict escalation. *Journal of Personality and Social Psychology, 52,* 41–46.

WITTMER, J. M., CARNEVALE, P., & WALKER, M. E. (1991). General alignment and overt support in biased mediation. *Journal of Conflict Resolution, 35,* 594–610.

WOLFGANG, M., & STROHM, R. B. (1956). The relationship between alcohol and criminal homicide. *Quarterly Journal of Studies on Alcohol, 17,* 411–425.

WOOD, J. V. (1989). Theory and research concerning social comparisons of personal attributes. *Psychological Bulletin, 106,* 231–248.

WORCHEL, S. (1979). Cooperation and the reduction of intergroup conflict: Some determining factors. In W. G. Austin & S. Worchel (Eds.), *The social psychology of intergroup relations* (pp. 262–273). Monterey, CA: Brooks/Cole.

WORCHEL, S., & ANDREOLI, V. A. (1978). Facilitation of social interaction through deindividuation of the target. *Journal of Personality and Social Psychology, 36,* 549–556.

WORCHEL, S., ANDREOLI, V. A., & FOLGER, R. (1977). Intergroup cooperation and intergroup attraction: The effect of previous interaction and outcome on combined effort. *Journal of Experimental Social Psychology, 13,* 131–140.

WORCHEL, S. & NORVELL, N. (1980). Effect of perceived environmental conditions during cooperation on intergroup attraction. *Journal of Personality and Social Psychology, 38,* 764–772.

WORTMAN, C. B., & LINSENMEIER, J. A. W. (1977). Interpersonal attraction and techniques of ingratiation in organizational settings. In B. M. Staw & G. R. Salancik (Eds.), *New directions in organizational behavior* (pp. 133–178). Chicago: St. Clair Press.

YAMAGISHI, T. (1986). The provision of a sanctioning system as a public good. *Journal of Personality and Social Psychology, 51,* 110–116.

YAMAGISHI, T., & SATO, K. (1986). Motivational bases of the public goods problem. *Journal of Personality and Social Psychology, 50,* 67–73.

YOUNG, O. R. (1968). *The politics of force.* Princeton, NJ: Princeton University Press.

YOUNGS, G. A., JR. (1986). Patterns of threat and punishment reciprocity in a conflict setting. *Journal of Personality and Social Psychology, 51,* 541–546.

YUKL, G. A., MALONE, M. P., HAYSLIP, B., & PAMIN, T. A. (1976). The effects of time pressure and issue settlement order on integrative bargaining. *Sociometry, 39,* 277–281.

ZAJONC, R. B. (1968). Attitudinal effects of mere exposure. *Journal of Personality and Social Psychology. Monograph Supplement, 9*(2, Pt. 2), 2–27.

ZARTMAN, I. W. (Ed.). (1977). *The negotiation process: Theories and applications.* Beverly Hills, CA: Sage.

ZARTMAN, I. W. (1981). Explaining disengagement. In J. Z. Rubin (Ed.), *Dynamics of third-party intervention* (pp. 148–167). New York: Praeger.

ZARTMAN, I. W. (1989). *Ripe for resolution: Conflict resolution in Africa* (2nd ed.). New York: Oxford.

ZARTMAN, I. W. (Ed.) (1994). *Multilateral negotiation.* San Francisco, CA: Jossey-Bass.

ZARTMAN, I. W., & BERMAN, M. R. (1982). *The practical negotiator.* New Haven, CT: Yale University Press.

ZILLMANN, D. (1971). Excitation transfer in communication-mediated aggressive behavior. *Journal of Experimental Social Psychology, 7,* 419–434.

ZILLMANN, D. (1979). *Hostility and aggression.* Hillsdale, NJ: Erlbaum.

ZILLMANN, D., BRYANT, J., CANTOR, J. R., & DAY, K. D. (1975). Irrelevance of mitigating circumstances in retaliatory behavior at high levels of excitation. *Journal of Research in Personality, 9,* 282–293.

ZILLMANN, D., JOHNSON, R. C., & DAY, K. D. (1974). Attribution of apparent arousal and proficiency of recovery from sympathetic activation affecting activation transfer to aggressive behavior. *Journal of Experimental Social Psychology, 10,* 503–515.

ZIMBARDO, P. G. (1970). The human choice: Individuation, reason, and order versus deindividuation, impulse, and chaos. In W. J. Arnold & D. Levine (Eds.), *Nebraska Symposium on Motivation, 1969* (Vol. 17, pp. 237–307). Lincoln: University of Nebraska Press.

ZIMBARDO, P. G., & LEIPPE, M. R. (1991). *The psychology of attitude change and social influence.* New York: McGraw-Hill.

ZUBEK, J. M., PRUITT, D. G., MCGILLICUDDY, N. B., PEIRCE, R. S., & SYNA, H. (1992). Short-term success in mediation: Its relationship to prior conditions and mediator and disputant behaviors. *Journal of Conflict Resolution, 36,* 546–572.

Glossary

accountability A representative's responsibility to report the outcome of its negotiations to powerful constituents.
aggression Intentionally hurting another person.
aggressor-defender model Explanation of escalation as due to Party's efforts to exploit Other, and Other's resistance to these efforts.
apology A special form of conciliatory initiative in which Party conveys to Other its regret over some prior, harmful behavior.
arbitrator A third party who is empowered to make a binding decision in order to settle a dispute.
arousal Activation of the autonomic nervous system.
aspirations A behavioral representation of the things that Party strives for or believes it must exceed. Aspirations may either take the form of goals that Party is striving for or standards that Party hopes to meet or exceed.
attitude Positive or negative feeling toward a person or object.
attribution Interpretation of the cause or motivation for Other's actions.
attribution theory A body of psychological theory that explains how people interpret the causes of behavior.
attributional distortion The tendency to attribute information that confirms Party's expectations about Other to Other's enduring and stable characteristics, while attributing information about Other that disconfirms Party's expectations to temporary environmental pressures on Other.
autistic hostility Antagonism that perpetuates itself by blocking further communication with Other.
aversive experience Unpleasant, frustrating, or painful experience.
avoiding A strategy that involves moving away from the settlement of conflict, either through inaction or withdrawing.
back-channel contacts Off-the-record meetings between disputing parties.
bad cop/good cop routine A two-stage, two-person contentious tactic. In the first stage, person A punishes the target. In the second stage, person B rewards the target, making it clear that person A will resume the punishment if the target fails to comply with a request. Also called "black hat/white hat" and "bad guy/good guy" routine.
balance of power Distribution of resources such that all members of a community are deterred from attacking one another.
blame Assignment of responsibility or fault for an aversive experience.

bond Felt or perceived link between Party and Other. May be due to attraction, kinship, common group identity, perceived similarity, or the expectation of future dependence.

bridging A type of integrative solution in which a new alternative is devised that satisfies the most important interests underlying the initial demands of Party and Other.

caucusing A technique that a third party uses to control the communication between Party and Other by physically separating them and engaging in private conversation with each side.

chicken A game in which the consequences of mutual noncooperation are so aversive that the first party to commit itself to noncooperation usually wins.

chilling effect The tendency for Party and Other to take tough and extreme positions in anticipation that an arbitrator will split the difference between the two positions.

chunking A method that Party can use to avoid entrapment by engaging in periodic reassessment of its commitment. Also a procedure for conflict settlement in which seemingly monolithic issues are addressed as bite-sized "chunks."

cohesiveness Group solidarity; overall attractiveness of a group to its members.

common group membership The perception that Other is a member of a group to which Party also belongs.

community polarization Disappearance of neutral third parties from the community surrounding a controversy as a result of recruitment to one side or the other.

compellent threat A threat that requests Other to adopt a particular action or solution.

compromise An obvious alternative that stands part way between Party's and Other's preferred positions.

concern about Other's outcomes Importance placed by Party on the outcomes of Other.

concern about Party's own outcomes Importance placed by Party on its own outcomes.

concern-likelihood model Explanation of mediator behavior as the interaction of two determining variables: (1) the mediator's likelihood assessment of a win-win agreement, and (2) the mediator's level of concern about the parties' outcomes.

conciliatory signals Hints of a willingness to make a particular concession or to take some other cooperative action.

confirmatory mechanisms Events and sequences of events that cause structural changes to endure; for example, selective perception and the self-fulfilling prophecy.

conflict Perceived divergence (conflict) of interest; a belief that the current aspirations of Party and Other cannot be achieved simultaneously.

conflict spiral model Explanation of escalation as due to a vicious circle of contentious action and reaction.

conflict style The way a person most commonly deals with conflict.

constituent A party represented in a conflict or negotiation.

contending A strategy that involves an effort by Party to impose its preferred solution on Other.

contractual intervention A type of third party intervention provided by a conflict management specialist who has expertise and experience with the issues under dispute.
conventional arbitration A form of outside intervention in which the third party is empowered to impose agreement in order to settle a conflict.
coping strategies Strategies that involve a relatively consistent, coherent effort to settle conflict. There are three types: contending, yielding, and problem solving.
cost cutting A type of integrative solution in which Party gets what it wants, while Other's costs are reduced or eliminated.
covert problem solving Problem solving that takes place behind the scenes or in the form of signals.
credibility Believability of a threat, promise, or irrevocable commitment.
crosscutting group memberships Configuration of bonds in which the major groups in a society have overlapping membership.
culture A set of shared and enduring meanings, values, and beliefs that characterize national, ethnic, or other groups and orient behavior.
cycle of escalation A four-part, recursive sequence of events in which Party's escalated behavior produces (1) changes in Other or in the surrounding community, leading to (2) escalated behavior by Other, which produces (3) changes in Party or the surrounding community, leading to (4) more escalated behavior by Party.
de-escalation Reduction in the intensity of conflict.
defensive spirals Escalation as a result of each party's efforts to protect itself from a threat it finds in the other's self-protective actions.
dehumanization Perception of Other as something less than human.
deindividuation Perception of Other as a member of a category rather than as an individual.
dependence Reliance on Other for Party's outcomes.
descriptive theory Theory about how people behave.
deterrence theory A theory about how to prevent Other from aggressing against Party or its allies.
deterrent threat A threat that requests Other to avoid a particular action.
diabolical enemy An image of Other as evil.
displacement Diversion of aggression from the party who is blamed for an aversive experience to a convenient target.
disposition A personality trait, attitude, or other characteristic of an individual.
dispute systems design A form of outside intervention in which the third party establishes conflict resolution procedures to help Party and Other settle the conflicts that may arise in the future.
dissonance theory A psychological theory explaining why attitudes and beliefs are consistent with prior actions.
distrust Perception of Other as not caring about, or being antagonistic to, Party's interests.
dual concern model Used in two senses: (1) A theory of strategic choice postulating that the strategy chosen is a function of the relative strength of Party's concern about its own outcomes and those of Other, and (2) a theory of individual differences in conflict style.
empathy Party's vicarious experience of feelings and thoughts about Other.

entrapment Persistence of unrewarding behavior in pursuit of a goal, characterized by the belief that one has too much invested to quit.
escalation Used in two senses: (1) The adoption by Party of heavier tactics now than before, and (2) an increase in the intensity of conflict as a whole.
ethnocentrism The tendency for Party to favor its own group over other groups and to derogate those groups to which Party does not belong.
evil-ruler enemy image Perception that the adversary consists of reasonable people who are dominated and misled by a small group of wicked leaders.
expanding the pie A type of integrative solution in which a way is found to augment a scarce resource.
final-offer arbitration A variant of conventional arbitration in which the third party must choose the position *either* of Party *or* of Other.
firm but conciliatory stance Strategy by Party of standing firm on its basic interests while trying to be responsive to the basic interests of Other.
firm flexibility Firmness with respect to ends, in conjunction with flexibility with respect to the means for achieving those ends.
formula A brief statement of the essential features of an agreement, which serves as a guide for later work on the fine details.
fractionation Division of large, all-encompassing issues into smaller, more manageable ones. *Also called* chunking.
framing Effect on Party's concern about its own or Other's outcomes of the way in which these outcomes are presented.
fraternalistic deprivation A sense that Party's own group has been deprived.
gamesmanship Contentious tactics that seek to win by throwing Other off guard.
geography of social bonds Overall pattern of bonding and antagonism among the members of a community.
graduated and reciprocated initiatives in tension reduction (GRIT) Unilateral conciliatory actions designed to de-escalate a conflict with Other.
group A set of people who are capable of coordinated action—a small group, organization, community, or nation. *Also called* a "collective."
group changes Changes in groups that result from escalation and produce more escalation.
group polarization Strengthening of the dominant attitude or belief in a group as a result of group discussion.
guilt trips Contentious tactics that seek to influence Other by making it feel responsible for an imagined injury to Party.
heavy tactics Contentious tactics that impose great costs on Other.
illusory conflict False perception of a divergence of interest.
image loss Loss of status or credibility in the eyes of either an antagonist or an observer of a conflict.
image-threats Threats to the way Party appears in the eyes of itself, Other, or observers of a conflict.
inaction A strategy that involves doing nothing.
individualistic orientation An outlook characterized by Party's efforts to maximize its own outcomes, regardless of Other's outcomes.
information loss Discovery by Other of the nature of Party's interests or the location of Party's lower limit.

ingratiation A strategy by which Party tries to increase its attractiveness to Other in order to exercise influence.
ingroup The group to which Party belongs.
integrative potential Availability of a mutually beneficial solution to a conflict.
integrative solution An alternative that reconciles Party's and Other's basic interests; a mutually beneficial solution. Also called a "win-win solution."
interest tree Hierarchical diagram showing more basic interests at lower levels, and more superficial interests at higher levels.
interests People's feelings about what is basically desirable; their values and needs.
intermediaries People who carry messages between Party and Other.
invidious comparison Perception that Other receives more reward in comparison to its worth than does Party.
irrevocable commitment Communication indicating that Party will under no circumstances deviate from its present position.
joint outcome space Geometric representation of the perceived value to two parties of the available alternatives.
light tactics Contentious tactics that impose relatively low cost on Other.
linkage Association of demands, goals, aspirations, and values in a package that seems inviolable. Unbundling such a package is often necessary for the development of an integrative solution.
logrolling A type of integrative solution in which Party and Other each concedes on issues that are of low priority to itself and of high priority to the other party.
mediation A form of outside intervention in which a third party helps the parties in conflict to reach a voluntary agreement.
mediation/arbitration (med/arb) A hybrid of mediation and arbitration in which arbitration is imposed only if Party and Other fail to reach agreement through mediation.
mediator power A mediator's capacity to reward or punish the parties.
metaconflict A situation in which the initial issues around which a conflict begins are outweighed by new issues.
mirror image Similarity of attitudes and perceptions on both sides of a conflict.
model An abstract pattern of thought from which explanations or predictions of particular events can be derived.
momentum The sense of forward motion in a conflict, resulting from prior success at achieving agreement.
narcotic effect Habitual dependence on a third party for resolving conflicts.
negotiation A form of conflict behavior; seeking to resolve divergence of interest by means of some form of interaction (typically the verbal exchange of offers) between the parties.
nonspecific compensation A type of integrative solution in which Party gets what it wants and Other is repaid in an unrelated coin.
norms Rules of behavior that a group imposes on its members.
ombuds A third party who is charged with the resolution of conflicts that arise between individuals and institutions.
outgroup A group to which Party does not belong and which Party contrasts with its own group.
overcommitment Resolution to follow an unwise course of action.

party A participant in conflict. Parties can be individuals, groups, organizations, communities, or nations.

perceived common ground (PCG) The perceived likelihood of finding an alternative that satisfies the aspirations of both Party and Other.

perceived divergence of interest A belief that Party and Other cannot achieve their aspirations simultaneously.

perceived feasibility The extent to which a strategy seems capable of achieving Party's aspirations at a reasonable cost.

perception Belief about a person or object.

persuasive argumentation Contentious tactics aimed at lowering Other's aspirations through a series of logical appeals.

position loss Other's perception that Party has conceded from an earlier demand.

power The capacity to persuade Other to yield.

prescriptive theory Theory about how people should behave.

priorities Preferences among interests, such as a preference for wealth over social approval.

problem solving A strategy that involves seeking a mutually satisfactory alternative.

problem-solving intervention A form of third party intervention in which scholar/practitioners use their stature and conflict expertise to educate the parties to change their perceptions so that they come to regard conflict as a problem to be solved together.

promise Commitment to reward Other if it complies with Party's wishes.

provocation Action by Party that produces an aversive experience for Other.

psychological changes Changes in individuals that result from escalation and produce more escalation.

relative deprivation Harsh experience resulting from Party's failure to achieve its aspirations.

residue Persistent structural change—in an individual, group, or community—which is due to past escalation and encourages further escalation.

retaliatory spirals Escalation as a result of each party's efforts to punish the other for actions it finds aversive.

ripeness of conflict Conditions in which Party and Other are motivated to take conflict seriously—and to do whatever is necessary to settle it through problem solving.

runaway norms Norms regarded by most members of the group as embodying right or correct thinking.

second strike A threat by Party to retaliate in the hope of deterring Other (from using nuclear weapons, for example).

selective perception Seeing only those things that fit one's needs or preconceptions.

self-fulfilling prophecy The tendency for Party's expectations to induce Other to behave in ways that confirm Party's initial expectations.

social categorization effect The finding that minimal differences between groups are sufficient to produce ethnocentrism. Also called minimal group effect.

social comparison Party's assessment of Other's characteristics or situation in comparison with Party's own.

social identity theory The theory that Party, in order to enhance its self-esteem, favors its own group over outgroups.

special envoy A third party dispatched to convey a particular message to Other on behalf of Party.

stability Low likelihood that conflict will escalate.

stalemate Condition in which Party (and often Other) comes to regard conflict as intolerable, as something that should be ended as soon as possible.

strategic choice Choice among the four basic strategies for dealing with conflict.

strategy A broad type of conflict behavior; a class of tactics. Four strategies are distinguished: contending, yielding, problem solving, and avoiding (withdrawing and inaction).

structural change model Explanation of escalation as due to persistent changes in individuals, groups, or communities.

struggle group A group that forms with the goal of obtaining concessions from the other side.

stubbornness Reluctance to yield.

superordinate goal An objective that is shared by Party and Other and requires them to work together.

superordinate identity The perception that Party and Other have achieved a shared identity as a result of belonging to a larger group that encompasses both of them.

surveillance Monitoring by constituents of their representatives' negotiation.

tactic A narrow type of conflict behavior. Various possible tactics are implied by a single strategy.

tar baby effect Reinforcement of an attitude or belief by the absence of behavior by Other.

third party An individual or collective that is external to a conflict between two or more people, and that tries to help them reach agreement.

threat Used in two different senses: (1) commitment to hurt Other if Other fails to comply with Party's wishes, and (2) perception of danger to something Party values.

transformations Changes in the parties and the nature of the conflict that occur during escalation; e.g., light to heavy, small to large.

trust The perception that Other is positively concerned about Party's interests.

vested interest The motive to retain one's group membership or leadership position because of the benefits that accrue from it.

vigor Amount of energy or effort put into strategy enactment.

withdrawing A strategy that involves leaving the conflict, either physically or psychologically.

yielding A conflict strategy in which Party lowers its aspirations.

zero-sum A conflict relationship in which Party can only do well if Other does poorly. Strictly speaking, the outcomes to Party and to Other sum to zero. Also called constant-sum.

zero-sum thinking The belief that my gain is your loss, and vice versa. Also known as the fixed-pie assumption.

Name Index

Subject Index